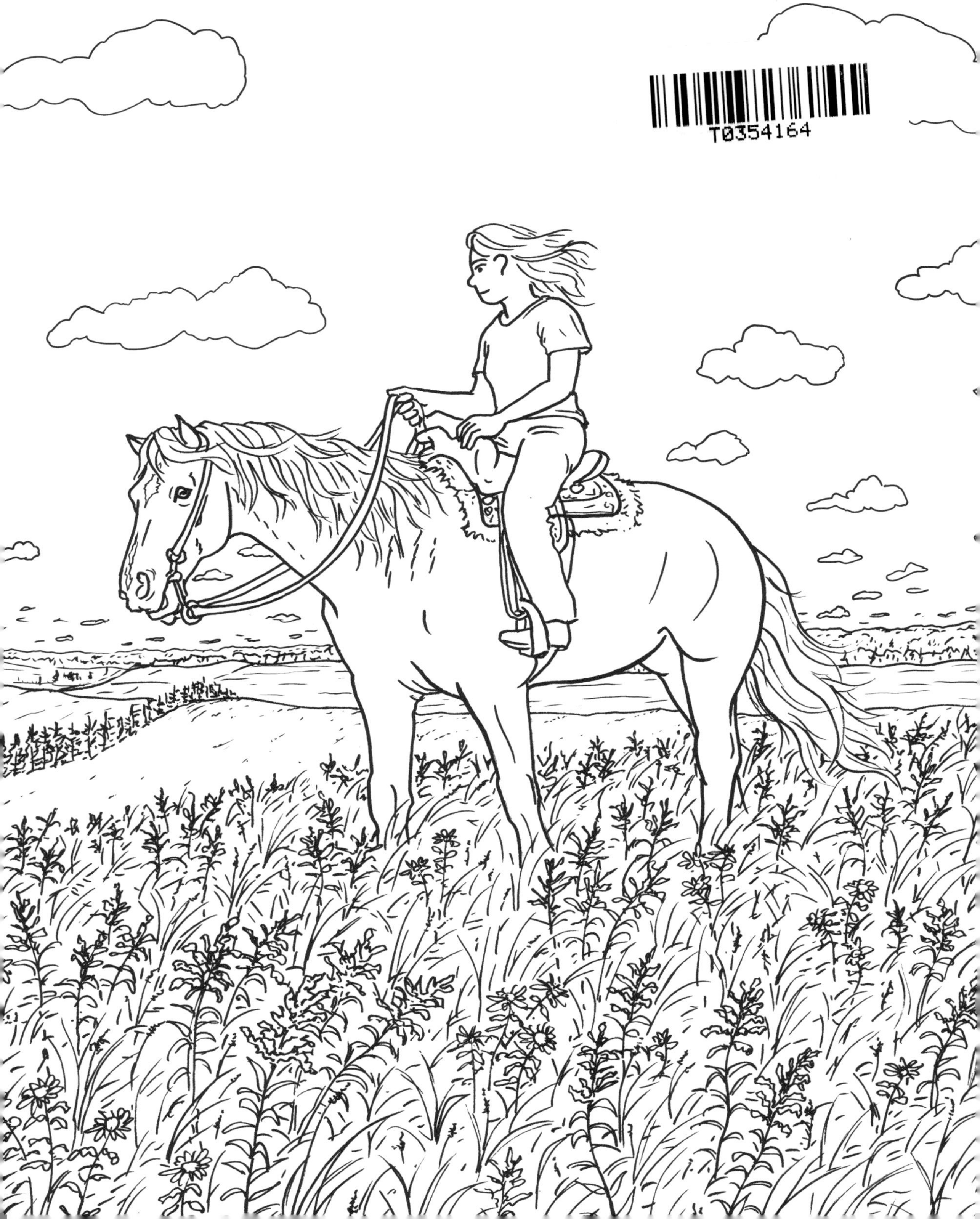

WARNING

This book references and portrays difficult scenes including childhood sexual abuse and may be triggering for some readers

A portion of the proceeds from this book will be donated to Covenant House, an organization that helps homeless and at-risk youth aged 16 to 24 who have fled physical, emotional, and sexual abuse; who have been forced from their homes; and who have aged out of foster care.

drawnandquarterly.com

ISBN 978-1-77046-546-6
first edition: January 2021
Printed in Turkey | 10 9 8 7 6 5 4 3 2 1

Cataloguing data available from Library and Archives Canada.

Published in the USA by Drawn & Quarterly, a client publisher of Farrar, Straus and Giroux.
Published in Canada by Drawn & Quarterly, a client publisher of Raincoast Books.
Published in the United Kingdom by Drawn & Quarterly, a client publisher of Publishers Group UK.

Canada ᴵ✦ᴵ Drawn & Quarterly acknowledges the support of the Government of Canada and the Canada Council for the Arts for our publishing program.

OUR little Secret

A Graphic Memoir
By Emily Carrington

Drawn & Quarterly

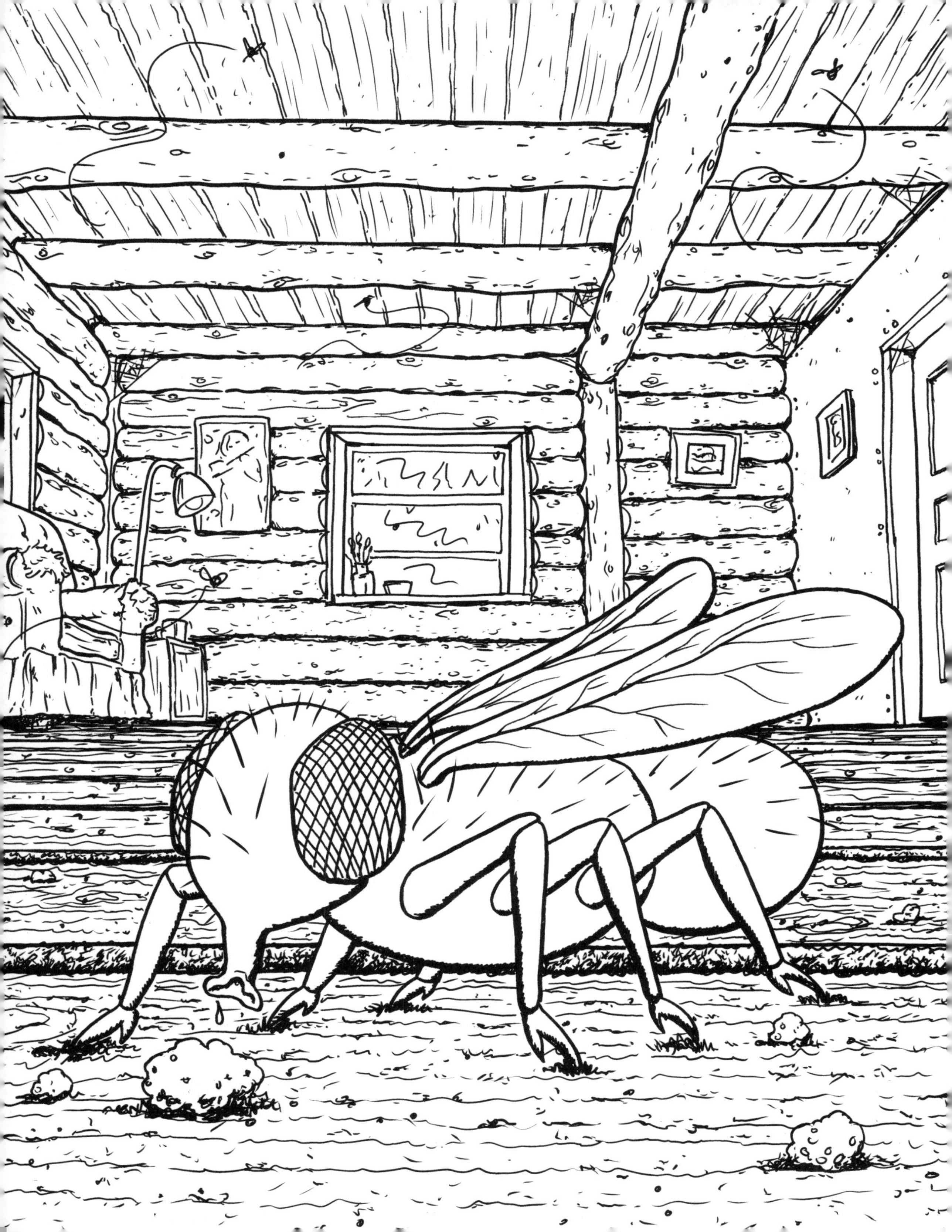

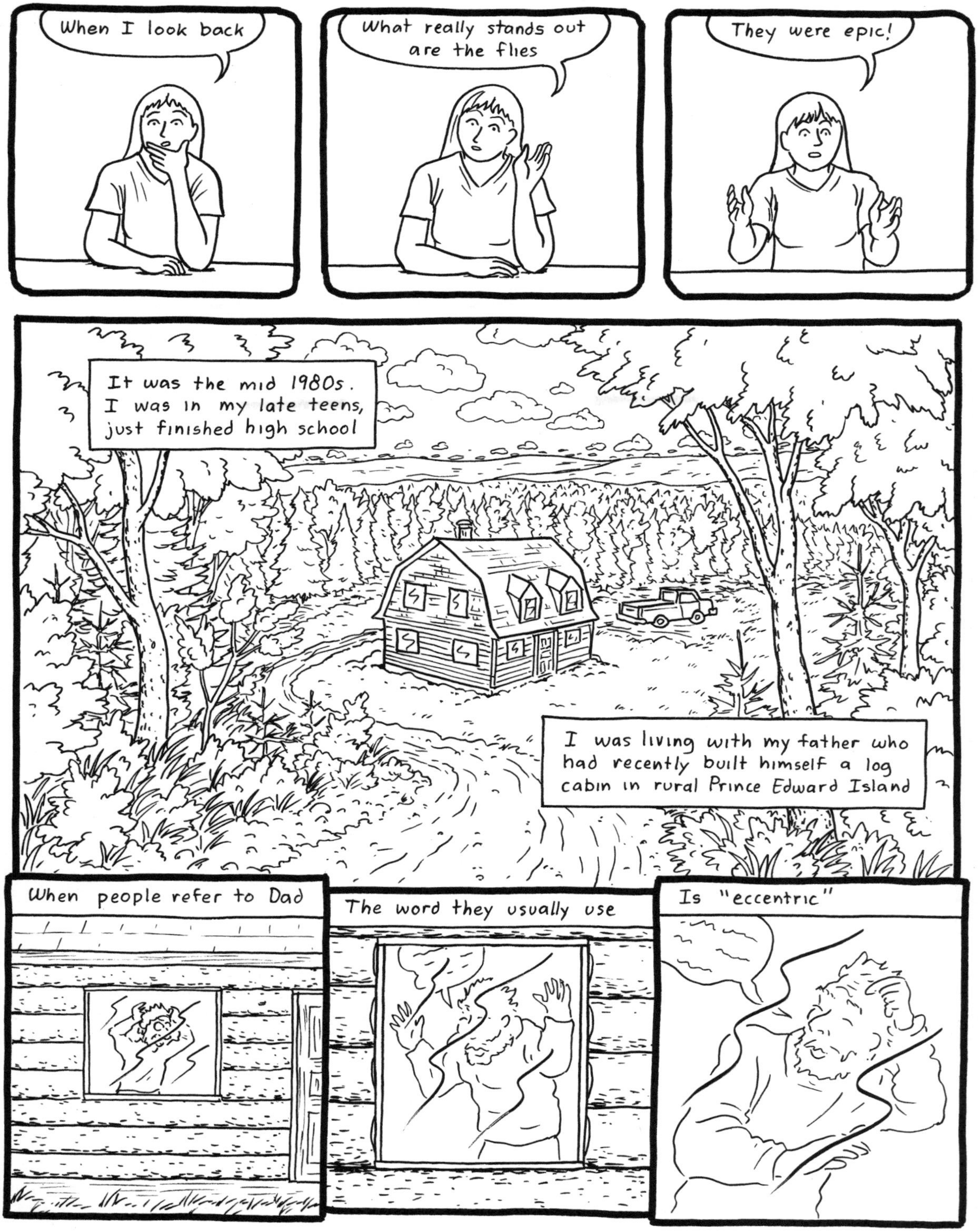
When I look back
What really stands out are the flies
They were epic!
It was the mid 1980s. I was in my late teens, just finished high school
I was living with my father who had recently built himself a log cabin in rural Prince Edward Island
When people refer to Dad
The word they usually use
Is "eccentric"

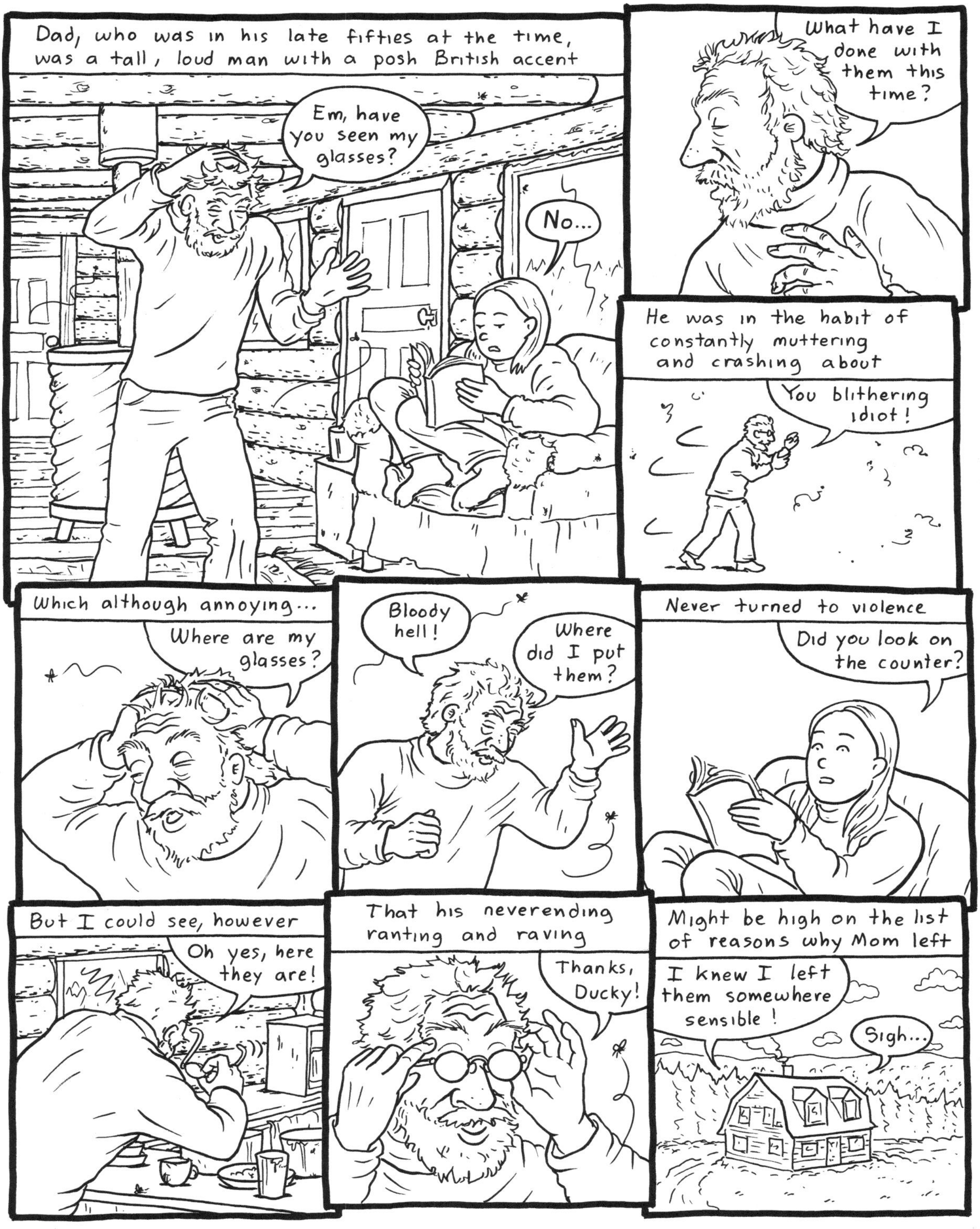
Dad, who was in his late fifties at the time, was a tall, loud man with a posh British accent
Em, have you seen my glasses?
No...
What have I done with them this time?
He was in the habit of constantly muttering and crashing about
You blithering idiot!
Which although annoying...
Where are my glasses?
Bloody hell!
Where did I put them?
Never turned to violence
Did you look on the counter?
But I could see, however
Oh yes, here they are!
That his neverending ranting and raving
Thanks, Ducky!
Might be high on the list of reasons why Mom left
I knew I left them somewhere sensible!
Sigh...

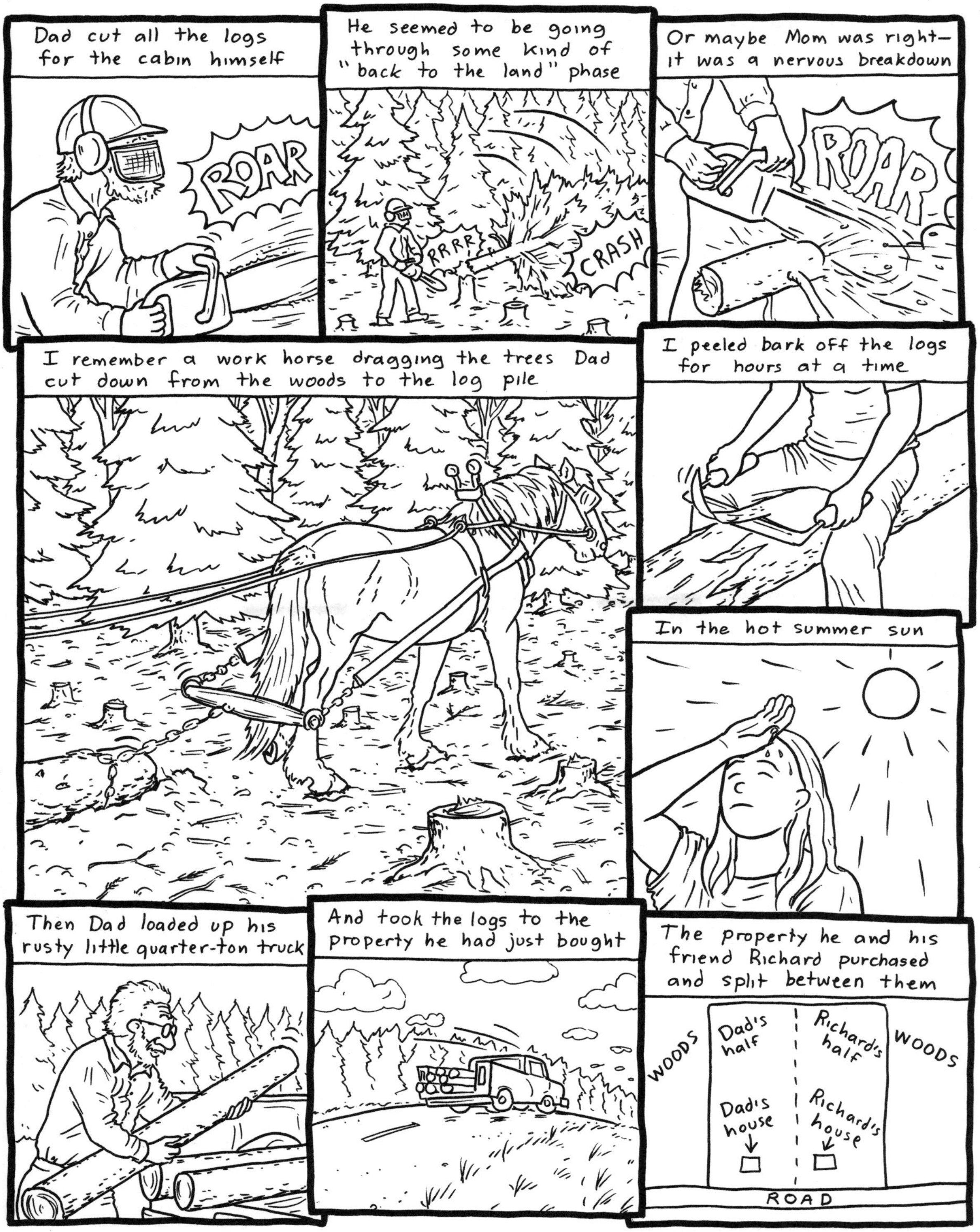
Dad cut all the logs for the cabin himself
ROAR
He seemed to be going through some kind of "back to the land" phase
RRRR
CRASH
Or maybe Mom was right—it was a nervous breakdown
ROAR
I remember a work horse dragging the trees Dad cut down from the woods to the log pile
I peeled bark off the logs for hours at a time
In the hot summer sun
Then Dad loaded up his rusty little quarter-ton truck
And took the logs to the property he had just bought
The property he and his friend Richard purchased and split between them
WOODS
Dad's half
Richard's half
WOODS
Dad's house
Richard's house
ROAD

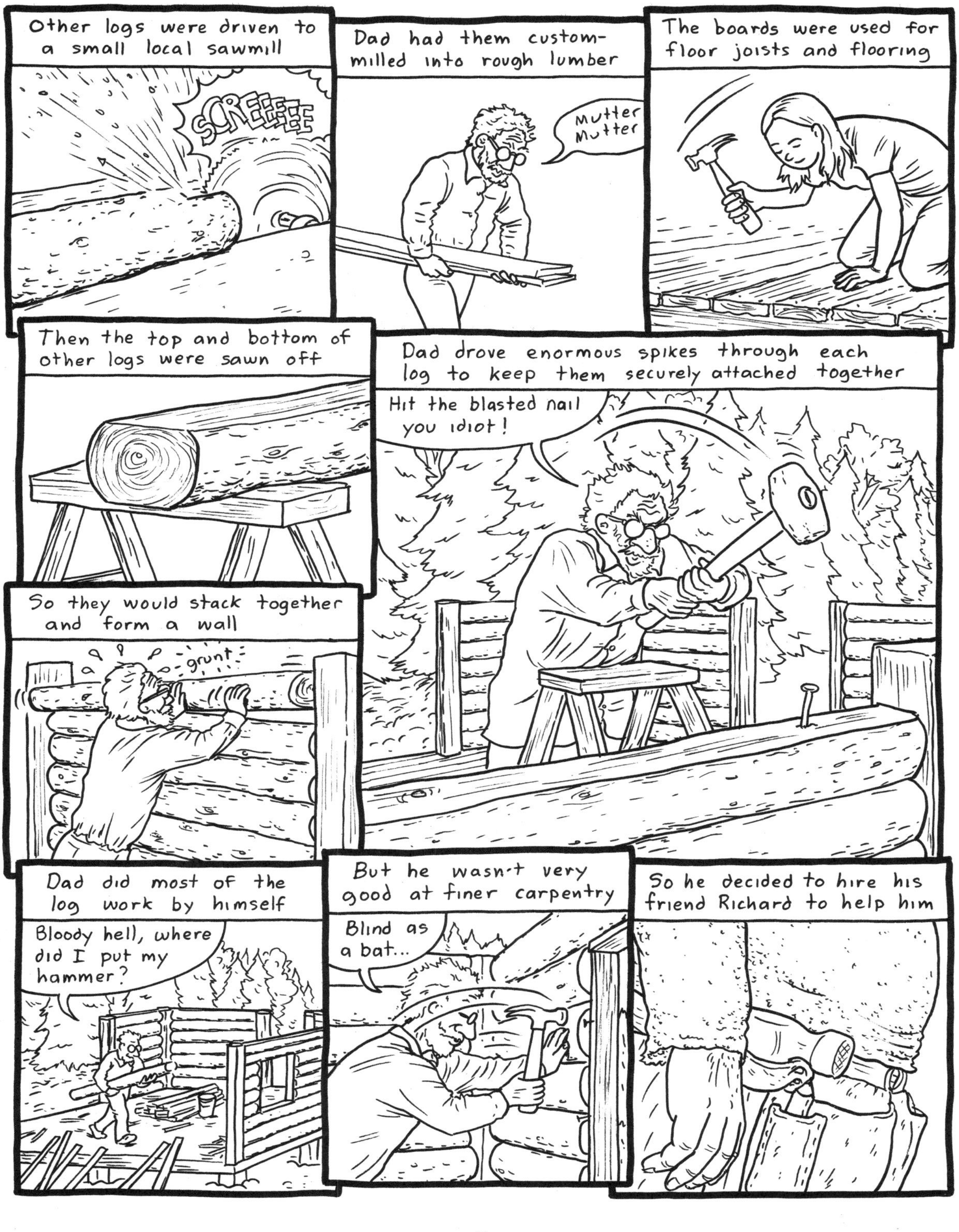
Other logs were driven to a small local sawmill
SCREEEEEE
Dad had them custom-milled into rough lumber
Mutter Mutter
The boards were used for floor joists and flooring
Then the top and bottom of other logs were sawn off
So they would stack together and form a wall
grunt
Dad drove enormous spikes through each log to keep them securely attached together
Hit the blasted nail you idiot!
Dad did most of the log work by himself
Bloody hell, where did I put my hammer?
But he wasn't very good at finer carpentry
Blind as a bat...
So he decided to hire his friend Richard to help him

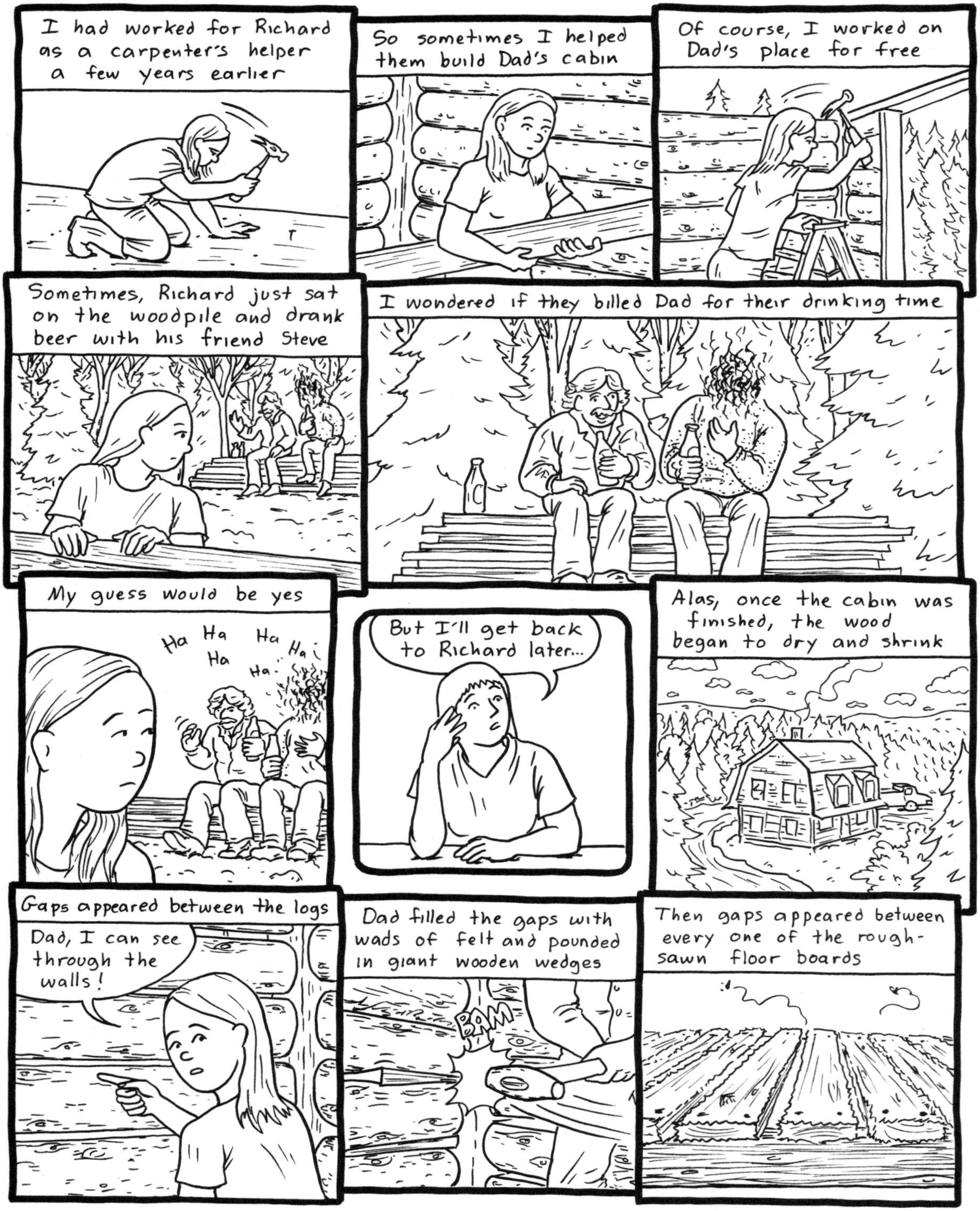
I had worked for Richard as a carpenter's helper a few years earlier
So sometimes I helped them build Dad's cabin
Of course, I worked on Dad's place for free
Sometimes, Richard just sat on the woodpile and drank beer with his friend Steve
I wondered if they billed Dad for their drinking time
My guess would be yes
Ha Ha Ha Ha Ha Ha
But I'll get back to Richard later...
Alas, once the cabin was finished, the wood began to dry and shrink
Gaps appeared between the logs
Dad, I can see through the walls!
Dad filled the gaps with wads of felt and pounded in giant wooden wedges
BAM
Then gaps appeared between every one of the rough-sawn floor boards

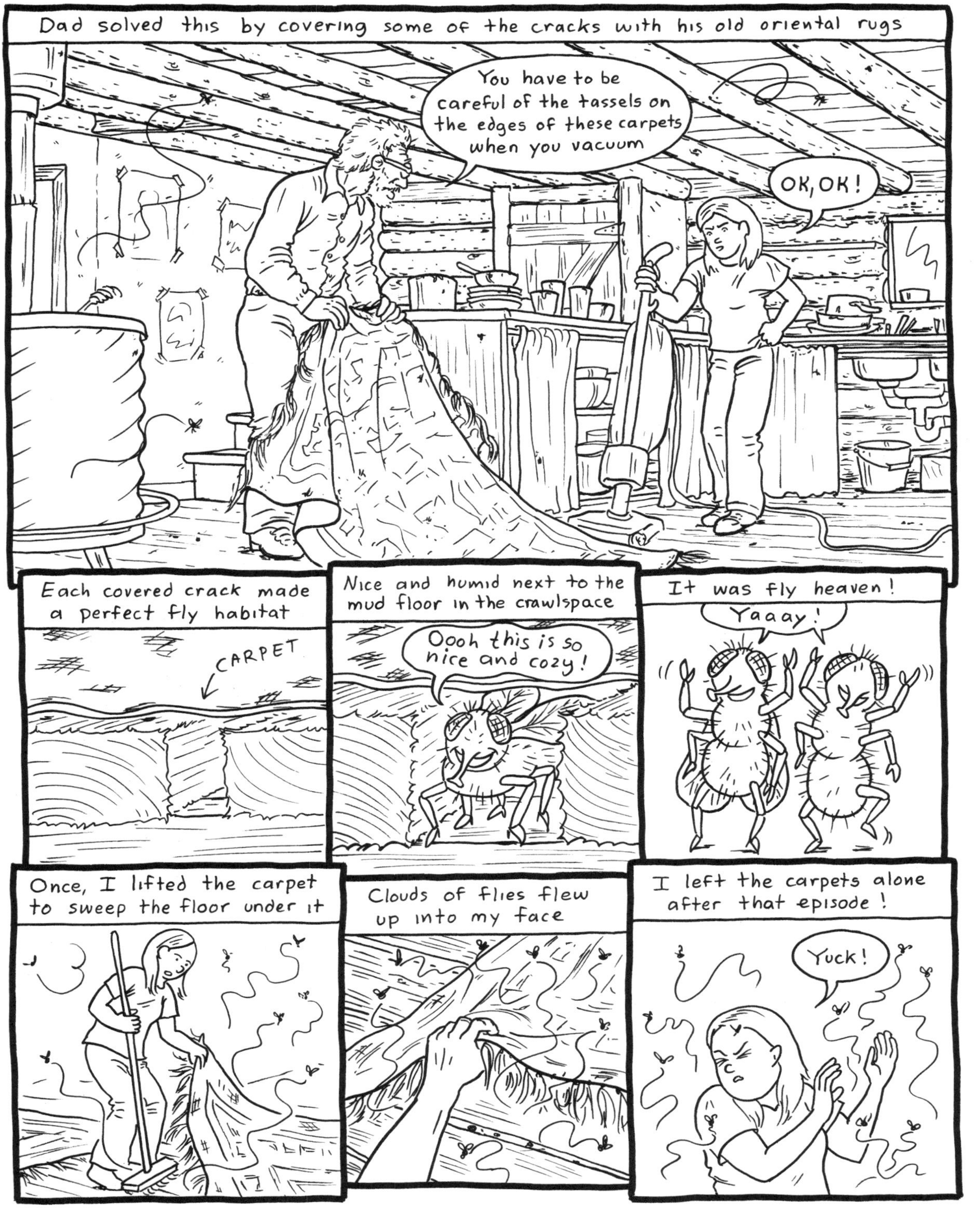

Dad solved this by covering some of the cracks with his old oriental rugs
You have to be careful of the tassels on the edges of these carpets when you vacuum
OK, OK!
Each covered crack made a perfect fly habitat
CARPET
Nice and humid next to the mud floor in the crawlspace
Oooh this is so nice and cozy!
It was fly heaven!
Yaaay!
Once, I lifted the carpet to sweep the floor under it
Clouds of flies flew up into my face
I left the carpets alone after that episode!
Yuck!

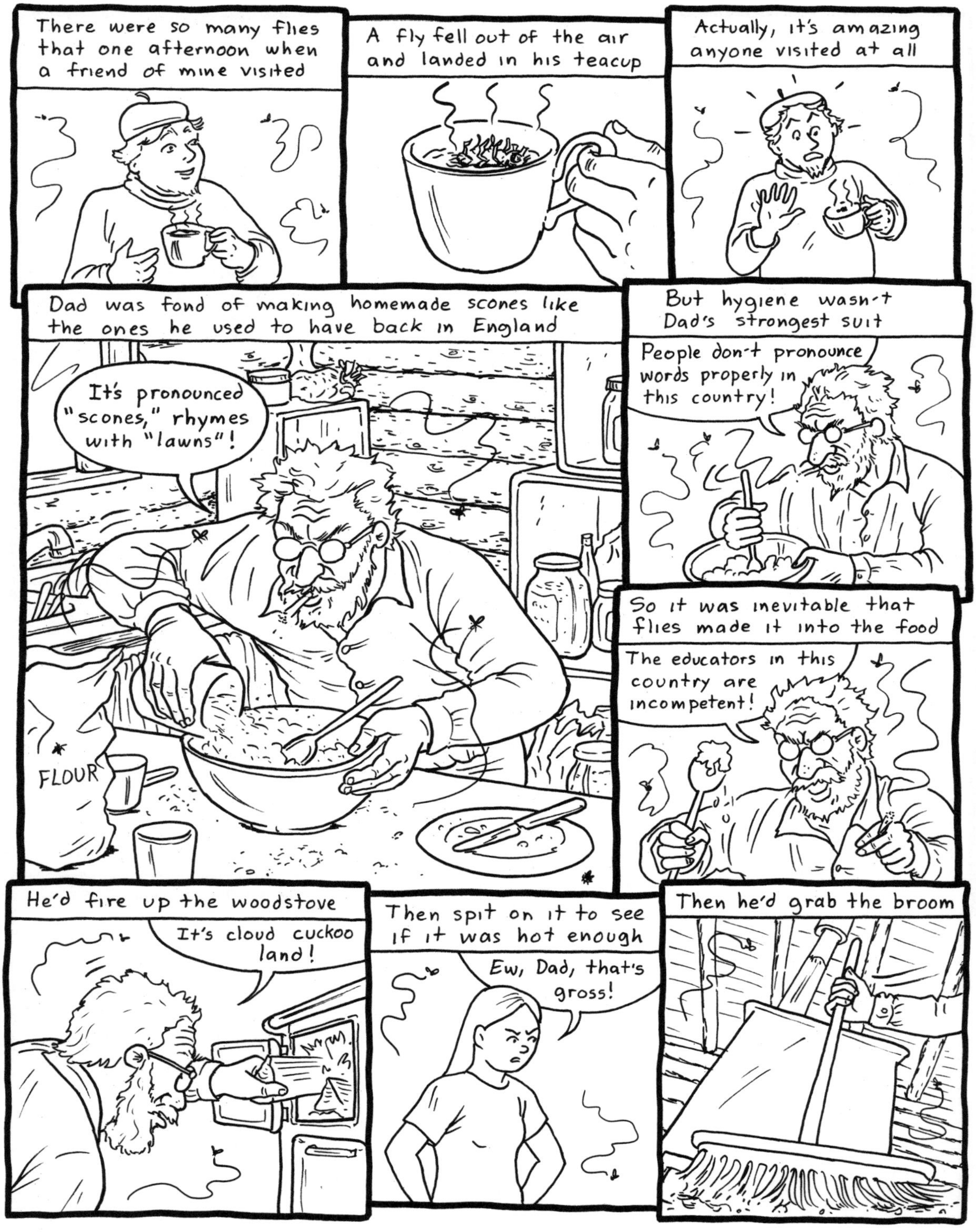
There were so many flies that one afternoon when a friend of mine visited
A fly fell out of the air and landed in his teacup
Actually, it's amazing anyone visited at all
Dad was fond of making homemade scones like the ones he used to have back in England
It's pronounced "scones," rhymes with "lawns"!
FLOUR
But hygiene wasn't Dad's strongest suit
People don't pronounce words properly in this country!
So it was inevitable that flies made it into the food
The educators in this country are incompetent!
He'd fire up the woodstove
It's cloud cuckoo land!
Then spit on it to see if it was hot enough
Ew, Dad, that's gross!
Then he'd grab the broom

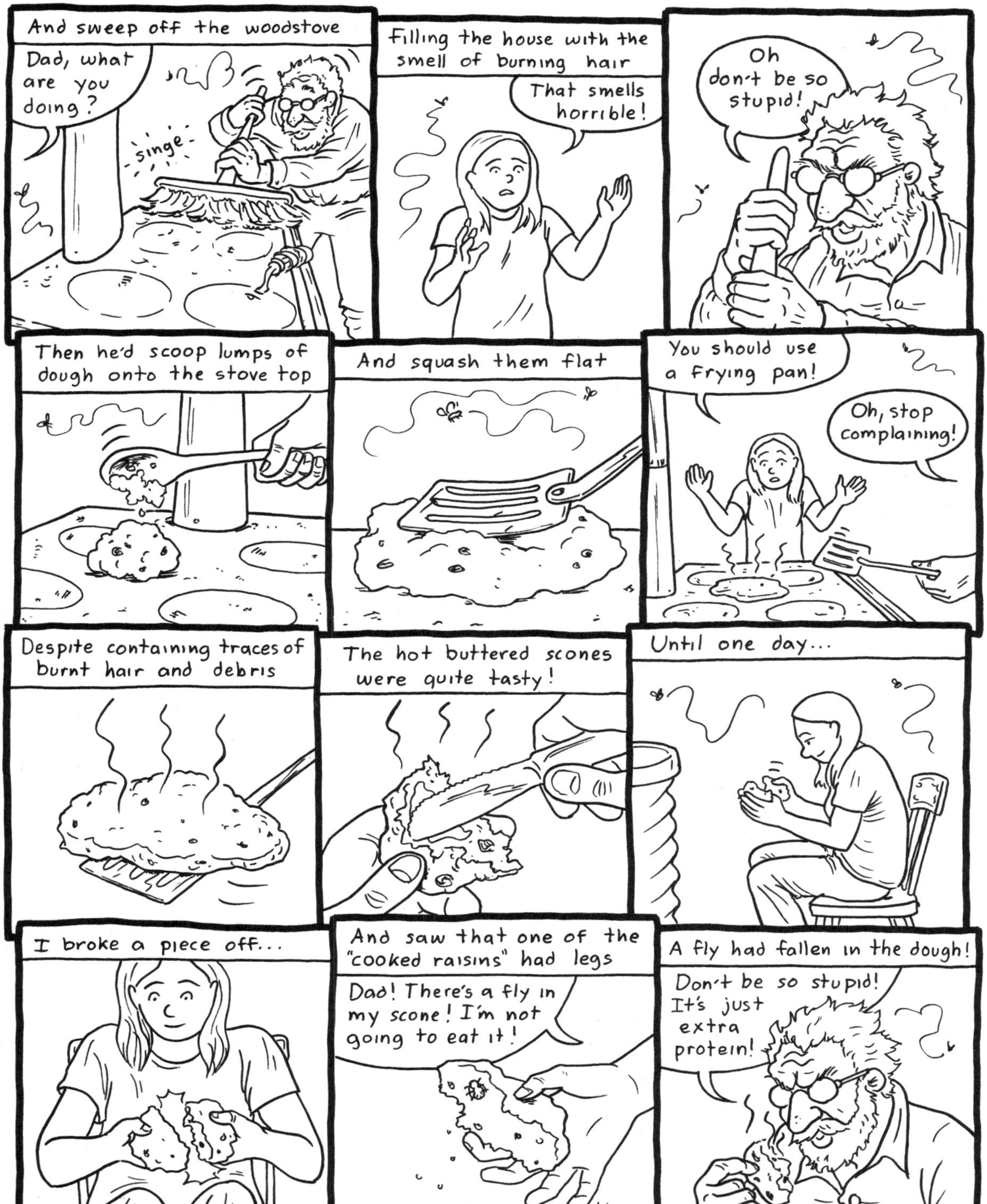
And sweep off the woodstove
Dad, what are you doing?
singe
Filling the house with the smell of burning hair
That smells horrible!
Oh don't be so stupid!
Then he'd scoop lumps of dough onto the stove top
And squash them flat
You should use a frying pan!
Oh, stop complaining!
Despite containing traces of burnt hair and debris
The hot buttered scones were quite tasty!
Until one day...
I broke a piece off...
And saw that one of the "cooked raisins" had legs
Dad! There's a fly in my scone! I'm not going to eat it!
A fly had fallen in the dough!
Don't be so stupid! It's just extra protein!

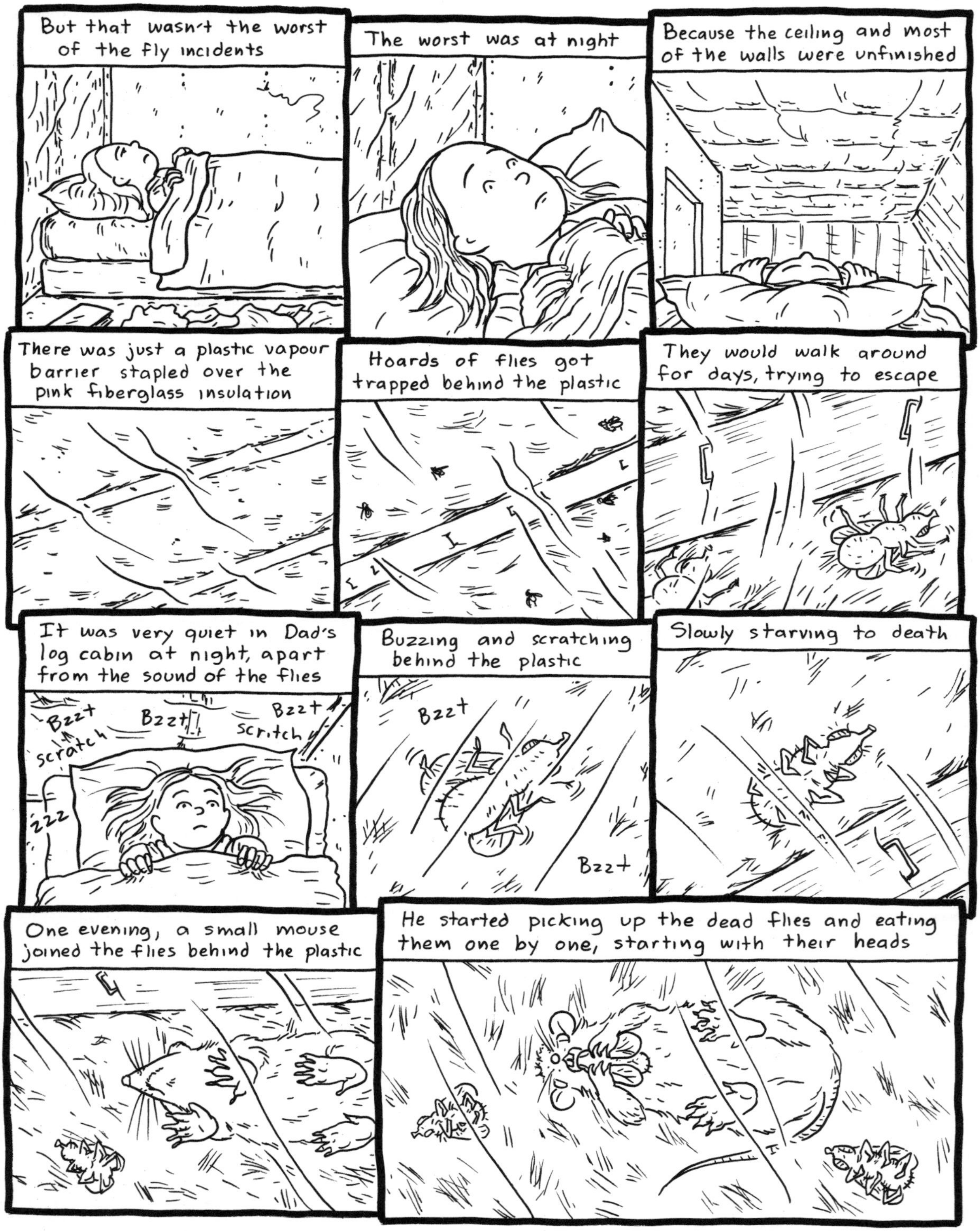
But that wasn't the worst of the fly incidents
The worst was at night
Because the ceiling and most of the walls were unfinished
There was just a plastic vapour barrier stapled over the pink fiberglass insulation
Hoards of flies got trapped behind the plastic
They would walk around for days, trying to escape
It was very quiet in Dad's log cabin at night, apart from the sound of the flies
Bzzt
Bzzt
Bzzt
scratch
scritch
zzz
Buzzing and scratching behind the plastic
Bzzt
Bzzt
Slowly starving to death
One evening, a small mouse joined the flies behind the plastic
He started picking up the dead flies and eating them one by one, starting with their heads

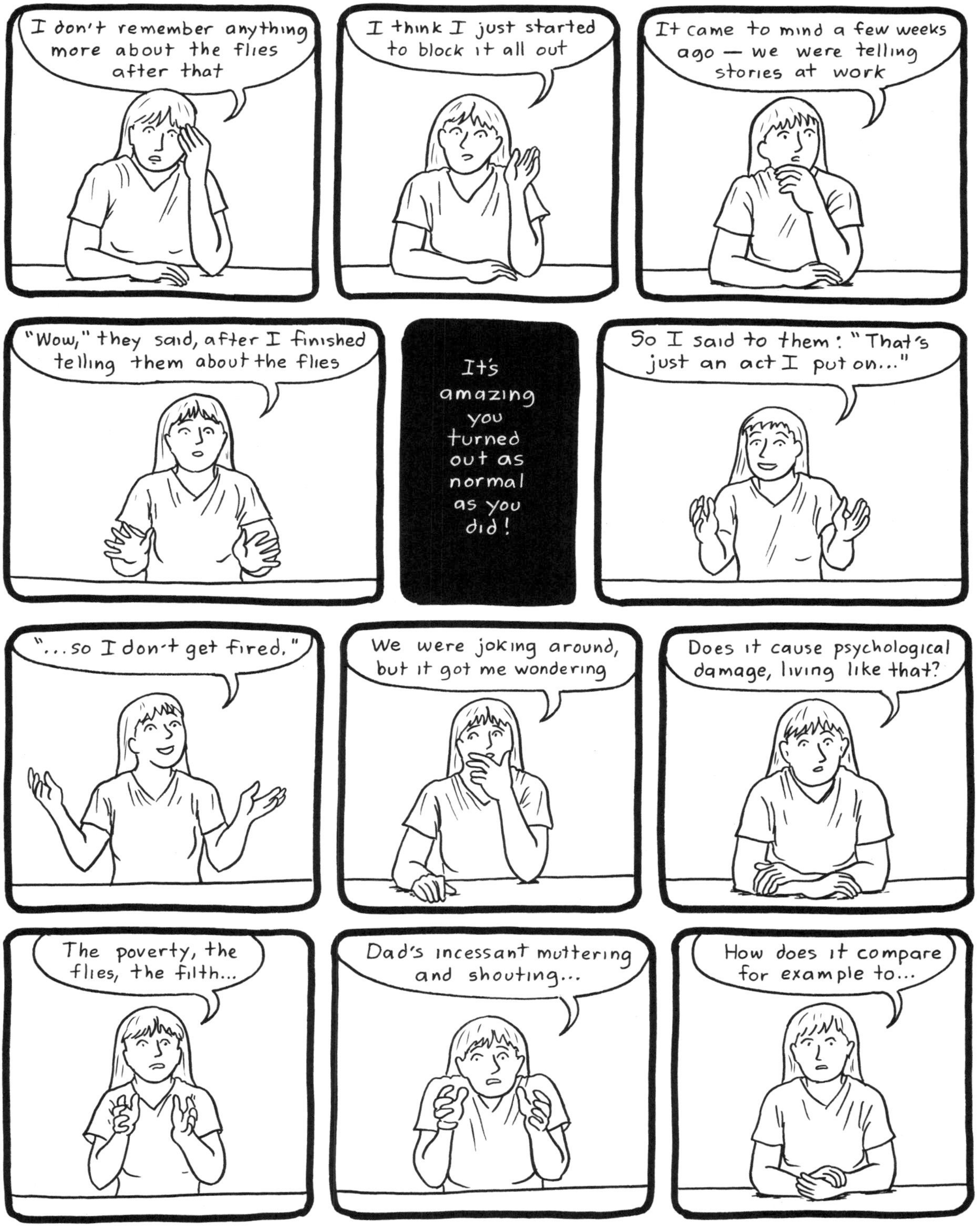
I don't remember anything more about the flies after that
I think I just started to block it all out
It came to mind a few weeks ago — we were telling stories at work
"Wow," they said, after I finished telling them about the flies
It's amazing you turned out as normal as you did!
So I said to them: "That's just an act I put on..."
"...so I don't get fired."
We were joking around, but it got me wondering
Does it cause psychological damage, living like that?
The poverty, the flies, the filth...
Dad's incessant muttering and shouting...
How does it compare for example to...

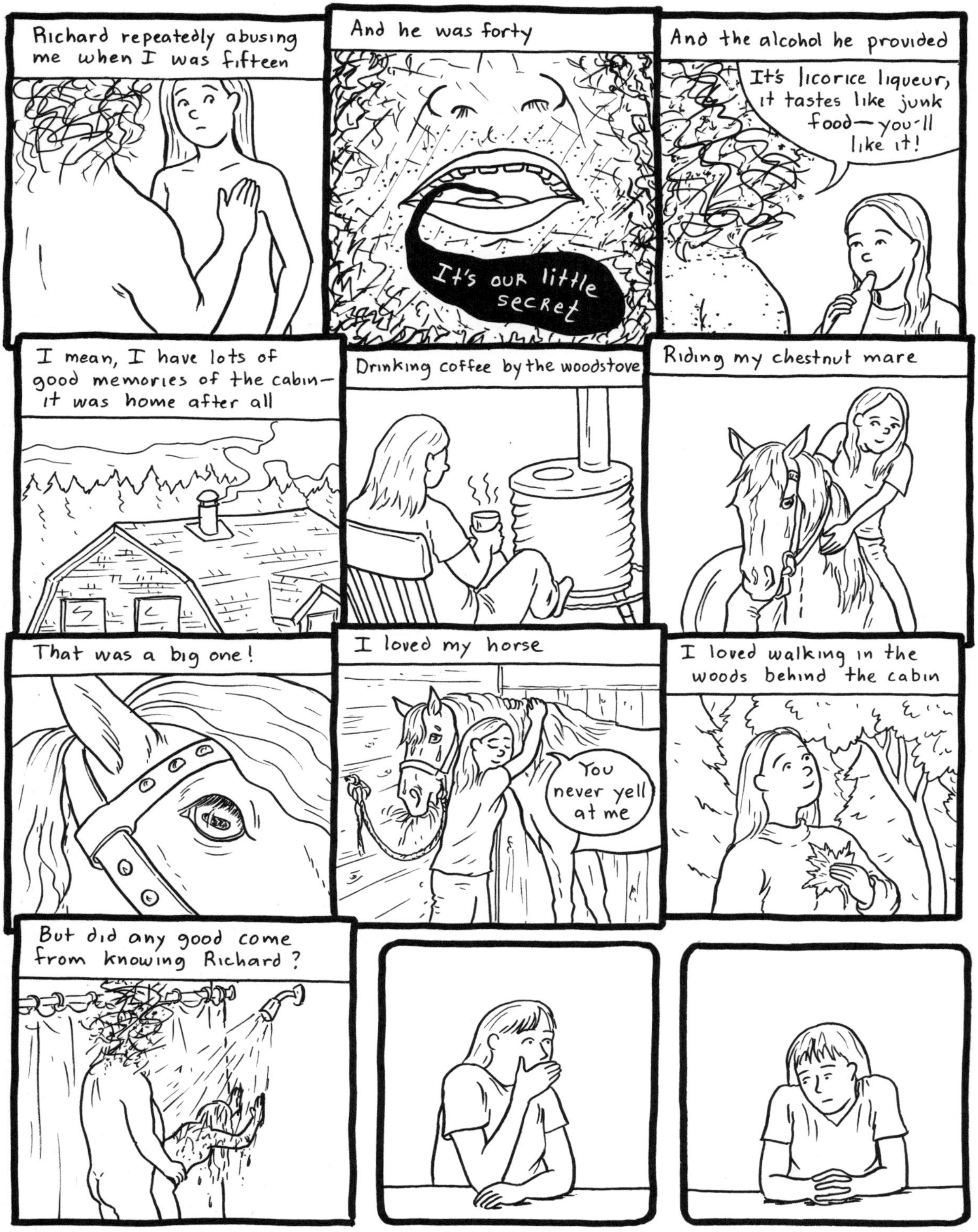
Richard repeatedly abusing me when I was fifteen
And he was forty
It's our little secret
And the alcohol he provided
It's licorice liqueur, it tastes like junk food— you'll like it!
I mean, I have lots of good memories of the cabin— it was home after all
Drinking coffee by the woodstove
Riding my chestnut mare
That was a big one!
I loved my horse
You never yell at me
I loved walking in the woods behind the cabin
But did any good come from knowing Richard?

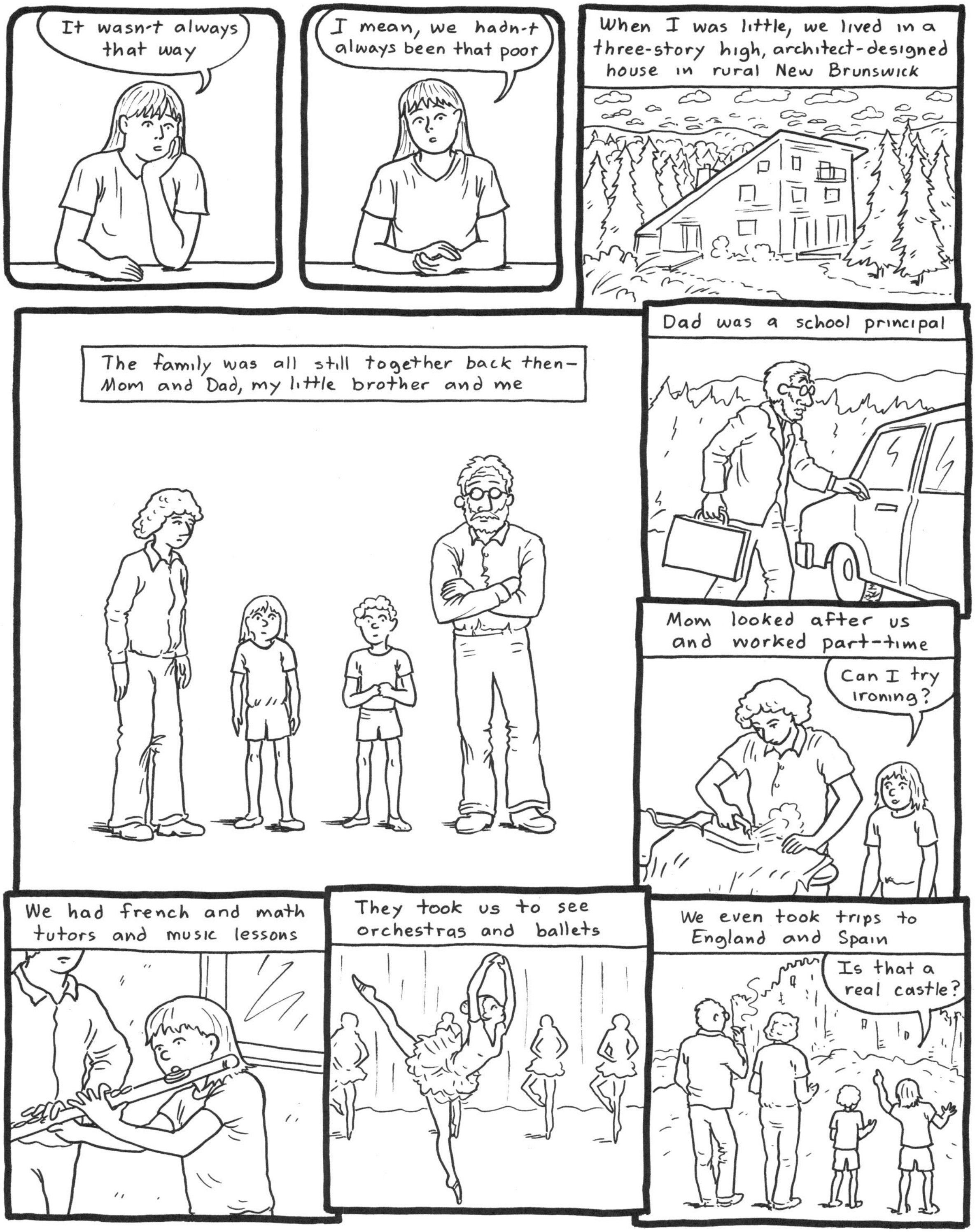

It wasn't always that way
I mean, we hadn't always been that poor
When I was little, we lived in a three-story high, architect-designed house in rural New Brunswick
The family was all still together back then— Mom and Dad, my little brother and me
Dad was a school principal
Mom looked after us and worked part-time
Can I try ironing?
We had french and math tutors and music lessons
They took us to see orchestras and ballets
We even took trips to England and Spain
Is that a real castle?

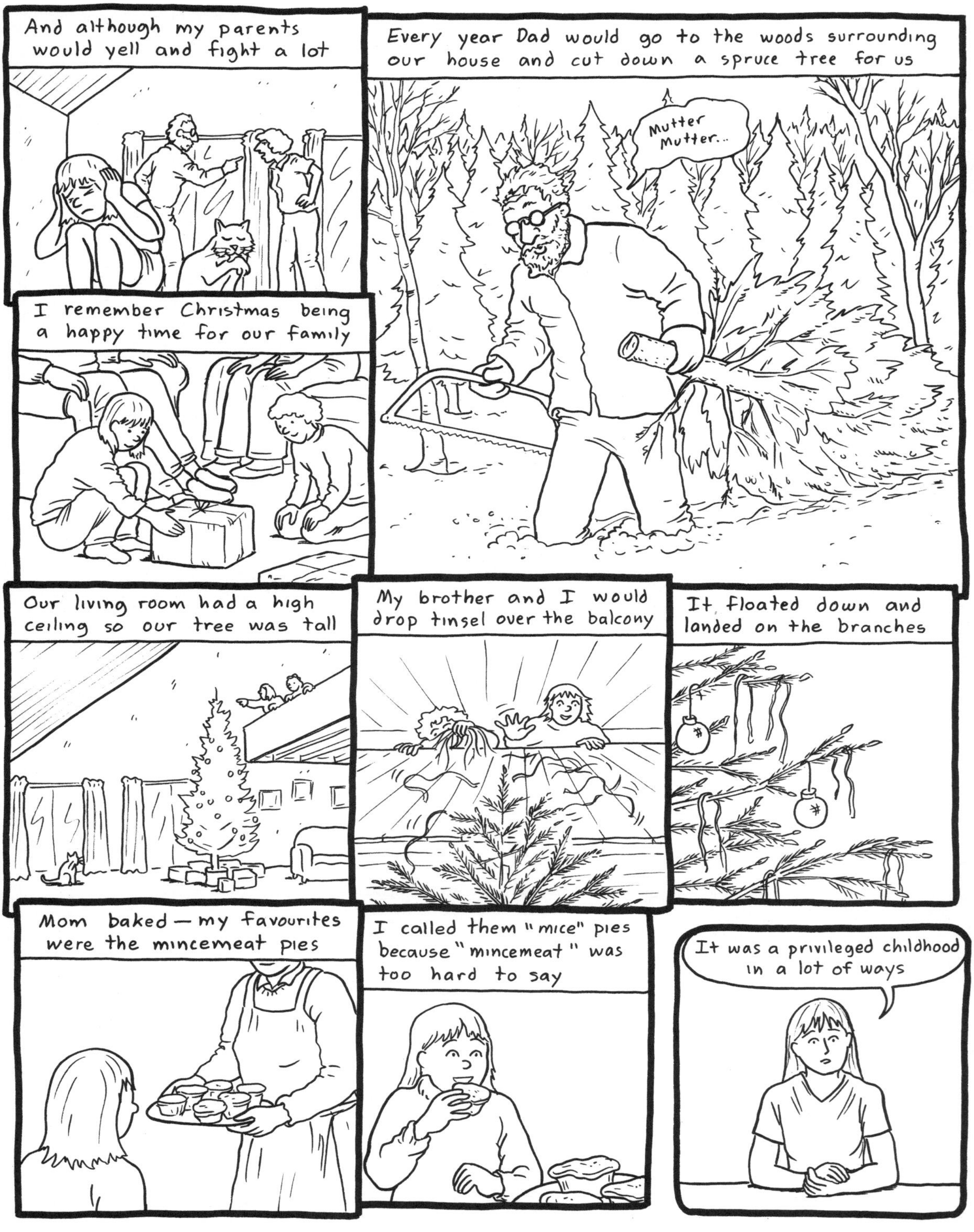
And although my parents would yell and fight a lot
Every year Dad would go to the woods surrounding our house and cut down a spruce tree for us
Mutter Mutter...
I remember Christmas being a happy time for our family
Our living room had a high ceiling so our tree was tall
My brother and I would drop tinsel over the balcony
It floated down and landed on the branches
Mom baked—my favourites were the mincemeat pies
I called them "mice" pies because "mincemeat" was too hard to say
It was a privileged childhood in a lot of ways

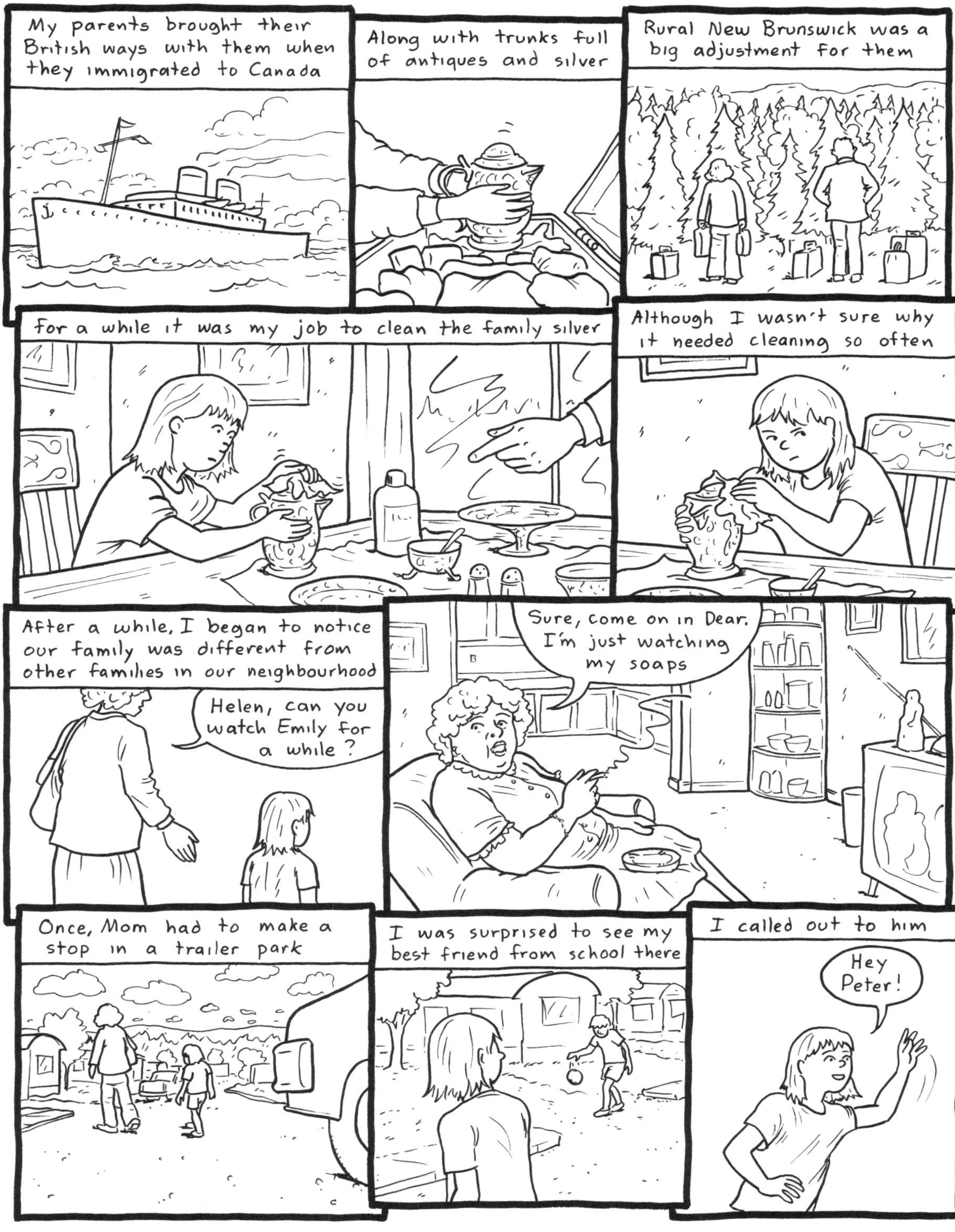
My parents brought their British ways with them when they immigrated to Canada
Along with trunks full of antiques and silver
Rural New Brunswick was a big adjustment for them
For a while it was my job to clean the family silver
Although I wasn't sure why it needed cleaning so often
After a while, I began to notice our family was different from other families in our neighbourhood
Helen, can you watch Emily for a while?
Sure, come on in Dear. I'm just watching my soaps
Once, Mom had to make a stop in a trailer park
I was surprised to see my best friend from school there
I called out to him
Hey Peter!

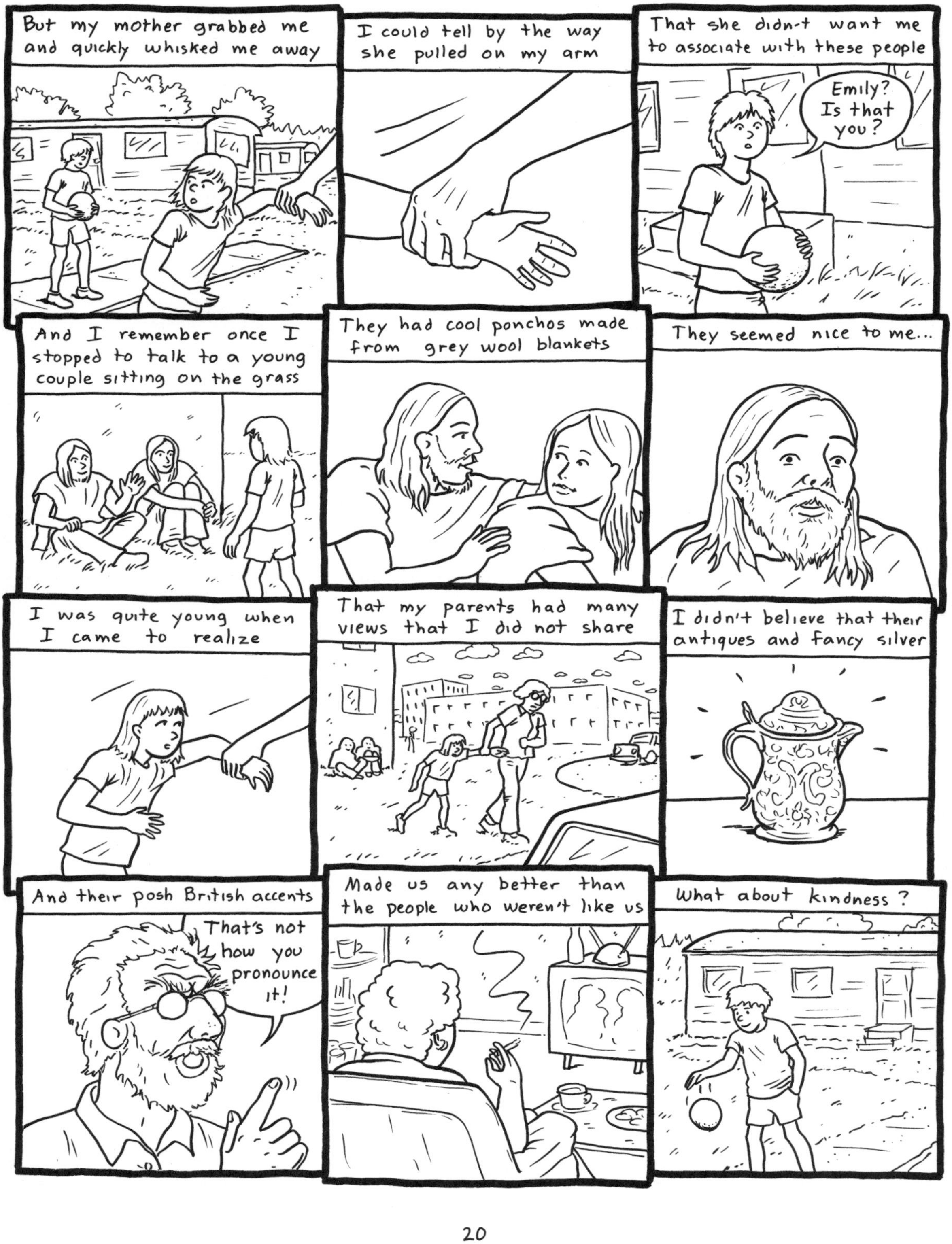
But my mother grabbed me and quickly whisked me away
I could tell by the way she pulled on my arm
That she didn't want me to associate with these people
Emily? Is that you?
And I remember once I stopped to talk to a young couple sitting on the grass
They had cool ponchos made from grey wool blankets
They seemed nice to me...
I was quite young when I came to realize
That my parents had many views that I did not share
I didn't believe that their antiques and fancy silver
And their posh British accents
That's not how you pronounce it!
Made us any better than the people who weren't like us
What about kindness?

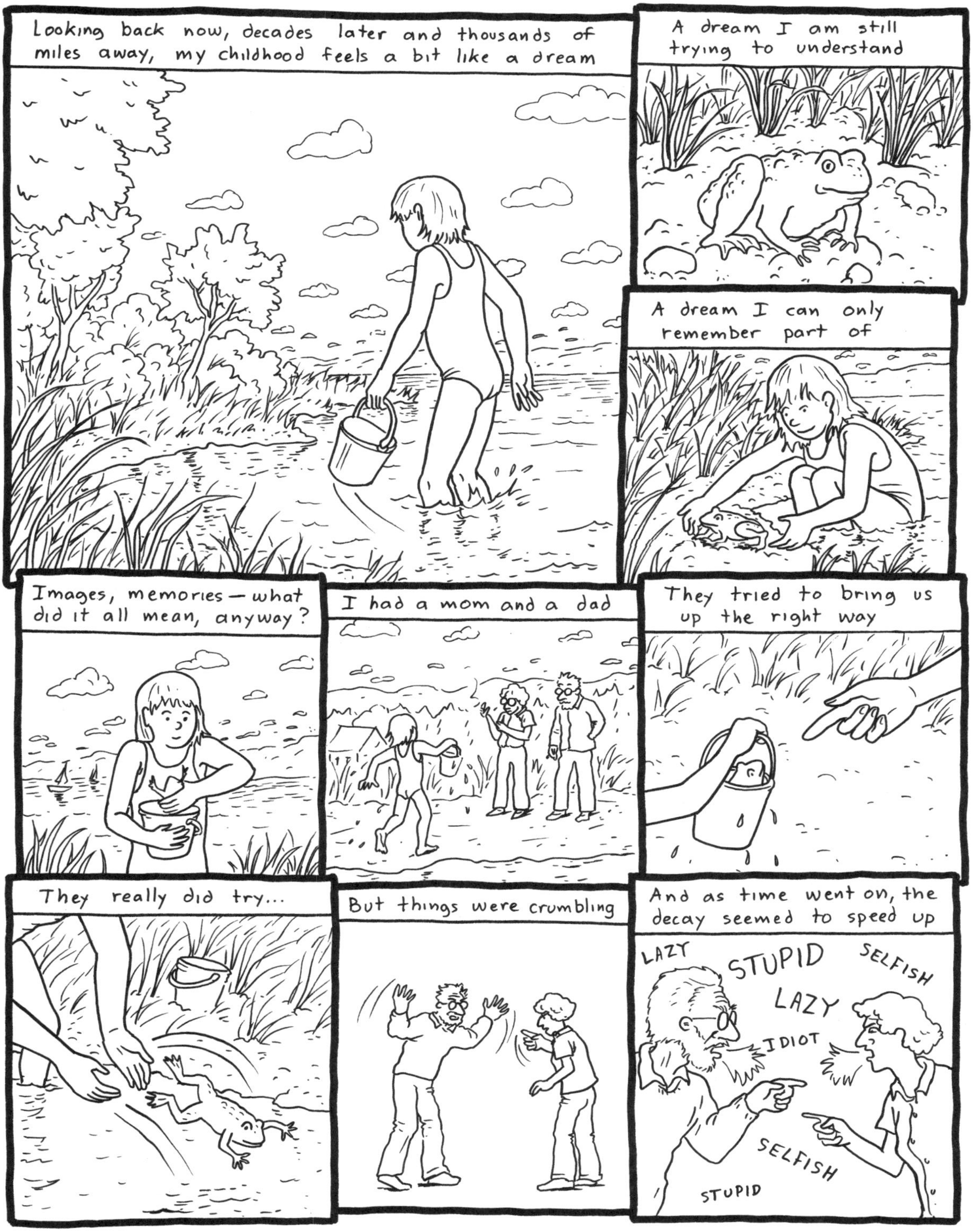
Looking back now, decades later and thousands of miles away, my childhood feels a bit like a dream
A dream I am still trying to understand
A dream I can only remember part of
Images, memories—what did it all mean, anyway?
I had a mom and a dad
They tried to bring us up the right way
They really did try...
But things were crumbling
And as time went on, the decay seemed to speed up
LAZY
STUPID
SELFISH
LAZY
IDIOT
SELFISH
STUPID

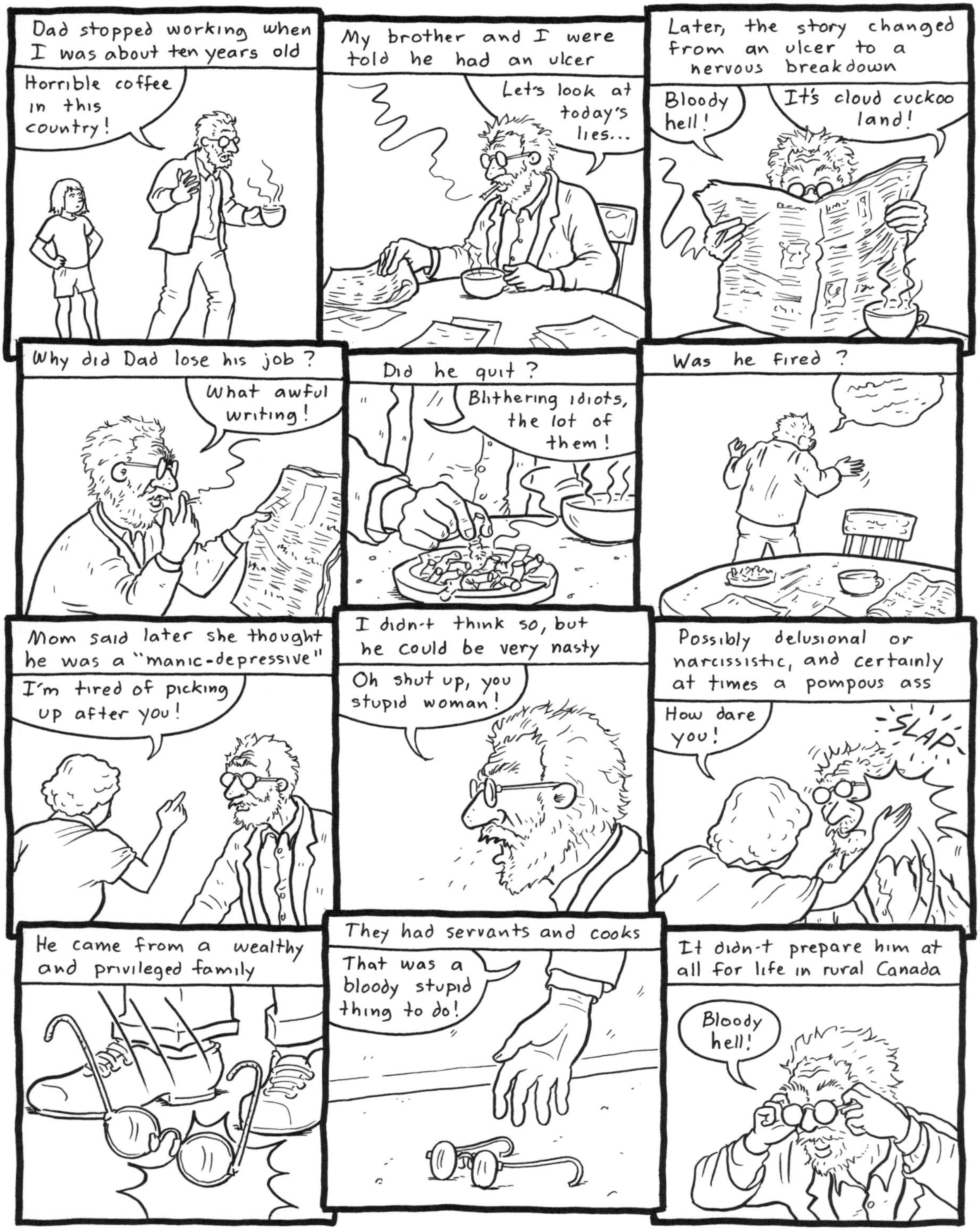

Dad stopped working when I was about ten years old
Horrible coffee in this country!
My brother and I were told he had an ulcer
Let's look at today's lies...
Later, the story changed from an ulcer to a nervous breakdown
Bloody hell!
It's cloud cuckoo land!
Why did Dad lose his job?
What awful writing!
Did he quit?
Blithering idiots, the lot of them!
Was he fired?
Mom said later she thought he was a "manic-depressive"
I'm tired of picking up after you!
I didn't think so, but he could be very nasty
Oh shut up, you stupid woman!
Possibly delusional or narcissistic, and certainly at times a pompous ass
How dare you!
SLAP
He came from a wealthy and privileged family
They had servants and cooks
That was a bloody stupid thing to do!
It didn't prepare him at all for life in rural Canada
Bloody hell!

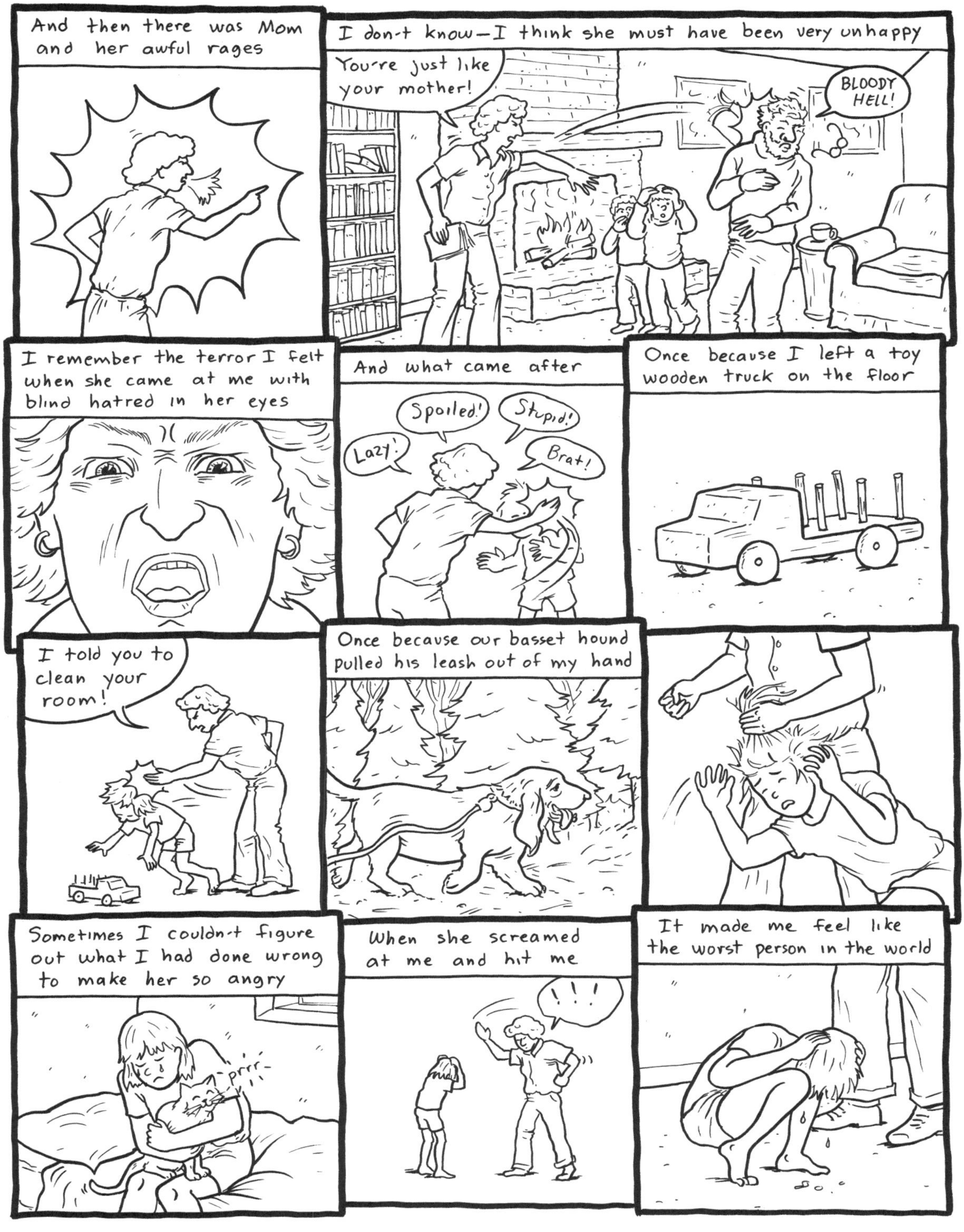
And then there was Mom and her awful rages
I don't know—I think she must have been very unhappy
You're just like your mother!
BLOODY HELL!
I remember the terror I felt when she came at me with blind hatred in her eyes
And what came after
Spoiled!
Stupid!
Lazy!
Brat!
Once because I left a toy wooden truck on the floor
I told you to clean your room!
Once because our basset hound pulled his leash out of my hand
Sometimes I couldn't figure out what I had done wrong to make her so angry
-prrr-
When she screamed at me and hit me
!!!
It made me feel like the worst person in the world

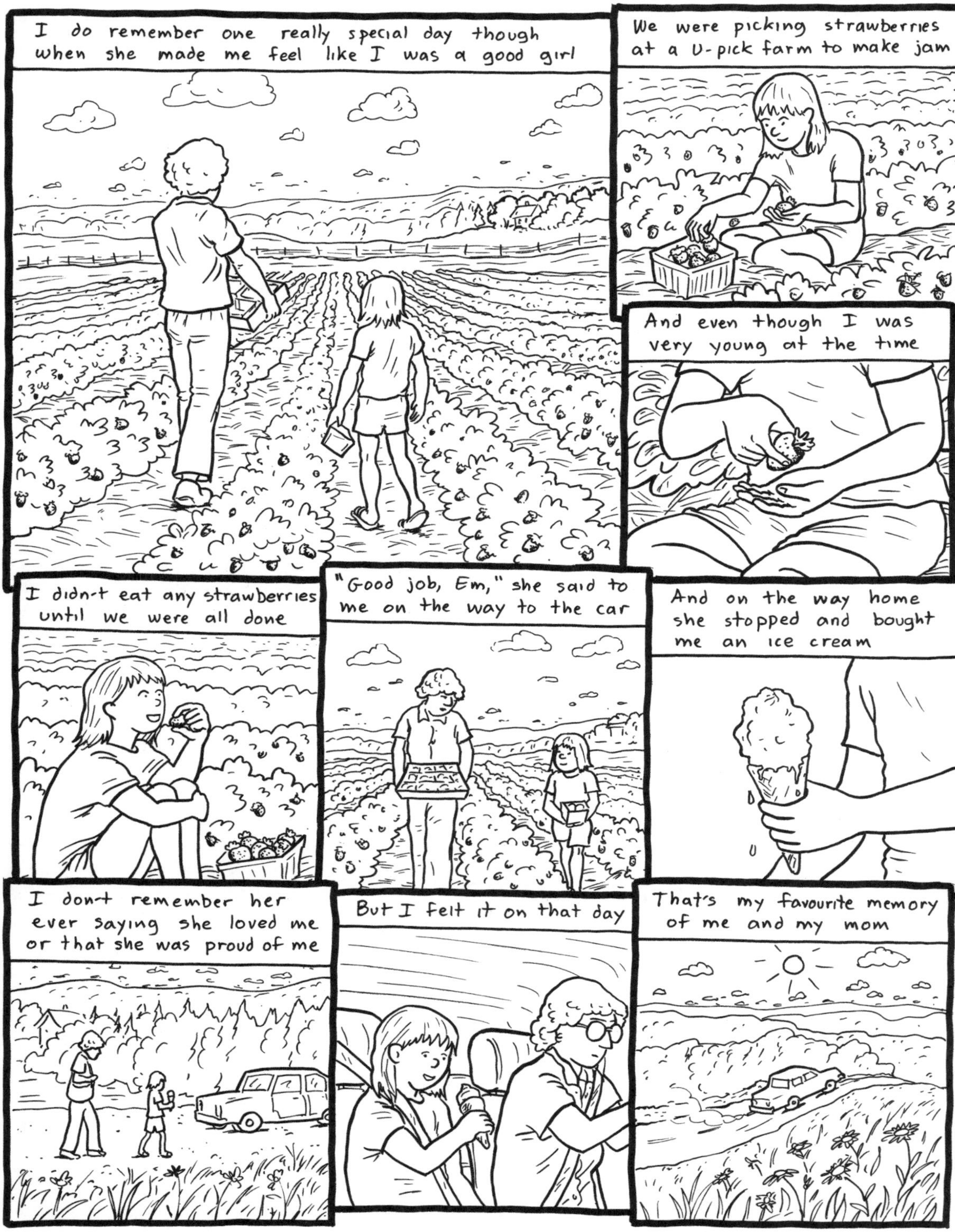
I do remember one really special day though when she made me feel like I was a good girl
We were picking strawberries at a U-pick farm to make jam
And even though I was very young at the time
I didn't eat any strawberries until we were all done
"Good job, Em," she said to me on the way to the car
And on the way home she stopped and bought me an ice cream
I don't remember her ever saying she loved me or that she was proud of me
But I felt it on that day
That's my favourite memory of me and my mom

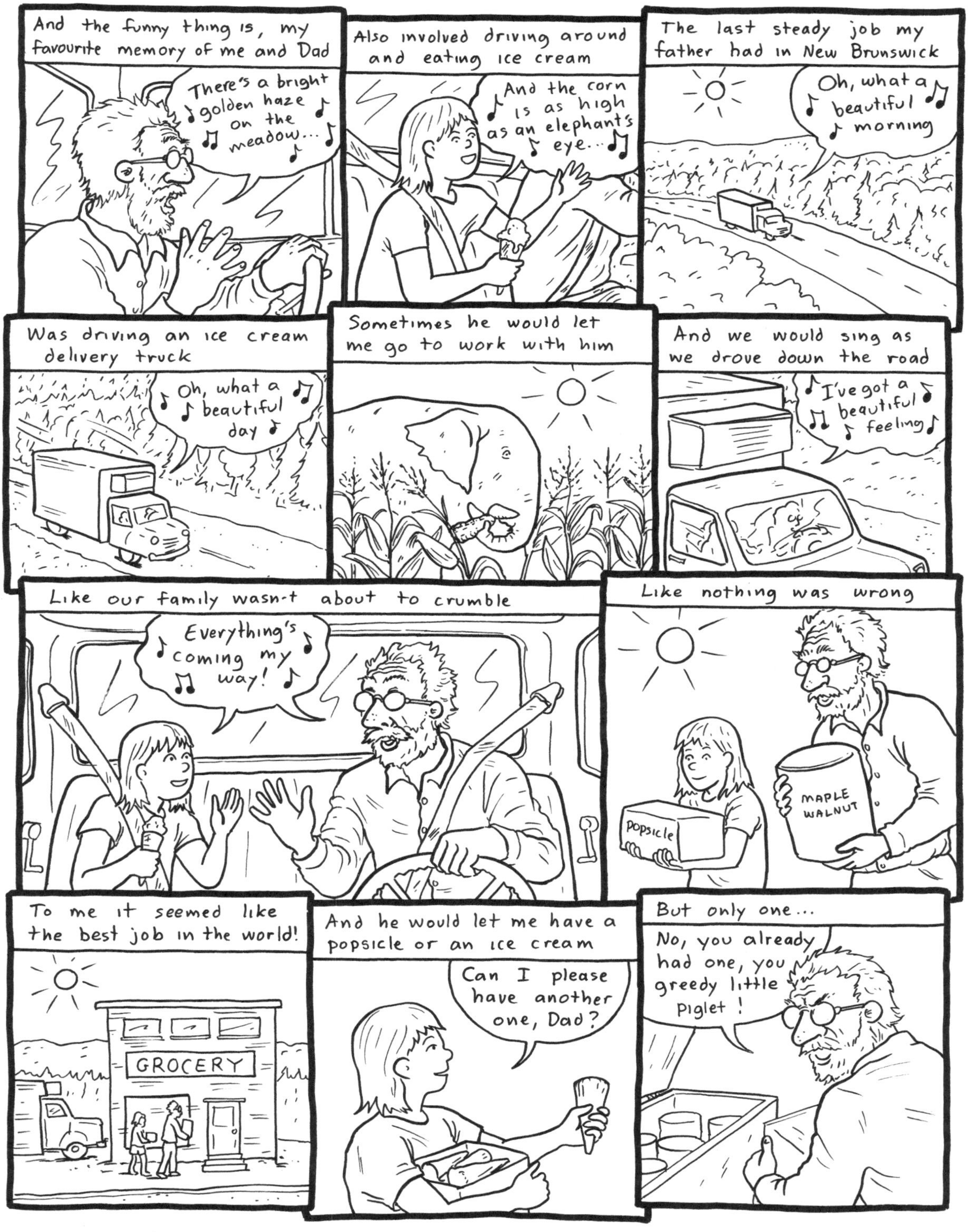

And the funny thing is, my favourite memory of me and Dad
There's a bright golden haze on the meadow...
Also involved driving around and eating ice cream
And the corn is as high as an elephant's eye...
The last steady job my father had in New Brunswick
Oh, what a beautiful morning
Was driving an ice cream delivery truck
Oh, what a beautiful day
Sometimes he would let me go to work with him
And we would sing as we drove down the road
I've got a beautiful feeling
Like our family wasn't about to crumble
Everything's coming my way!
Like nothing was wrong
Popsicle
MAPLE WALNUT
To me it seemed like the best job in the world!
GROCERY
And he would let me have a popsicle or an ice cream
Can I please have another one, Dad?
But only one...
No, you already had one, you greedy little piglet!

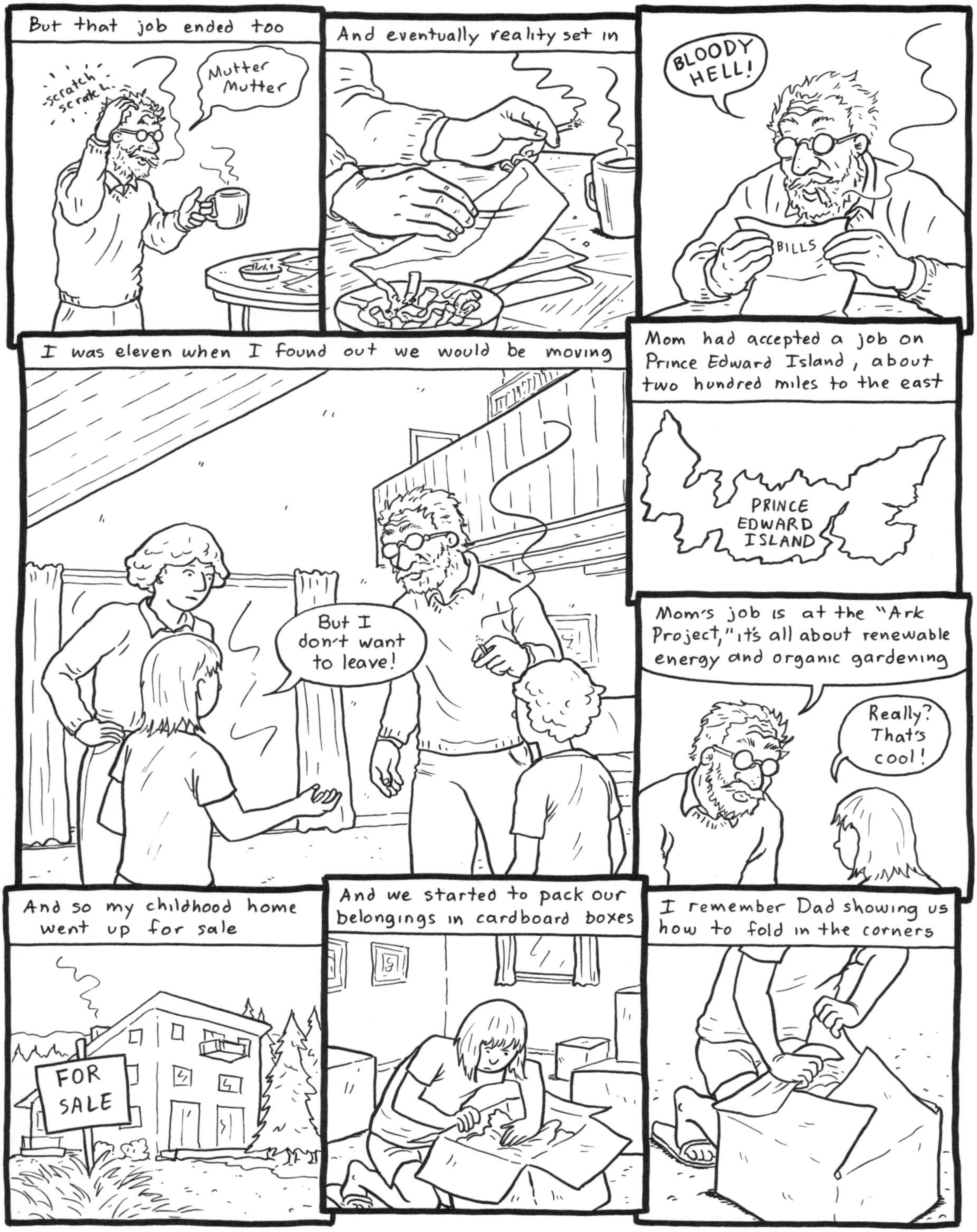

But that job ended too
-scratch scratch-
Mutter Mutter
And eventually reality set in
BLOODY HELL!
BILLS
I was eleven when I found out we would be moving
But I don't want to leave!
Mom had accepted a job on Prince Edward Island, about two hundred miles to the east
PRINCE EDWARD ISLAND
Mom's job is at the "Ark Project," it's all about renewable energy and organic gardening
Really? That's cool!
And so my childhood home went up for sale
FOR SALE
And we started to pack our belongings in cardboard boxes
I remember Dad showing us how to fold in the corners

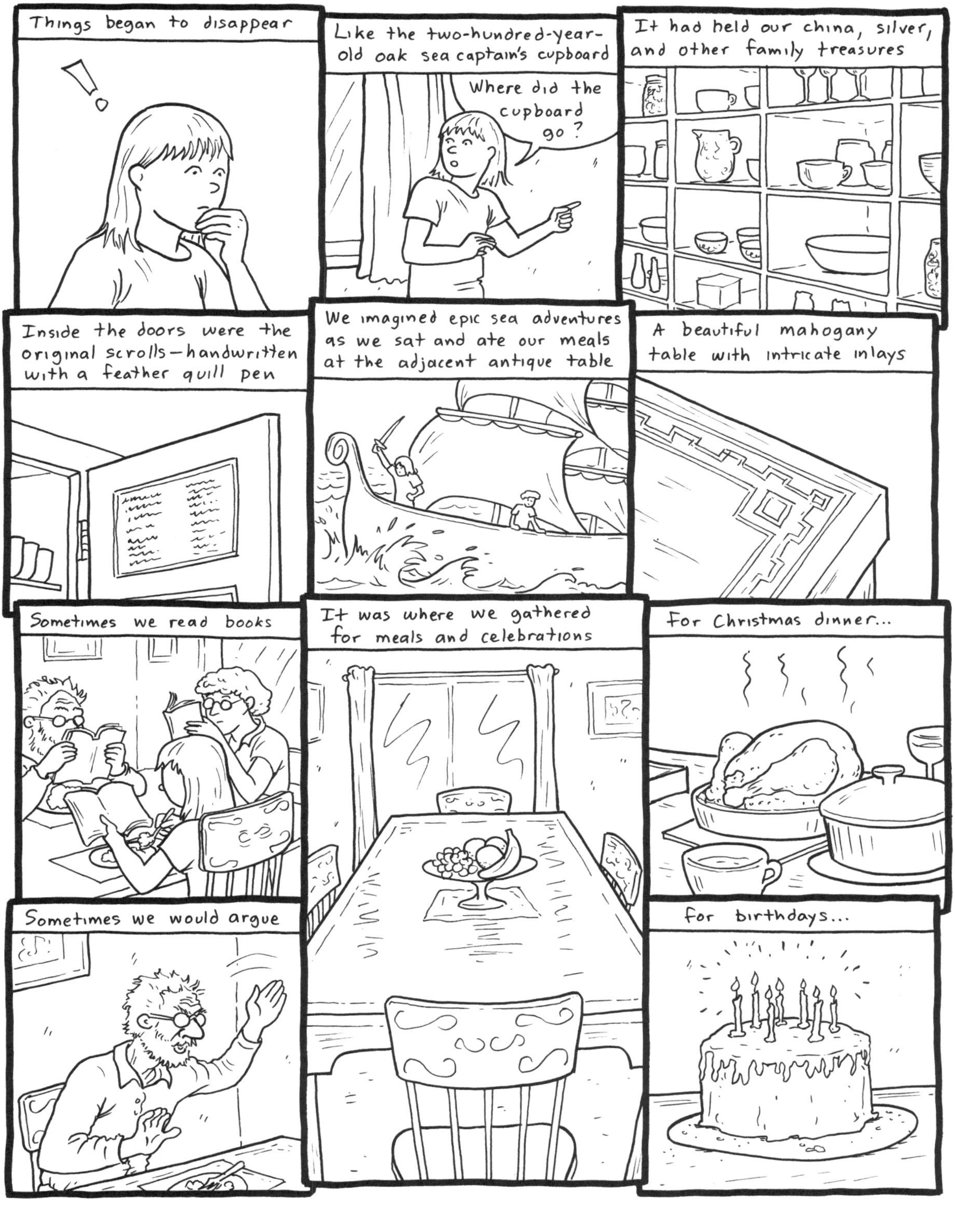
Things began to disappear
!
Like the two-hundred-year-old oak sea captain's cupboard
Where did the cupboard go?
It had held our china, silver, and other family treasures
Inside the doors were the original scrolls—handwritten with a feather quill pen
We imagined epic sea adventures as we sat and ate our meals at the adjacent antique table
A beautiful mahogany table with intricate inlays
Sometimes we read books
It was where we gathered for meals and celebrations
For Christmas dinner...
Sometimes we would argue
for birthdays...

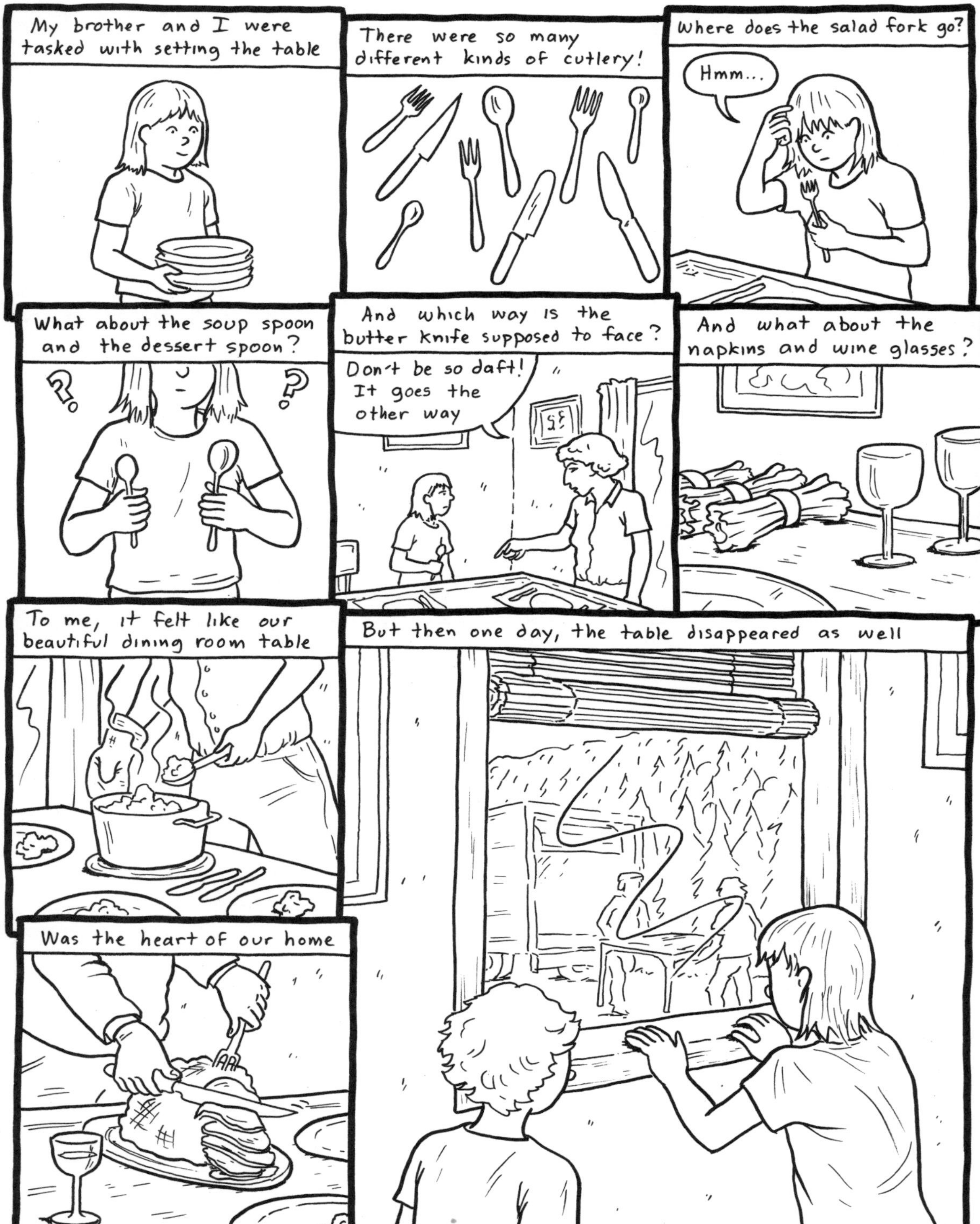
My brother and I were tasked with setting the table
There were so many different kinds of cutlery!
Where does the salad fork go?
Hmm...
What about the soup spoon and the dessert spoon?
And which way is the butter knife supposed to face?
Don't be so daft! It goes the other way
And what about the napkins and wine glasses?
To me, it felt like our beautiful dining room table
Was the heart of our home
But then one day, the table disappeared as well

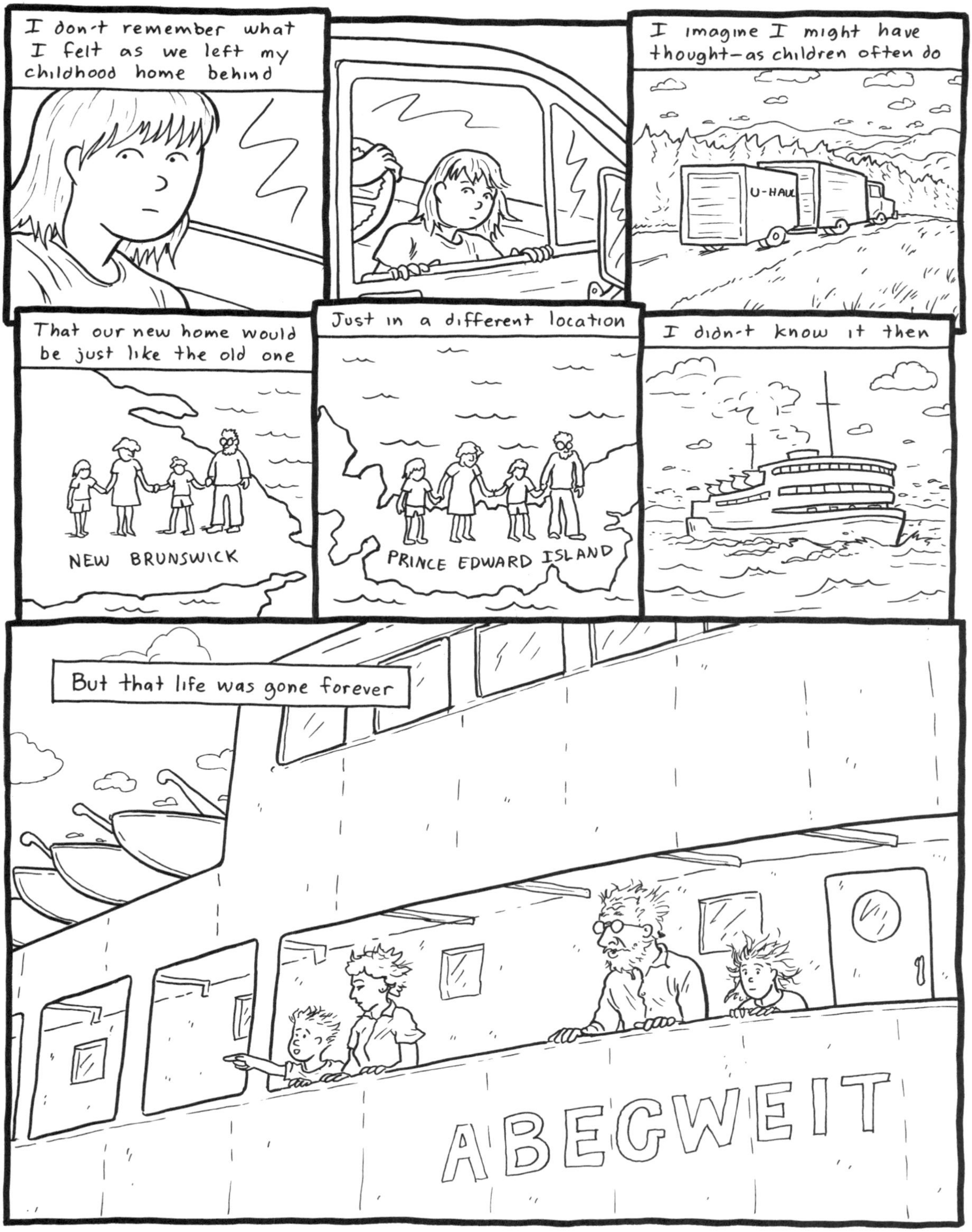
I don't remember what I felt as we left my childhood home behind
I imagine I might have thought—as children often do
U-HAUL
That our new home would be just like the old one
NEW BRUNSWICK
Just in a different location
PRINCE EDWARD ISLAND
I didn't know it then
But that life was gone forever
ABEGWEIT

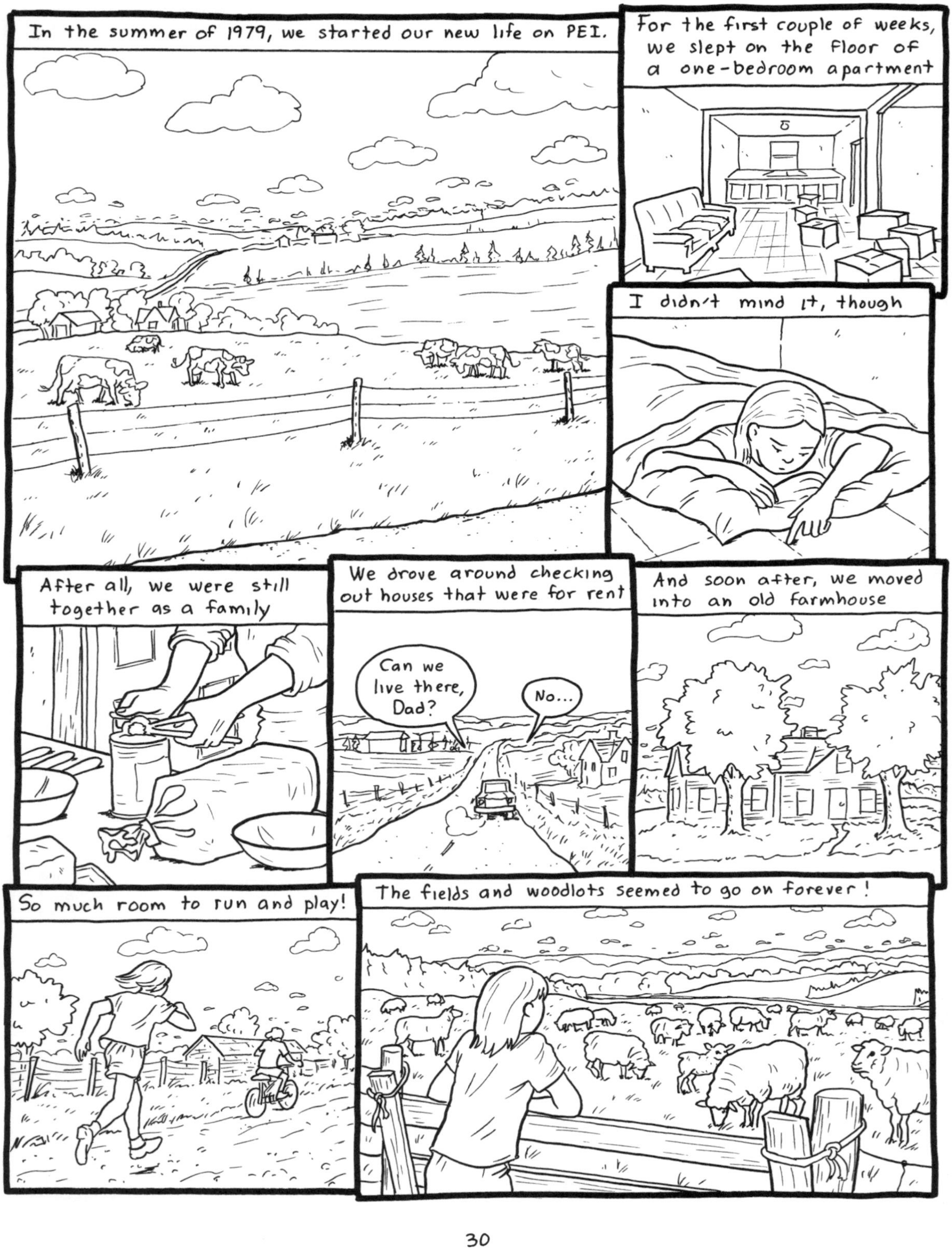
In the summer of 1979, we started our new life on PEI.
For the first couple of weeks, we slept on the floor of a one-bedroom apartment
I didn't mind it, though
After all, we were still together as a family
We drove around checking out houses that were for rent
Can we live there, Dad?
No...
And soon after, we moved into an old farmhouse
So much room to run and play!
The fields and woodlots seemed to go on forever!

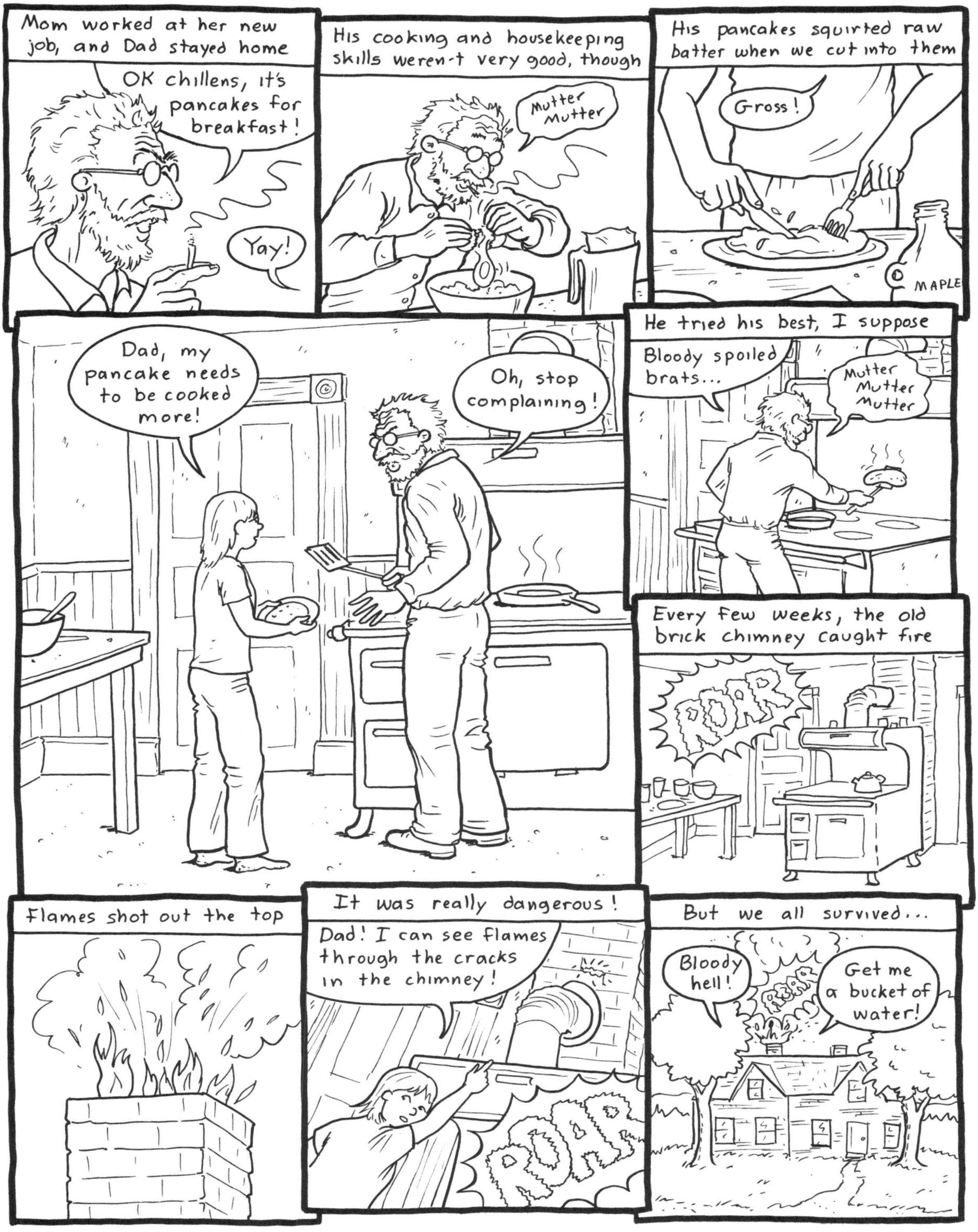

Mom worked at her new job, and Dad stayed home
OK chillens, it's pancakes for breakfast!
Yay!
His cooking and housekeeping skills weren't very good, though
Mutter Mutter
His pancakes squirted raw batter when we cut into them
Gross!
MAPLE
Dad, my pancake needs to be cooked more!
Oh, stop complaining!
He tried his best, I suppose
Bloody spoiled brats...
Mutter Mutter Mutter
Every few weeks, the old brick chimney caught fire
ROAR
Flames shot out the top
It was really dangerous!
Dad! I can see flames through the cracks in the chimney!
ROAR
But we all survived...
Bloody hell!
ROAR
Get me a bucket of water!

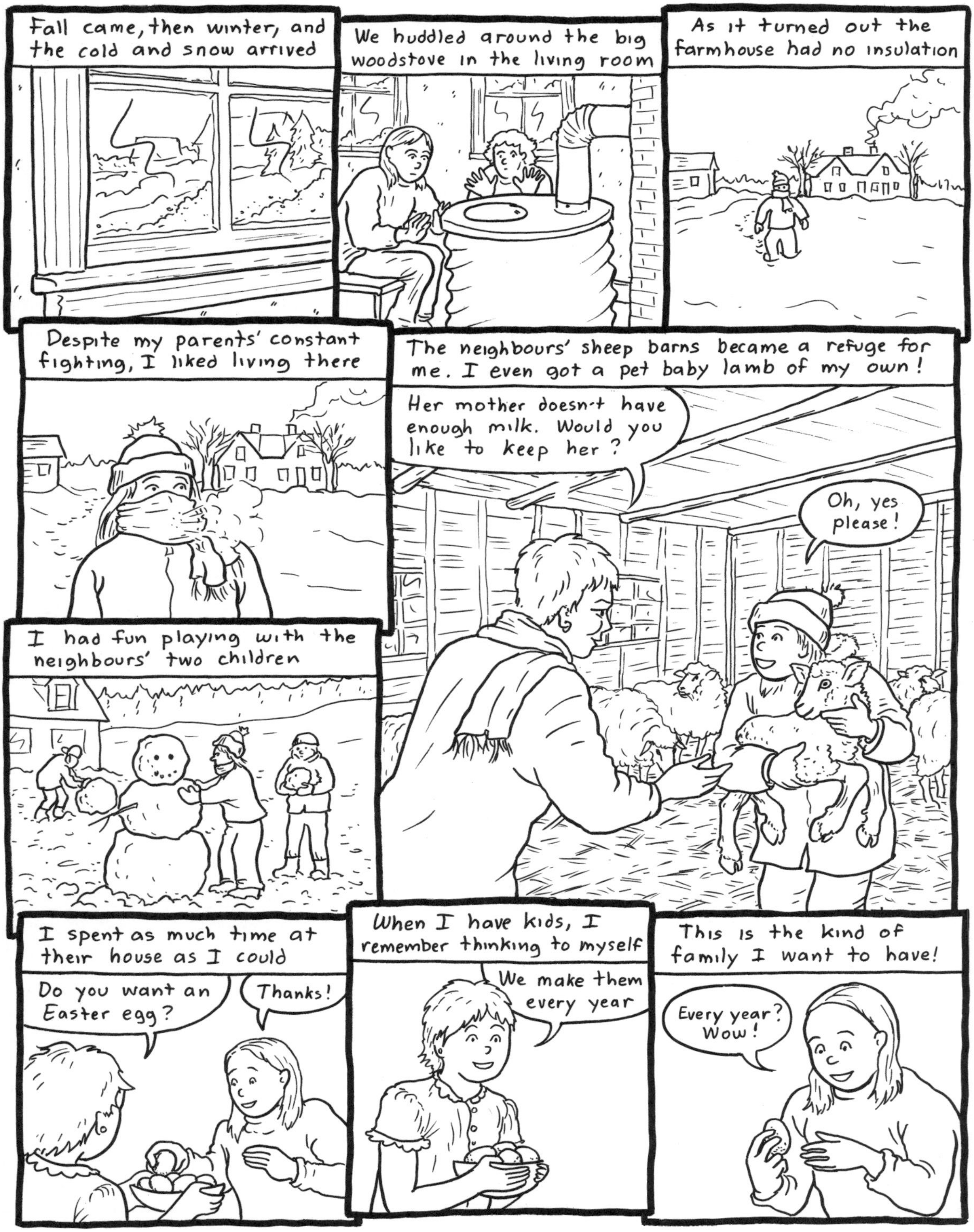
Fall came, then winter, and the cold and snow arrived
We huddled around the big woodstove in the living room
As it turned out the farmhouse had no insulation
Despite my parents' constant fighting, I liked living there
The neighbours' sheep barns became a refuge for me. I even got a pet baby lamb of my own!
Her mother doesn't have enough milk. Would you like to keep her?
Oh, yes please!
I had fun playing with the neighbours' two children
I spent as much time at their house as I could
Do you want an Easter egg?
Thanks!
When I have kids, I remember thinking to myself
We make them every year
This is the kind of family I want to have!
Every year? Wow!

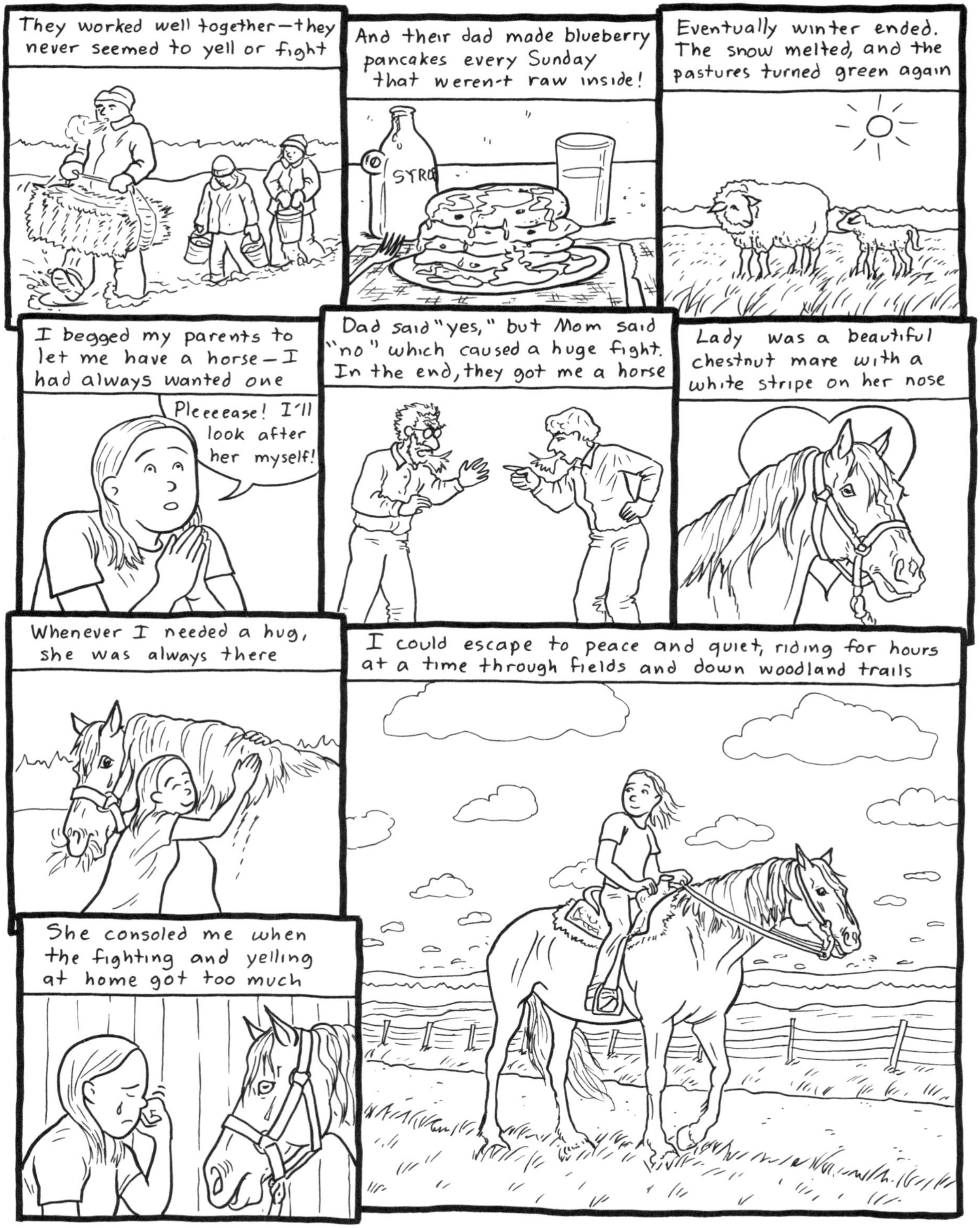
They worked well together—they never seemed to yell or fight
And their dad made blueberry pancakes every Sunday that weren't raw inside!
SYR
Eventually winter ended. The snow melted, and the pastures turned green again
I begged my parents to let me have a horse—I had always wanted one
Pleeeease! I'll look after her myself!
Dad said "yes," but Mom said "no" which caused a huge fight. In the end, they got me a horse
Lady was a beautiful chestnut mare with a white stripe on her nose
Whenever I needed a hug, she was always there
She consoled me when the fighting and yelling at home got too much
I could escape to peace and quiet, riding for hours at a time through fields and down woodland trails

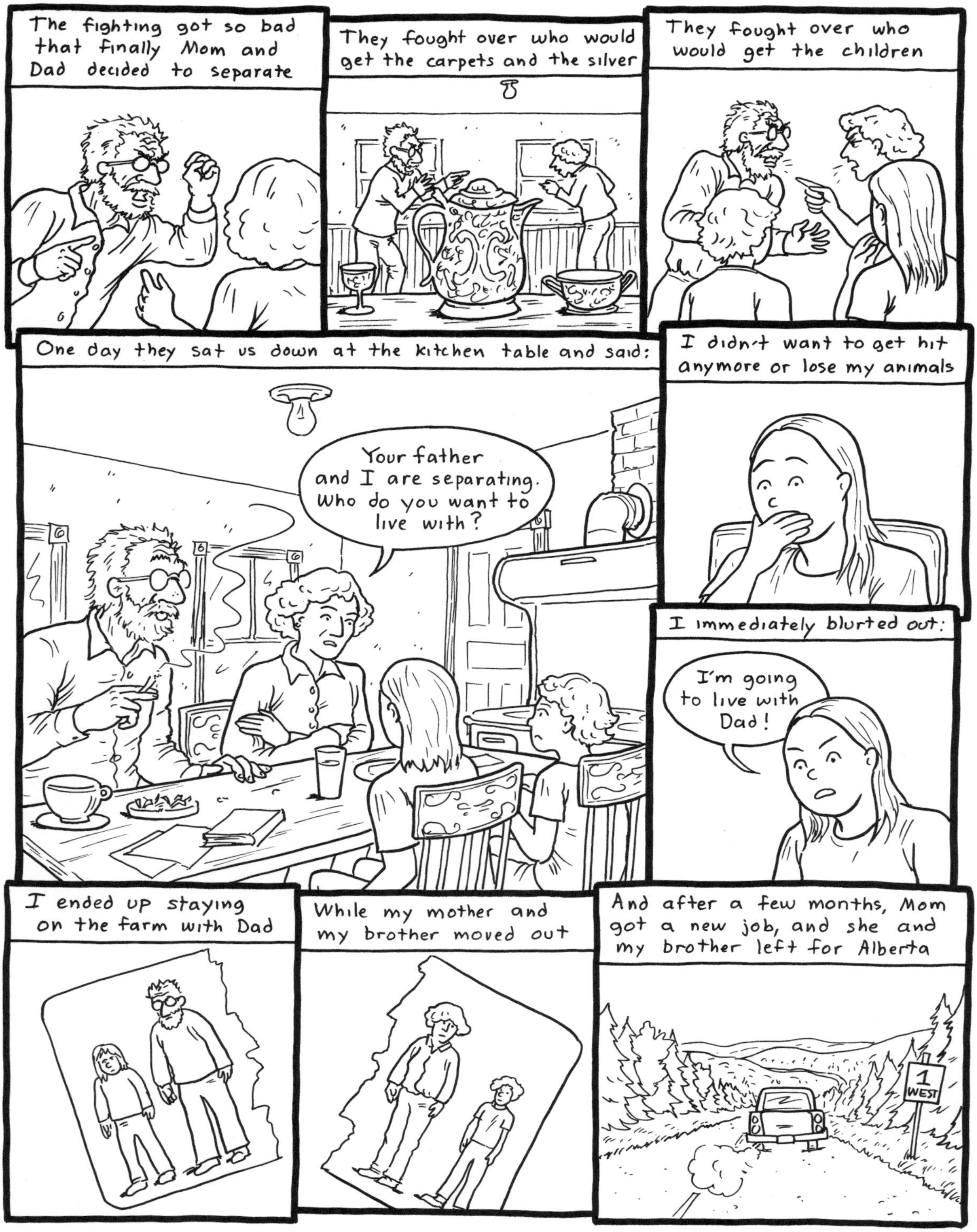
The fighting got so bad that finally Mom and Dad decided to separate
They fought over who would get the carpets and the silver
They fought over who would get the children
One day they sat us down at the kitchen table and said:
Your father and I are separating. Who do you want to live with?
I didn't want to get hit anymore or lose my animals
I immediately blurted out:
I'm going to live with Dad!
I ended up staying on the farm with Dad
While my mother and my brother moved out
And after a few months, Mom got a new job, and she and my brother left for Alberta
1
WEST

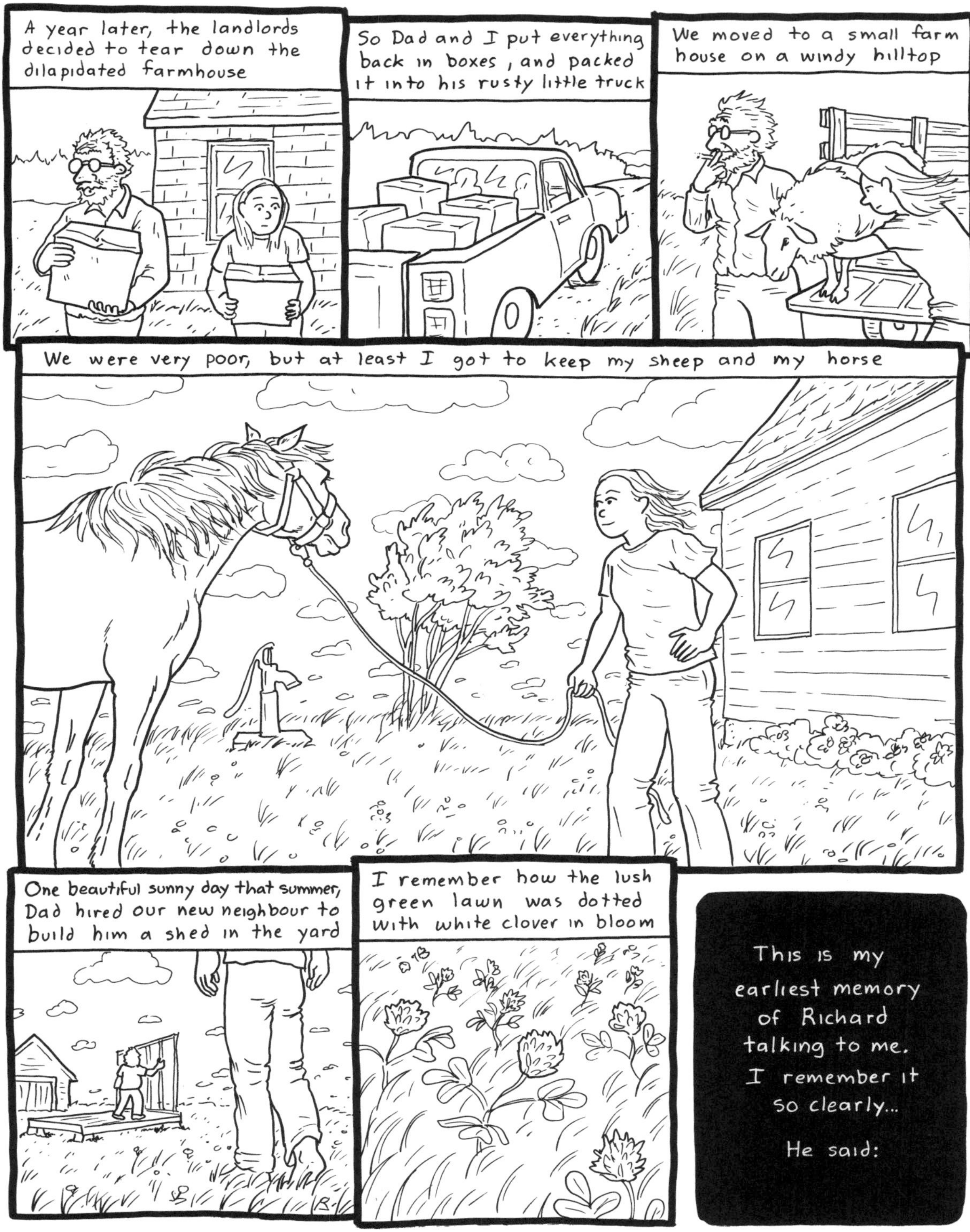
A year later, the landlords decided to tear down the dilapidated farmhouse
So Dad and I put everything back in boxes, and packed it into his rusty little truck
We moved to a small farm house on a windy hilltop
We were very poor, but at least I got to keep my sheep and my horse
One beautiful sunny day that summer, Dad hired our new neighbour to build him a shed in the yard
I remember how the lush green lawn was dotted with white clover in bloom
This is my earliest memory of Richard talking to me. I remember it so clearly...
He said:

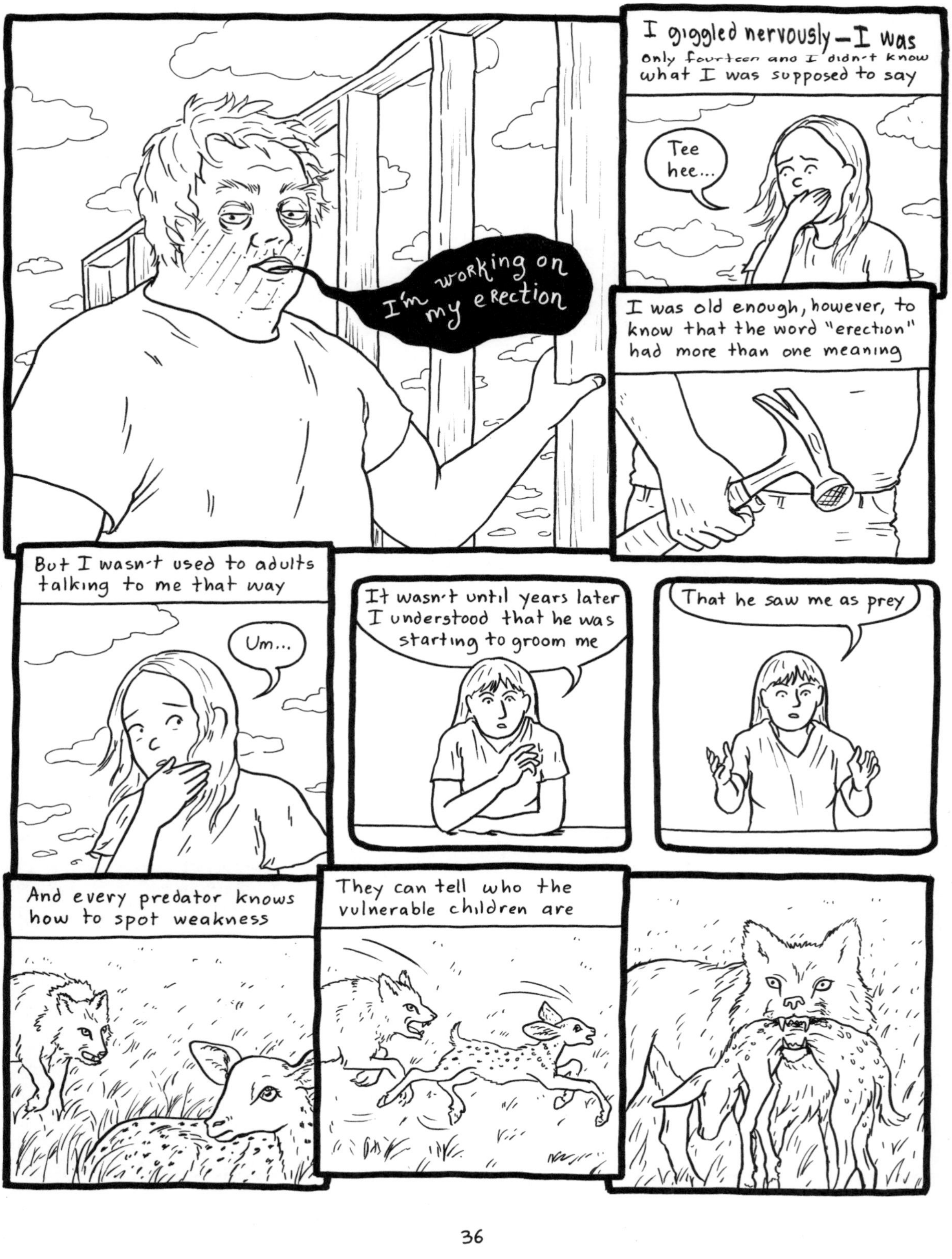
I'm working on my erection
I giggled nervously—I was only fourteen and I didn't know what I was supposed to say
Tee hee...
I was old enough, however, to know that the word "erection" had more than one meaning
But I wasn't used to adults talking to me that way
Um...
It wasn't until years later I understood that he was starting to groom me
That he saw me as prey
And every predator knows how to spot weakness
They can tell who the vulnerable children are

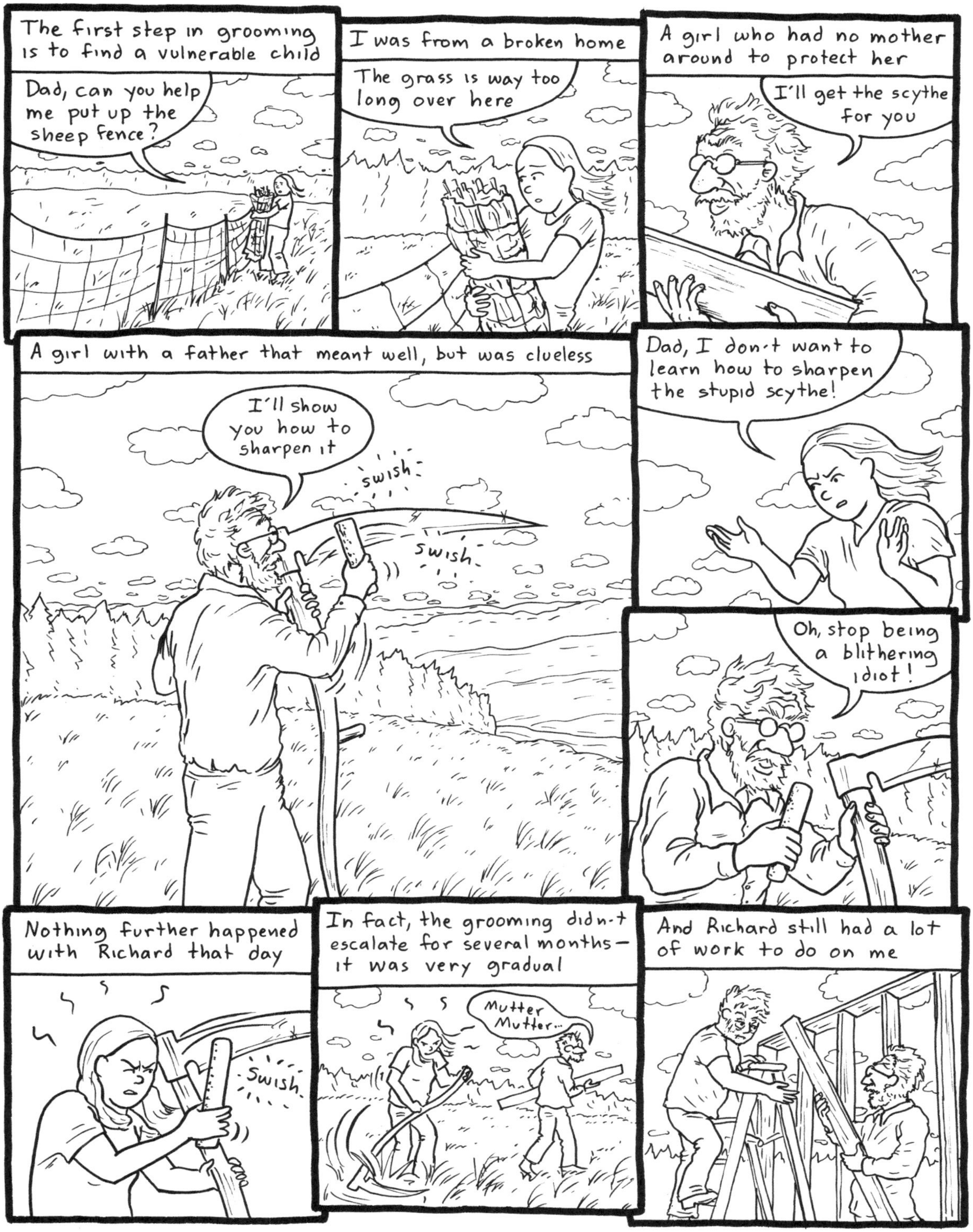
The first step in grooming is to find a vulnerable child
Dad, can you help me put up the sheep fence?
I was from a broken home
The grass is way too long over here
A girl who had no mother around to protect her
I'll get the scythe for you
A girl with a father that meant well, but was clueless
I'll show you how to sharpen it
swish
swish
Dad, I don't want to learn how to sharpen the stupid scythe!
Oh, stop being a blithering idiot!
Nothing further happened with Richard that day
Swish
In fact, the grooming didn't escalate for several months—it was very gradual
Mutter Mutter...
And Richard still had a lot of work to do on me

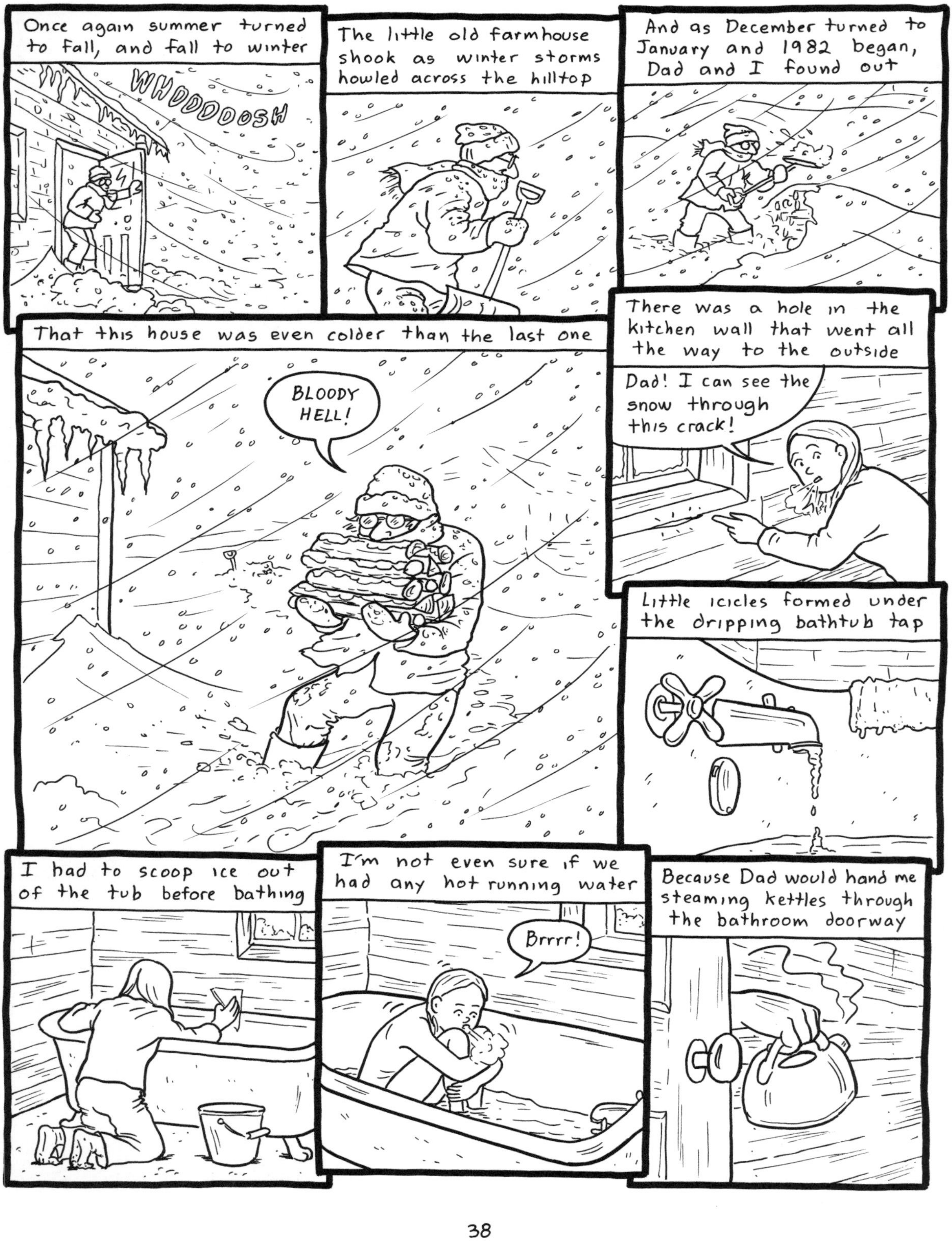
Once again summer turned to fall, and fall to winter
WHOOOOOOSH
The little old farmhouse shook as winter storms howled across the hilltop
And as December turned to January and 1982 began, Dad and I found out
That this house was even colder than the last one
BLOODY HELL!
There was a hole in the kitchen wall that went all the way to the outside
Dad! I can see the snow through this crack!
Little icicles formed under the dripping bathtub tap
I had to scoop ice out of the tub before bathing
I'm not even sure if we had any hot running water
Brrrr!
Because Dad would hand me steaming kettles through the bathroom doorway

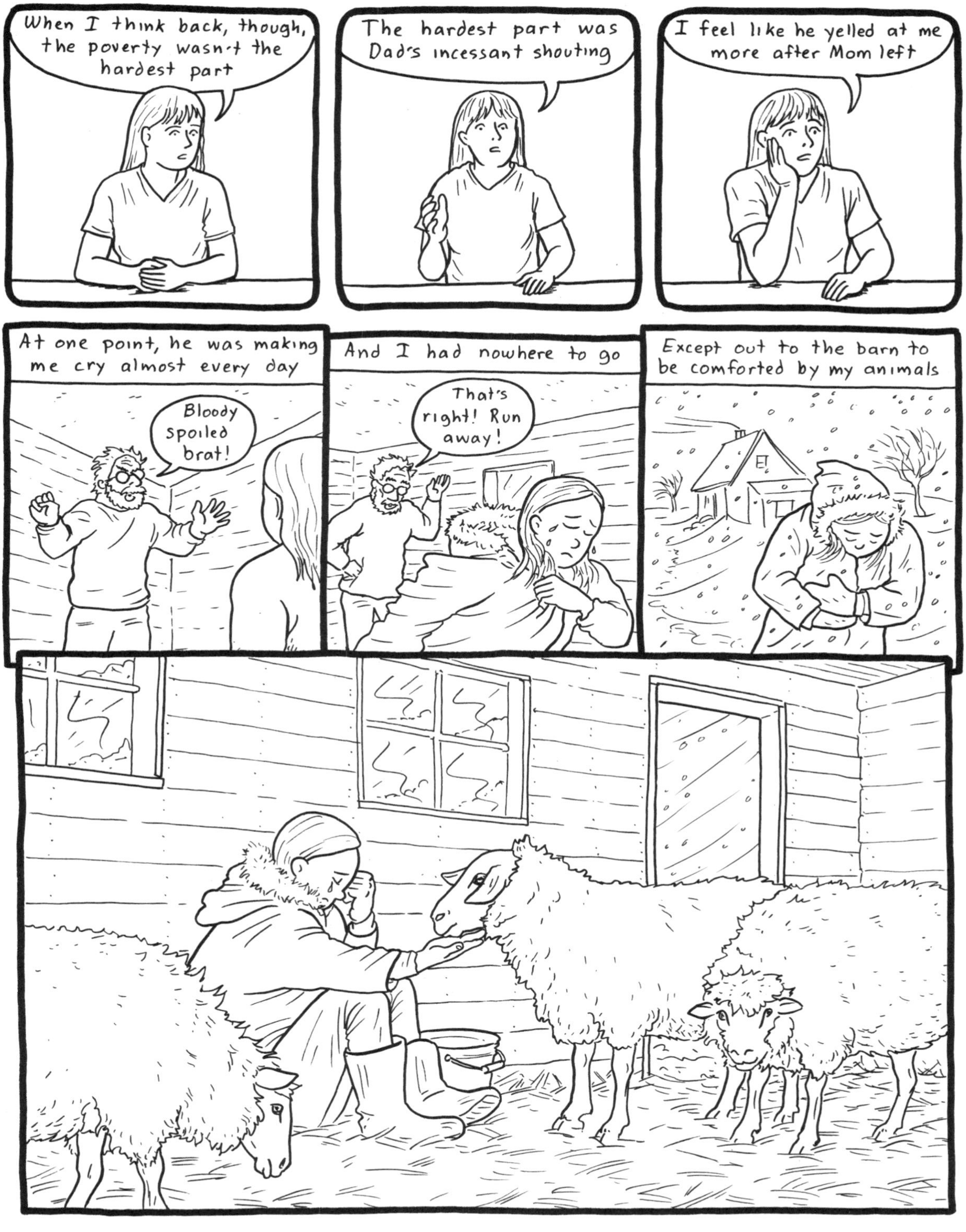
When I think back, though, the poverty wasn't the hardest part
The hardest part was Dad's incessant shouting
I feel like he yelled at me more after Mom left
At one point, he was making me cry almost every day
Bloody spoiled brat!
And I had nowhere to go
That's right! Run away!
Except out to the barn to be comforted by my animals

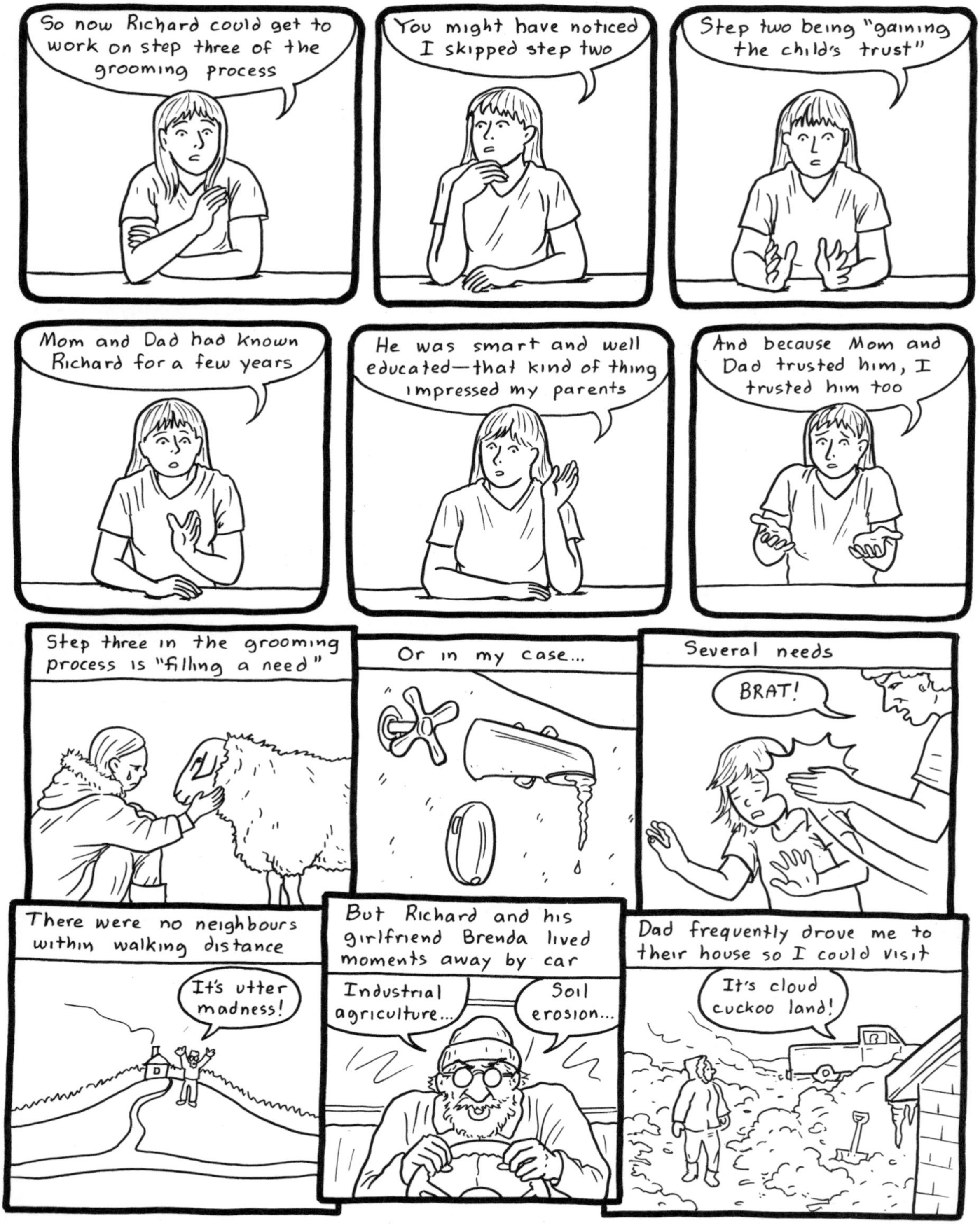
So now Richard could get to work on step three of the grooming process
You might have noticed I skipped step two
Step two being "gaining the child's trust"
Mom and Dad had known Richard for a few years
He was smart and well educated—that kind of thing impressed my parents
And because Mom and Dad trusted him, I trusted him too
Step three in the grooming process is "filling a need"
Or in my case...
Several needs
BRAT!
There were no neighbours within walking distance
It's utter madness!
But Richard and his girlfriend Brenda lived moments away by car
Industrial agriculture...
Soil erosion...
Dad frequently drove me to their house so I could visit
It's cloud cuckoo land!

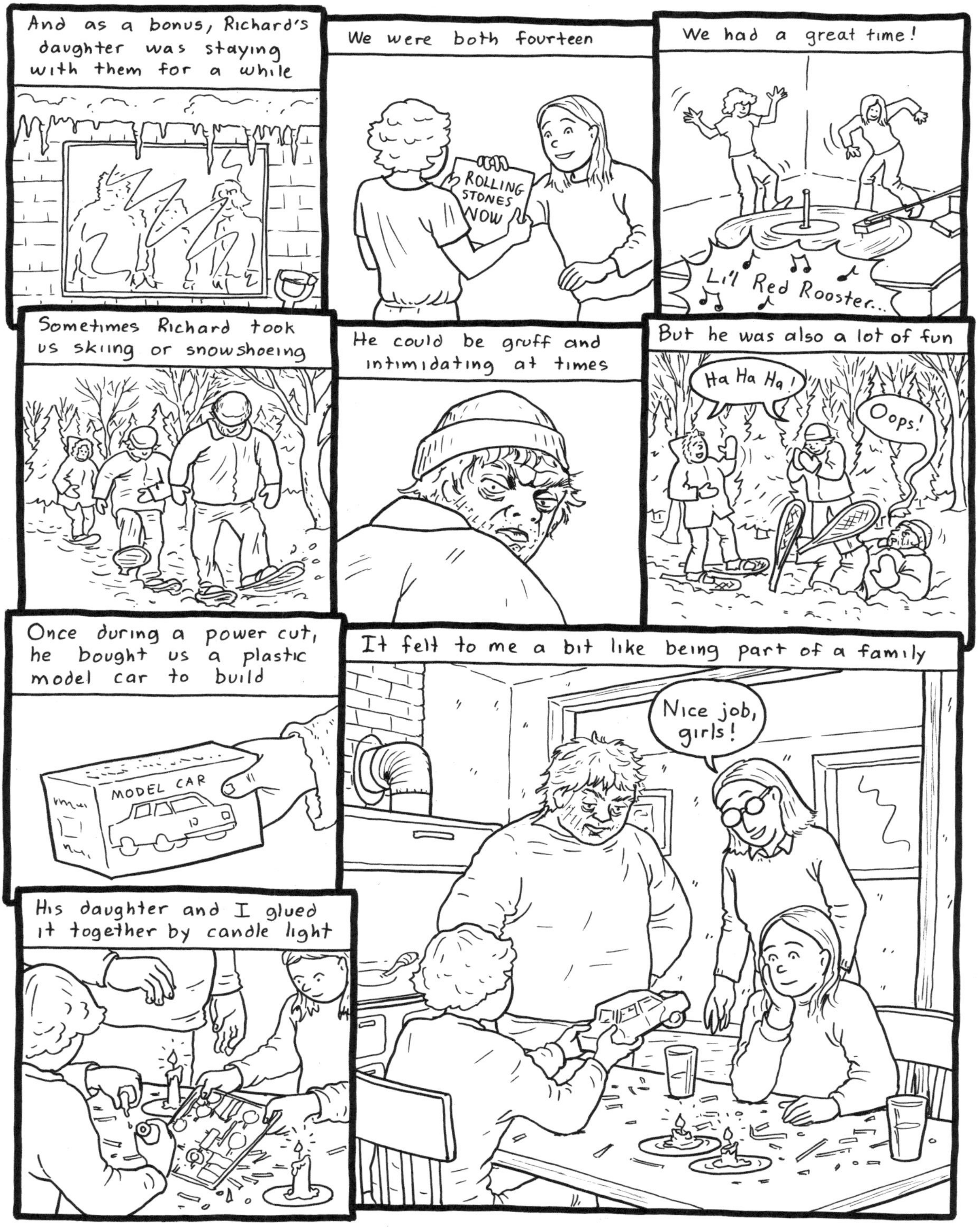
And as a bonus, Richard's daughter was staying with them for a while
We were both fourteen
ROLLING STONES NOW
We had a great time!
Li'l Red Rooster...
Sometimes Richard took us skiing or snowshoeing
He could be gruff and intimidating at times
But he was also a lot of fun
Ha Ha Ha!
Oops!
Once during a power cut, he bought us a plastic model car to build
MODEL CAR
His daughter and I glued it together by candle light
It felt to me a bit like being part of a family
Nice job, girls!

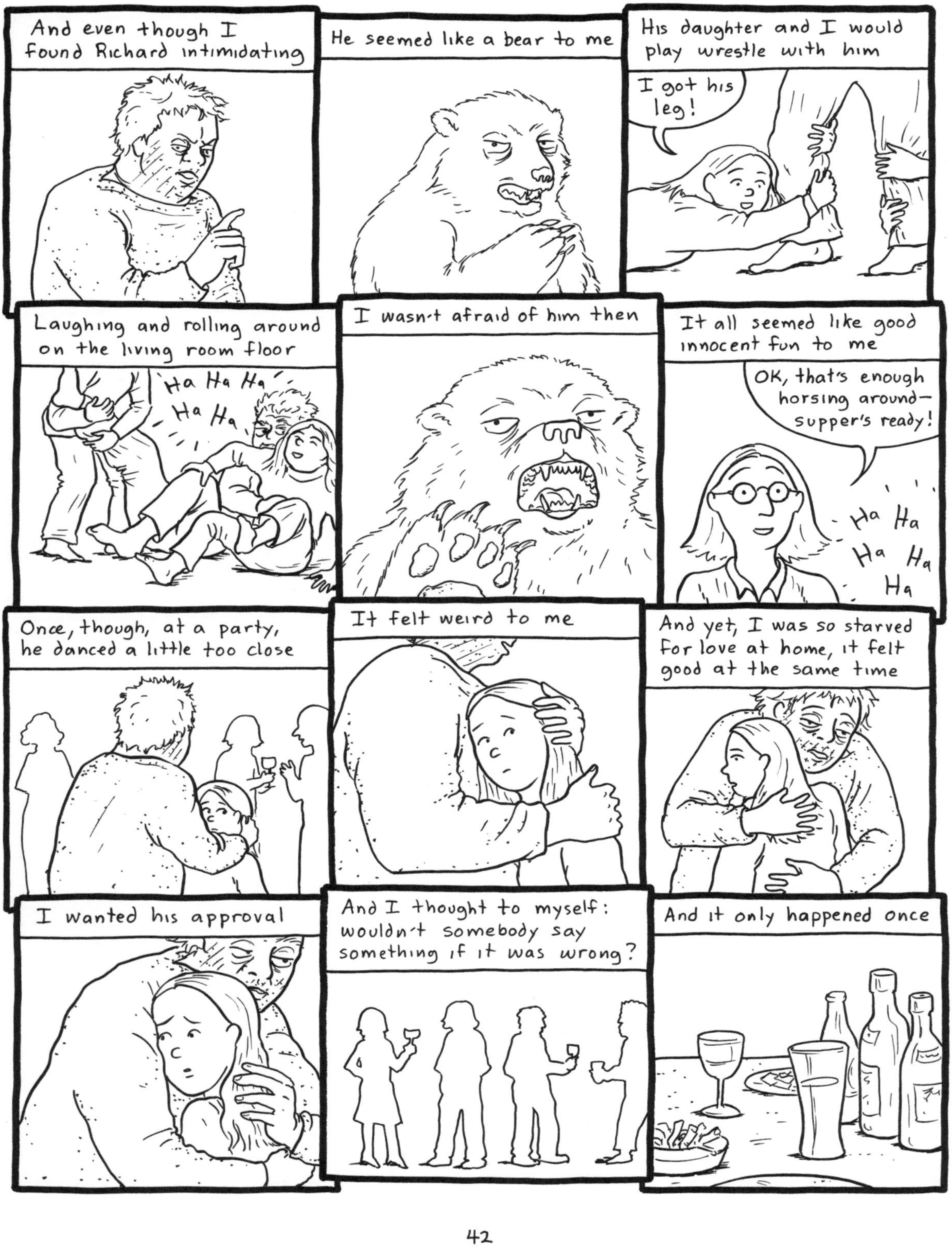
And even though I found Richard intimidating
He seemed like a bear to me
His daughter and I would play wrestle with him
I got his leg!
Laughing and rolling around on the living room floor
Ha Ha Ha Ha Ha
I wasn't afraid of him then
It all seemed like good innocent fun to me
OK, that's enough horsing around— supper's ready!
Ha Ha Ha Ha Ha
Once, though, at a party, he danced a little too close
It felt weird to me
And yet, I was so starved for love at home, it felt good at the same time
I wanted his approval
And I thought to myself: wouldn't somebody say something if it was wrong?
And it only happened once

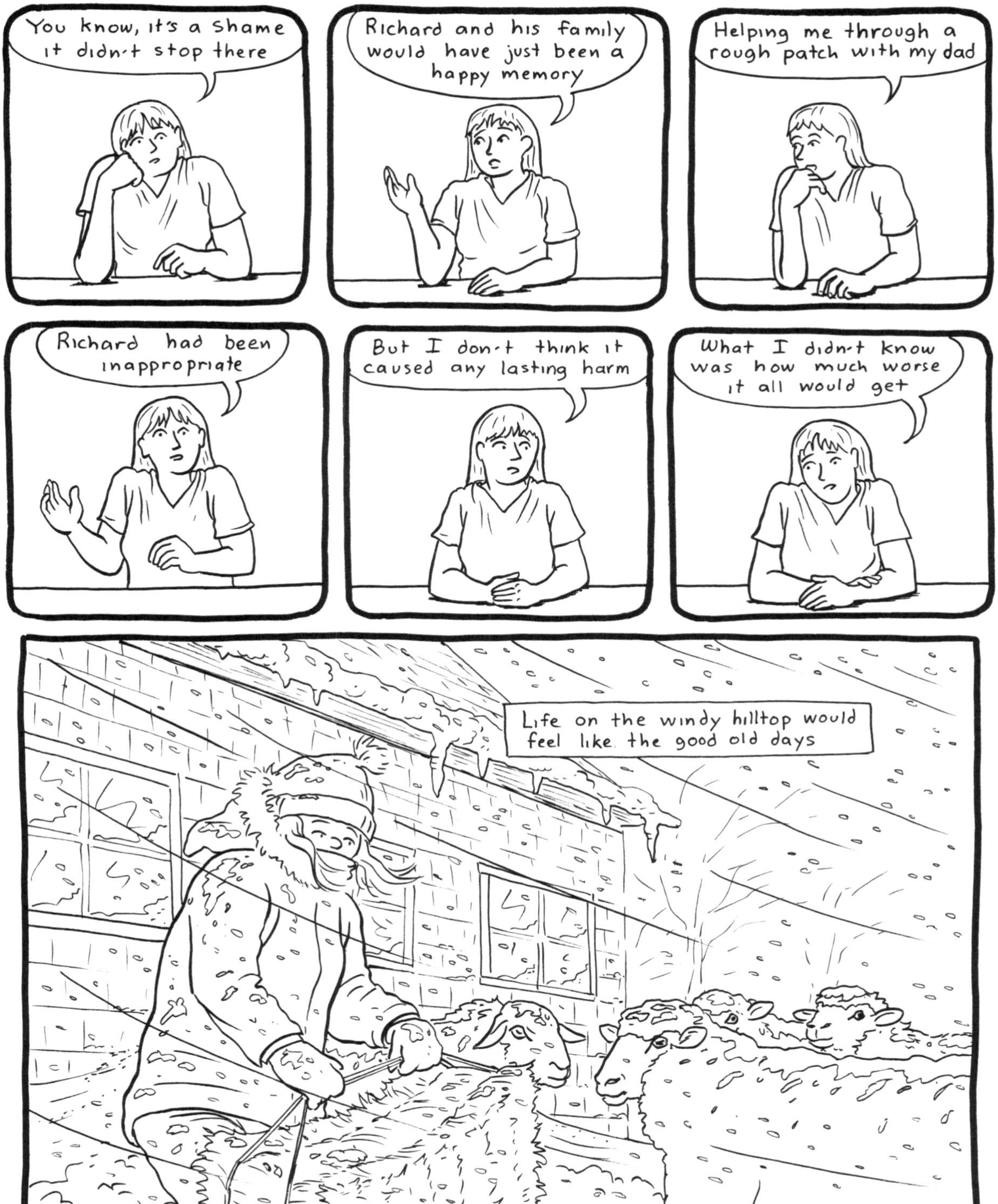
You know, it's a shame it didn't stop there
Richard and his family would have just been a happy memory
Helping me through a rough patch with my dad
Richard had been inappropriate
But I don't think it caused any lasting harm
What I didn't know was how much worse it all would get
Life on the windy hilltop would feel like the good old days

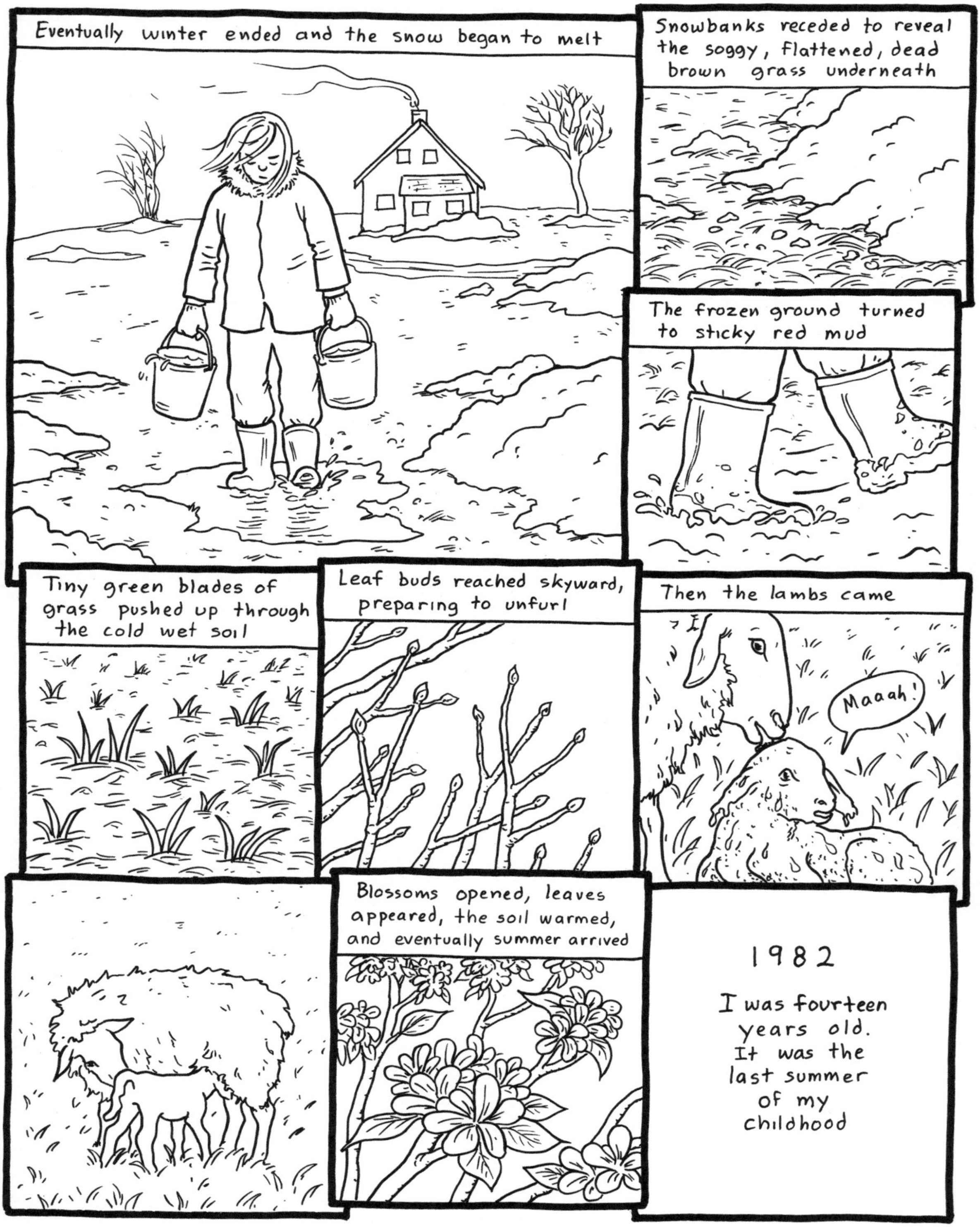
Eventually winter ended and the snow began to melt
Snowbanks receded to reveal the soggy, flattened, dead brown grass underneath
The frozen ground turned to sticky red mud
Tiny green blades of grass pushed up through the cold wet soil
Leaf buds reached skyward, preparing to unfurl
Then the lambs came
Maaah!
Blossoms opened, leaves appeared, the soil warmed, and eventually summer arrived
1982
I was fourteen years old. It was the last summer of my childhood

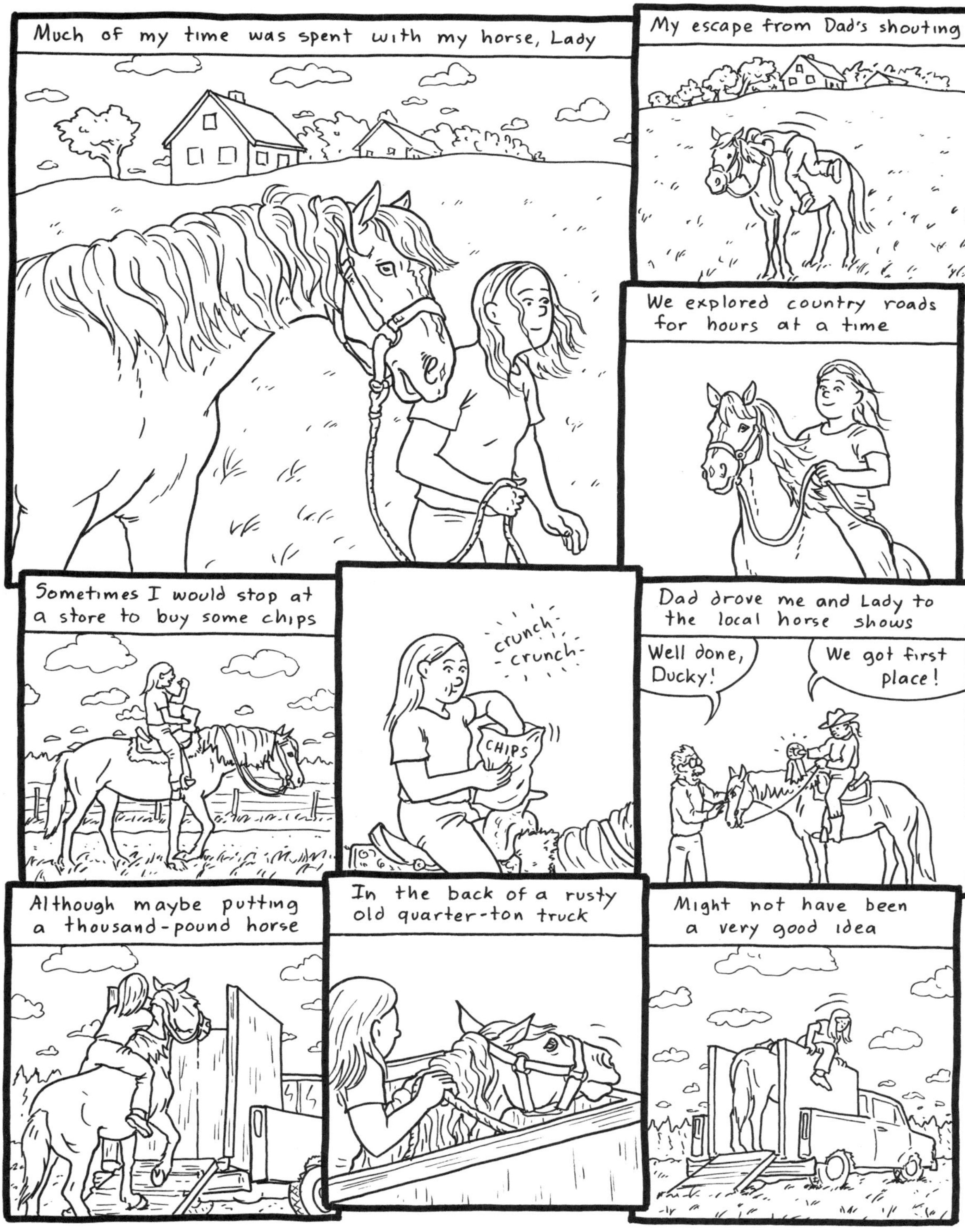
Much of my time was spent with my horse, Lady
My escape from Dad's shouting
We explored country roads for hours at a time
Sometimes I would stop at a store to buy some chips
crunch crunch
CHIPS
Dad drove me and Lady to the local horse shows
Well done, Ducky!
We got first place!
Although maybe putting a thousand-pound horse
In the back of a rusty old quarter-ton truck
Might not have been a very good idea

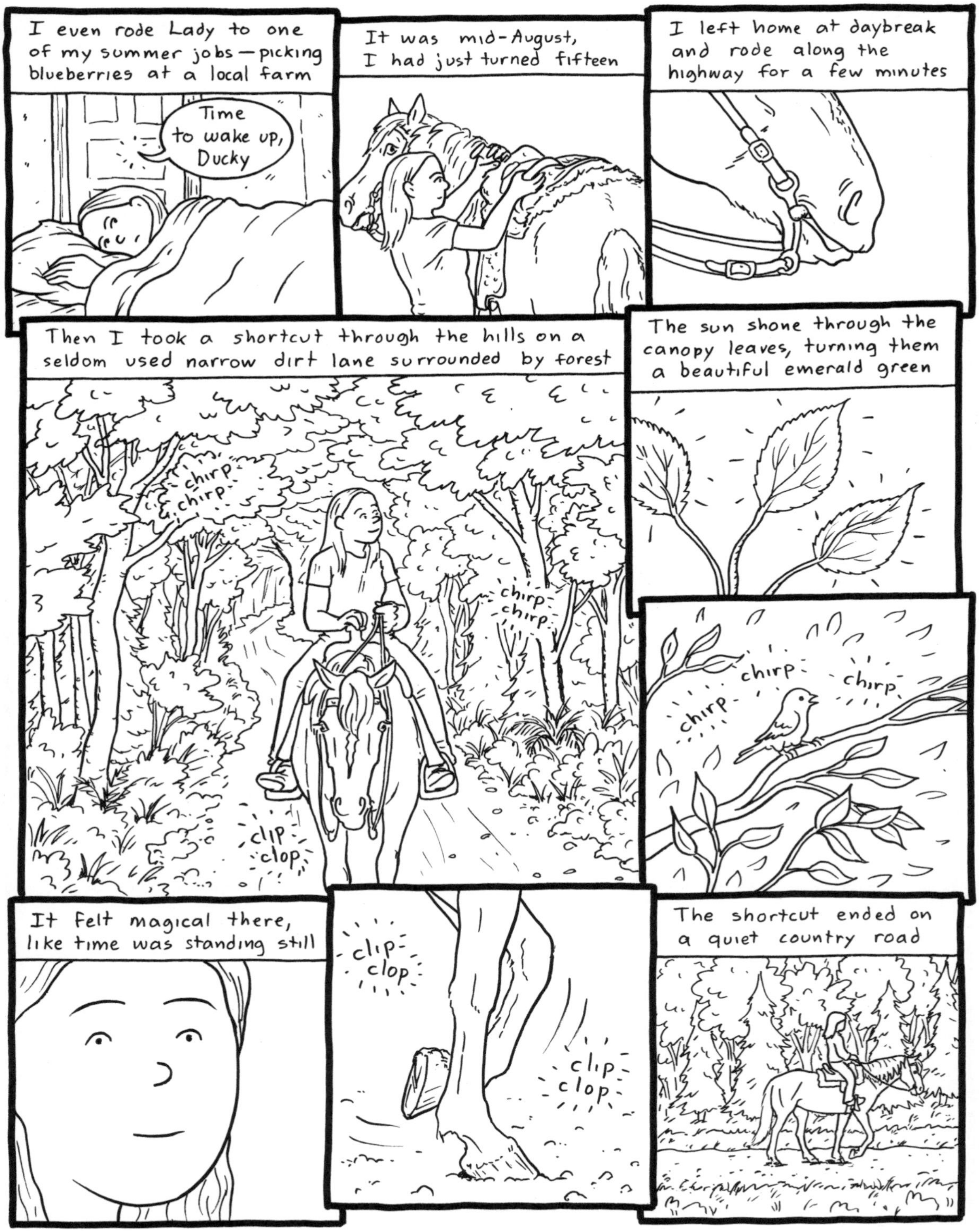
I even rode Lady to one of my summer jobs—picking blueberries at a local farm
Time to wake up, Ducky
It was mid-August, I had just turned fifteen
I left home at daybreak and rode along the highway for a few minutes
Then I took a shortcut through the hills on a seldom used narrow dirt lane surrounded by forest
chirp chirp
chirp chirp
clip clop
The sun shone through the canopy leaves, turning them a beautiful emerald green
chirp
chirp
chirp
It felt magical there, like time was standing still
clip clop
clip clop
The shortcut ended on a quiet country road

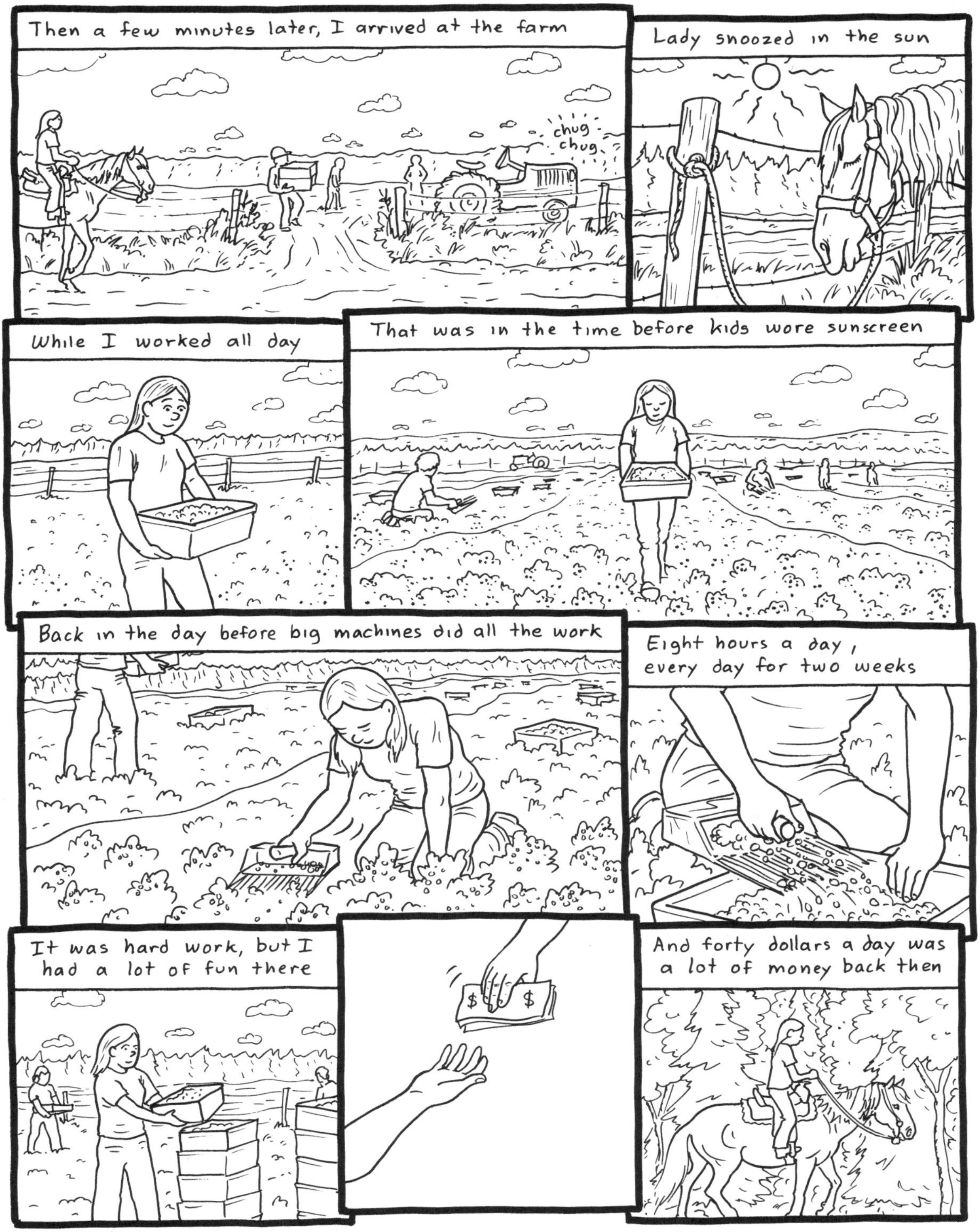

Then a few minutes later, I arrived at the farm
chug chug
Lady snoozed in the sun
While I worked all day
That was in the time before kids wore sunscreen
Back in the day before big machines did all the work
Eight hours a day, every day for two weeks
It was hard work, but I had a lot of fun there
$ $
And forty dollars a day was a lot of money back then

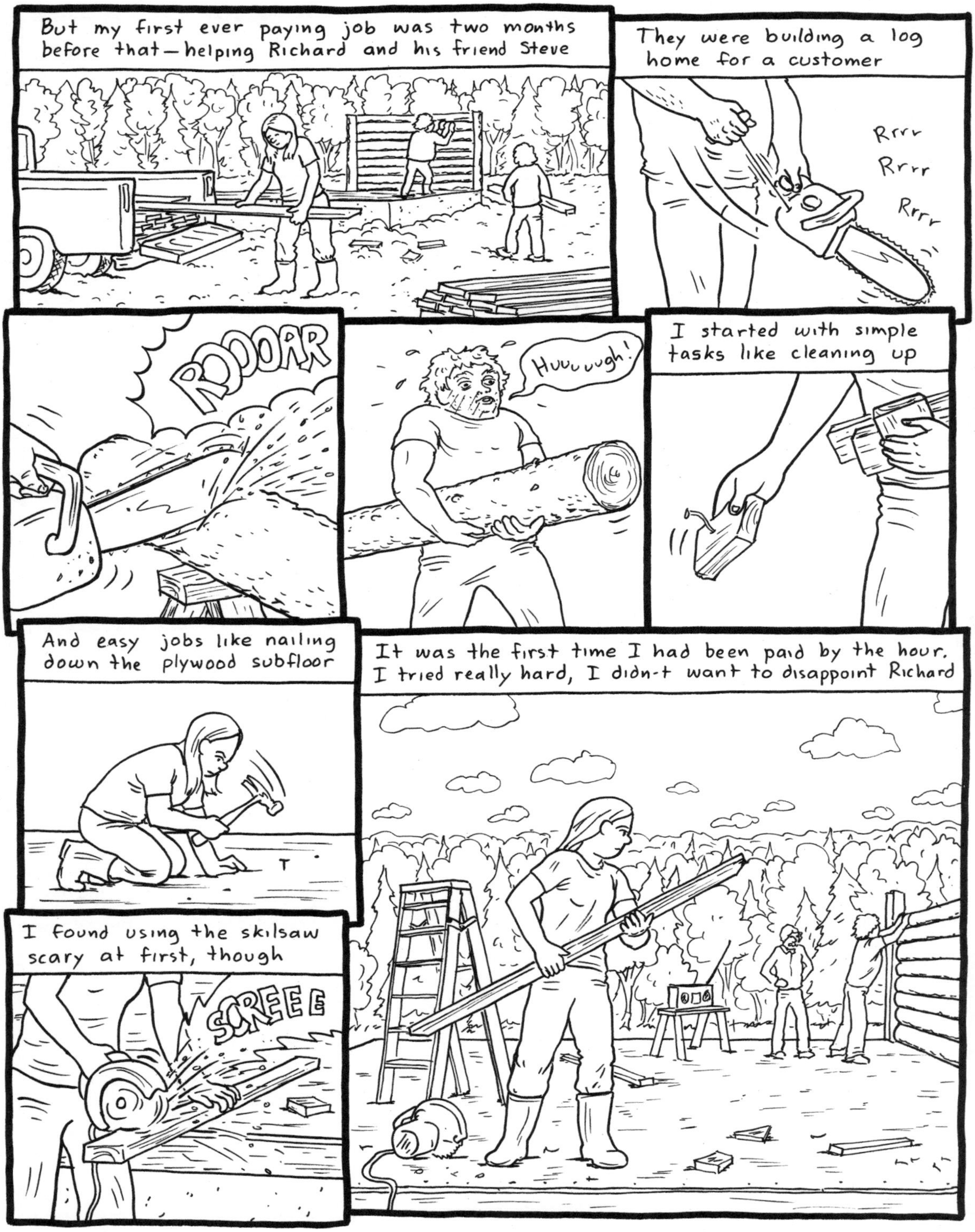
But my first ever paying job was two months before that—helping Richard and his friend Steve
They were building a log home for a customer
Rrrr
Rrrr
Rrrr
ROOOAR
Huuuuugh!
I started with simple tasks like cleaning up
And easy jobs like nailing down the plywood subfloor
It was the first time I had been paid by the hour. I tried really hard, I didn-t want to disappoint Richard
I found using the skilsaw scary at first, though
SCREEEE

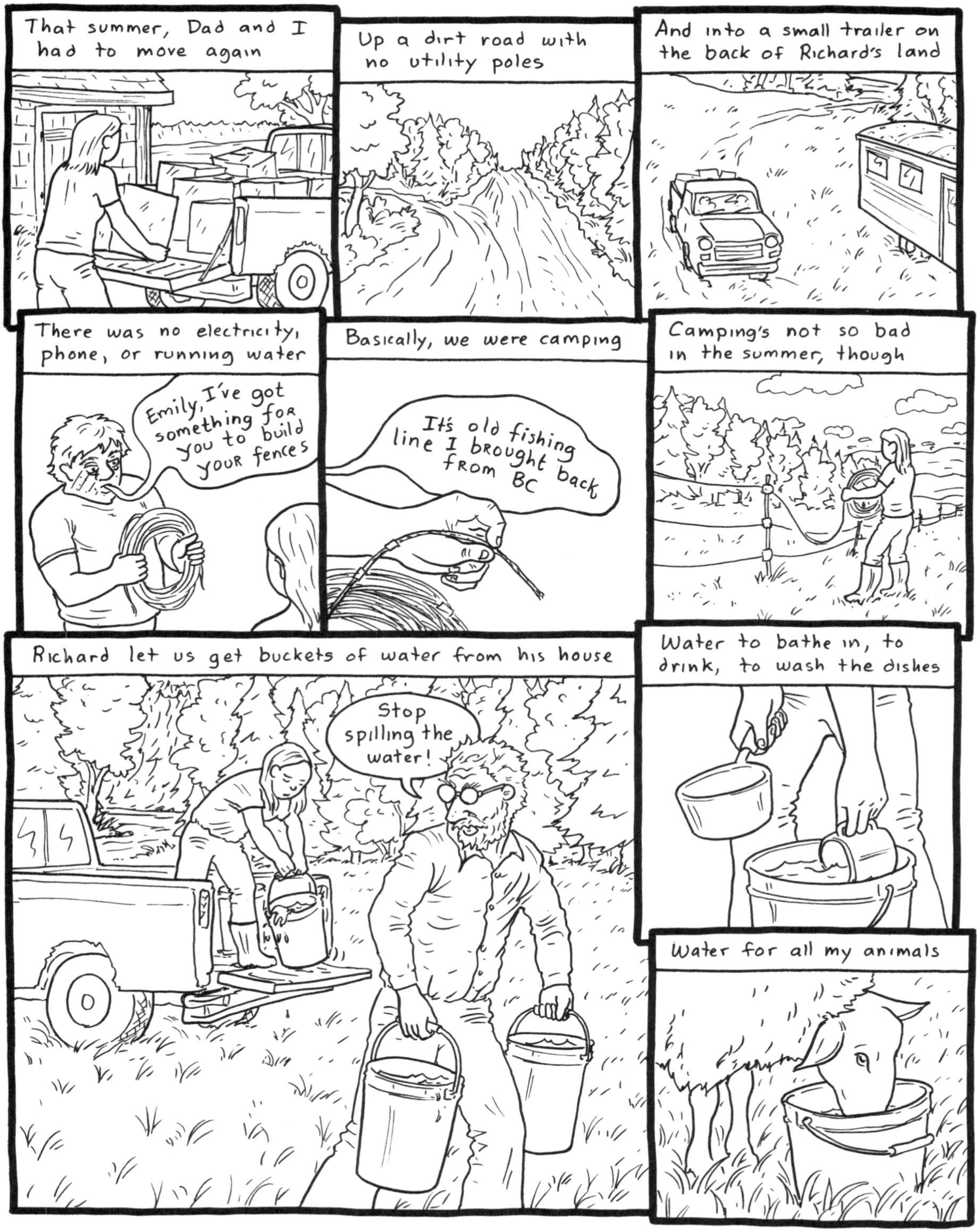
That summer, Dad and I had to move again
Up a dirt road with no utility poles
And into a small trailer on the back of Richard's land
There was no electricity, phone, or running water
Emily, I've got something for you to build your fences
Basically, we were camping
It's old fishing line I brought back from BC
Camping's not so bad in the summer, though
Richard let us get buckets of water from his house
Stop spilling the water!
Water to bathe in, to drink, to wash the dishes
Water for all my animals

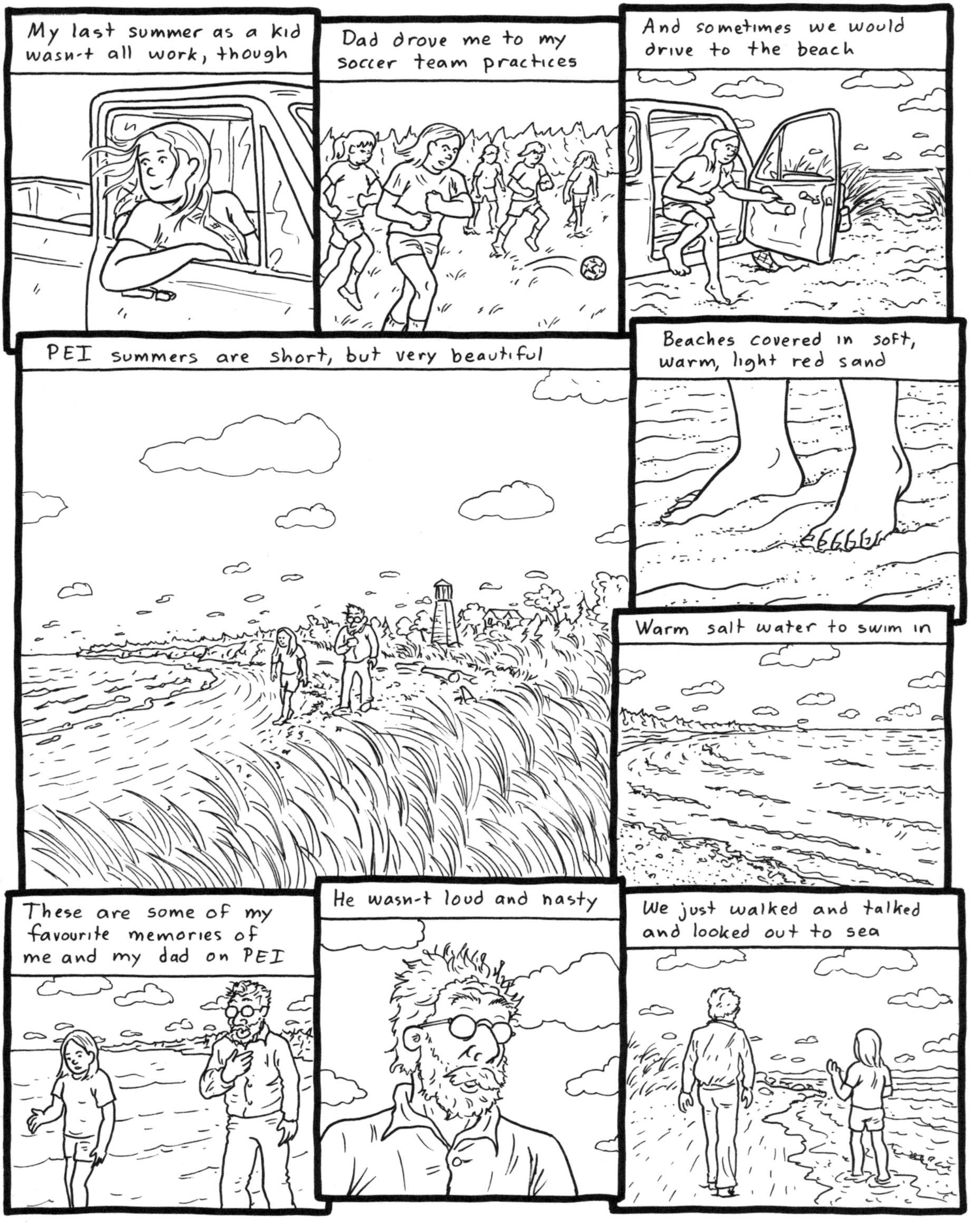
My last summer as a kid wasn-t all work, though
Dad drove me to my soccer team practices
And sometimes we would drive to the beach
PEI summers are short, but very beautiful
Beaches covered in soft, warm, light red sand
Warm salt water to swim in
These are some of my favourite memories of me and my dad on PEI
He wasn-t loud and nasty
We just walked and talked and looked out to sea

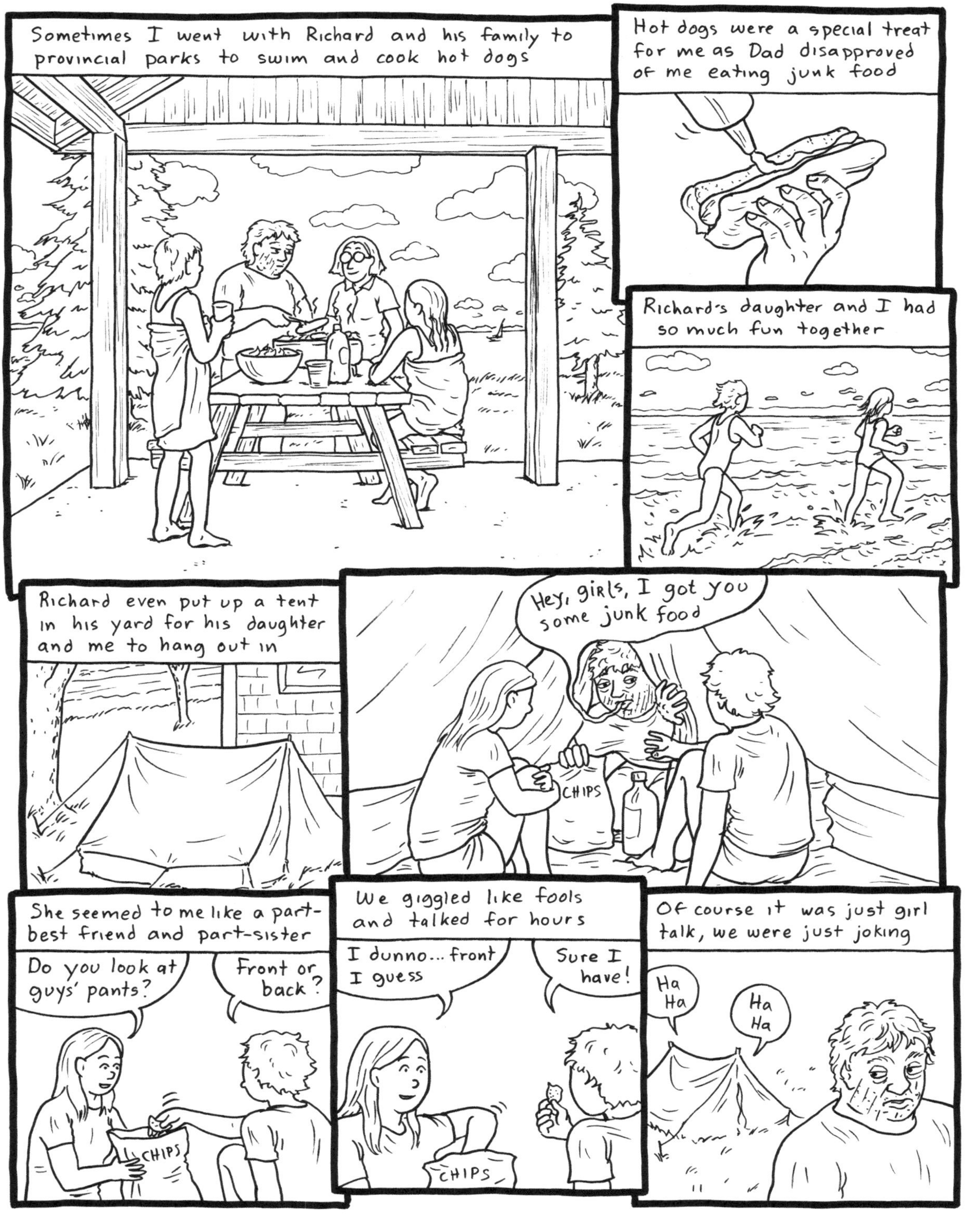
Sometimes I went with Richard and his family to provincial parks to swim and cook hot dogs
Hot dogs were a special treat for me as Dad disapproved of me eating junk food
Richard's daughter and I had so much fun together
Richard even put up a tent in his yard for his daughter and me to hang out in
Hey, girls, I got you some junk food
CHIPS
She seemed to me like a part-best friend and part-sister
Do you look at guys' pants?
Front or back?
CHIPS
We giggled like fools and talked for hours
I dunno... front I guess
Sure I have!
CHIPS
Of course it was just girl talk, we were just joking
Ha Ha
Ha Ha

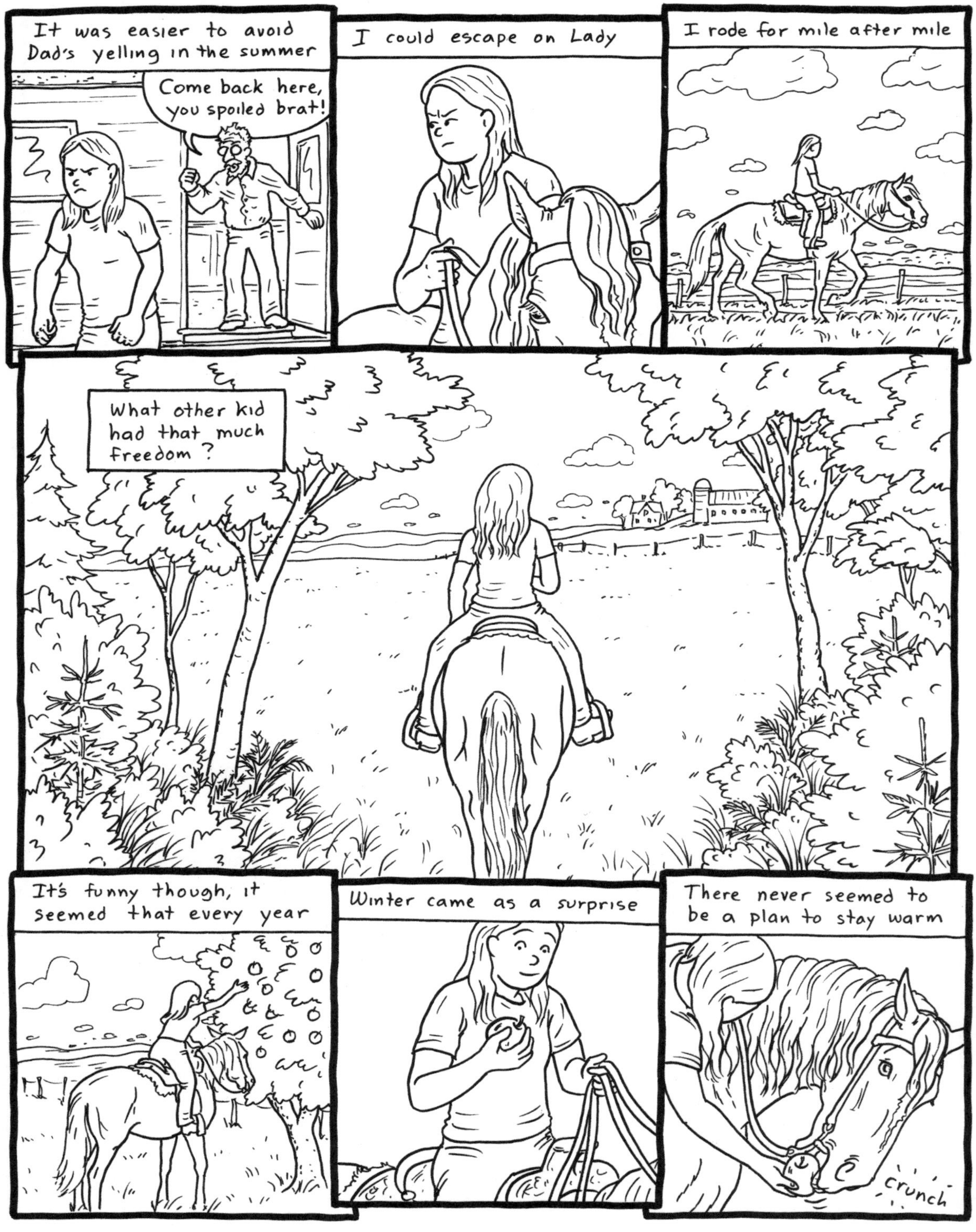
It was easier to avoid Dad's yelling in the summer
Come back here, you spoiled brat!
I could escape on Lady
I rode for mile after mile
What other kid had that much freedom?
It's funny though, it seemed that every year
Winter came as a surprise
There never seemed to be a plan to stay warm
crunch

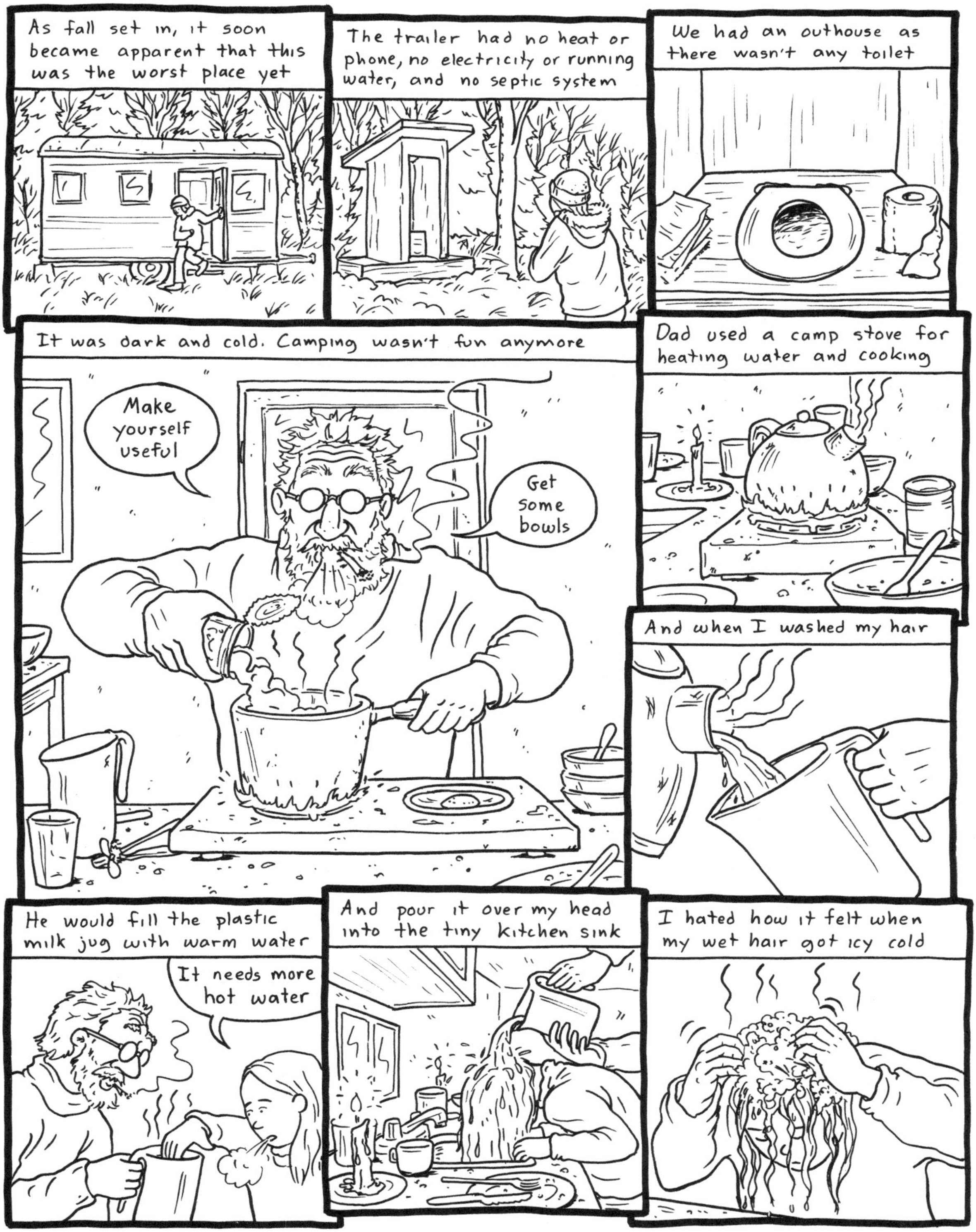
As fall set in, it soon became apparent that this was the worst place yet
The trailer had no heat or phone, no electricity or running water, and no septic system
We had an outhouse as there wasn't any toilet
It was dark and cold. Camping wasn't fun anymore
Make yourself useful
Get some bowls
Dad used a camp stove for heating water and cooking
And when I washed my hair
He would fill the plastic milk jug with warm water
It needs more hot water
And pour it over my head into the tiny kitchen sink
I hated how it felt when my wet hair got icy cold

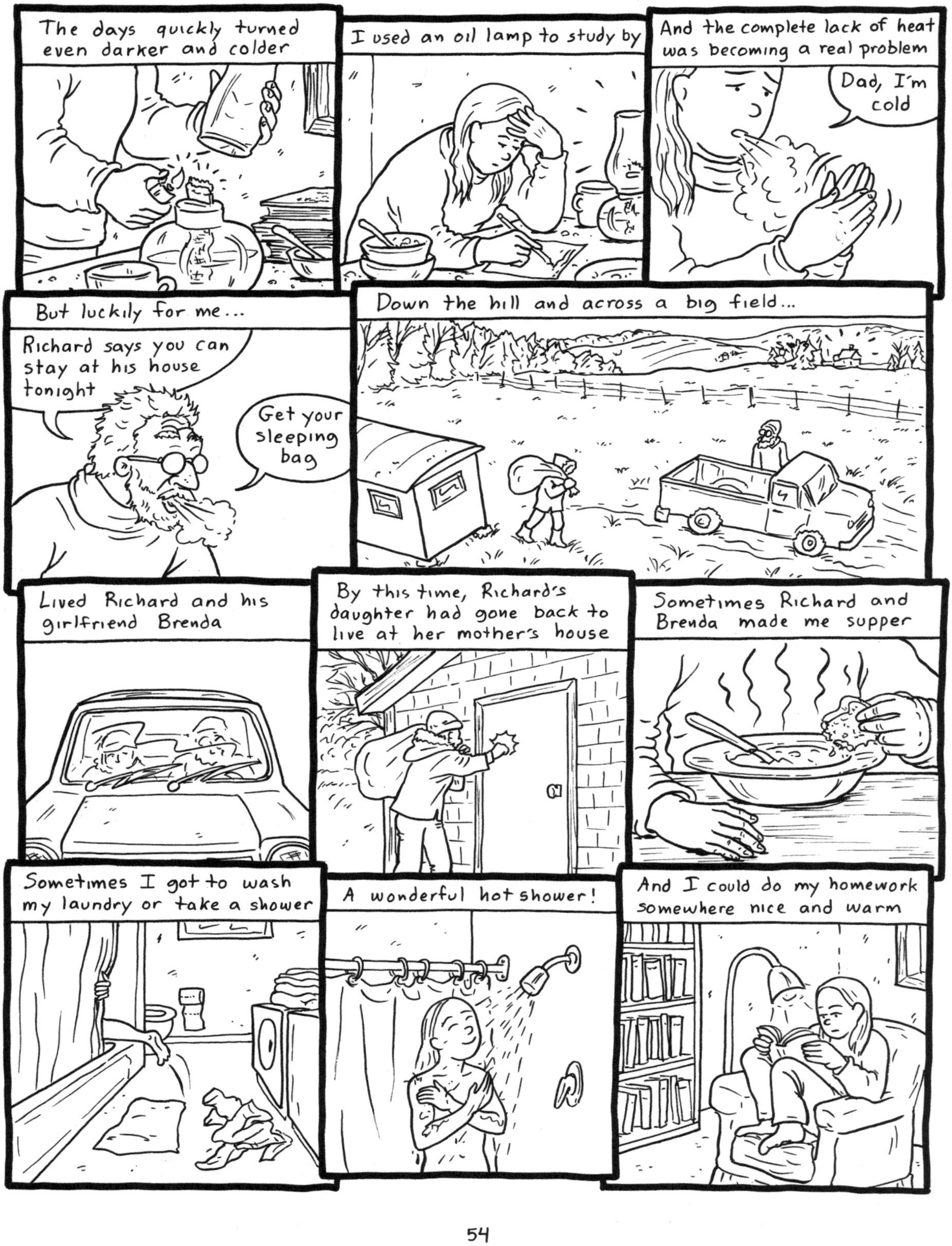

The days quickly turned even darker and colder
I used an oil lamp to study by
And the complete lack of heat was becoming a real problem
Dad, I'm cold
But luckily for me...
Richard says you can stay at his house tonight
Get your sleeping bag
Down the hill and across a big field...
Lived Richard and his girlfriend Brenda
By this time, Richard's daughter had gone back to live at her mother's house
Sometimes Richard and Brenda made me supper
Sometimes I got to wash my laundry or take a shower
A wonderful hot shower!
And I could do my homework somewhere nice and warm

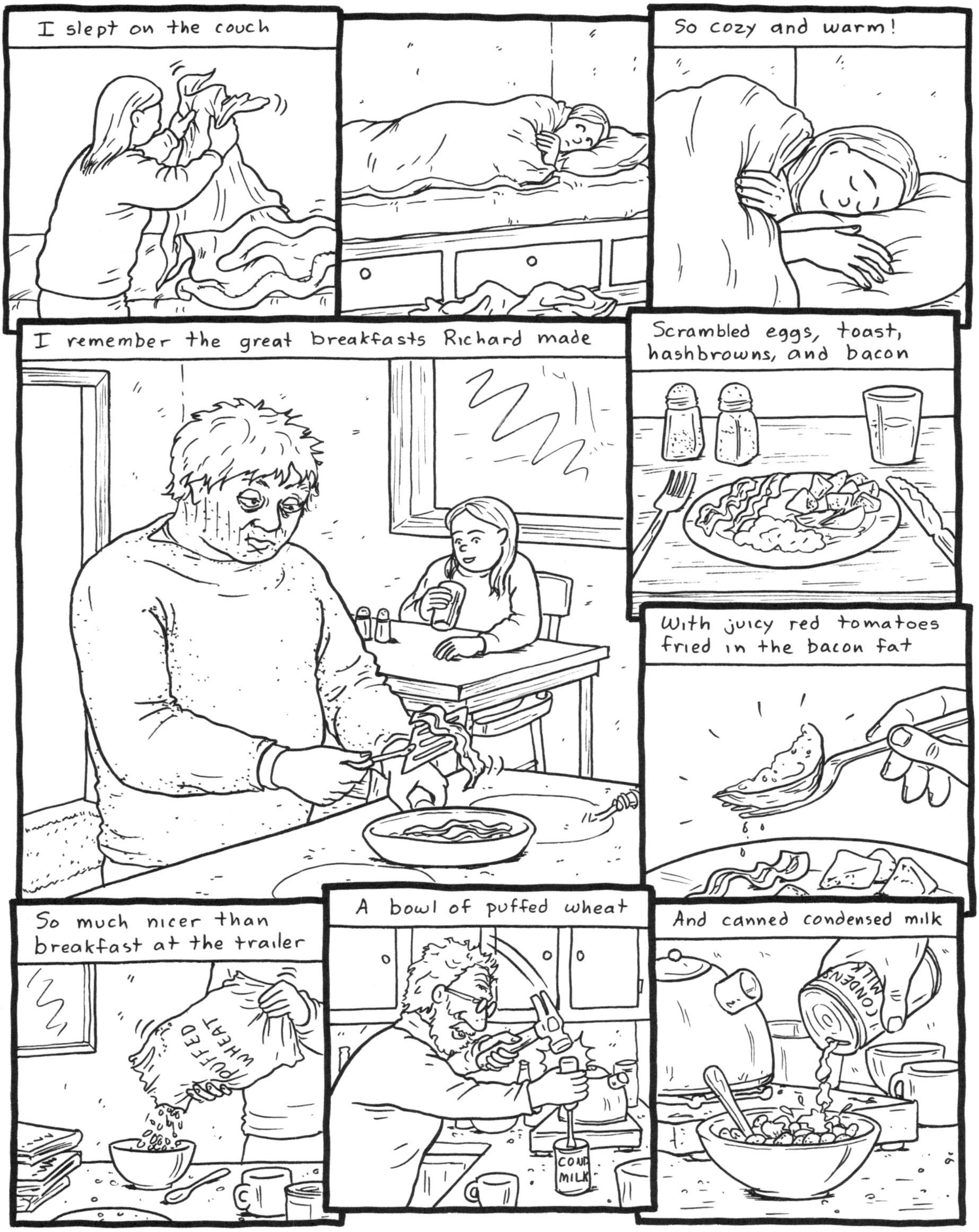
I slept on the couch
So cozy and warm!
I remember the great breakfasts Richard made
Scrambled eggs, toast, hashbrowns, and bacon
With juicy red tomatoes fried in the bacon fat
So much nicer than breakfast at the trailer
PUFFED WHEAT
A bowl of puffed wheat
COND MILK
And canned condensed milk
CONDENS MILK

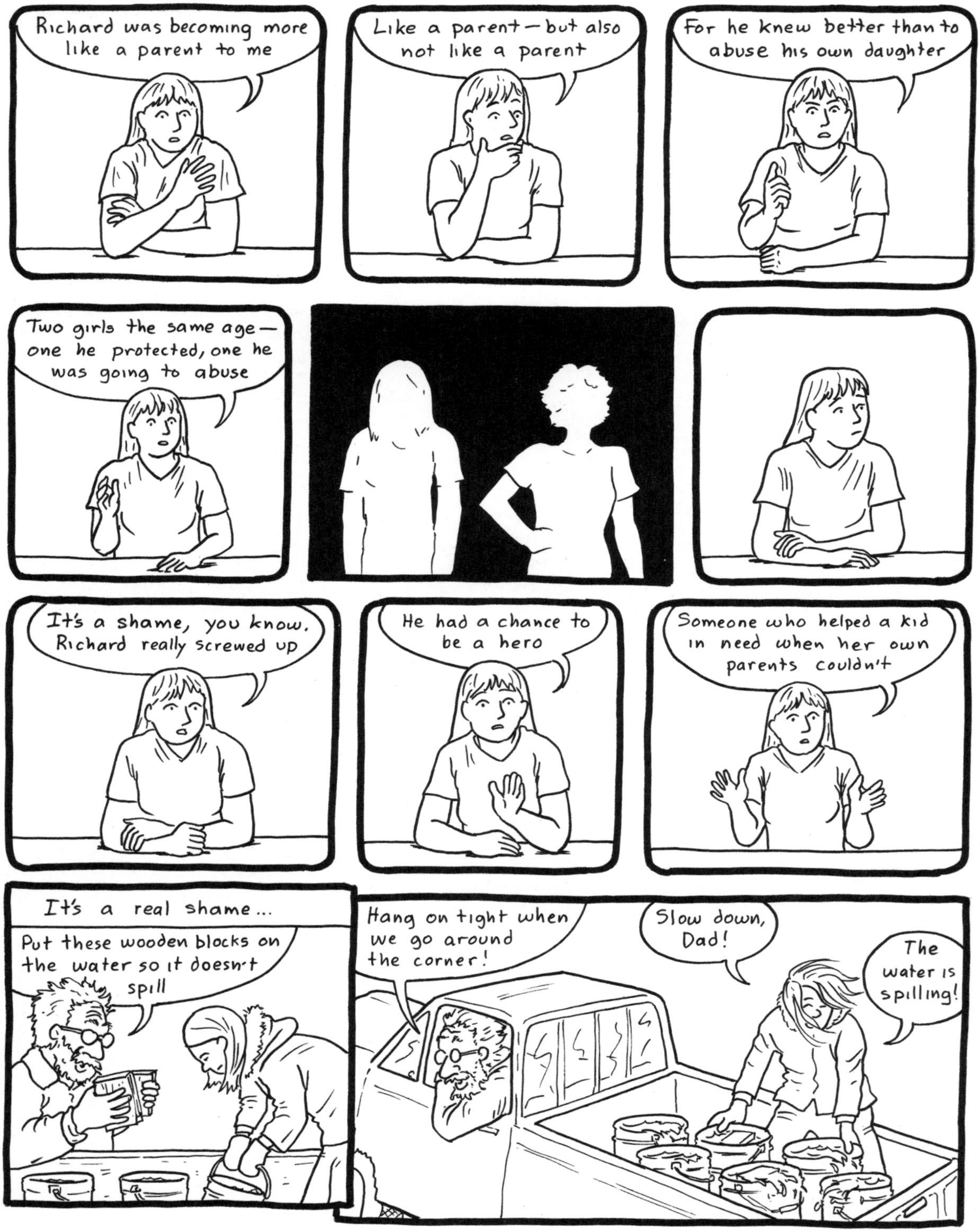
Richard was becoming more like a parent to me
Like a parent—but also not like a parent
For he knew better than to abuse his own daughter
Two girls the same age—one he protected, one he was going to abuse
It's a shame, you know. Richard really screwed up
He had a chance to be a hero
Someone who helped a kid in need when her own parents couldn't
It's a real shame...
Put these wooden blocks on the water so it doesn't spill
Hang on tight when we go around the corner!
Slow down, Dad!
The water is spilling!

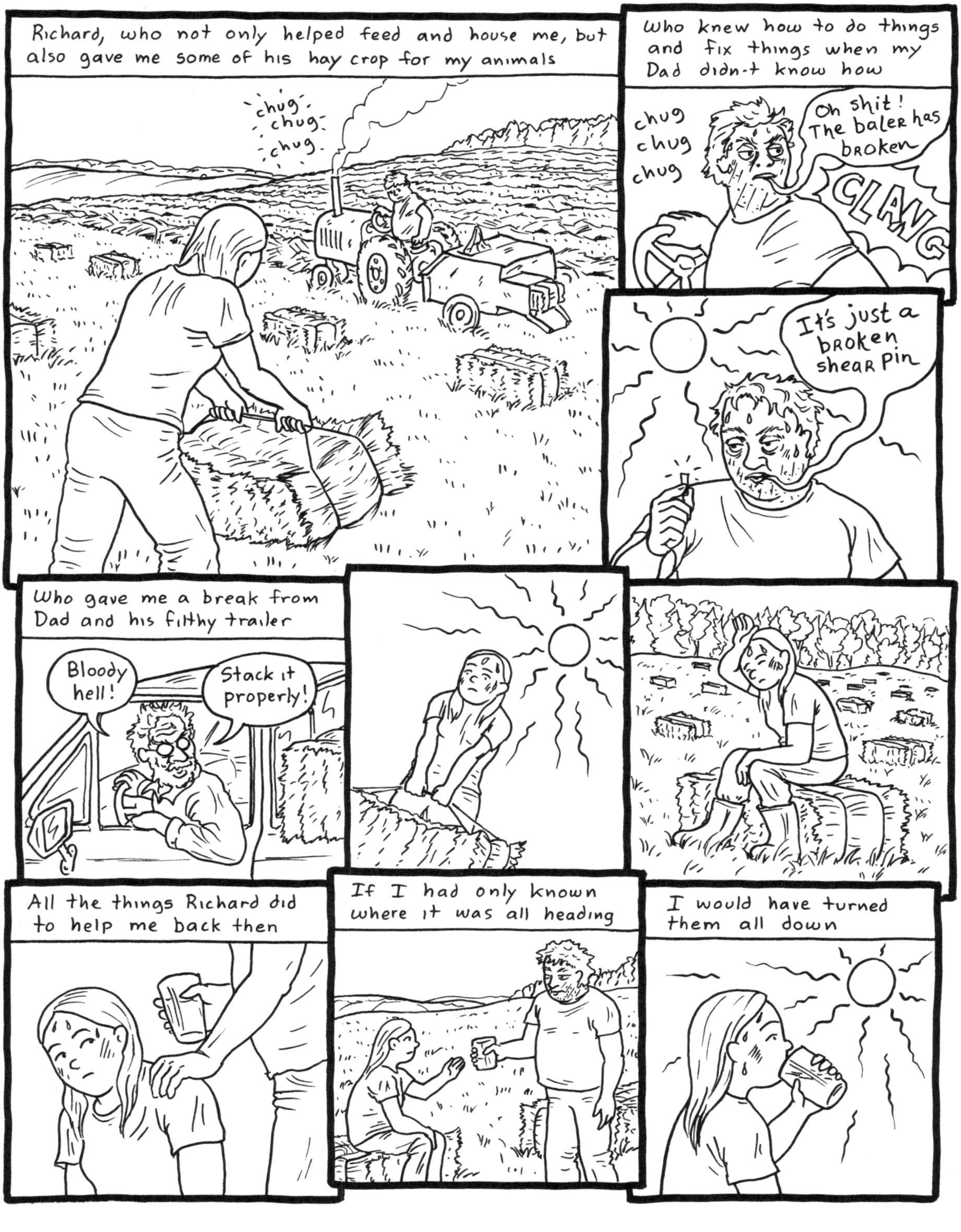
Richard, who not only helped feed and house me, but also gave me some of his hay crop for my animals
chug chug chug
Who knew how to do things and fix things when my Dad didn't know how
chug chug chug
Oh shit! The baler has broken
CLANG
It's just a broken shear pin
Who gave me a break from Dad and his filthy trailer
Bloody hell!
Stack it properly!
All the things Richard did to help me back then
If I had only known where it was all heading
I would have turned them all down

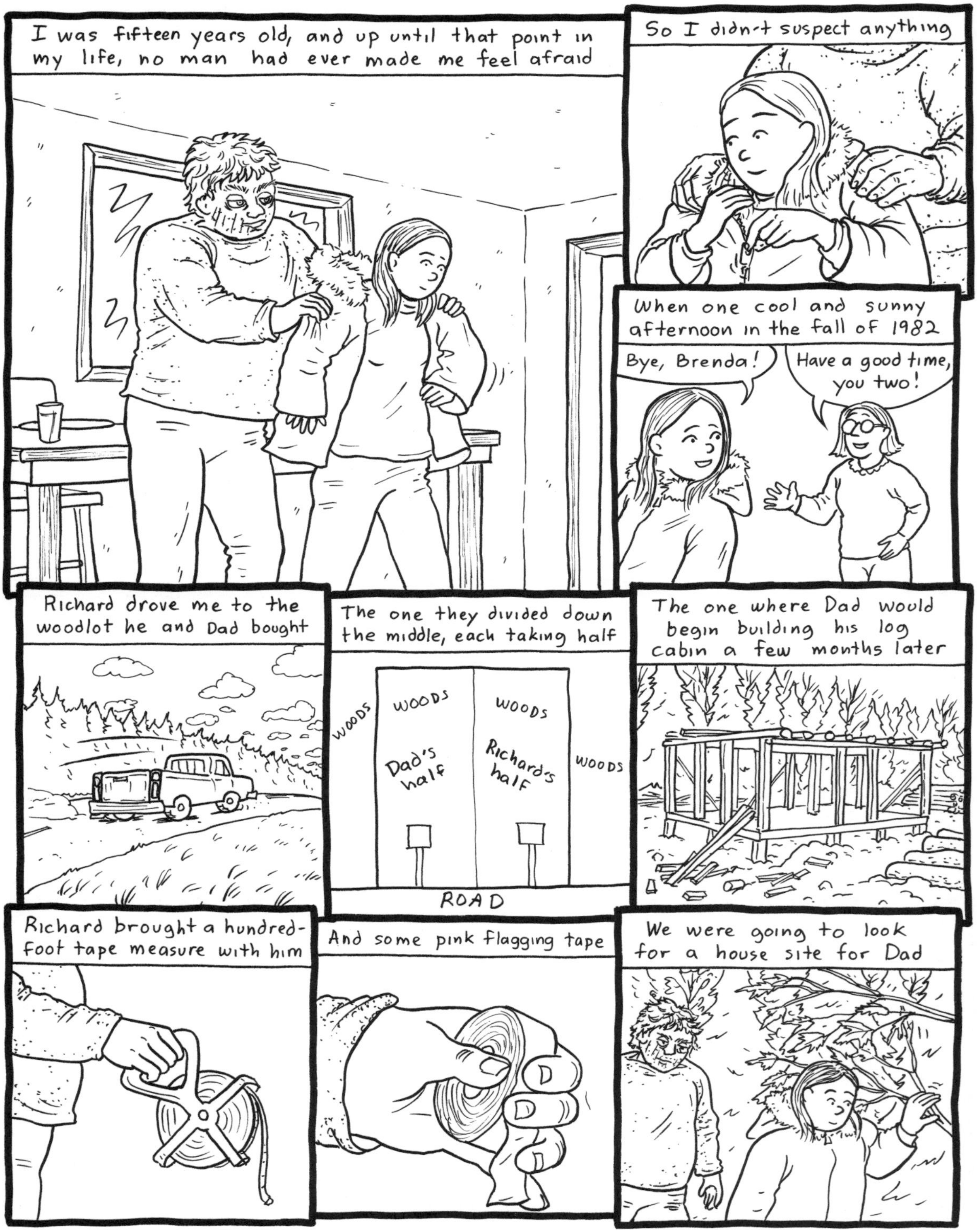

I was fifteen years old, and up until that point in my life, no man had ever made me feel afraid
So I didn't suspect anything
When one cool and sunny afternoon in the fall of 1982
Bye, Brenda!
Have a good time, you two!
Richard drove me to the woodlot he and Dad bought
The one they divided down the middle, each taking half
WOODS
WOODS
WOODS
WOODS
Dad's half
Richard's half
ROAD
The one where Dad would begin building his log cabin a few months later
Richard brought a hundred-foot tape measure with him
And some pink flagging tape
We were going to look for a house site for Dad

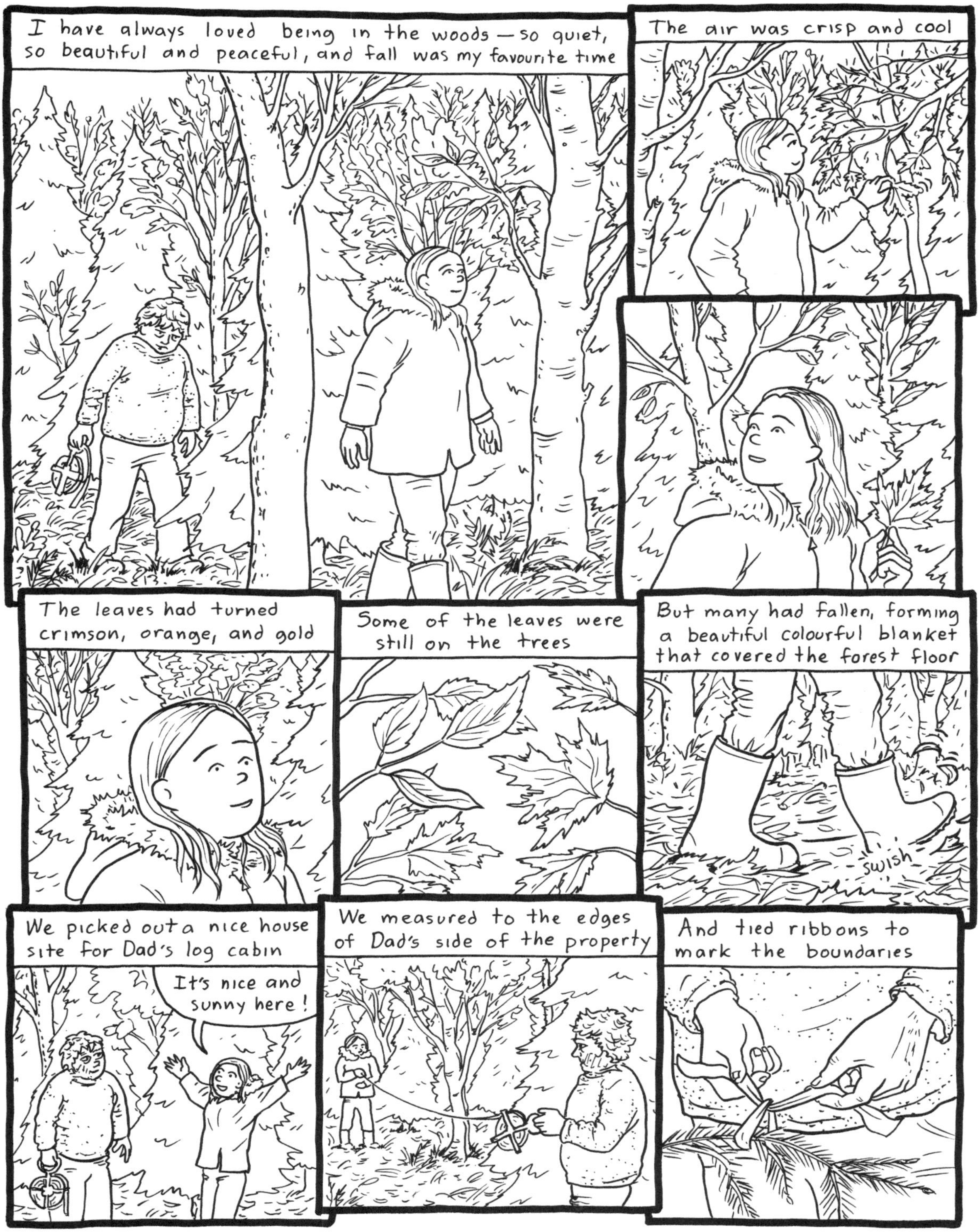
I have always loved being in the woods — so quiet, so beautiful and peaceful, and fall was my favourite time
The air was crisp and cool
The leaves had turned crimson, orange, and gold
Some of the leaves were still on the trees
But many had fallen, forming a beautiful colourful blanket that covered the forest floor
SWISH
We picked out a nice house site for Dad's log cabin
It's nice and sunny here!
We measured to the edges of Dad's side of the property
And tied ribbons to mark the boundaries

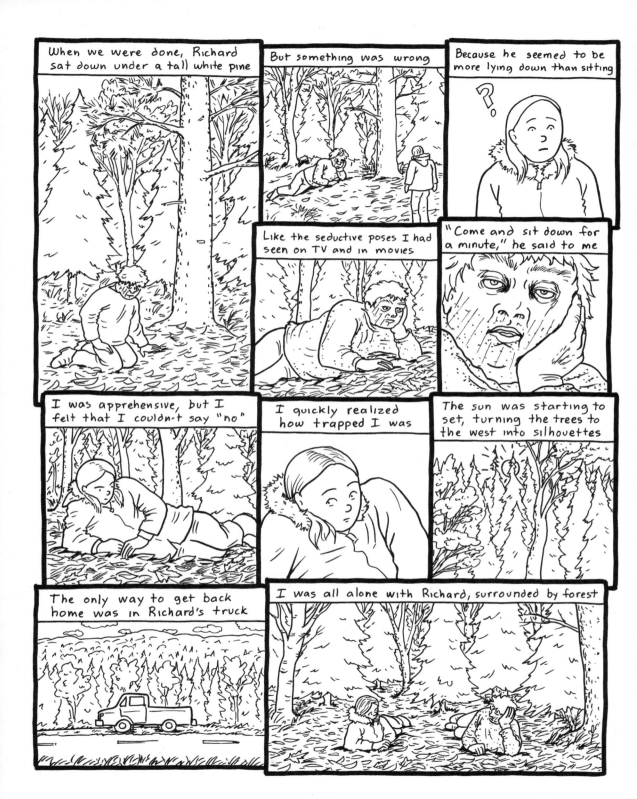

When we were done, Richard sat down under a tall white pine

But something was wrong

Because he seemed to be more lying down than sitting

Like the seductive poses I had seen on TV and in movies

"Come and sit down for a minute," he said to me

I was apprehensive, but I felt that I couldn't say "no"

I quickly realized how trapped I was

The sun was starting to set, turning the trees to the west into silhouettes

The only way to get back home was in Richard's truck

I was all alone with Richard, surrounded by forest

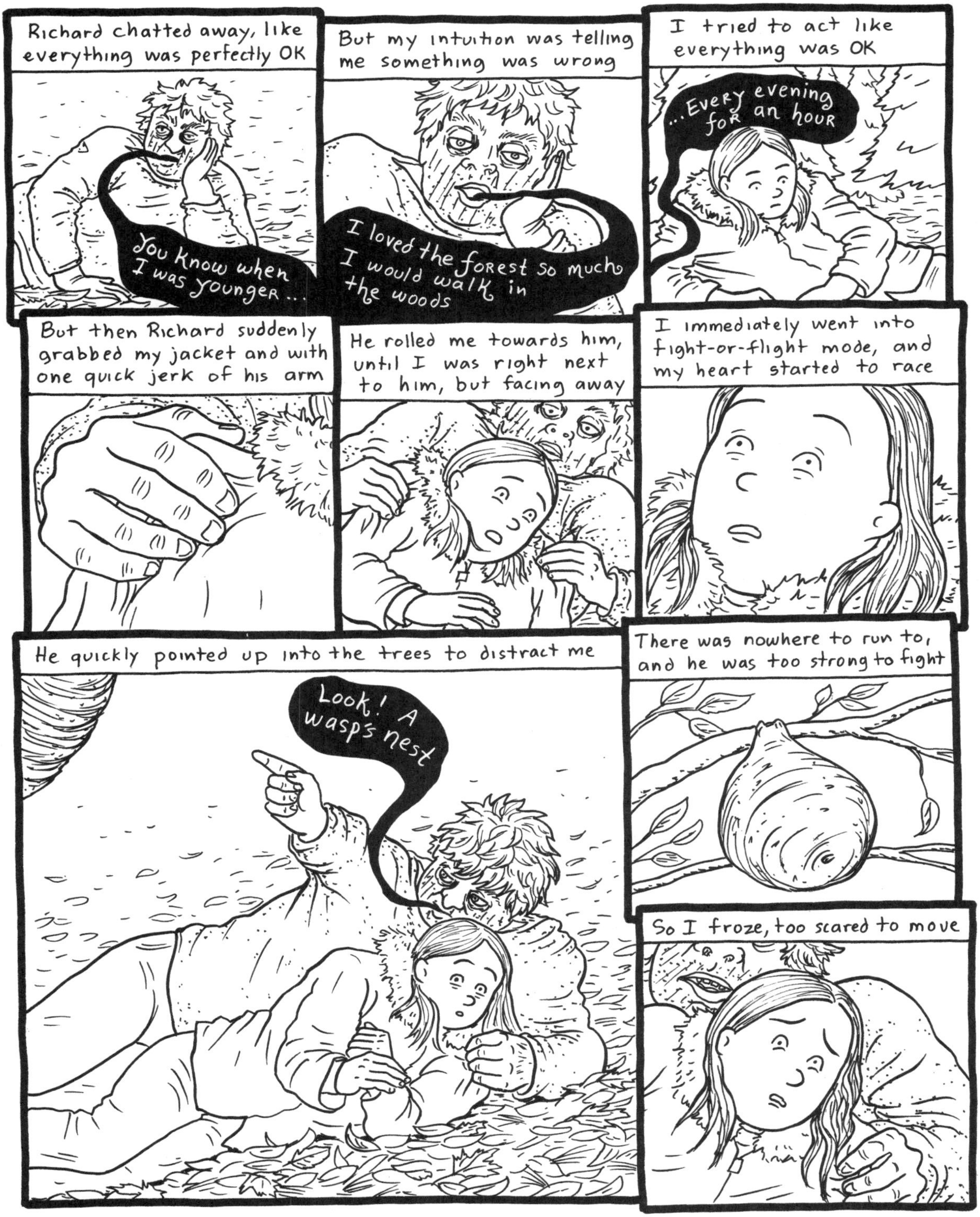
Richard chatted away, like everything was perfectly OK
You know when I was younger...
But my intuition was telling me something was wrong
I loved the forest so much I would walk in the woods
I tried to act like everything was OK
...Every evening for an hour
But then Richard suddenly grabbed my jacket and with one quick jerk of his arm
He rolled me towards him, until I was right next to him, but facing away
I immediately went into fight-or-flight mode, and my heart started to race
He quickly pointed up into the trees to distract me
Look! A wasp's nest
There was nowhere to run to, and he was too strong to fight
So I froze, too scared to move

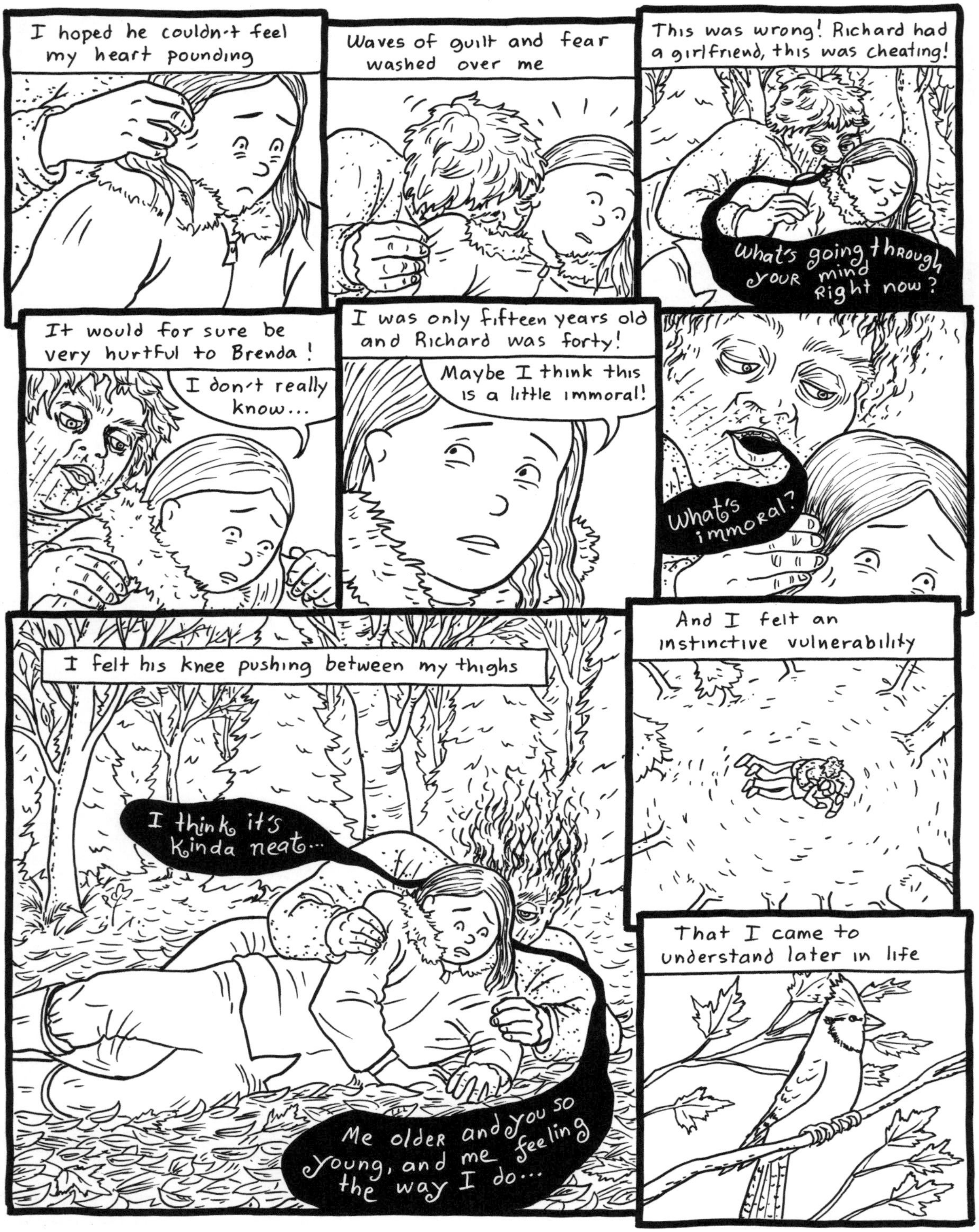

I hoped he couldn't feel my heart pounding
Waves of guilt and fear washed over me
This was wrong! Richard had a girlfriend, this was cheating!
What's going through your mind right now?
It would for sure be very hurtful to Brenda!
I don't really know...
I was only fifteen years old and Richard was forty!
Maybe I think this is a little immoral!
What's immoral?
I felt his knee pushing between my thighs
I think it's kinda neat...
Me older and you so young, and me feeling the way I do...
And I felt an instinctive vulnerability
That I came to understand later in life

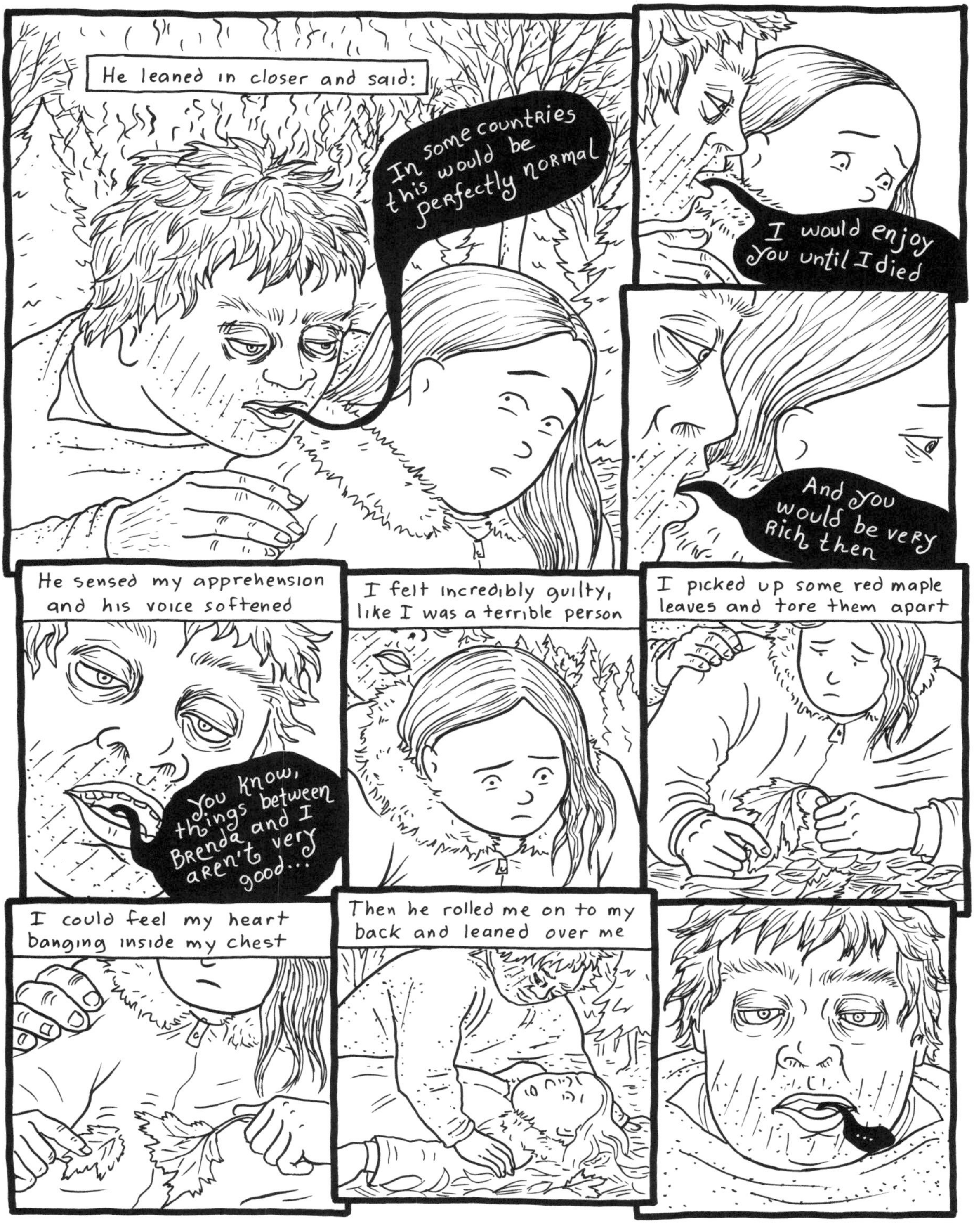
He leaned in closer and said:
In some countries this would be perfectly normal
I would enjoy you until I died
And you would be very rich then
He sensed my apprehension and his voice softened
You know, things between Brenda and I aren't very good...
I felt incredibly guilty, like I was a terrible person
I picked up some red maple leaves and tore them apart
I could feel my heart banging inside my chest
Then he rolled me on to my back and leaned over me
...

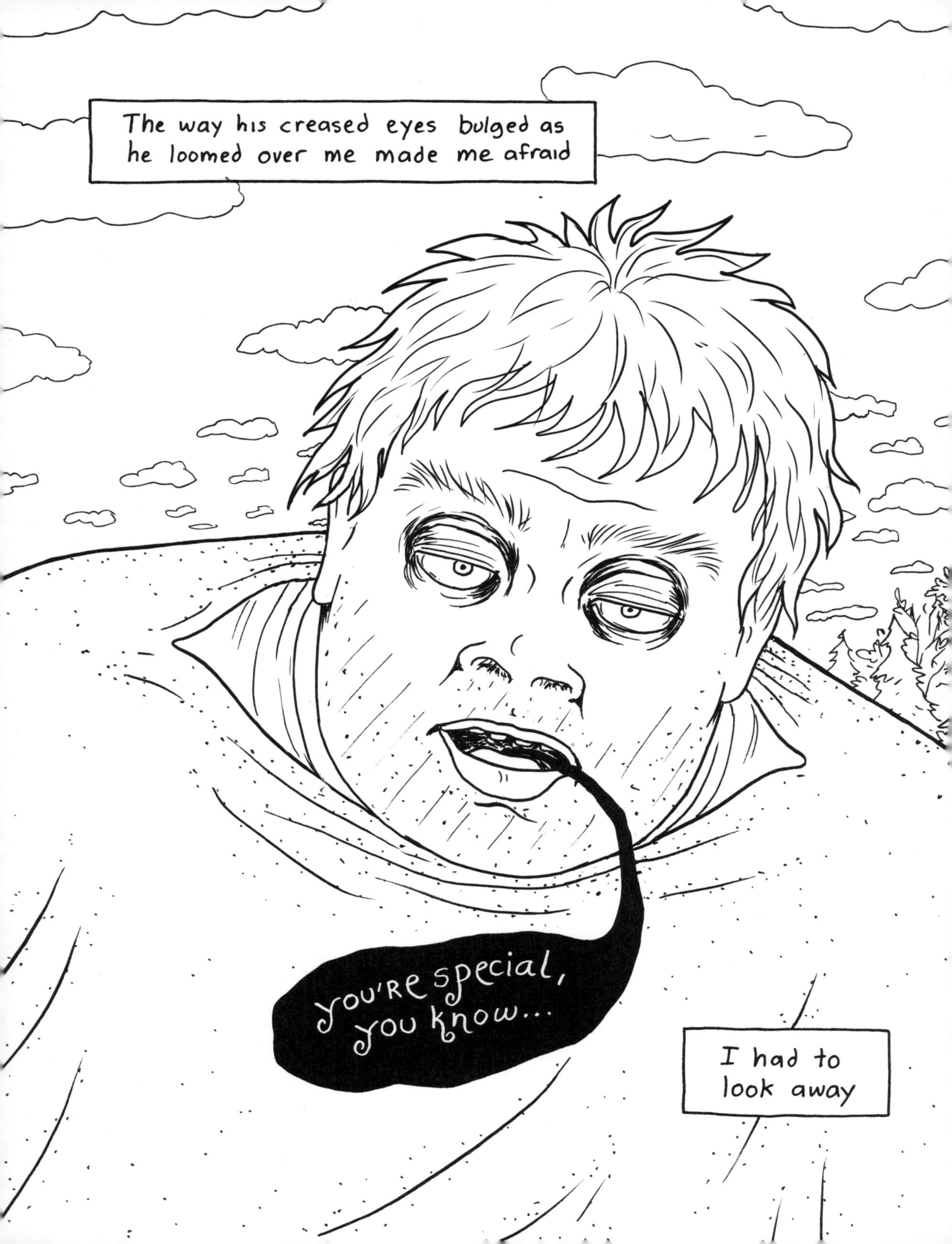
The way his creased eyes bulged as he loomed over me made me afraid
you're special, you know...
I had to look away

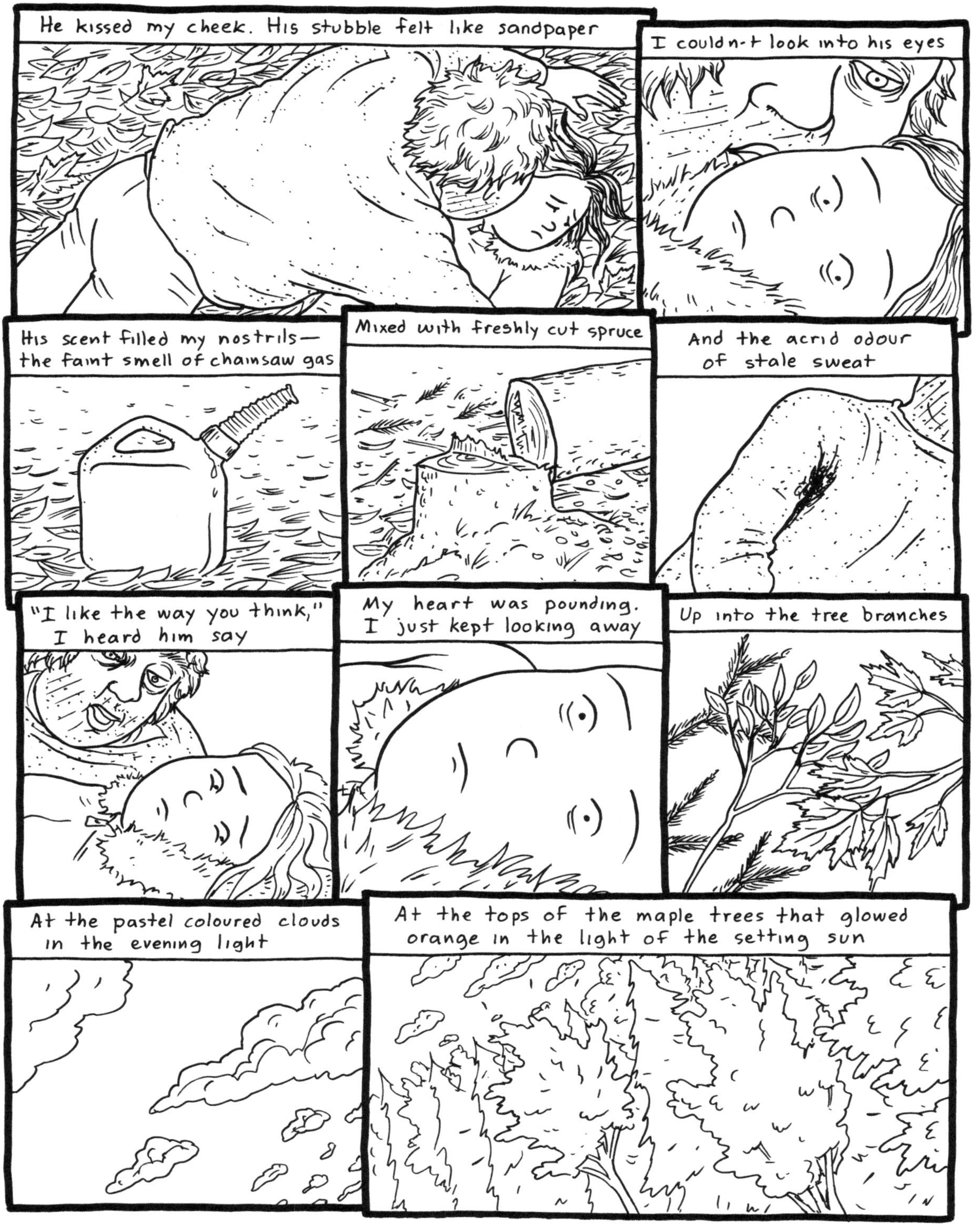
He kissed my cheek. His stubble felt like sandpaper
I couldn-t look into his eyes
His scent filled my nostrils— the faint smell of chainsaw gas
Mixed with freshly cut spruce
And the acrid odour of stale sweat
"I like the way you think," I heard him say
My heart was pounding. I just kept looking away
Up into the tree branches
At the pastel coloured clouds in the evening light
At the tops of the maple trees that glowed orange in the light of the setting sun

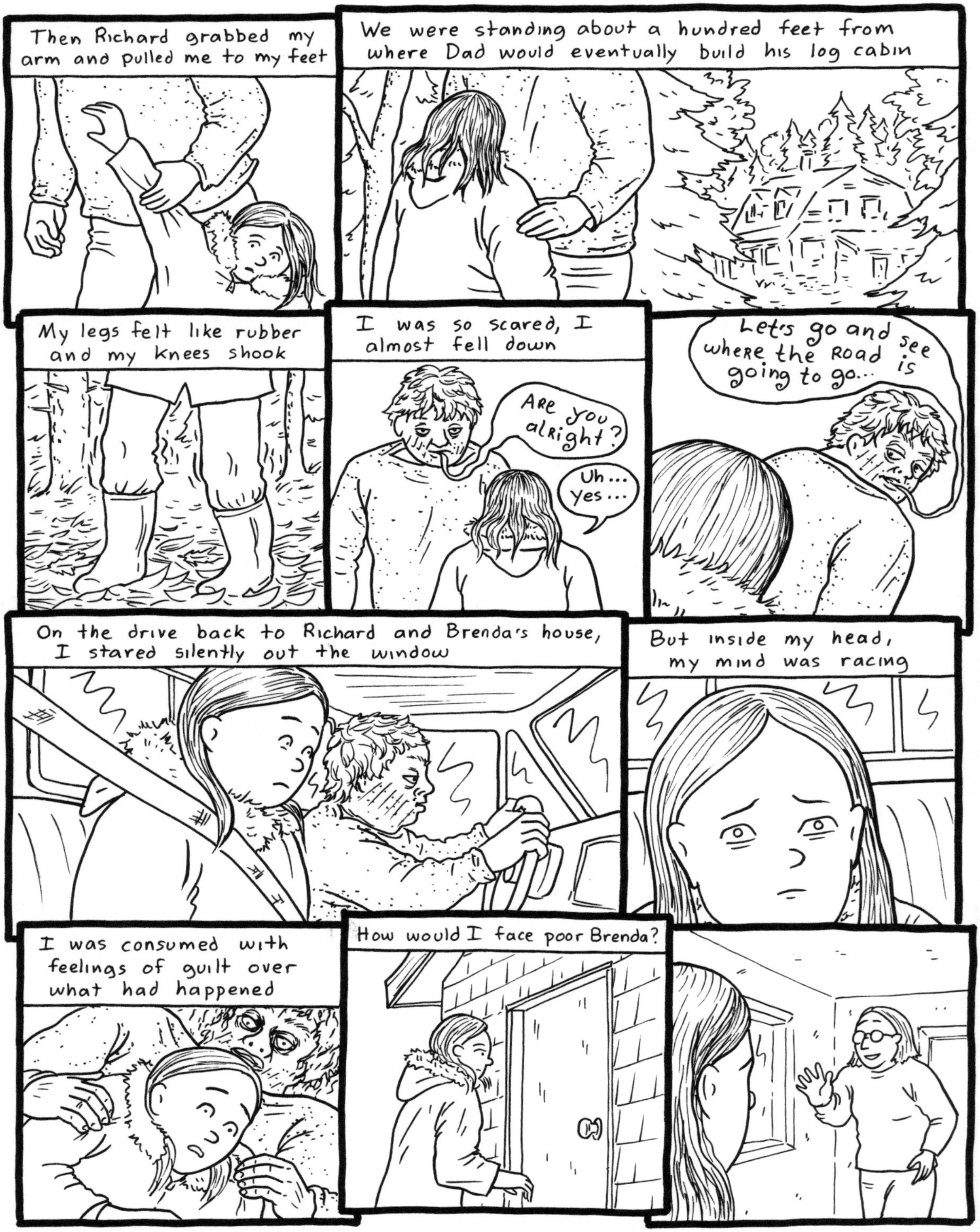
Then Richard grabbed my arm and pulled me to my feet
We were standing about a hundred feet from where Dad would eventually build his log cabin
My legs felt like rubber and my knees shook
I was so scared, I almost fell down
Are you alright?
Uh... yes...
Let's go and see where the Road is going to go...
On the drive back to Richard and Brenda's house, I stared silently out the window
But inside my head, my mind was racing
I was consumed with feelings of guilt over what had happened
How would I face poor Brenda?

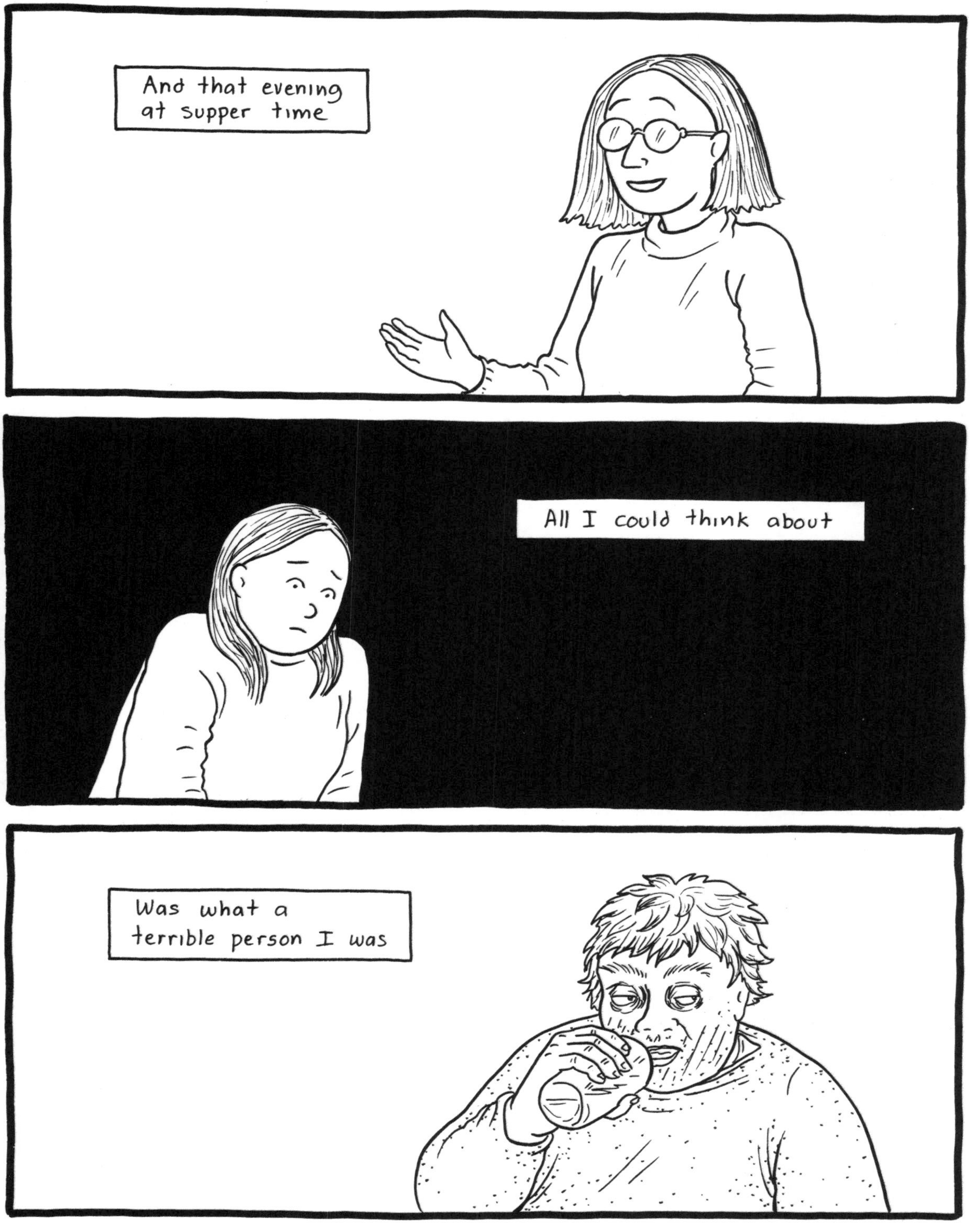
And that evening at supper time
All I could think about
Was what a terrible person I was

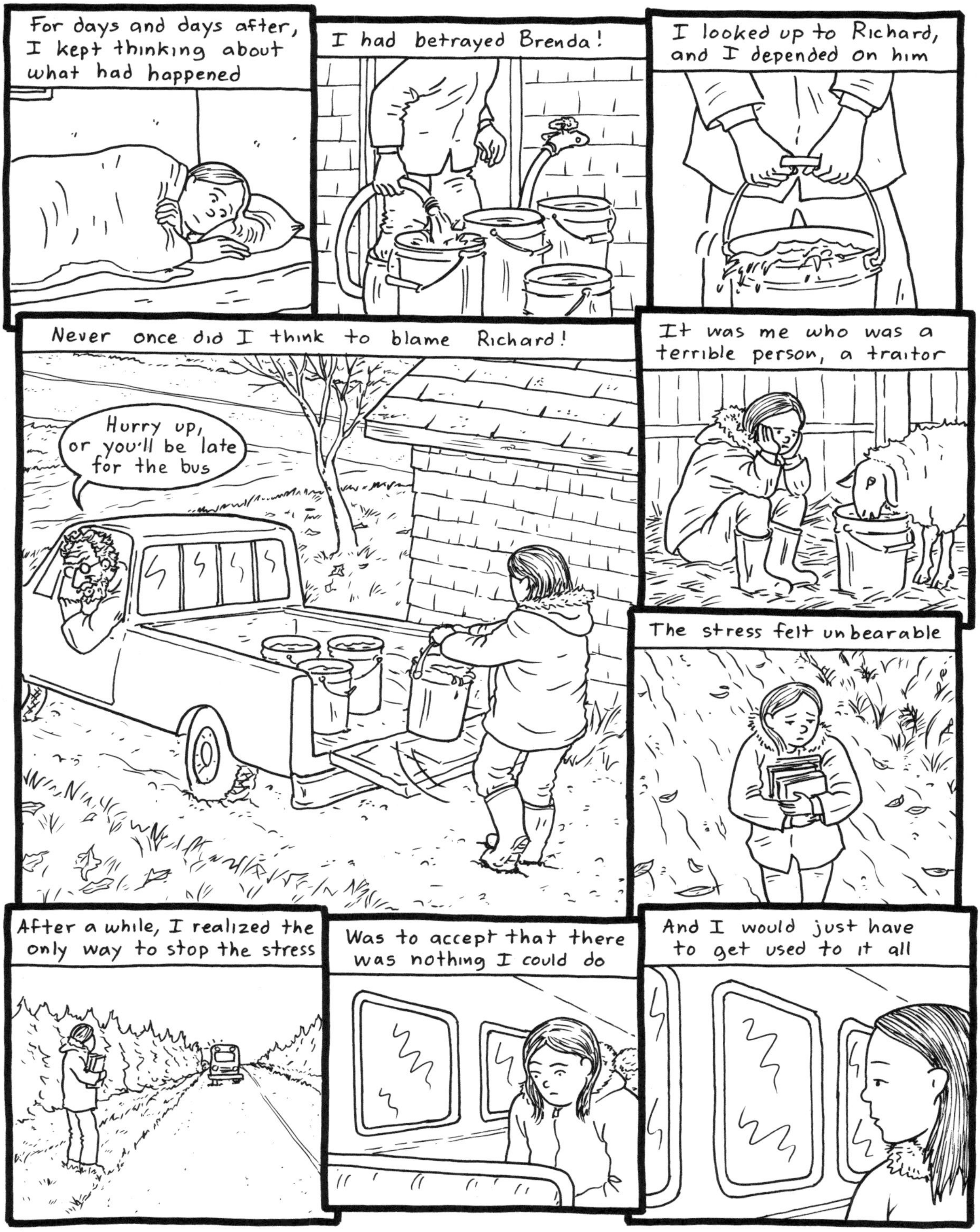
For days and days after, I kept thinking about what had happened
I had betrayed Brenda!
I looked up to Richard, and I depended on him
Never once did I think to blame Richard!
Hurry up, or you'll be late for the bus
It was me who was a terrible person, a traitor
The stress felt unbearable
After a while, I realized the only way to stop the stress
Was to accept that there was nothing I could do
And I would just have to get used to it all

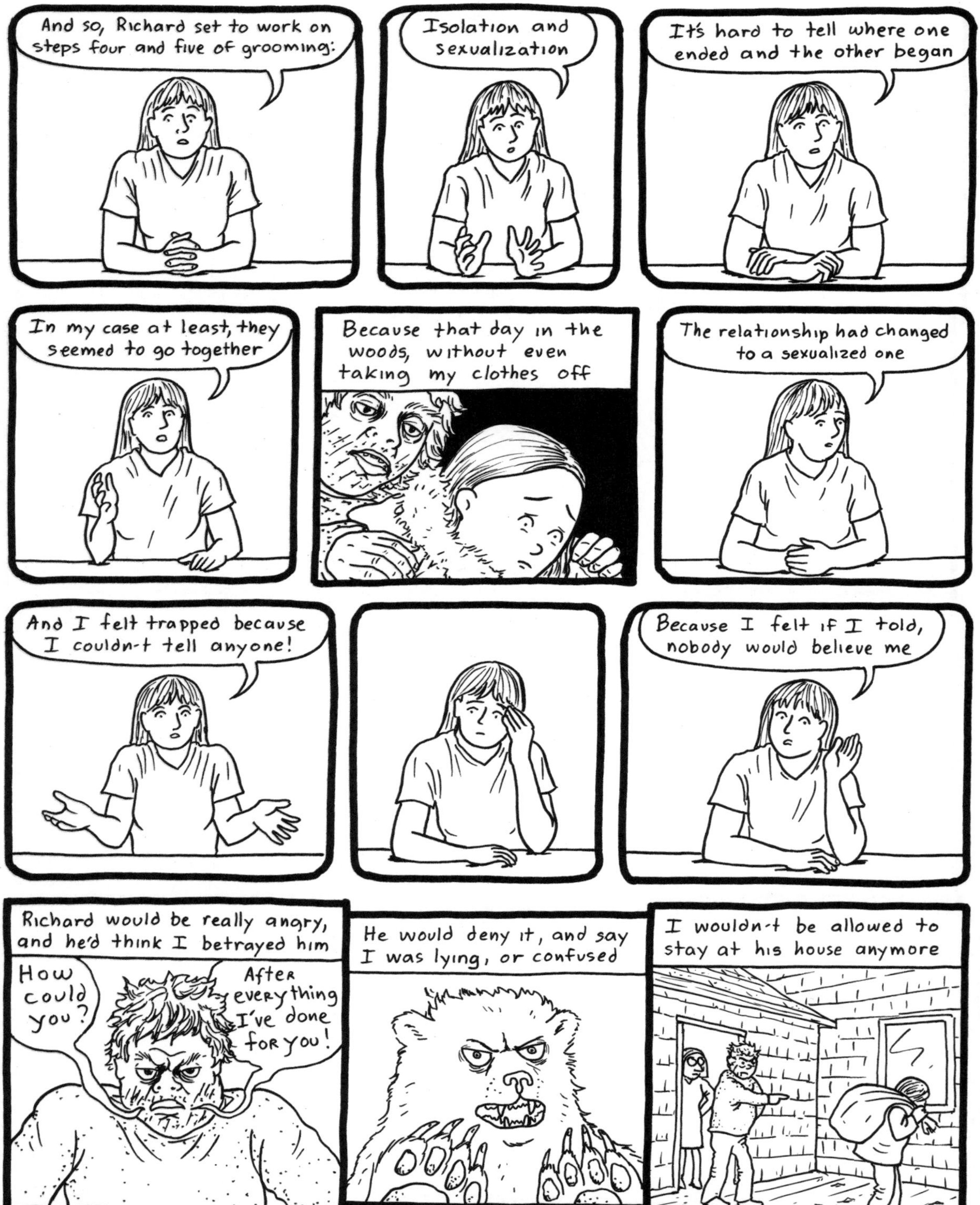

And so, Richard set to work on steps four and five of grooming:
Isolation and sexualization
It's hard to tell where one ended and the other began
In my case at least, they seemed to go together
Because that day in the woods, without even taking my clothes off
The relationship had changed to a sexualized one
And I felt trapped because I couldn't tell anyone!
Because I felt if I told, nobody would believe me
Richard would be really angry, and he'd think I betrayed him
How could you?
After everything I've done for you!
He would deny it, and say I was lying, or confused
I wouldn't be allowed to stay at his house anymore

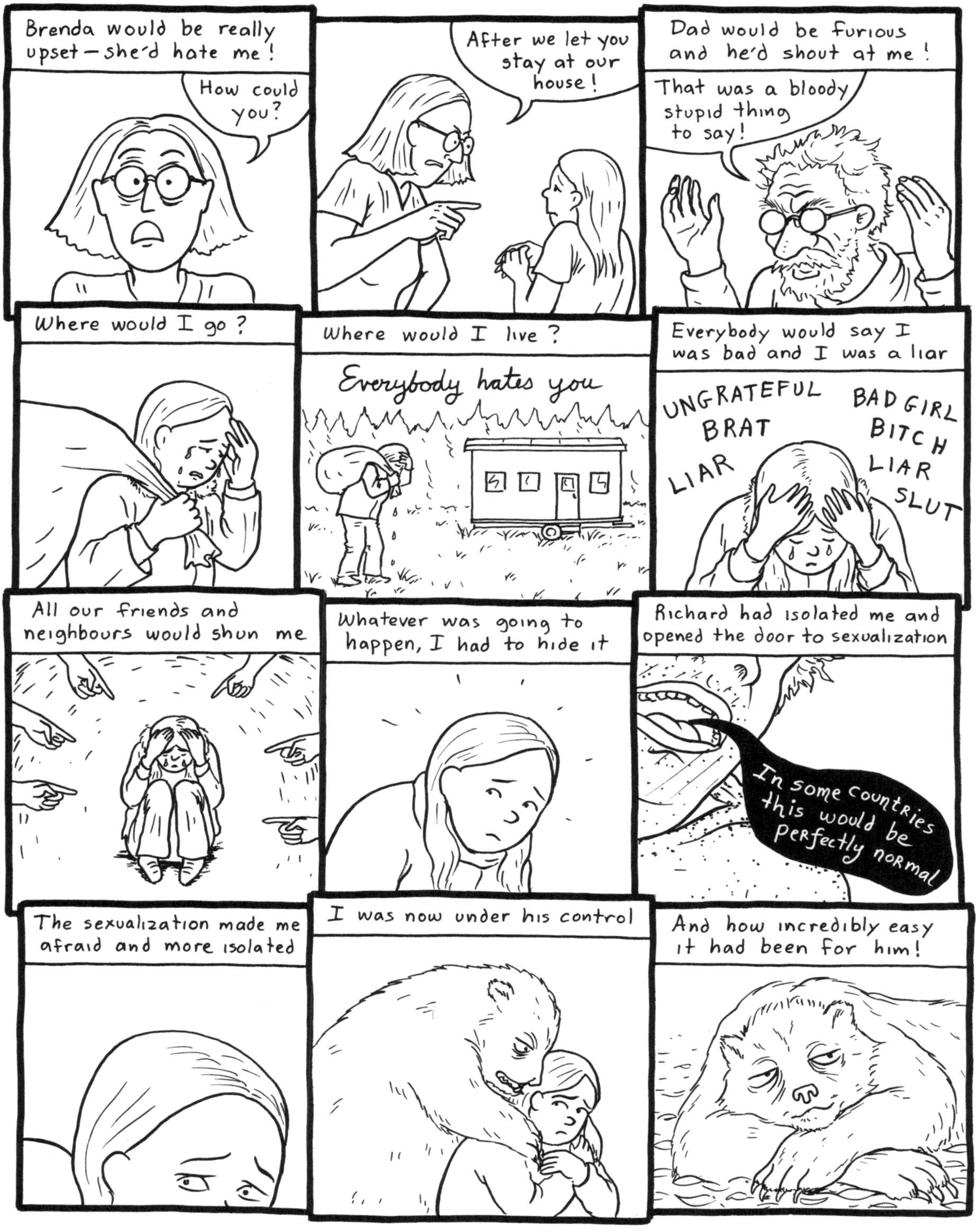
Brenda would be really upset—she'd hate me!
How could you?
After we let you stay at our house!
Dad would be furious and he'd shout at me!
That was a bloody stupid thing to say!
Where would I go?
Where would I live?
Everybody hates you
Everybody would say I was bad and I was a liar
UNGRATEFUL
BRAT
LIAR
BAD GIRL
BITCH
LIAR
SLUT
All our friends and neighbours would shun me
Whatever was going to happen, I had to hide it
Richard had isolated me and opened the door to sexualization
In some countries this would be perfectly normal
The sexualization made me afraid and more isolated
I was now under his control
And how incredibly easy it had been for him!

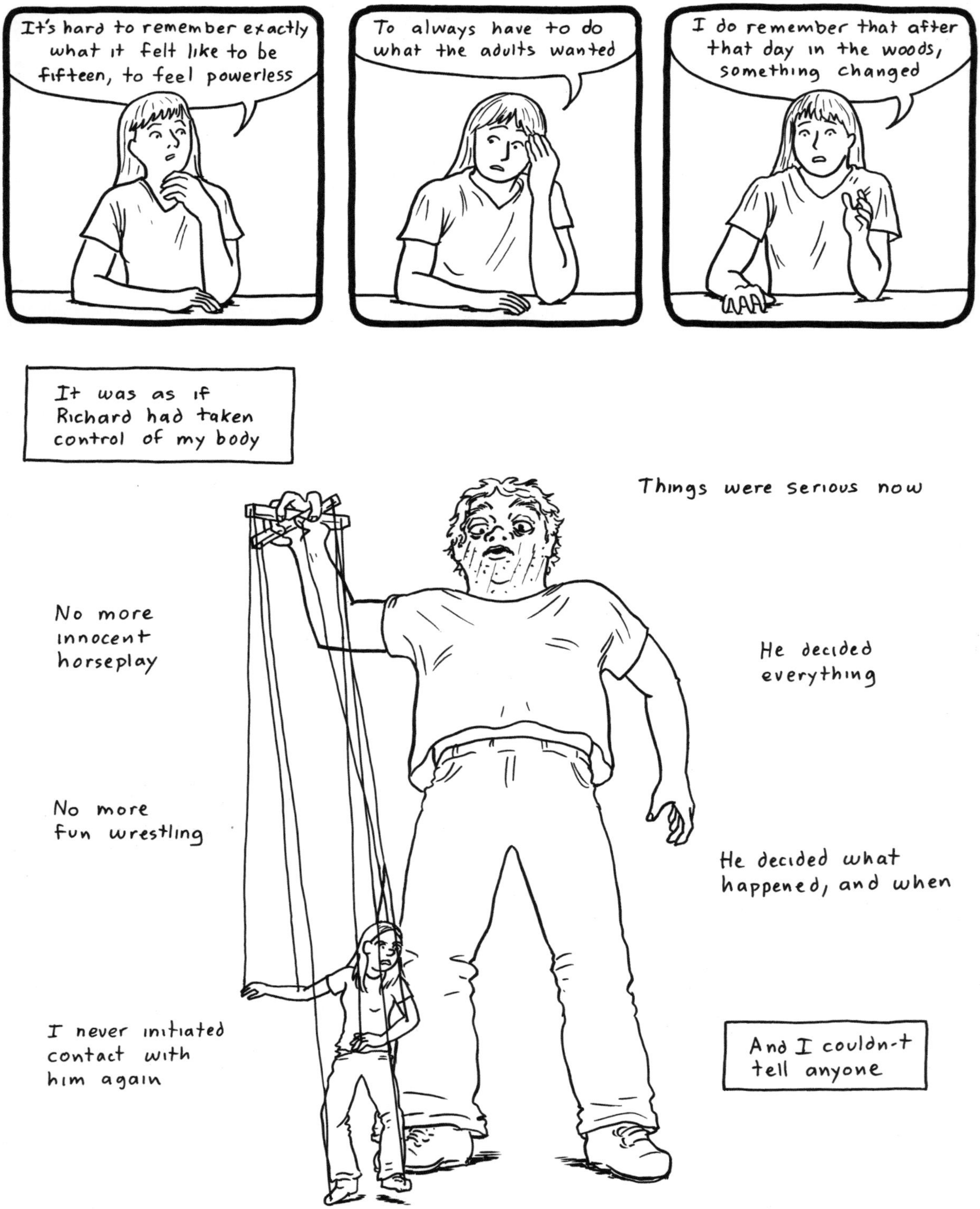
It's hard to remember exactly what it felt like to be fifteen, to feel powerless
To always have to do what the adults wanted
I do remember that after that day in the woods, something changed
It was as if Richard had taken control of my body
Things were serious now
No more innocent horseplay
He decided everything
No more fun wrestling
He decided what happened, and when
I never initiated contact with him again
And I couldn-t tell anyone

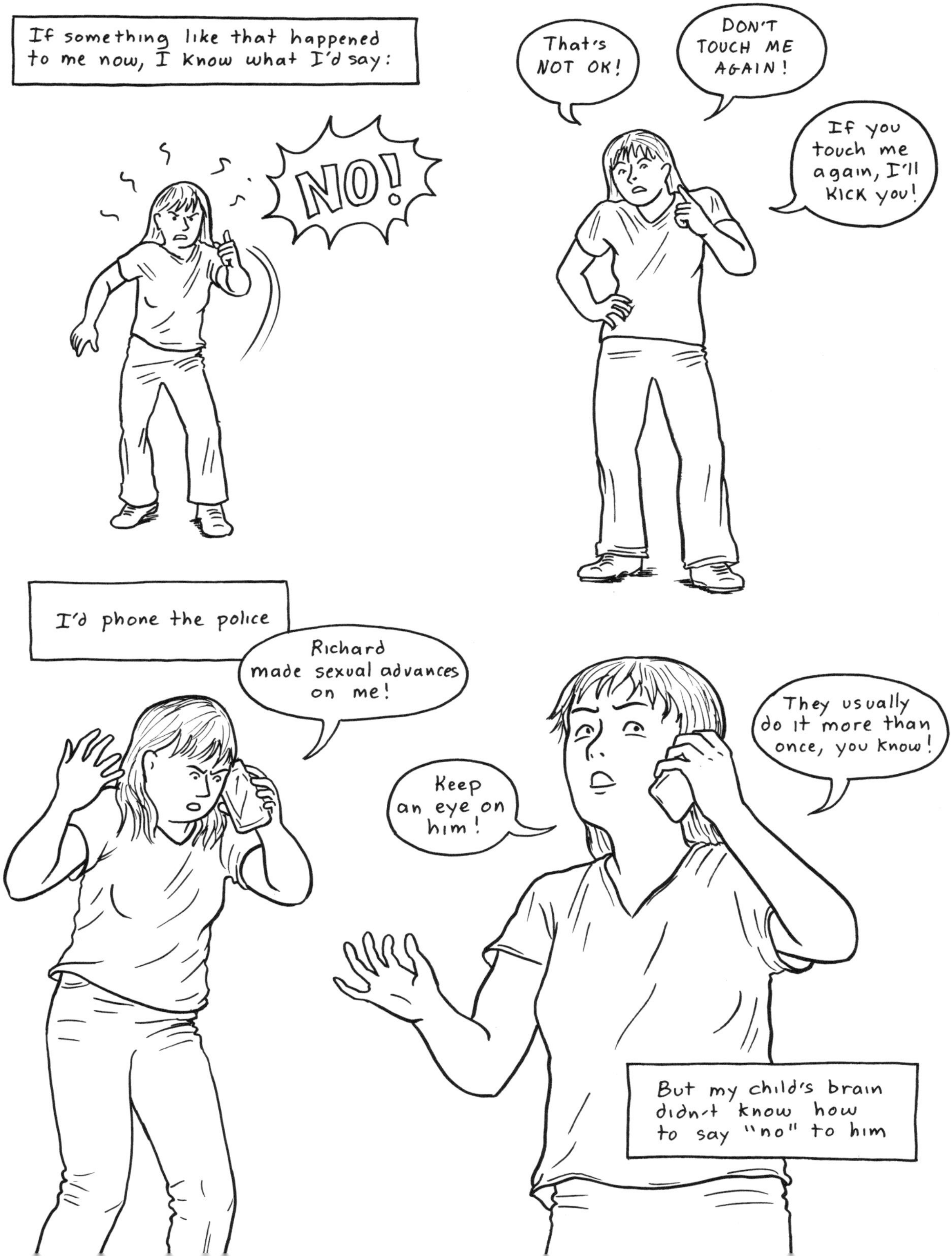
If something like that happened to me now, I know what I'd say:
NO!
That's NOT OK!
DON'T TOUCH ME AGAIN!
If you touch me again, I'll KICK you!
I'd phone the police
Richard made sexual advances on me!
Keep an eye on him!
They usually do it more than once, you know!
But my child's brain didn't know how to say "no" to him

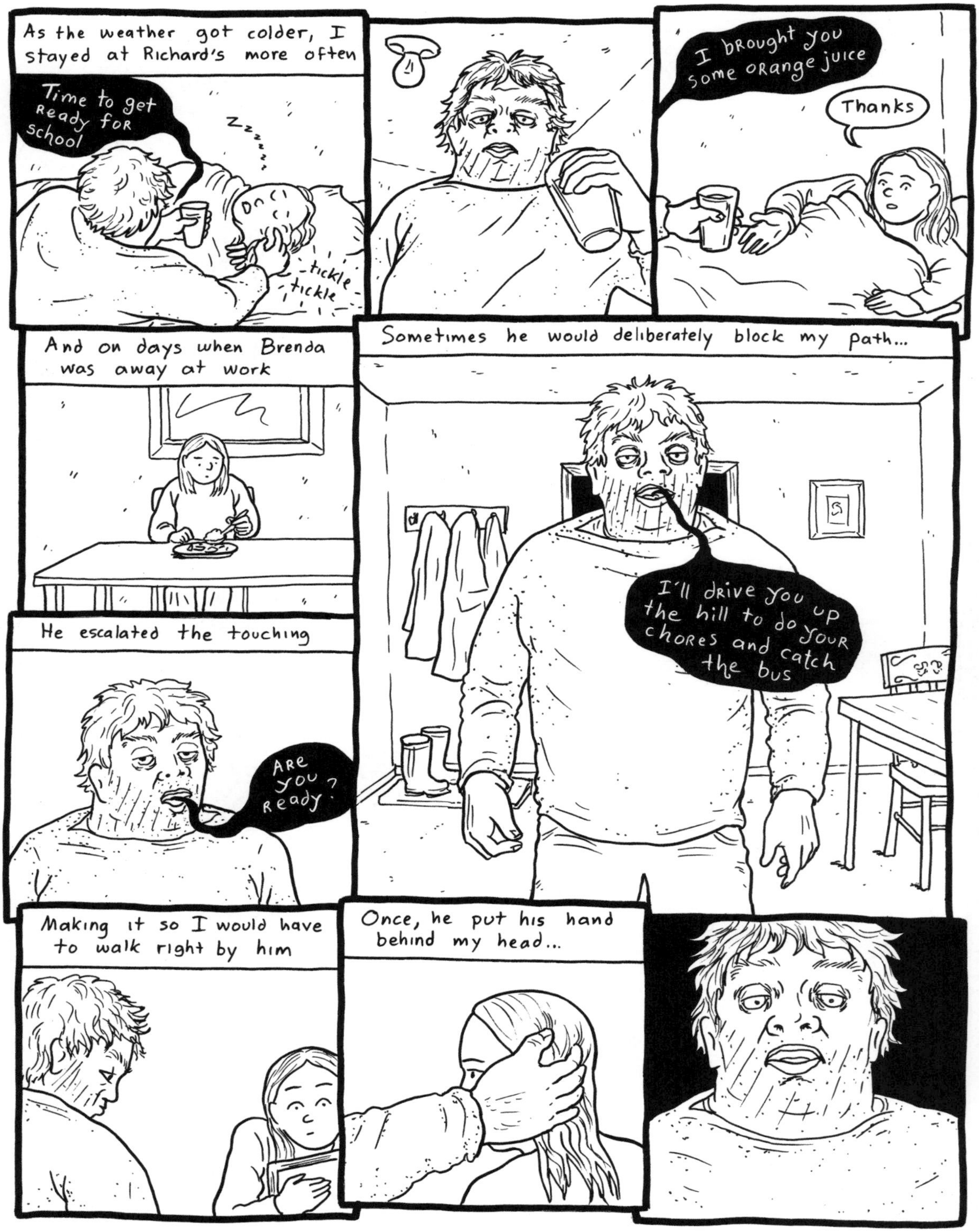
As the weather got colder, I stayed at Richard's more often
Time to get ready for school
Zzzzzz
tickle tickle
I brought you some orange juice
Thanks
And on days when Brenda was away at work
Sometimes he would deliberately block my path...
I'll drive you up the hill to do your chores and catch the bus
He escalated the touching
Are you ready?
Making it so I would have to walk right by him
Once, he put his hand behind my head...

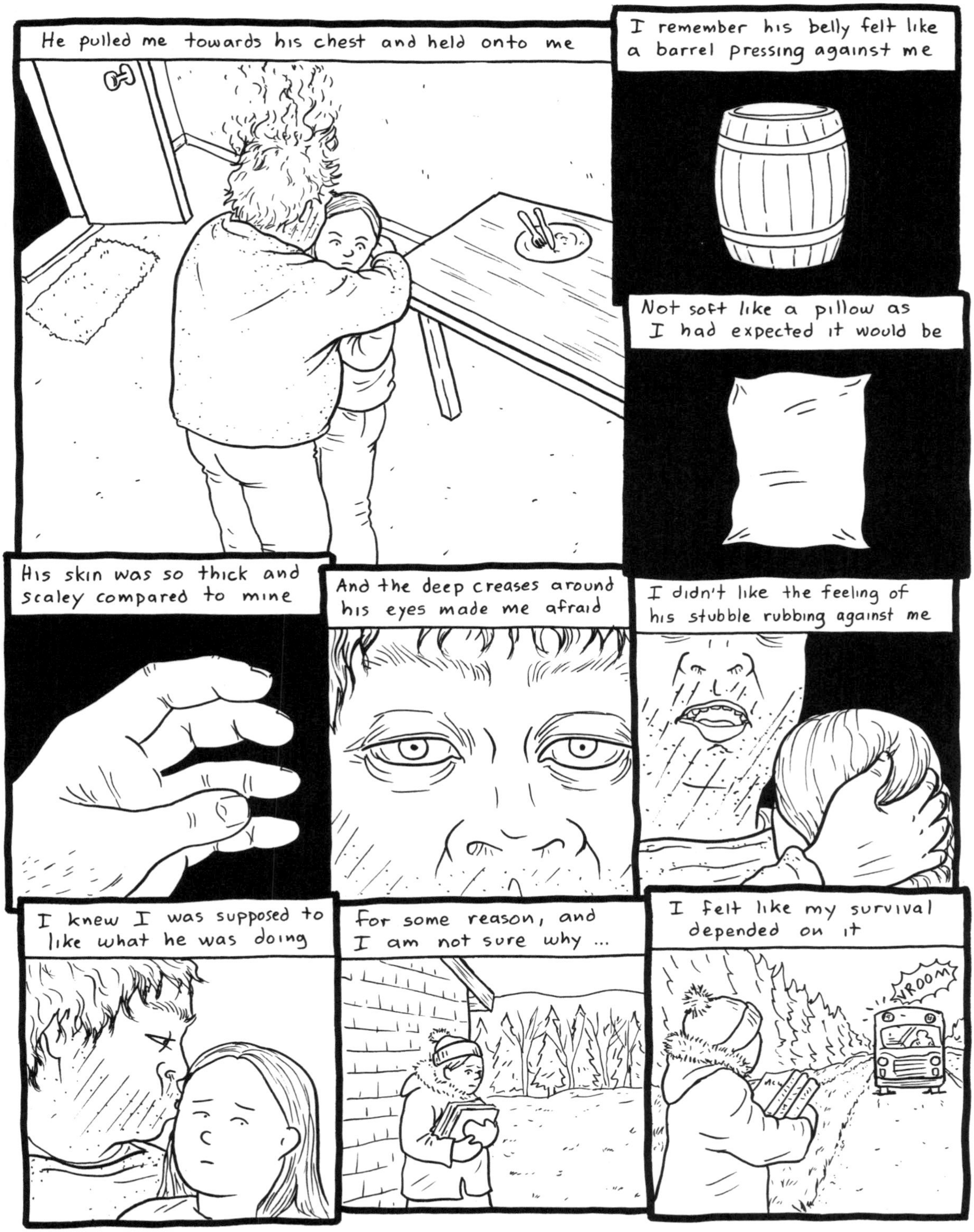
He pulled me towards his chest and held onto me
I remember his belly felt like a barrel pressing against me
Not soft like a pillow as I had expected it would be
His skin was so thick and scaley compared to mine
And the deep creases around his eyes made me afraid
I didn't like the feeling of his stubble rubbing against me
I knew I was supposed to like what he was doing
For some reason, and I am not sure why ...
I felt like my survival depended on it
VROOM

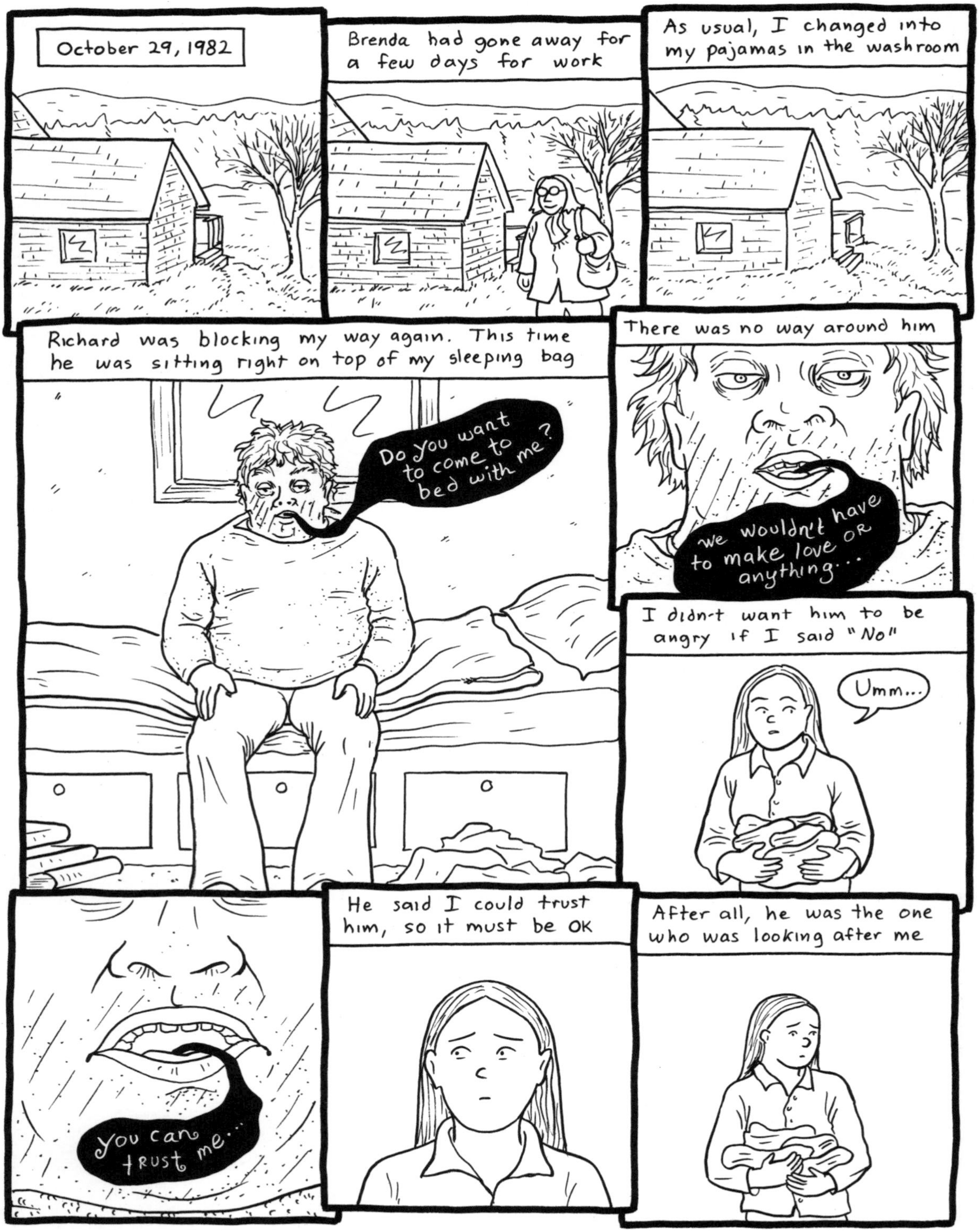
October 29, 1982
Brenda had gone away for a few days for work
As usual, I changed into my pajamas in the washroom
Richard was blocking my way again. This time he was sitting right on top of my sleeping bag
Do you want to come to bed with me?
There was no way around him
we wouldn't have to make love or anything...
I didn't want him to be angry if I said "No"
Umm...
you can trust me...
He said I could trust him, so it must be OK
After all, he was the one who was looking after me

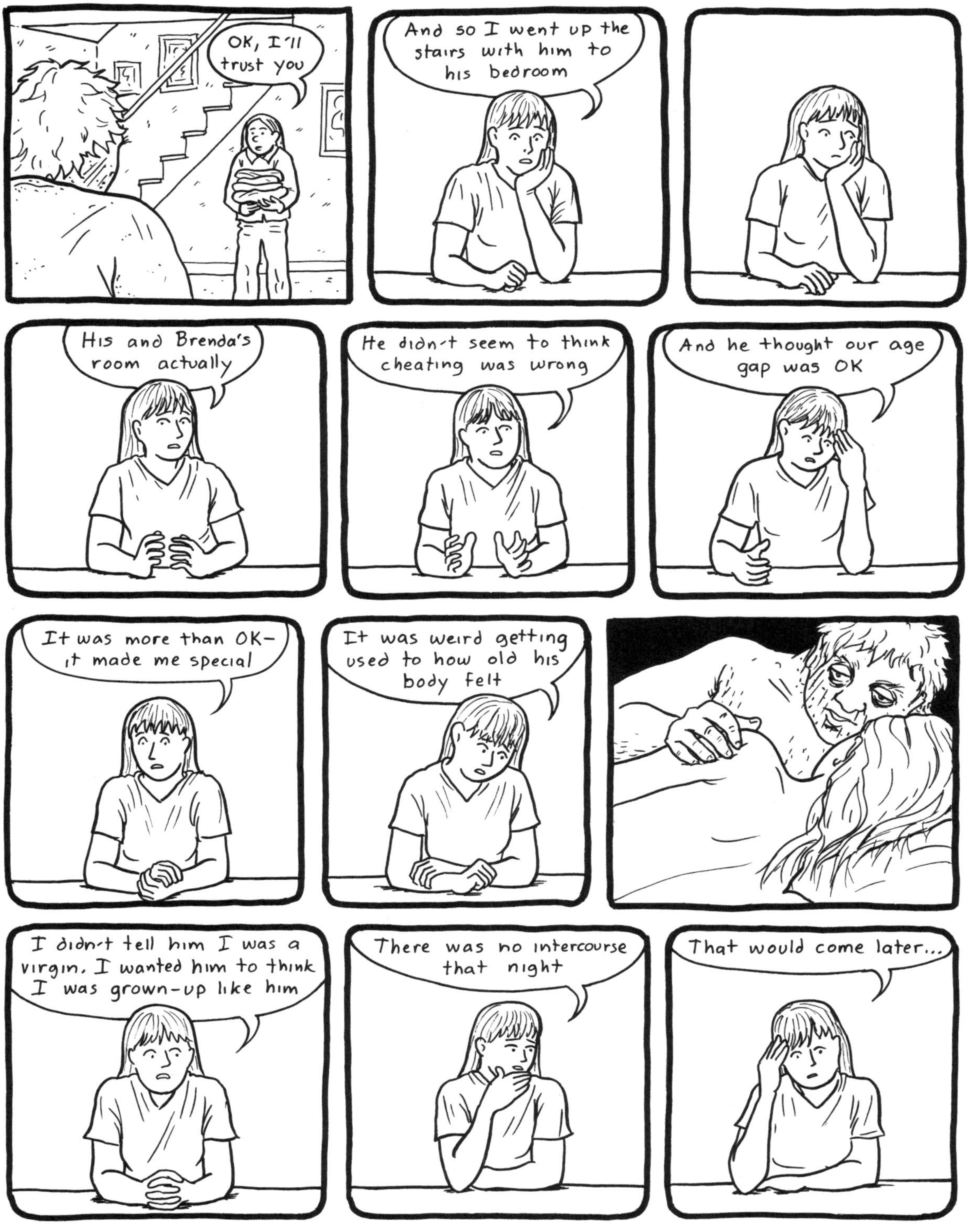
OK, I'll trust you
And so I went up the stairs with him to his bedroom
His and Brenda's room actually
He didn't seem to think cheating was wrong
And he thought our age gap was OK
It was more than OK— it made me special
It was weird getting used to how old his body felt
I didn't tell him I was a virgin. I wanted him to think I was grown-up like him
There was no intercourse that night
That would come later...

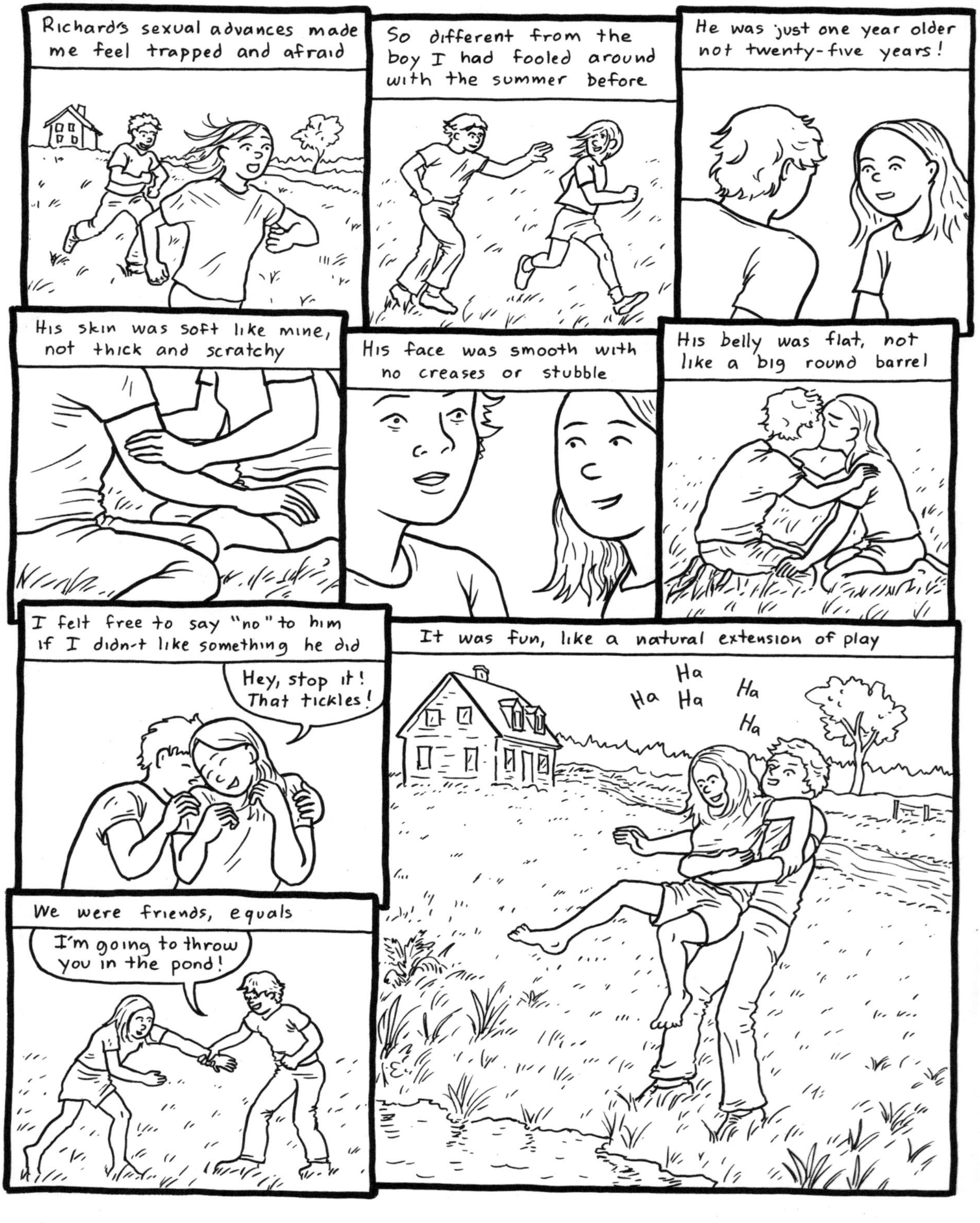
Richard's sexual advances made me feel trapped and afraid
So different from the boy I had fooled around with the summer before
He was just one year older not twenty-five years!
His skin was soft like mine, not thick and scratchy
His face was smooth with no creases or stubble
His belly was flat, not like a big round barrel
I felt free to say "no" to him if I didn't like something he did
Hey, stop it! That tickles!
We were friends, equals
I'm going to throw you in the pond!
It was fun, like a natural extension of play
Ha Ha Ha Ha Ha Ha

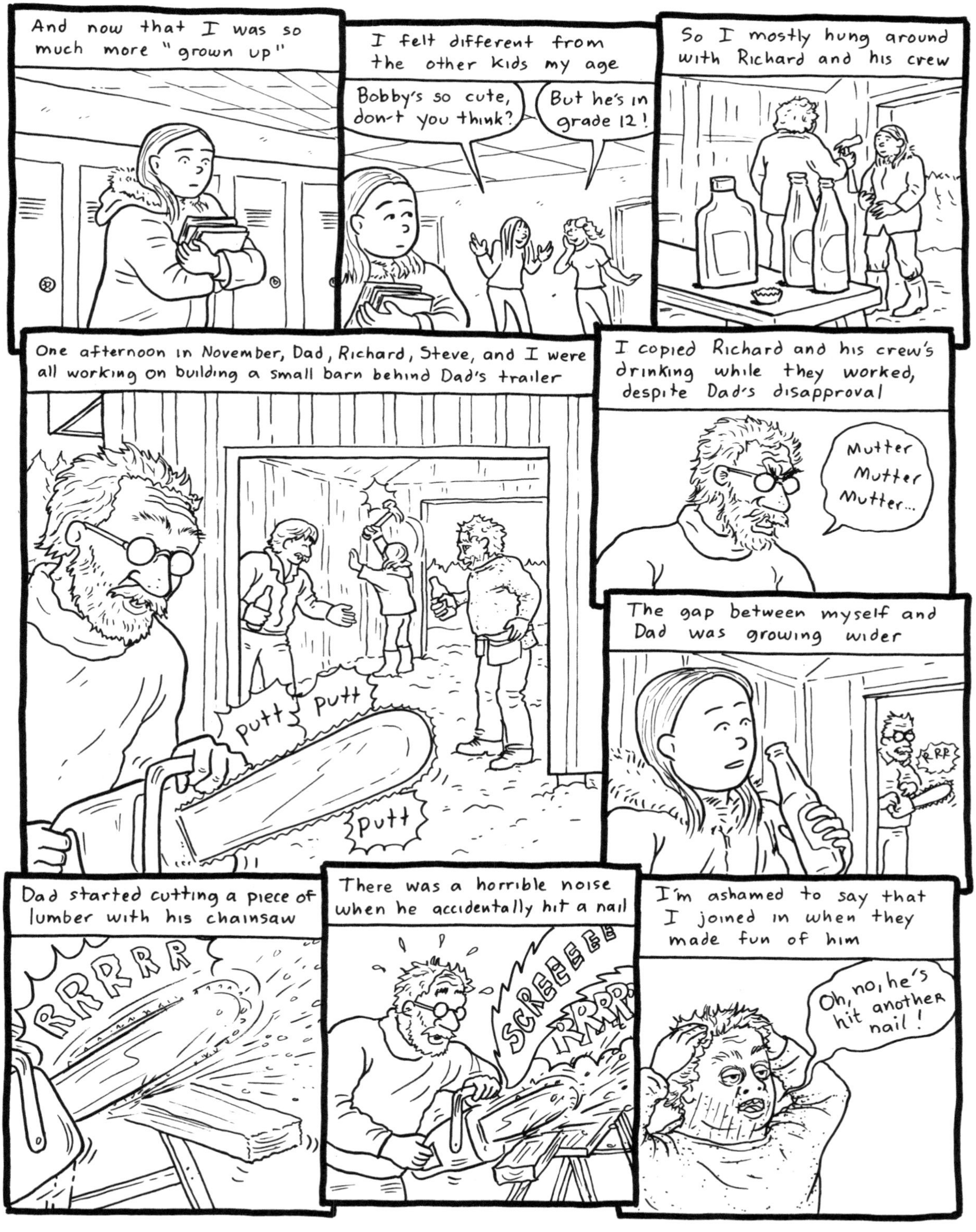
And now that I was so much more "grown up"
I felt different from the other kids my age
Bobby's so cute, don't you think?
But he's in grade 12!
So I mostly hung around with Richard and his crew
One afternoon in November, Dad, Richard, Steve, and I were all working on building a small barn behind Dad's trailer
putt putt
putt
I copied Richard and his crew's drinking while they worked, despite Dad's disapproval
Mutter Mutter Mutter...
The gap between myself and Dad was growing wider
RRR
Dad started cutting a piece of lumber with his chainsaw
RRRRR
There was a horrible noise when he accidentally hit a nail
SCREEEEE
I'm ashamed to say that I joined in when they made fun of him
Oh, no, he's hit another nail!

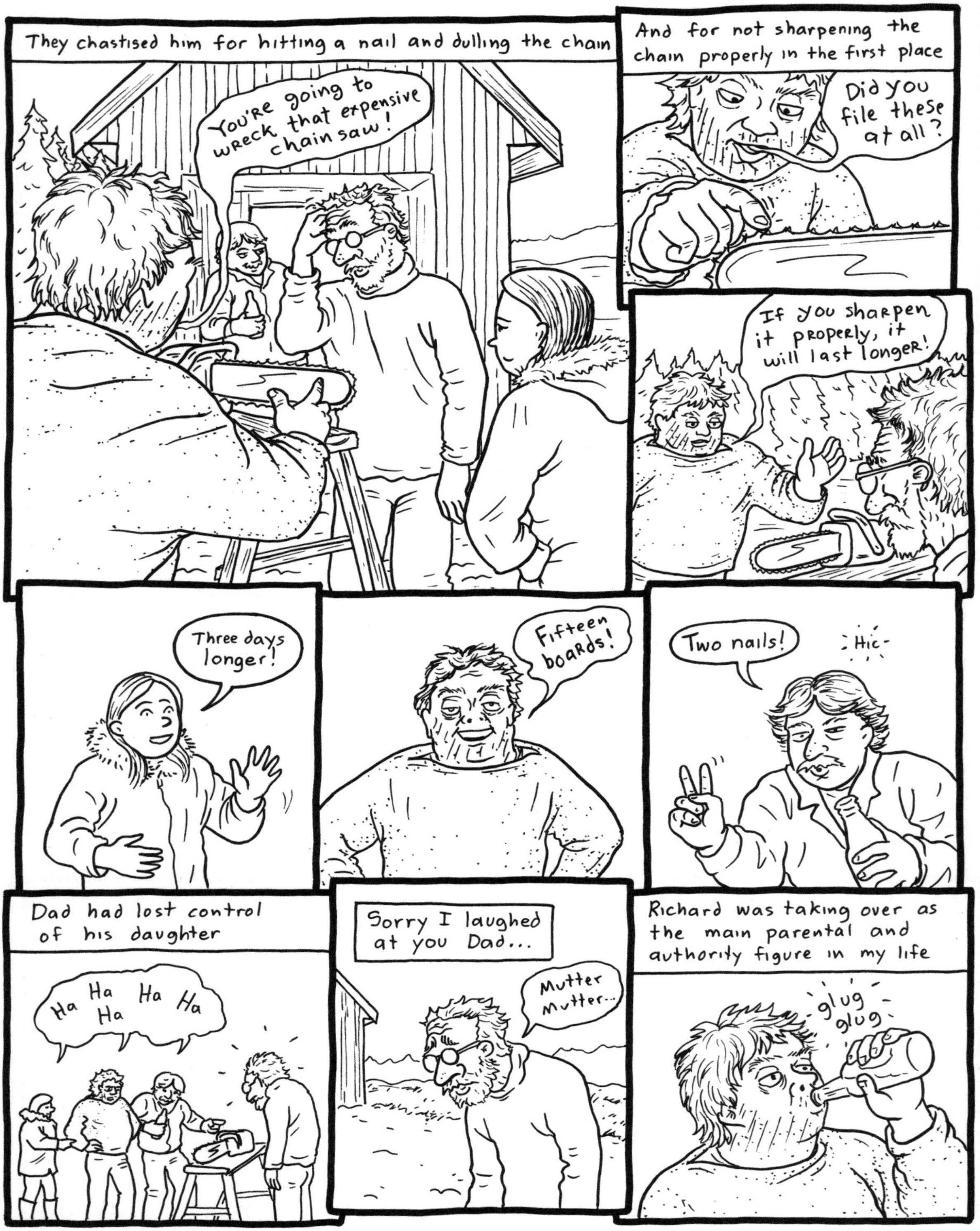

They chastised him for hitting a nail and dulling the chain
You're going to wreck that expensive chainsaw!
And for not sharpening the chain properly in the first place
Did you file these at all?
If you sharpen it properly, it will last longer!
Three days longer!
Fifteen boards!
Two nails!
Hic
Dad had lost control of his daughter
Ha Ha Ha Ha Ha
Sorry I laughed at you Dad...
Mutter Mutter...
Richard was taking over as the main parental and authority figure in my life
glug glug

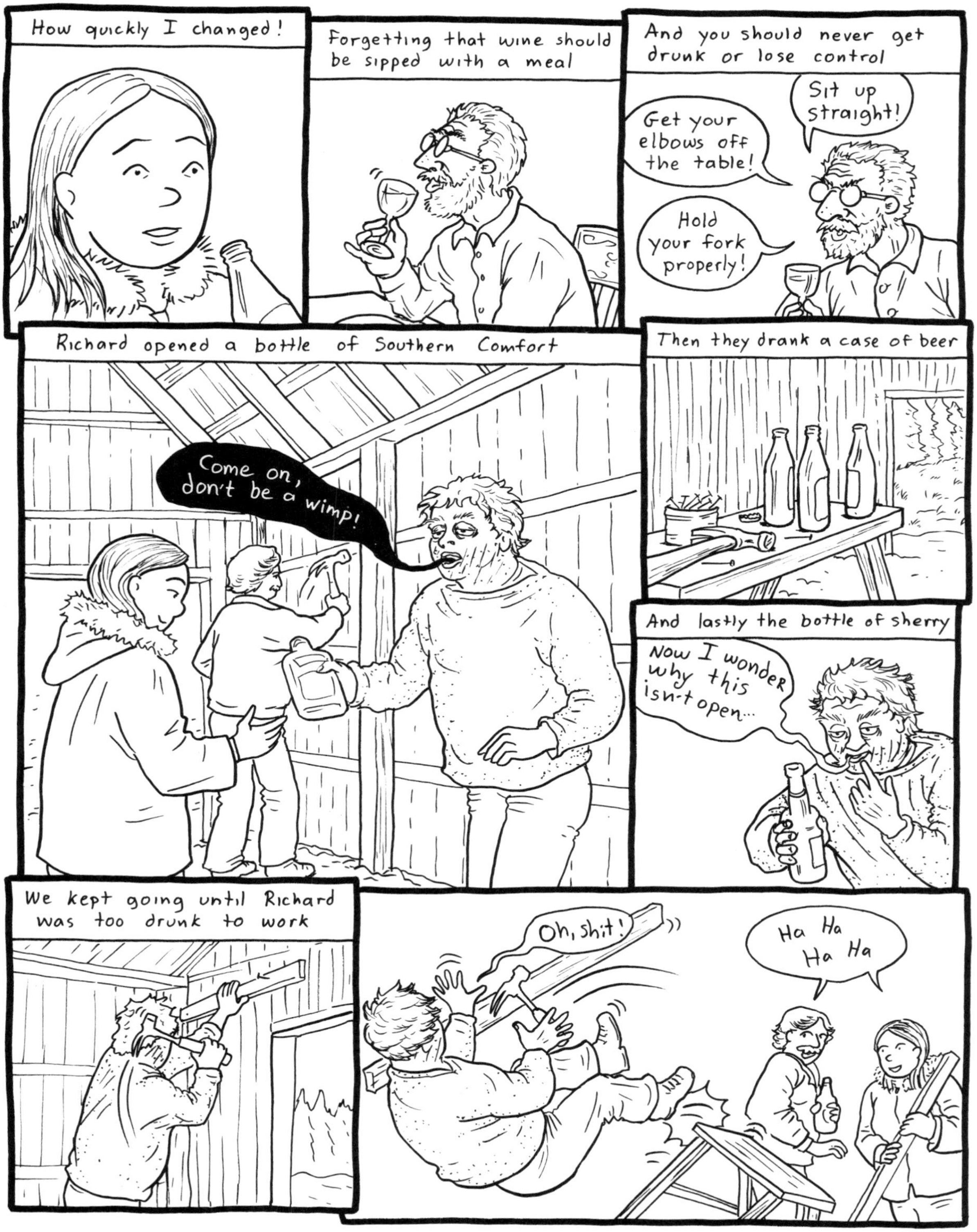
How quickly I changed!
Forgetting that wine should be sipped with a meal
And you should never get drunk or lose control
Sit up straight!
Get your elbows off the table!
Hold your fork properly!
Richard opened a bottle of Southern Comfort
Come on, don't be a wimp!
Then they drank a case of beer
And lastly the bottle of sherry
Now I wonder why this isn't open...
We kept going until Richard was too drunk to work
Oh, shit!
Ha Ha Ha Ha

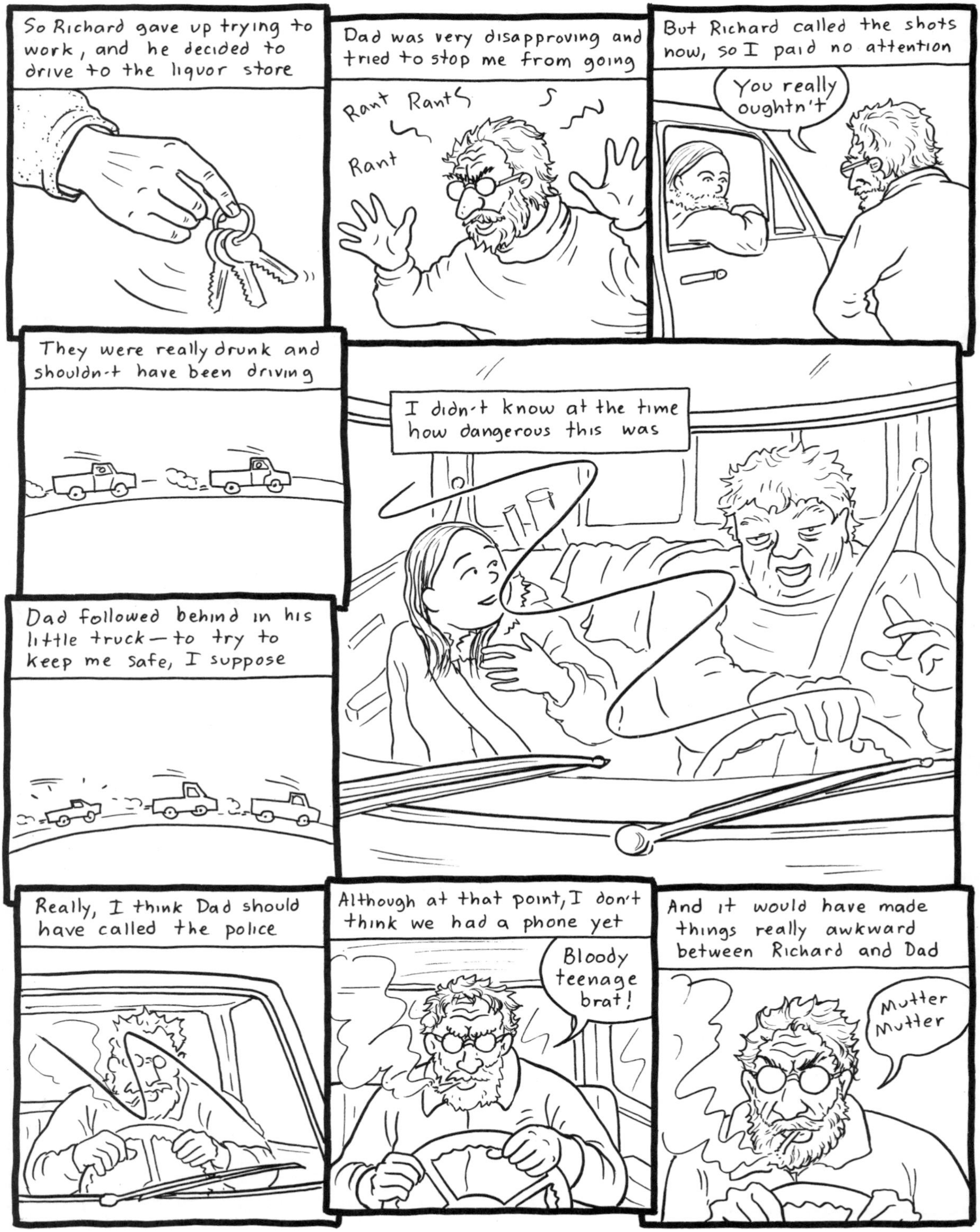

So Richard gave up trying to work, and he decided to drive to the liquor store
Dad was very disapproving and tried to stop me from going
Rant Rant Rant
But Richard called the shots now, so I paid no attention
You really oughtn't
They were really drunk and shouldn't have been driving
I didn't know at the time how dangerous this was
Dad followed behind in his little truck—to try to keep me safe, I suppose
Really, I think Dad should have called the police
Although at that point, I don't think we had a phone yet
Bloody teenage brat!
And it would have made things really awkward between Richard and Dad
Mutter Mutter

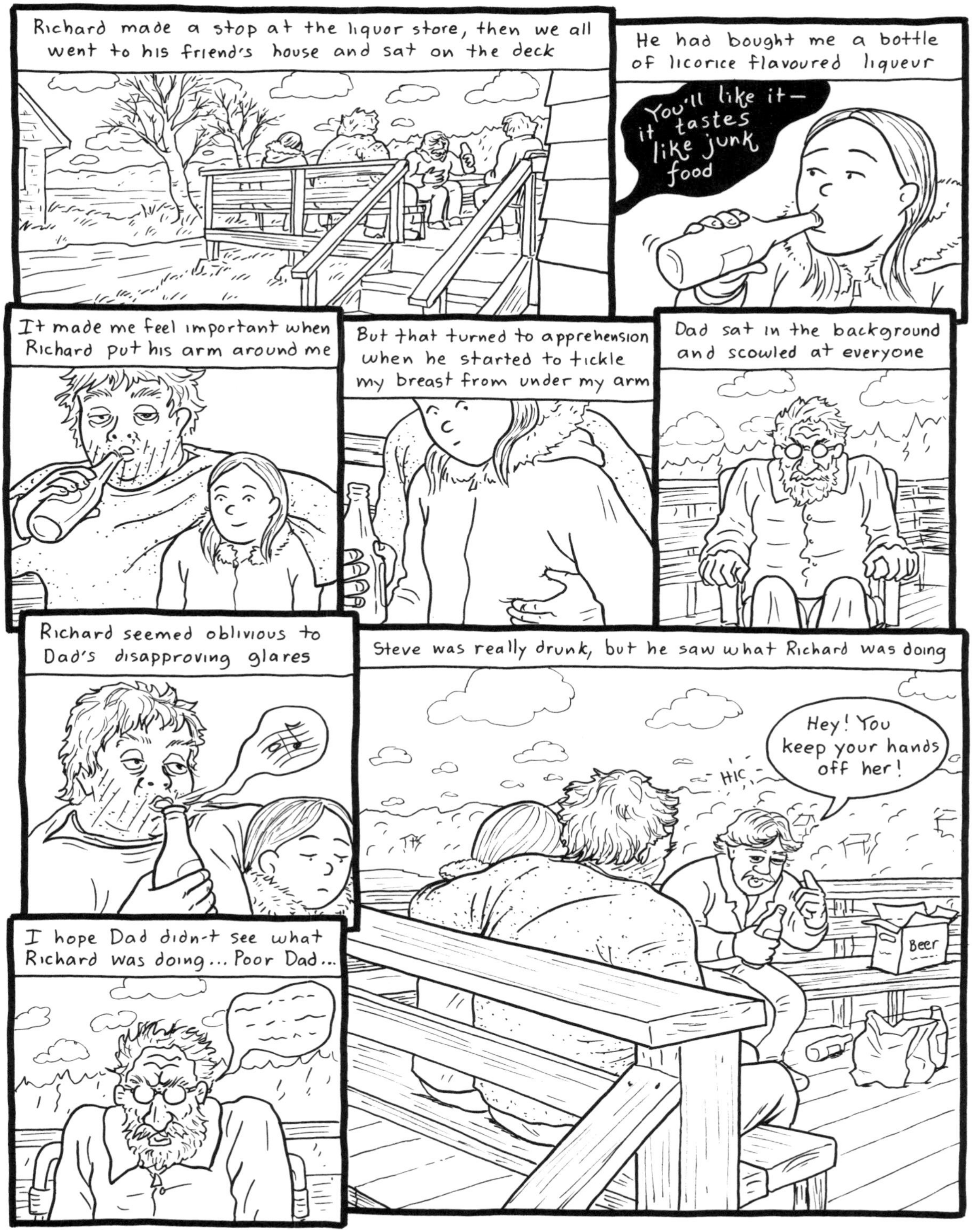
Richard made a stop at the liquor store, then we all went to his friend's house and sat on the deck
He had bought me a bottle of licorice flavoured liqueur
You'll like it— it tastes like junk food
It made me feel important when Richard put his arm around me
But that turned to apprehension when he started to tickle my breast from under my arm
Dad sat in the background and scowled at everyone
Richard seemed oblivious to Dad's disapproving glares
Steve was really drunk, but he saw what Richard was doing
HIC
Hey! You keep your hands off her!
Beer
I hope Dad didn't see what Richard was doing... Poor Dad...

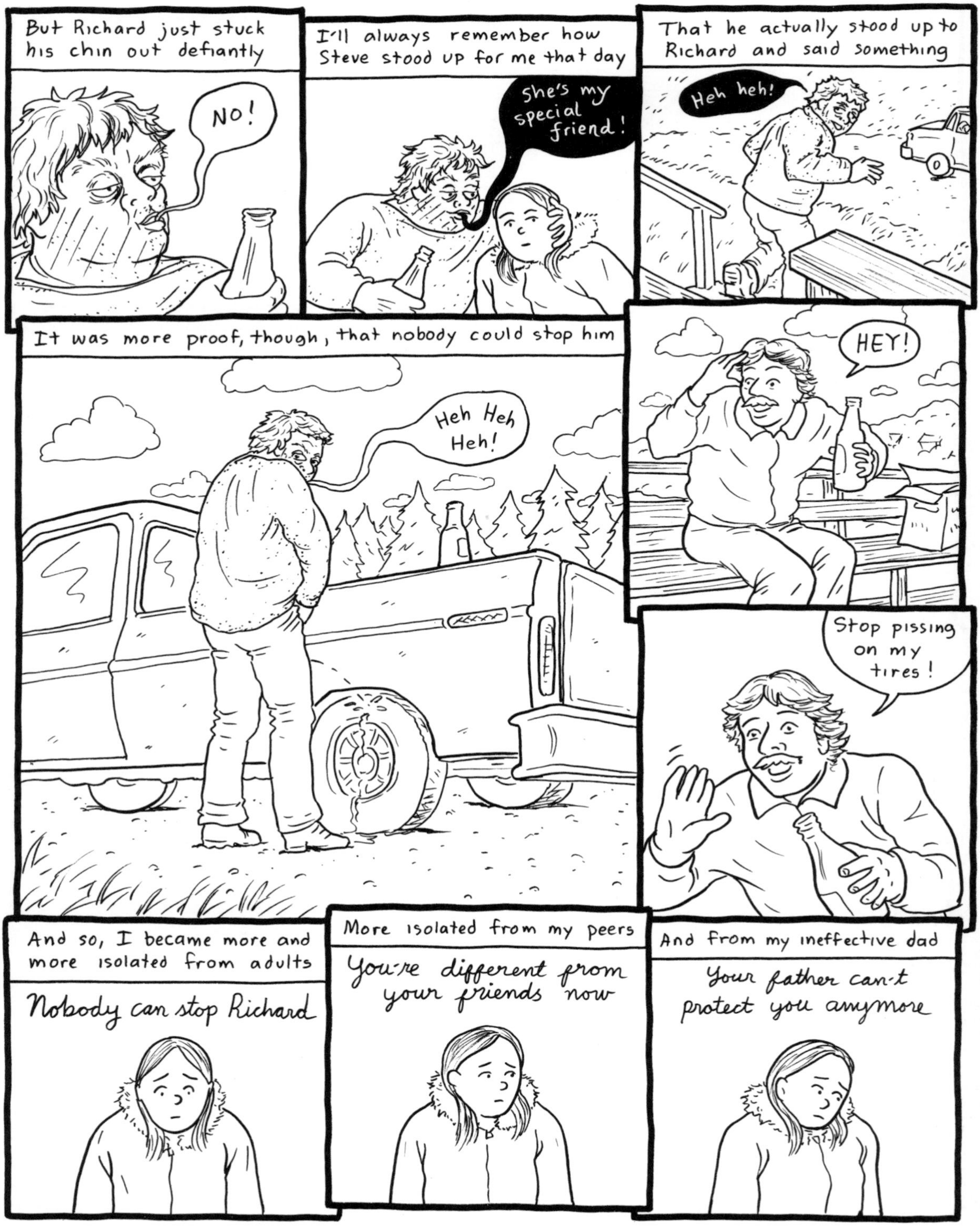
But Richard just stuck his chin out defiantly
NO!
I'll always remember how Steve stood up for me that day
She's my special friend!
That he actually stood up to Richard and said something
Heh heh!
It was more proof, though, that nobody could stop him
Heh Heh Heh!
HEY!
Stop pissing on my tires!
And so, I became more and more isolated from adults
Nobody can stop Richard
More isolated from my peers
You're different from your friends now
And from my ineffective dad
Your father can't protect you anymore

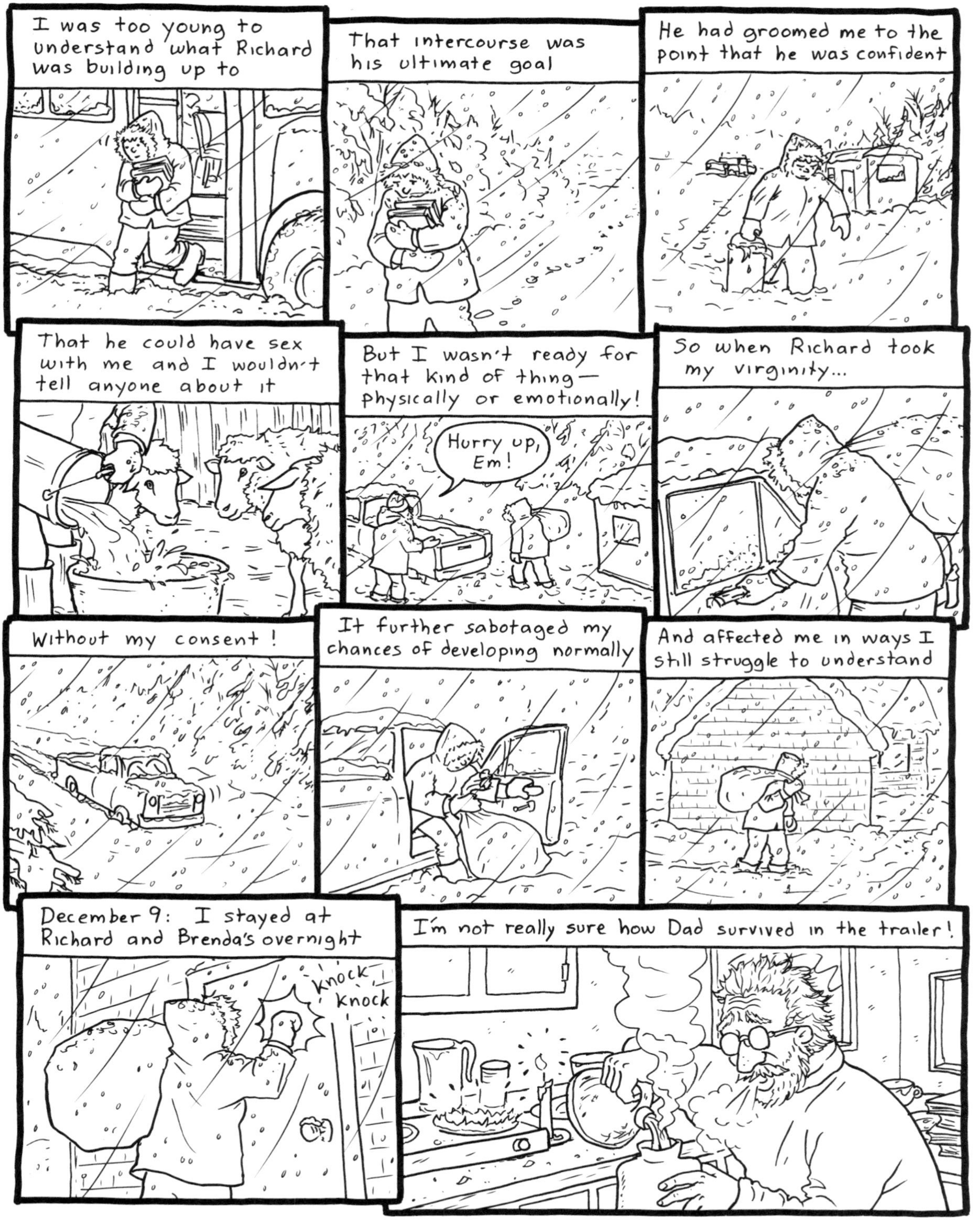
I was too young to understand what Richard was building up to
That intercourse was his ultimate goal
He had groomed me to the point that he was confident
That he could have sex with me and I wouldn't tell anyone about it
But I wasn't ready for that kind of thing— physically or emotionally!
Hurry up, Em!
So when Richard took my virginity...
Without my consent!
It further sabotaged my chances of developing normally
And affected me in ways I still struggle to understand
December 9: I stayed at Richard and Brenda's overnight
knock knock
I'm not really sure how Dad survived in the trailer!

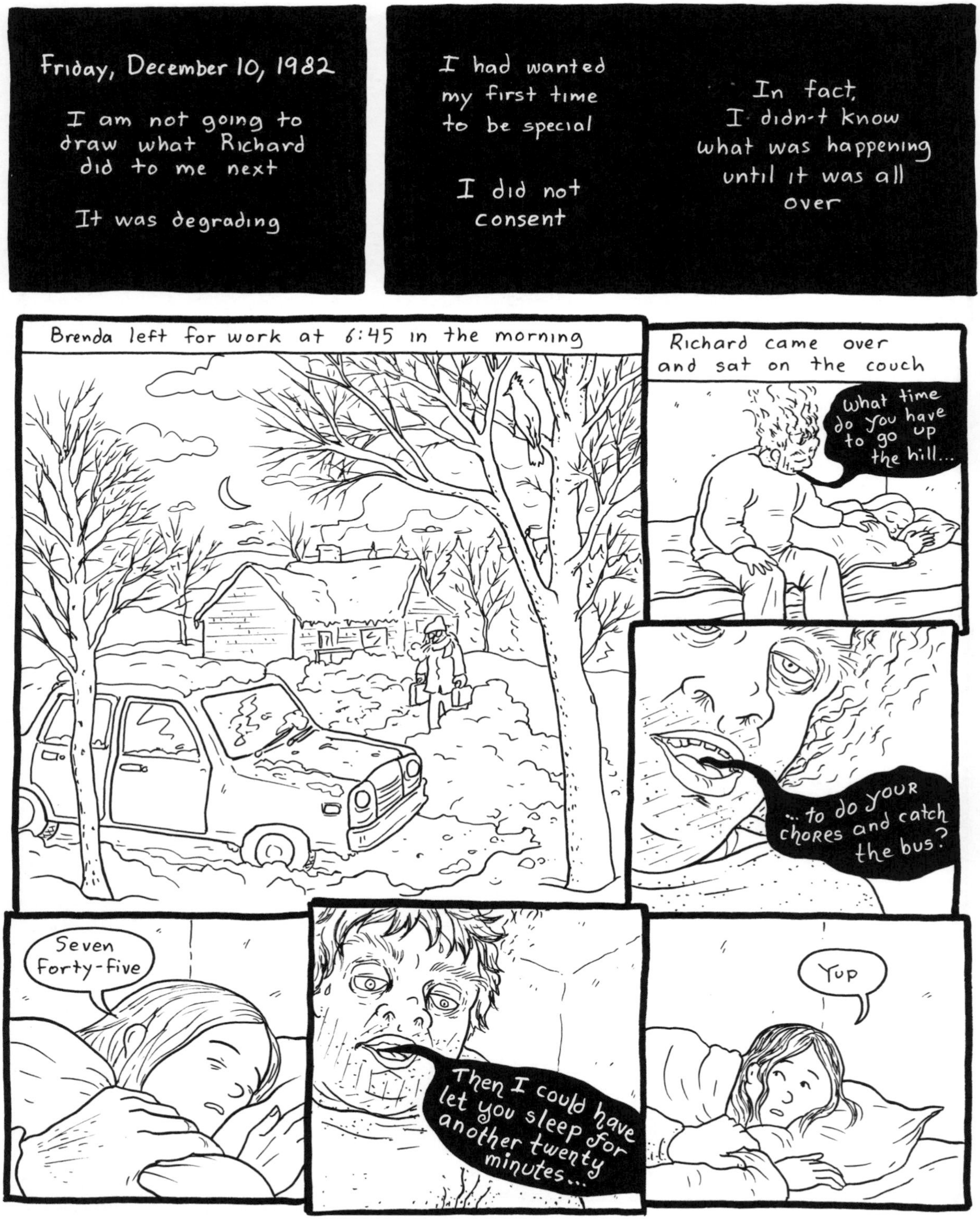
Friday, December 10, 1982
I am not going to draw what Richard did to me next
It was degrading
I had wanted my first time to be special
I did not consent
In fact, I didn't know what was happening until it was all over
Brenda left for work at 6:45 in the morning
Richard came over and sat on the couch
What time do you have to go up the hill...
... to do your chores and catch the bus?
Seven Forty-five
Then I could have let you sleep for another twenty minutes...
Yup

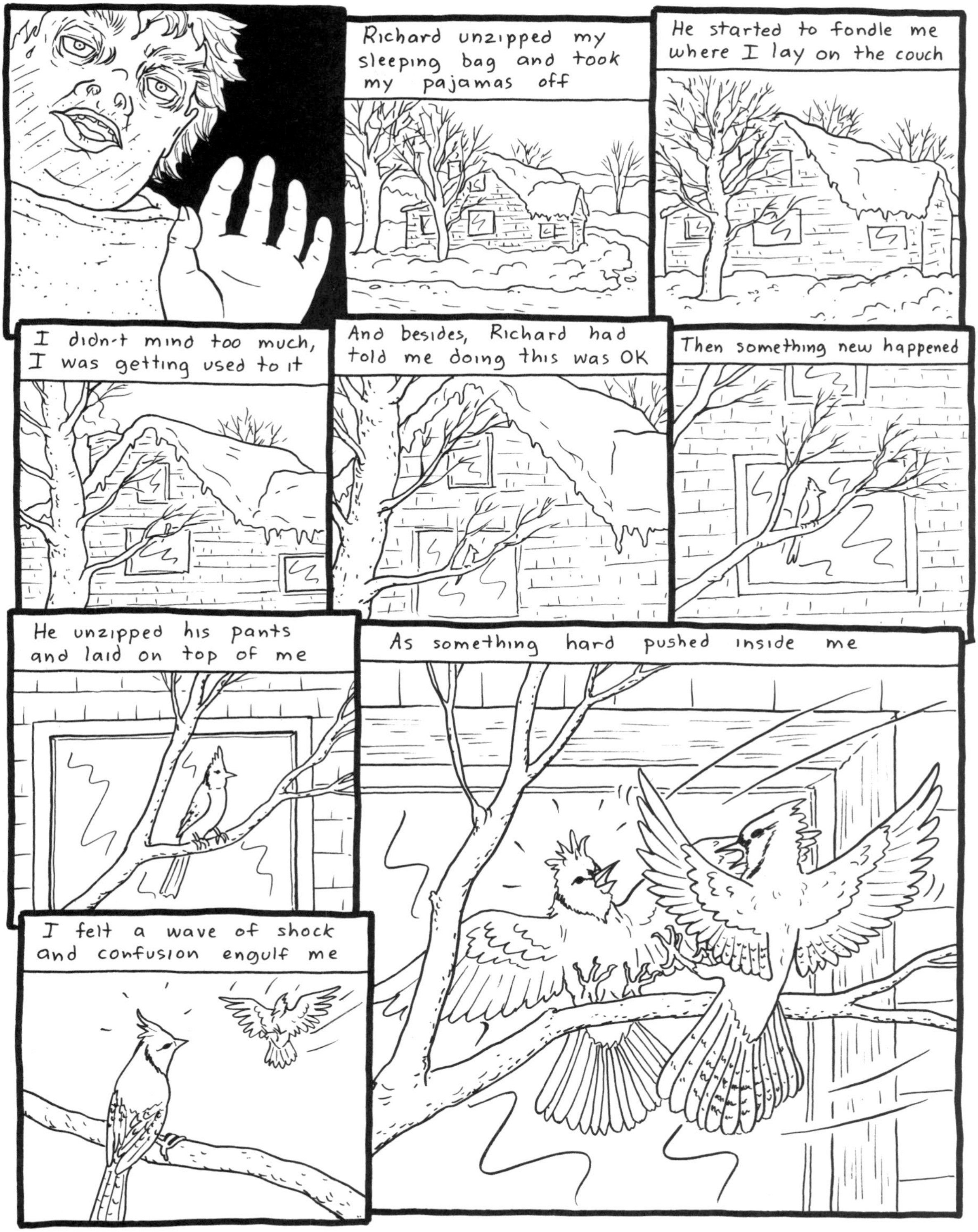
Richard unzipped my sleeping bag and took my pajamas off
He started to fondle me where I lay on the couch
I didn't mind too much, I was getting used to it
And besides, Richard had told me doing this was OK
Then something new happened
He unzipped his pants and laid on top of me
As something hard pushed inside me
I felt a wave of shock and confusion engulf me

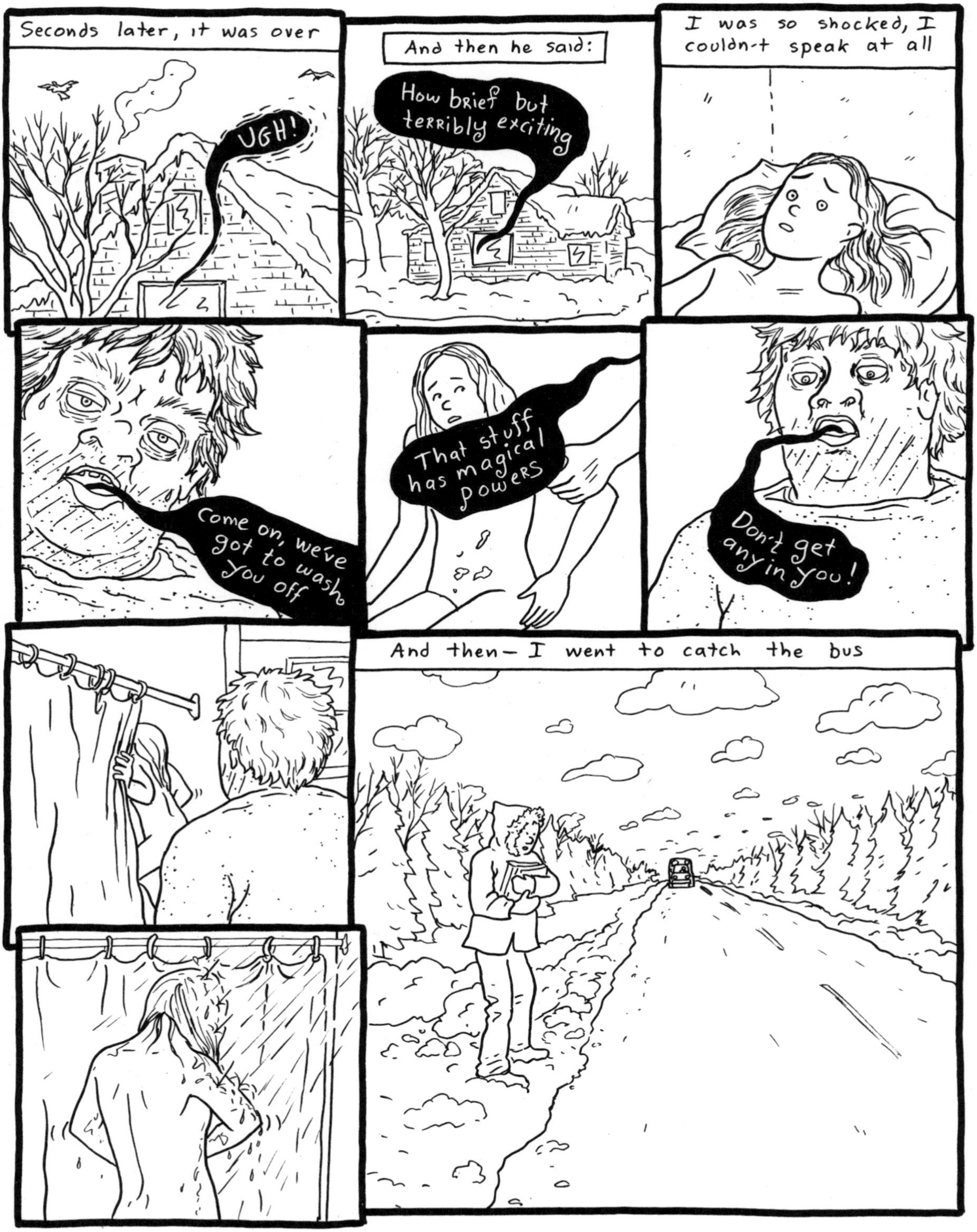
Seconds later, it was over
UGH!
And then he said:
How brief but terribly exciting
I was so shocked, I couldn't speak at all
Come on, we've got to wash you off
That stuff has magical powers
Don't get any in you!
And then— I went to catch the bus

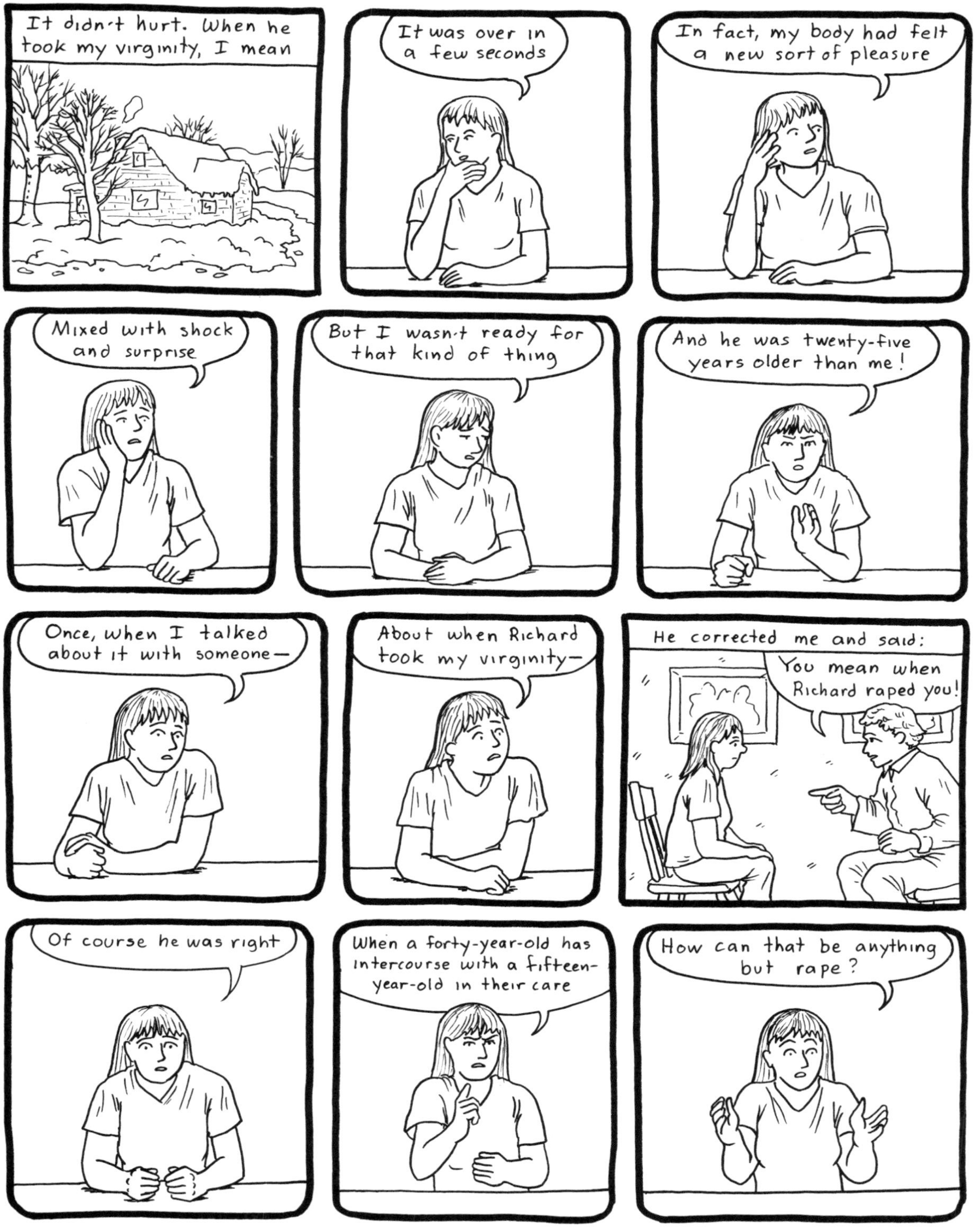
It didn't hurt. When he took my virginity, I mean
It was over in a few seconds
In fact, my body had felt a new sort of pleasure
Mixed with shock and surprise
But I wasn't ready for that kind of thing
And he was twenty-five years older than me!
Once, when I talked about it with someone—
About when Richard took my virginity—
He corrected me and said:
You mean when Richard raped you!
Of course he was right
When a forty-year-old has intercourse with a fifteen-year-old in their care
How can that be anything but rape?

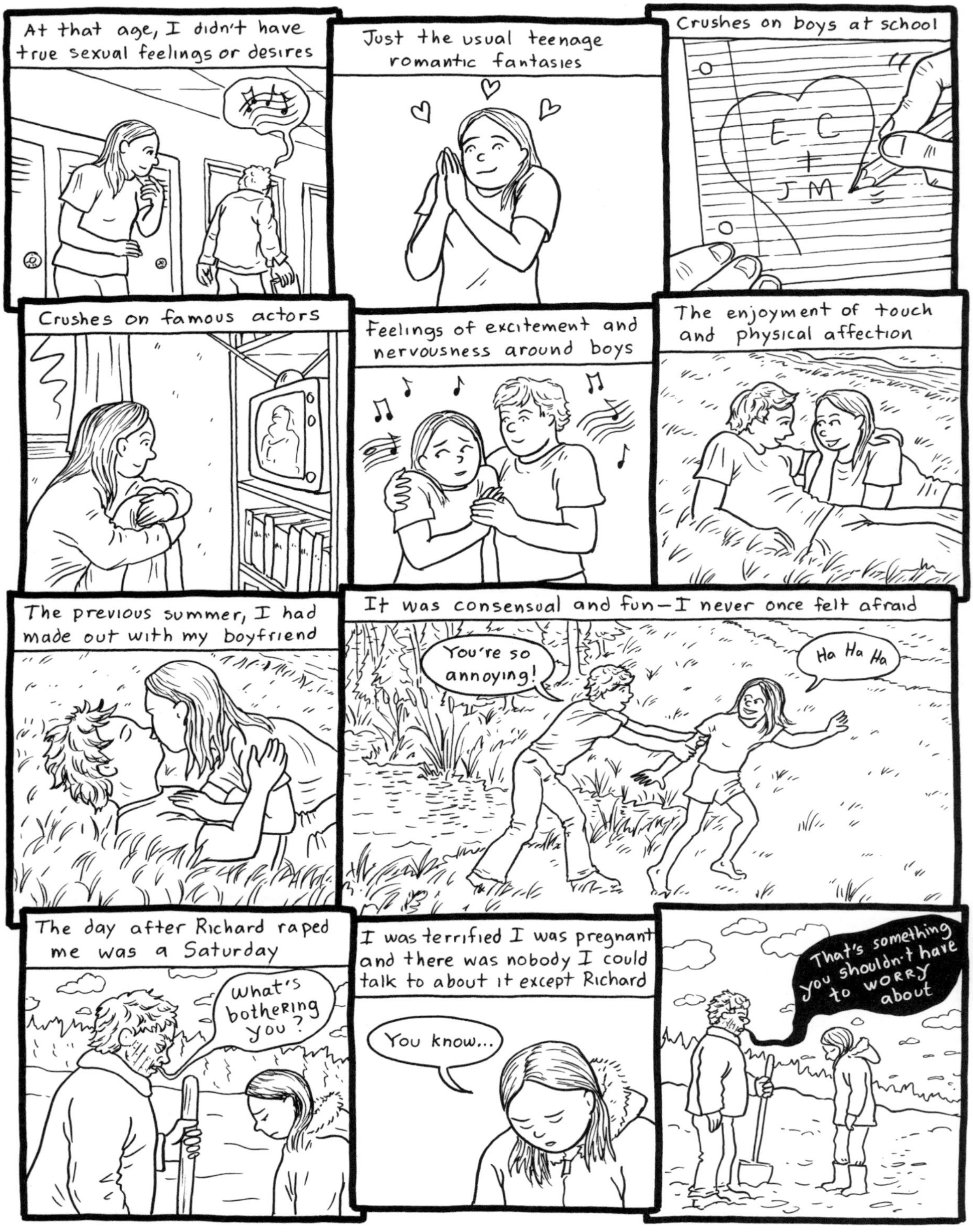
At that age, I didn't have true sexual feelings or desires
Just the usual teenage romantic fantasies
Crushes on boys at school
E C + J M
Crushes on famous actors
Feelings of excitement and nervousness around boys
The enjoyment of touch and physical affection
The previous summer, I had made out with my boyfriend
It was consensual and fun—I never once felt afraid
You're so annoying!
Ha Ha Ha
The day after Richard raped me was a Saturday
What's bothering you?
I was terrified I was pregnant and there was nobody I could talk to about it except Richard
You know...
That's something you shouldn't have to WORRY about

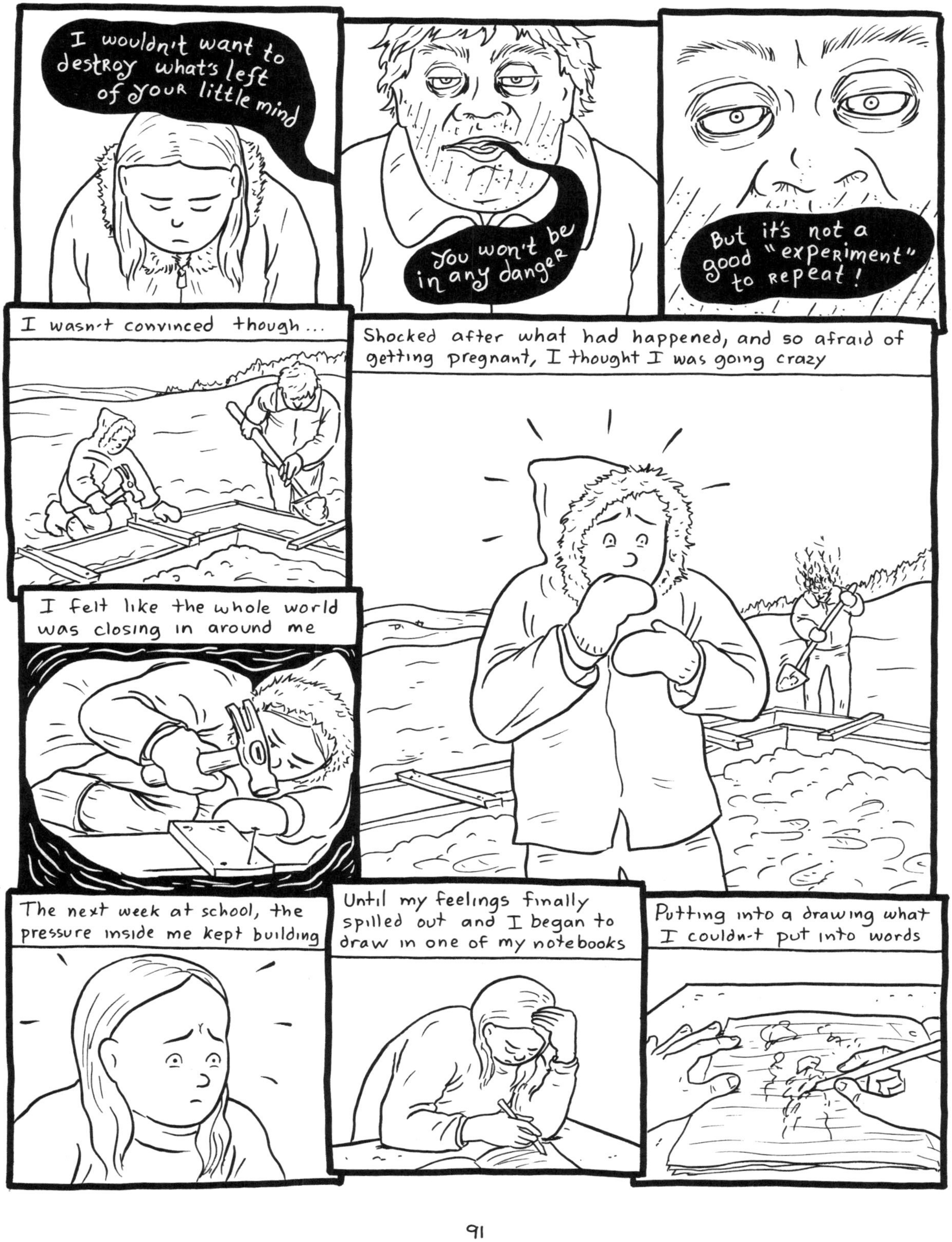
I wouldn't want to destroy what's left of your little mind
You won't be in any danger
But it's not a good "experiment" to repeat!
I wasn't convinced though...
Shocked after what had happened, and so afraid of getting pregnant, I thought I was going crazy
I felt like the whole world was closing in around me
The next week at school, the pressure inside me kept building
Until my feelings finally spilled out and I began to draw in one of my notebooks
Putting into a drawing what I couldn't put into words

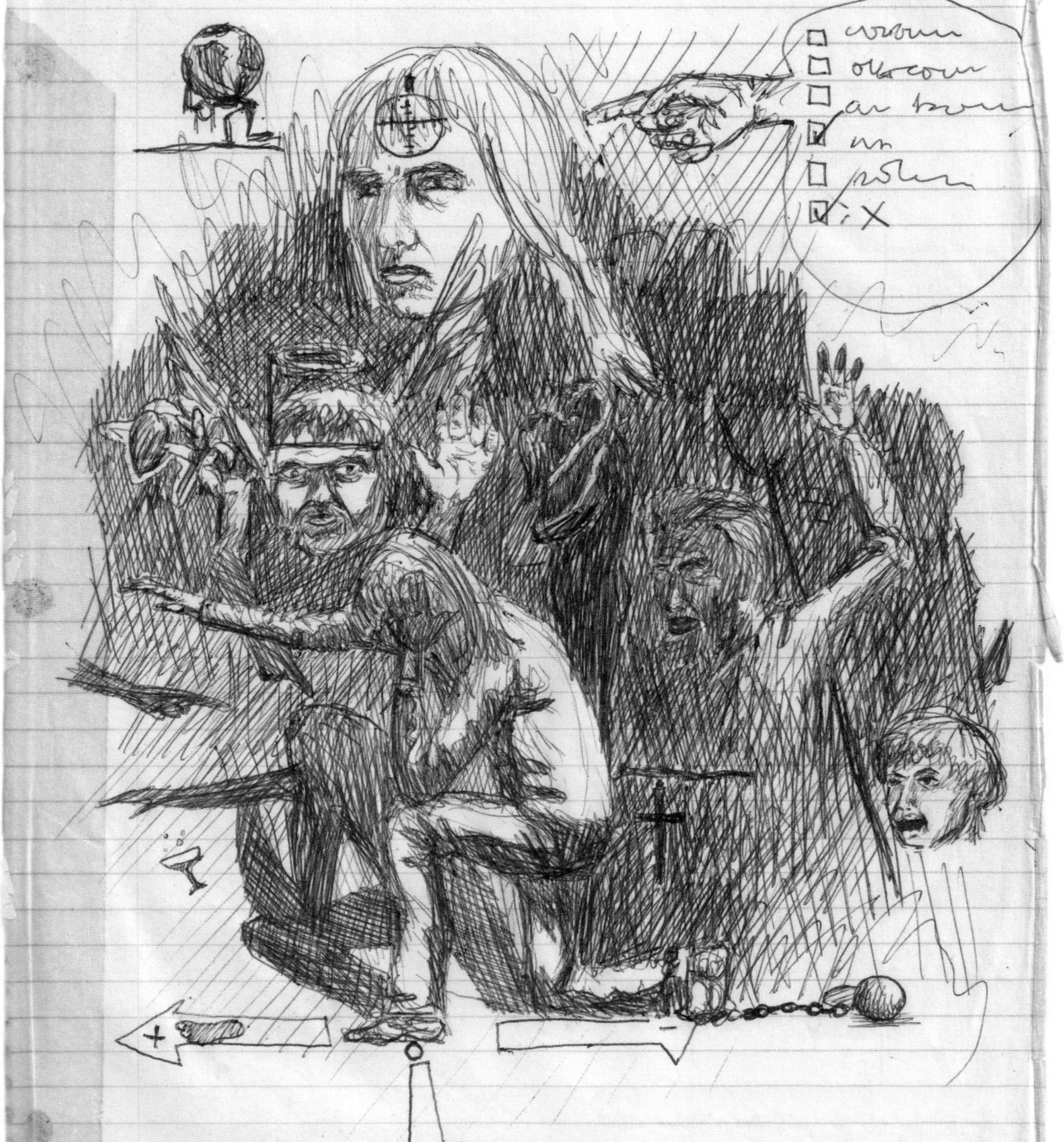

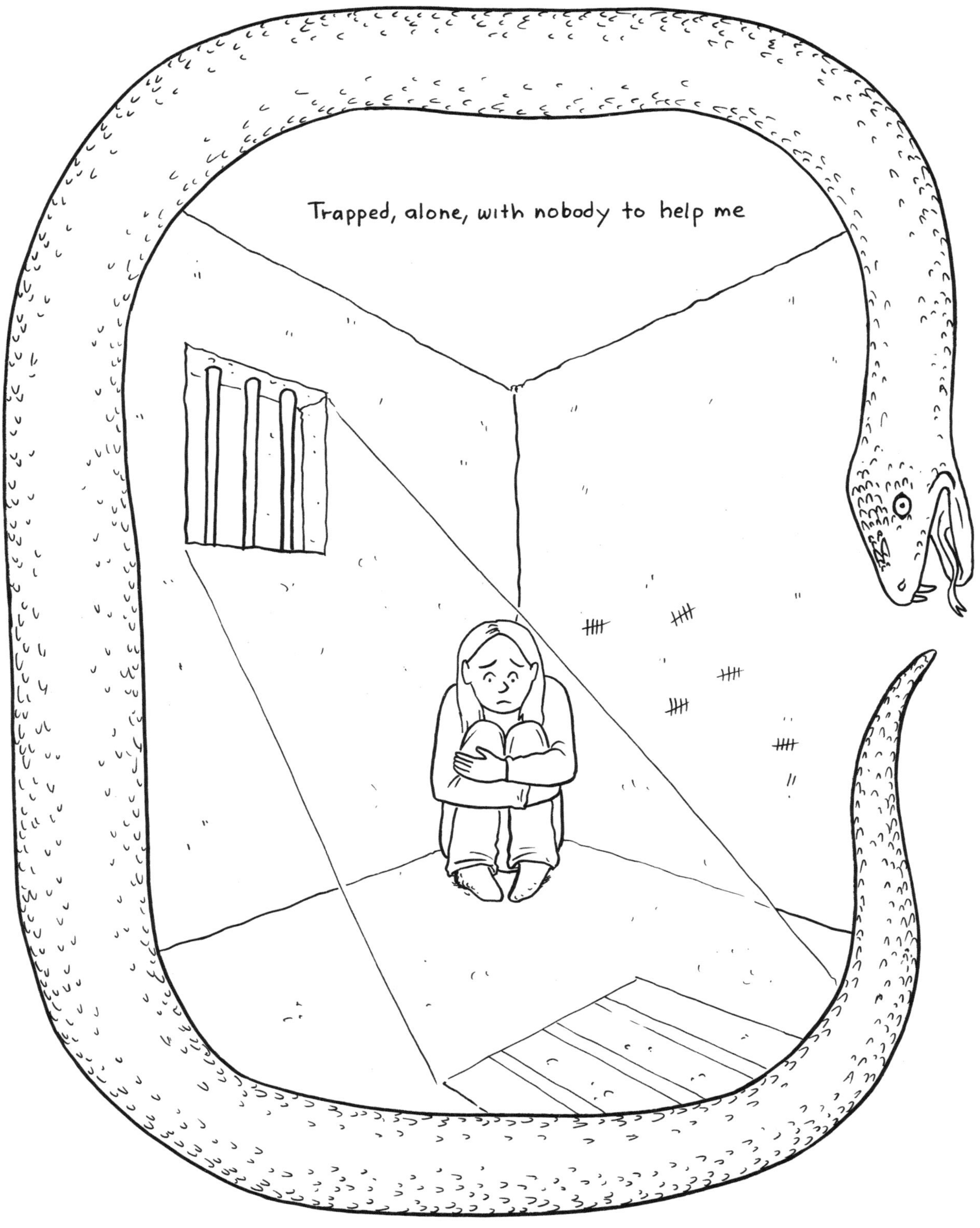
Trapped, alone, with nobody to help me

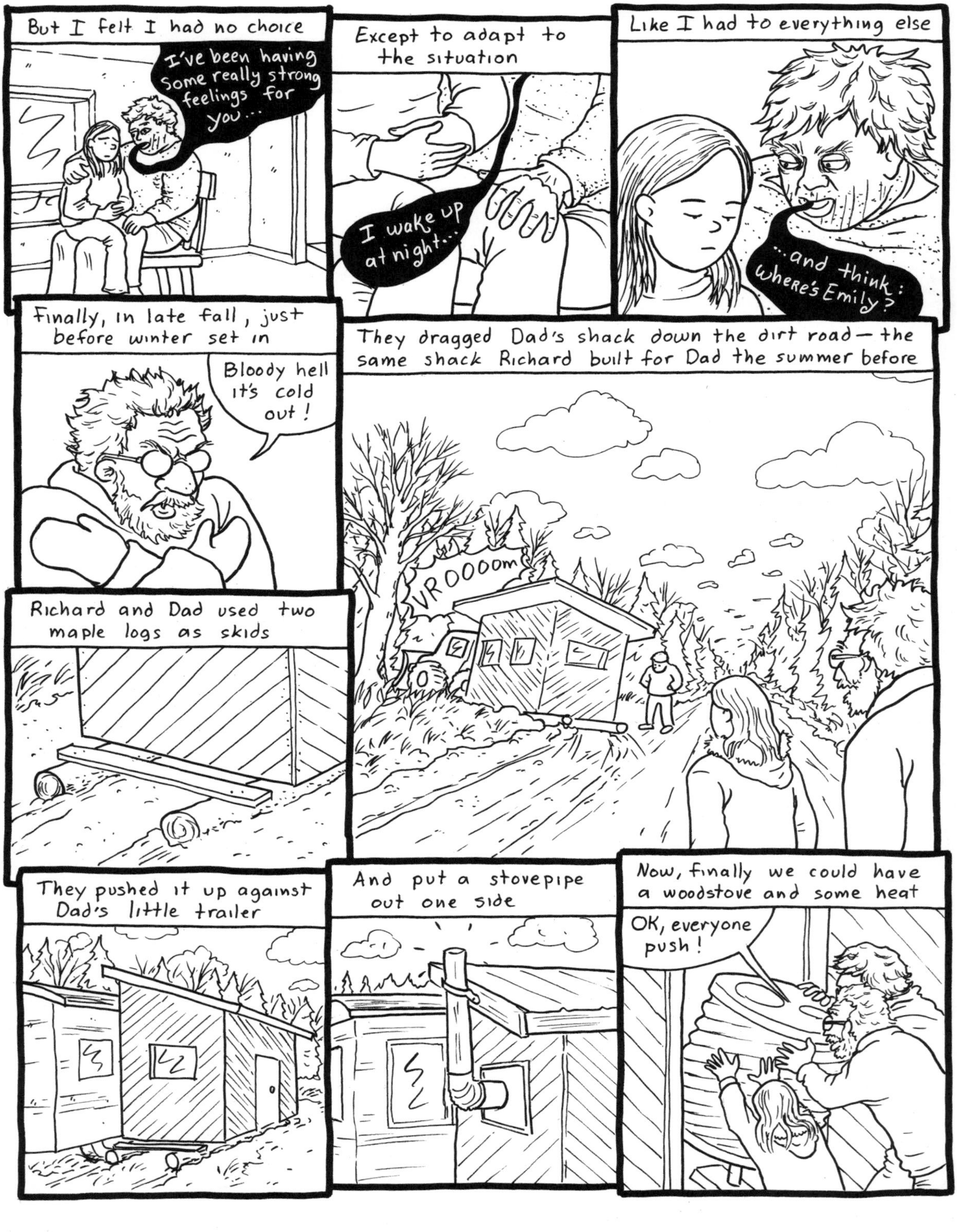
But I felt I had no choice
I've been having some really strong feelings for you...
Except to adapt to the situation
I wake up at night...
Like I had to everything else
...and think: where's Emily?
Finally, in late fall, just before winter set in
Bloody hell it's cold out!
They dragged Dad's shack down the dirt road—the same shack Richard built for Dad the summer before
VROOOOm
Richard and Dad used two maple logs as skids
They pushed it up against Dad's little trailer
And put a stovepipe out one side
Now, finally we could have a woodstove and some heat
OK, everyone push!

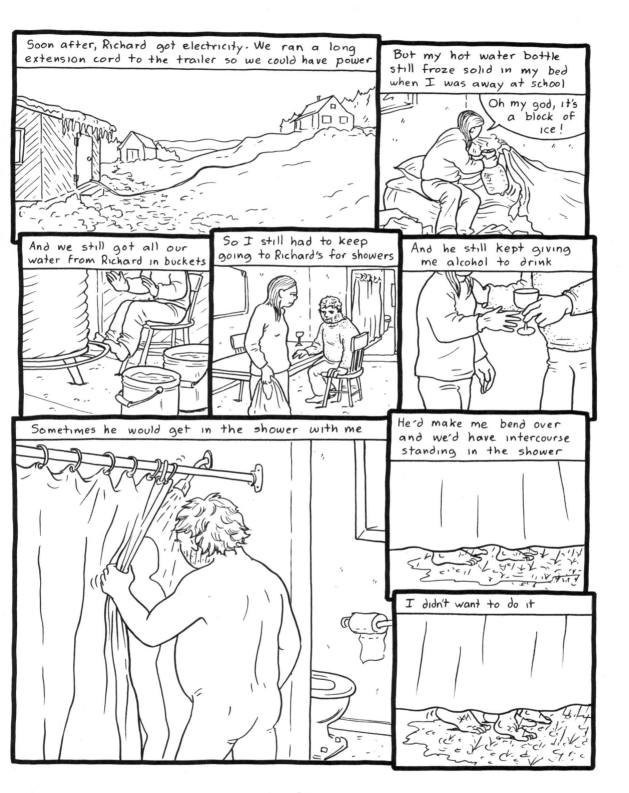

Soon after, Richard got electricity. We ran a long extension cord to the trailer so we could have power

But my hot water bottle still froze solid in my bed when I was away at school

Oh my god, it's a block of ice!

And we still got all our water from Richard in buckets

So I still had to keep going to Richard's for showers

And he still kept giving me alcohol to drink

Sometimes he would get in the shower with me

He'd make me bend over and we'd have intercourse standing in the shower

I didn't want to do it

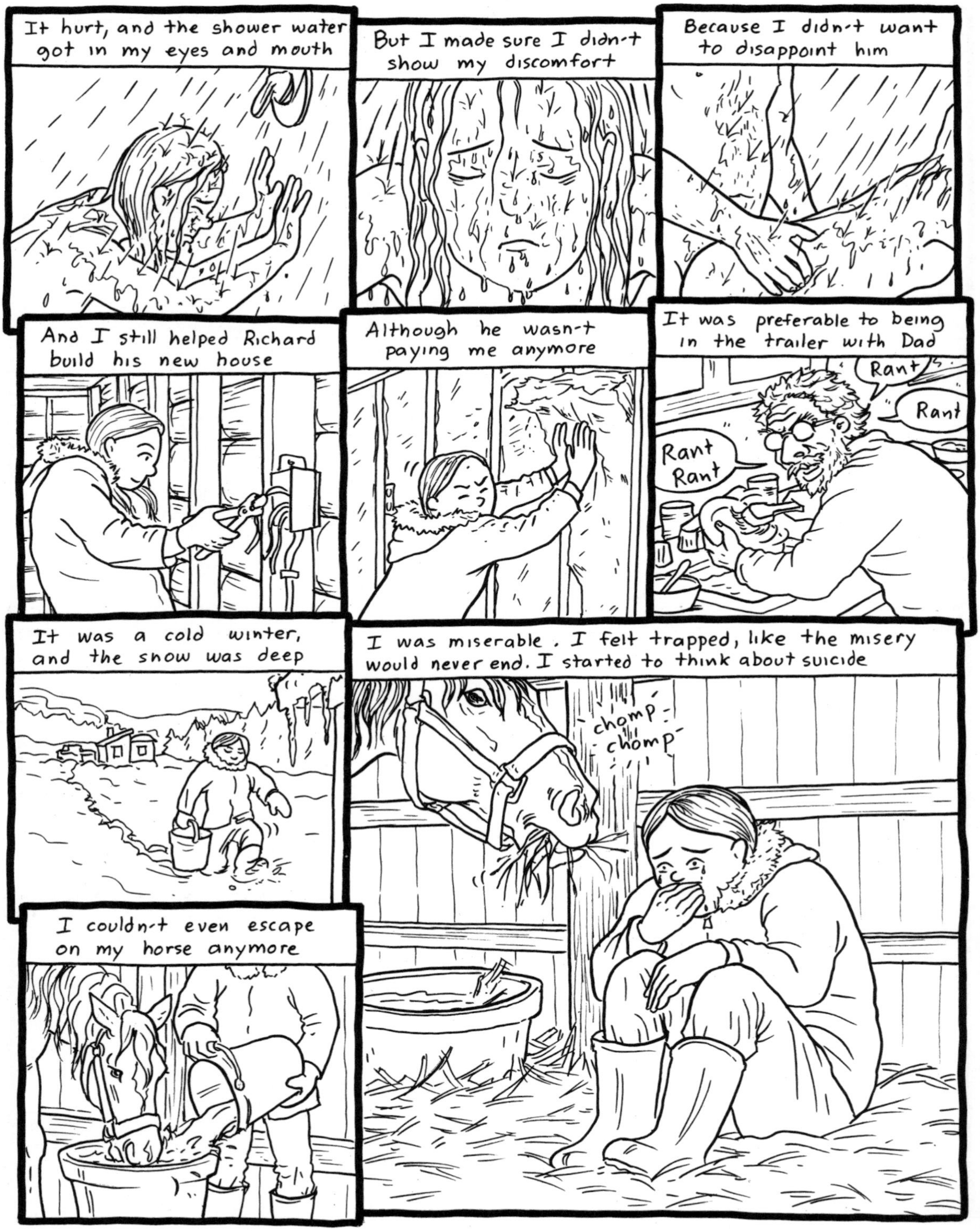
It hurt, and the shower water got in my eyes and mouth
But I made sure I didn't show my discomfort
Because I didn't want to disappoint him
And I still helped Richard build his new house
Although he wasn't paying me anymore
It was preferable to being in the trailer with Dad
Rant
Rant
Rant Rant
It was a cold winter, and the snow was deep
I couldn't even escape on my horse anymore
I was miserable. I felt trapped, like the misery would never end. I started to think about suicide
chomp
chomp

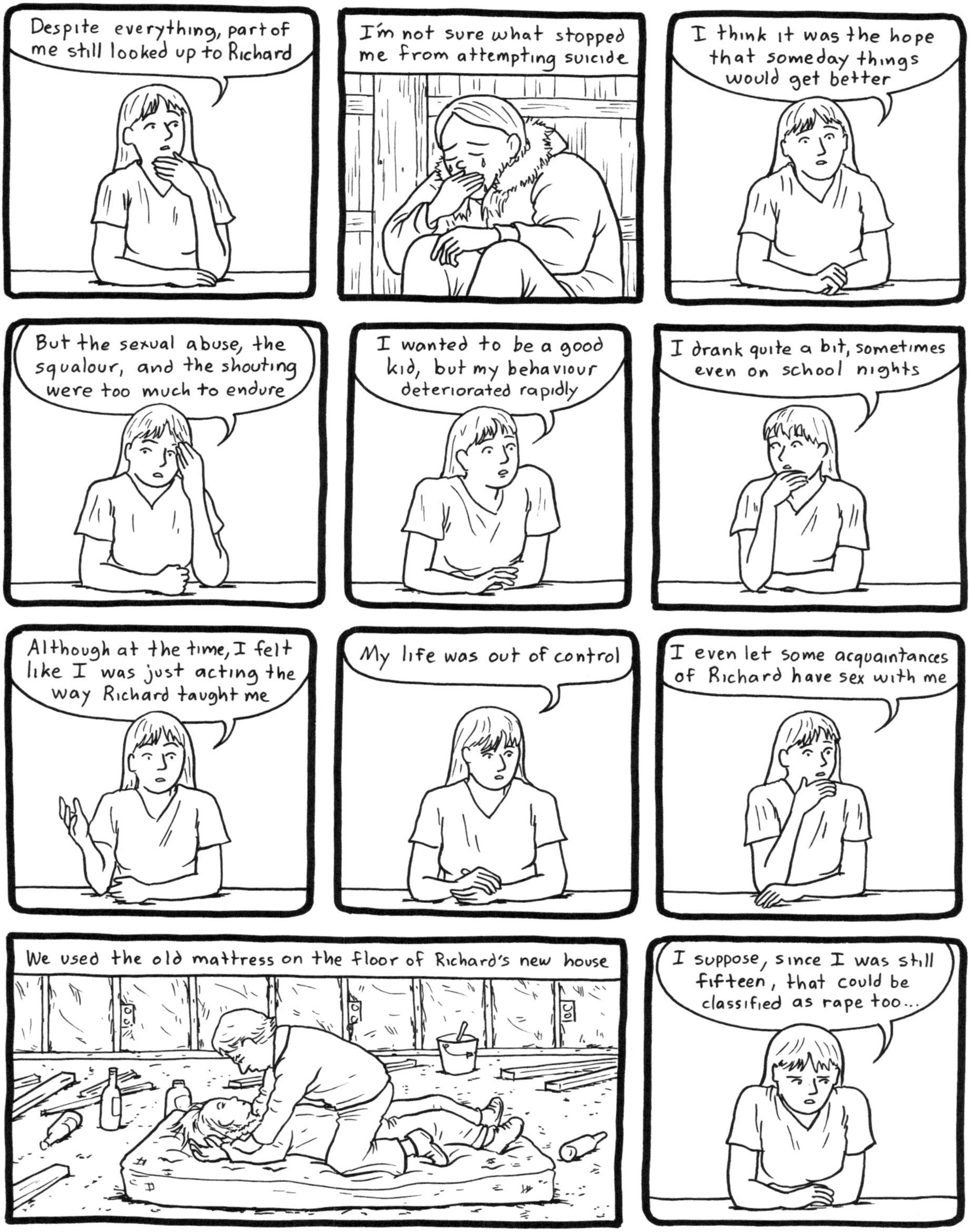
Despite everything, part of me still looked up to Richard
I'm not sure what stopped me from attempting suicide
I think it was the hope that someday things would get better
But the sexual abuse, the squalour, and the shouting were too much to endure
I wanted to be a good kid, but my behaviour deteriorated rapidly
I drank quite a bit, sometimes even on school nights
Although at the time, I felt like I was just acting the way Richard taught me
My life was out of control
I even let some acquaintances of Richard have sex with me
We used the old mattress on the floor of Richard's new house
I suppose, since I was still fifteen, that could be classified as rape too...

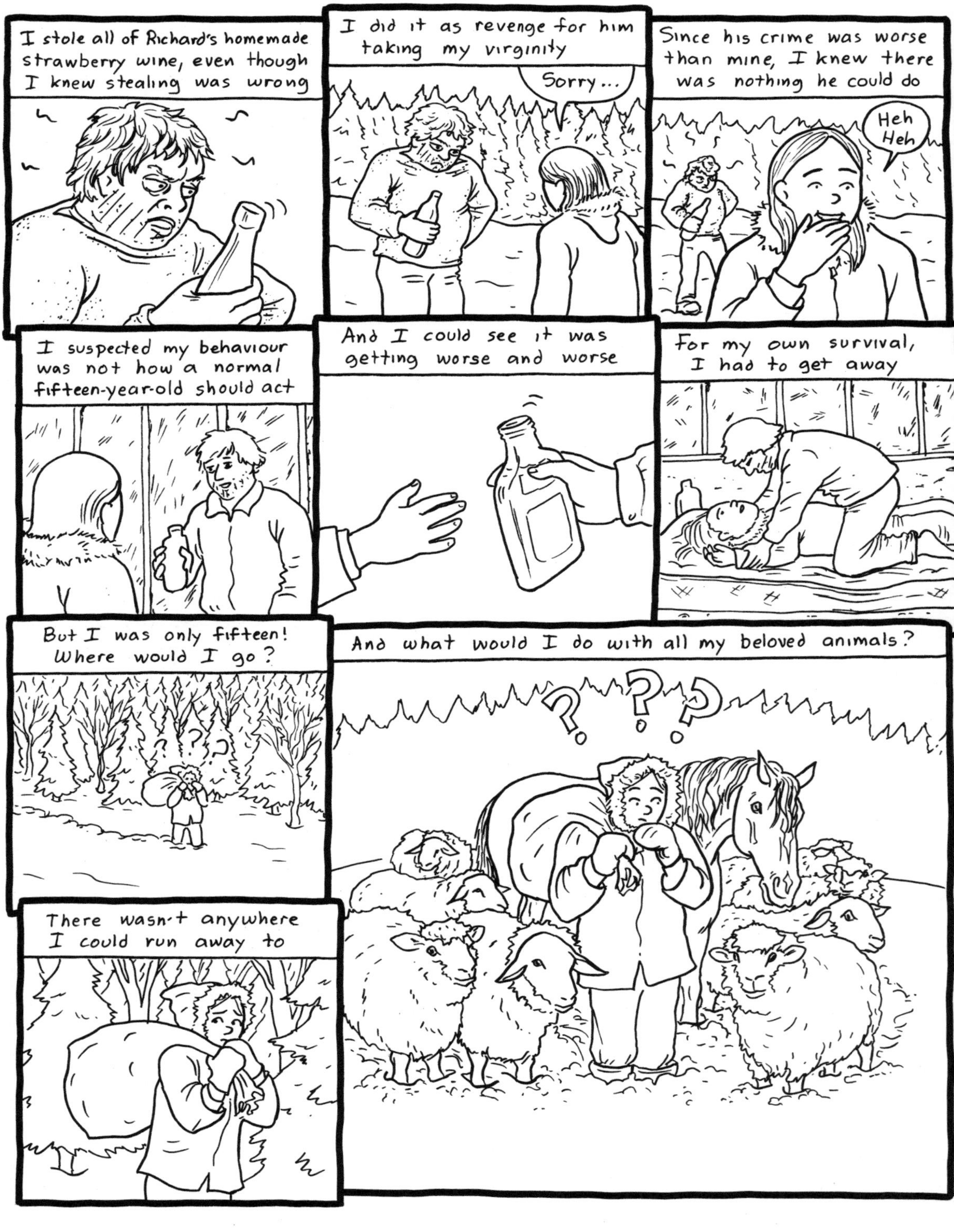
I stole all of Richard's homemade strawberry wine, even though I knew stealing was wrong
I did it as revenge for him taking my virginity
Sorry...
Since his crime was worse than mine, I knew there was nothing he could do
Heh Heh
I suspected my behaviour was not how a normal fifteen-year-old should act
And I could see it was getting worse and worse
For my own survival, I had to get away
But I was only fifteen! Where would I go?
And what would I do with all my beloved animals?
There wasn't anywhere I could run away to

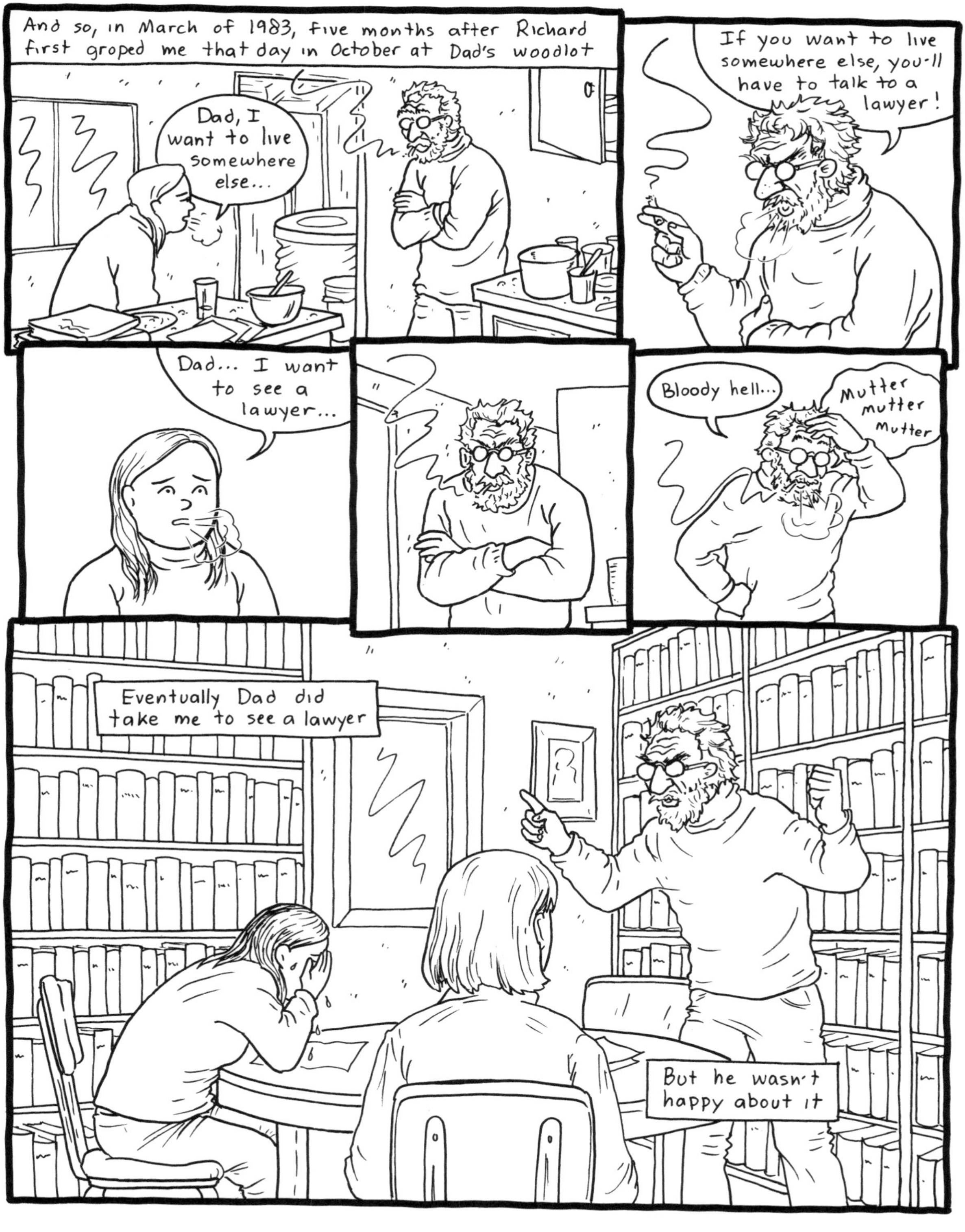
And so, in March of 1983, five months after Richard first groped me that day in October at Dad's woodlot
Dad, I want to live somewhere else...
If you want to live somewhere else, you'll have to talk to a lawyer!
Dad... I want to see a lawyer...
Bloody hell...
Mutter mutter mutter
Eventually Dad did take me to see a lawyer
But he wasn't happy about it

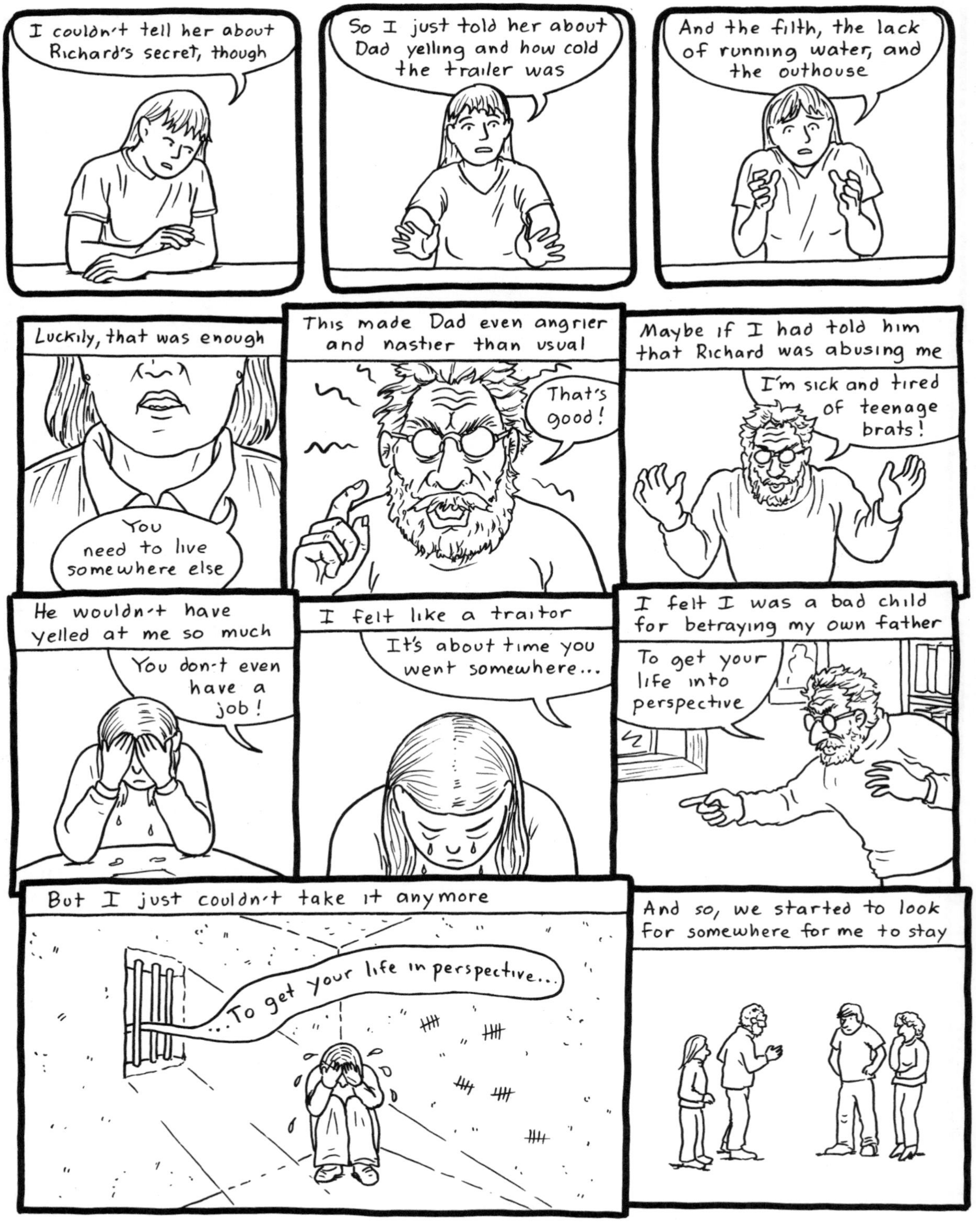
I couldn't tell her about Richard's secret, though
So I just told her about Dad yelling and how cold the trailer was
And the filth, the lack of running water, and the outhouse
Luckily, that was enough
You need to live somewhere else
This made Dad even angrier and nastier than usual
That's good!
Maybe if I had told him that Richard was abusing me
I'm sick and tired of teenage brats!
He wouldn't have yelled at me so much
You don't even have a job!
I felt like a traitor
It's about time you went somewhere...
I felt I was a bad child for betraying my own father
To get your life into perspective
But I just couldn't take it anymore
...To get your life in perspective...
And so, we started to look for somewhere for me to stay

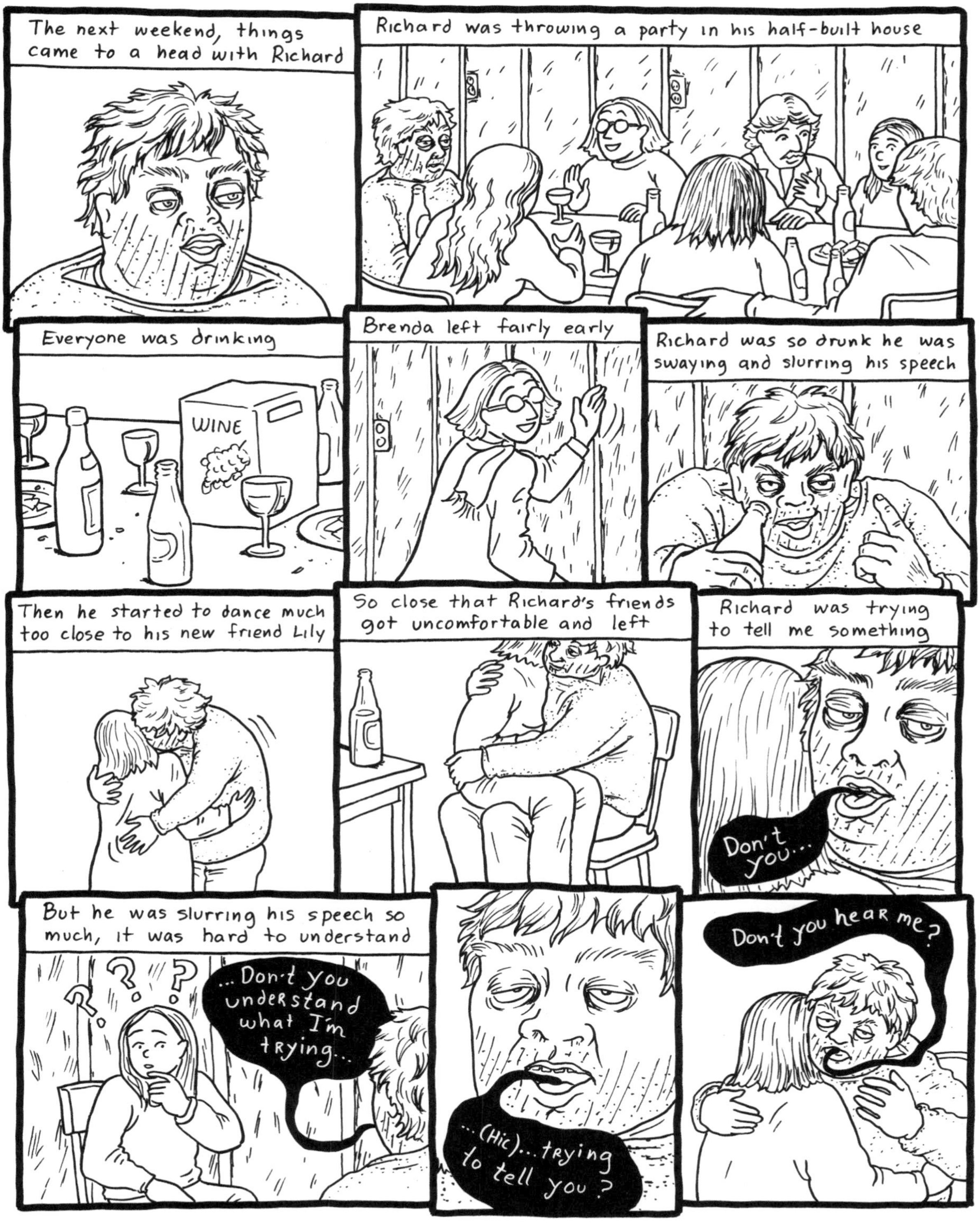
The next weekend, things came to a head with Richard
Richard was throwing a party in his half-built house
Everyone was drinking
WINE
Brenda left fairly early
Richard was so drunk he was swaying and slurring his speech
Then he started to dance much too close to his new friend Lily
So close that Richard's friends got uncomfortable and left
Richard was trying to tell me something
Don't you...
But he was slurring his speech so much, it was hard to understand
? ? ?
...Don't you understand what I'm trying...
...(Hic)...trying to tell you?
Don't you hear me?

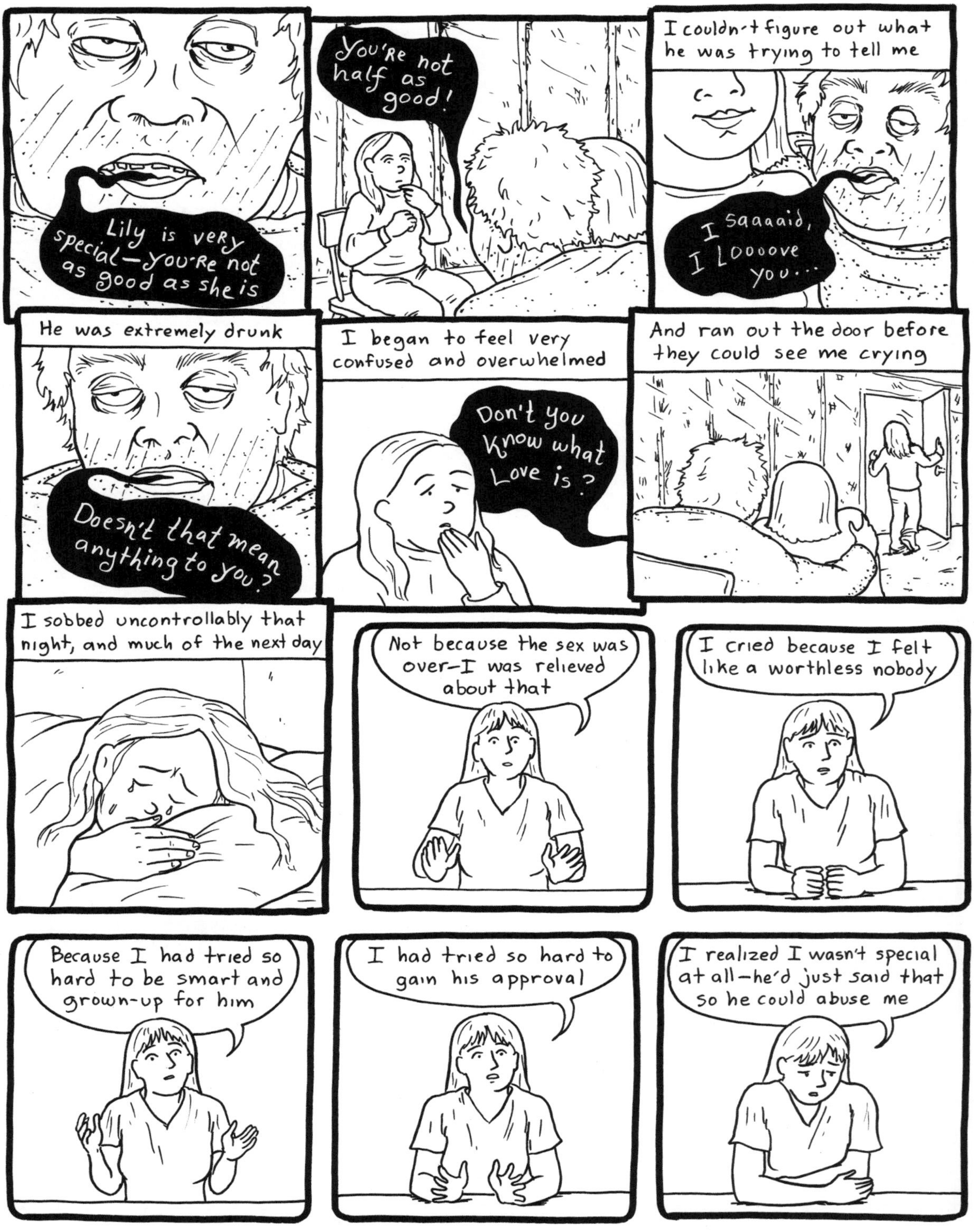
Lily is very special—you're not as good as she is
You're not half as good!
I couldn't figure out what he was trying to tell me
I saaaaid, I Looooove you...
He was extremely drunk
Doesn't that mean anything to you?
I began to feel very confused and overwhelmed
Don't you know what Love is?
And ran out the door before they could see me crying
I sobbed uncontrollably that night, and much of the next day
Not because the sex was over—I was relieved about that
I cried because I felt like a worthless nobody
Because I had tried so hard to be smart and grown-up for him
I had tried so hard to gain his approval
I realized I wasn't special at all—he'd just said that so he could abuse me

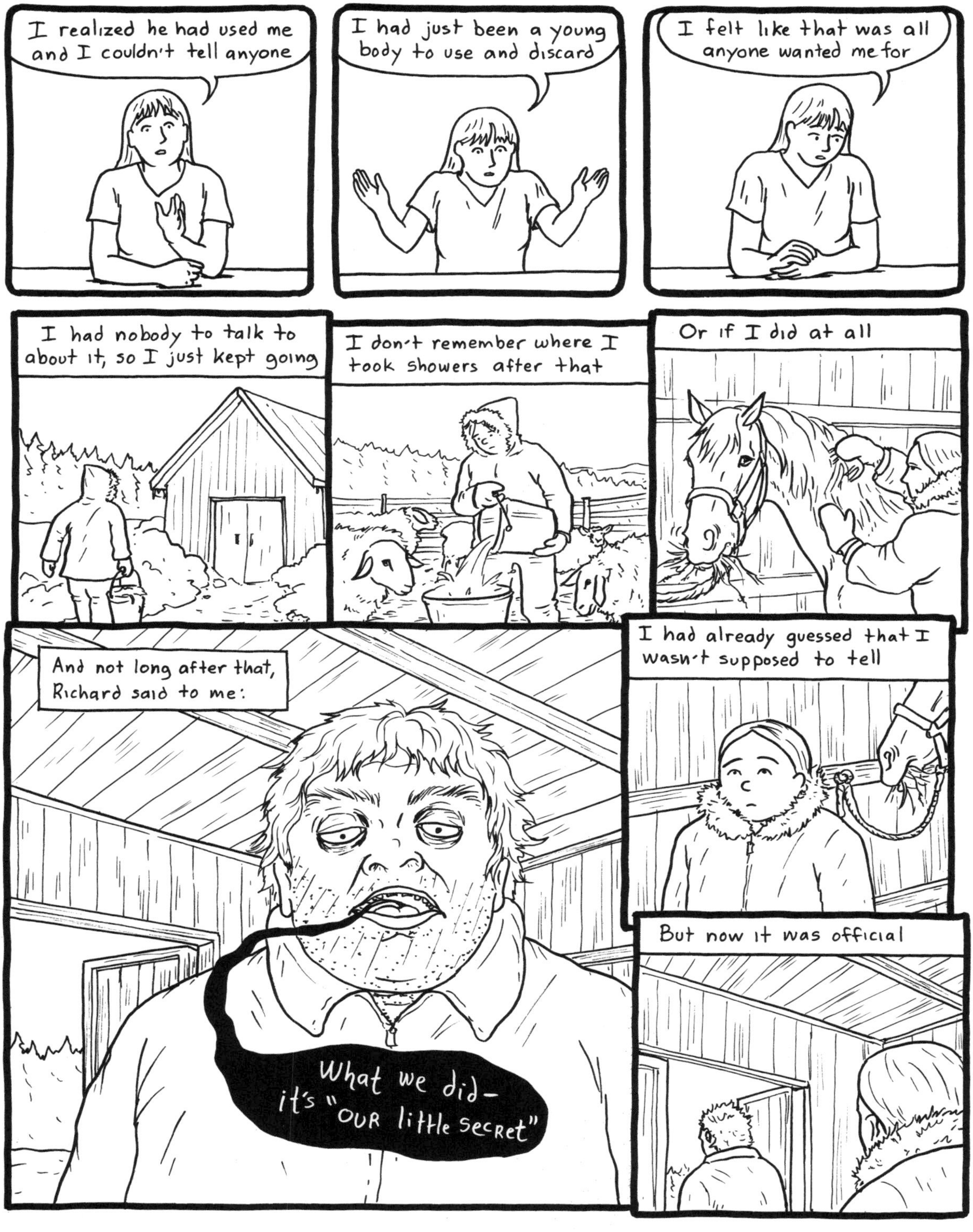

I realized he had used me and I couldn't tell anyone
I had just been a young body to use and discard
I felt like that was all anyone wanted me for
I had nobody to talk to about it, so I just kept going
I don't remember where I took showers after that
Or if I did at all
And not long after that, Richard said to me:
What we did- it's "our little secret"
I had already guessed that I wasn't supposed to tell
But now it was official

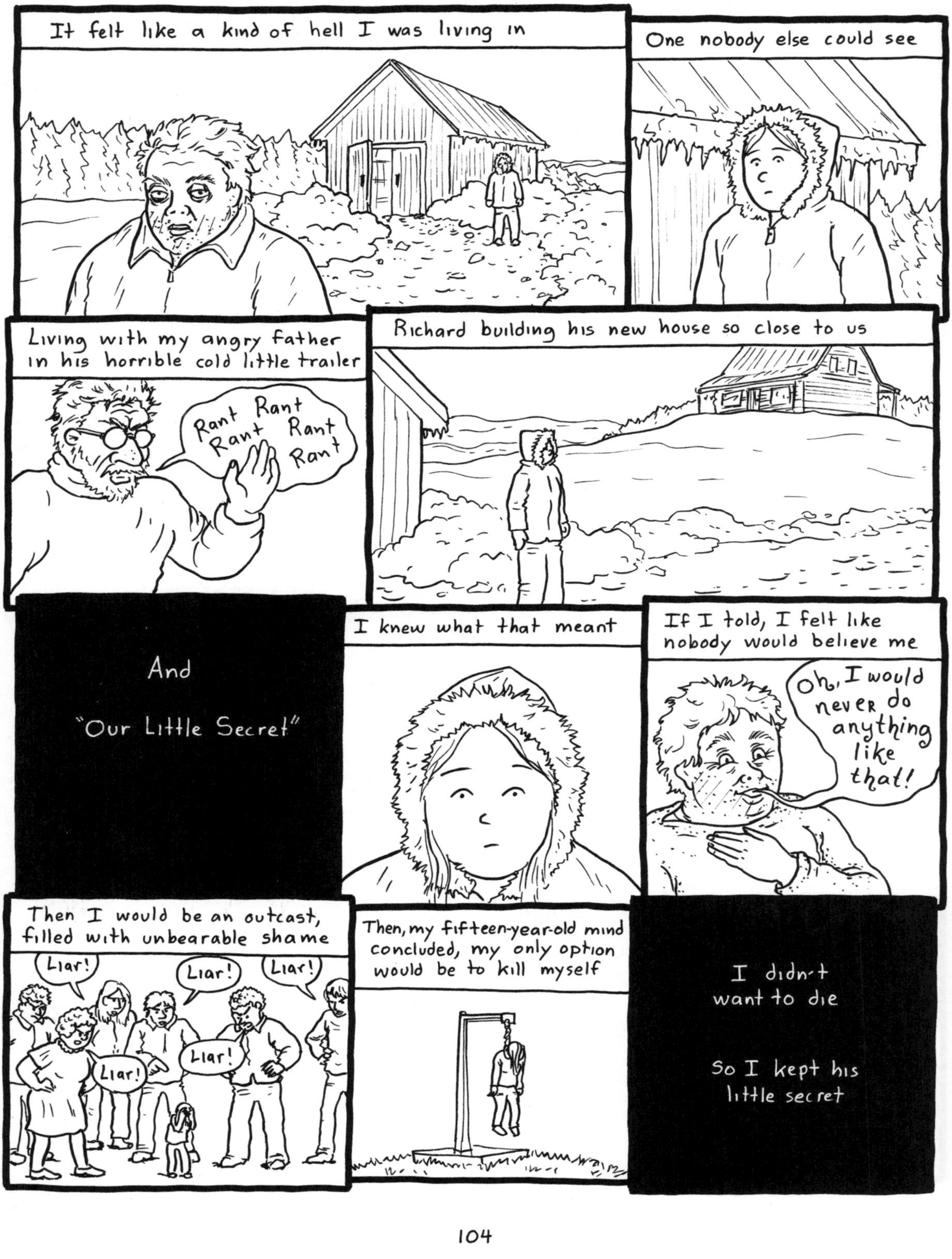

It felt like a kind of hell I was living in
One nobody else could see
Living with my angry father in his horrible cold little trailer
Rant Rant Rant Rant Rant
Richard building his new house so close to us
And
"Our Little Secret"
I knew what that meant
If I told, I felt like nobody would believe me
Oh, I would never do anything like that!
Then I would be an outcast, filled with unbearable shame
Liar!
Liar!
Liar!
Liar!
Liar!
Then, my fifteen-year-old mind concluded, my only option would be to kill myself
I didn't want to die
So I kept his little secret

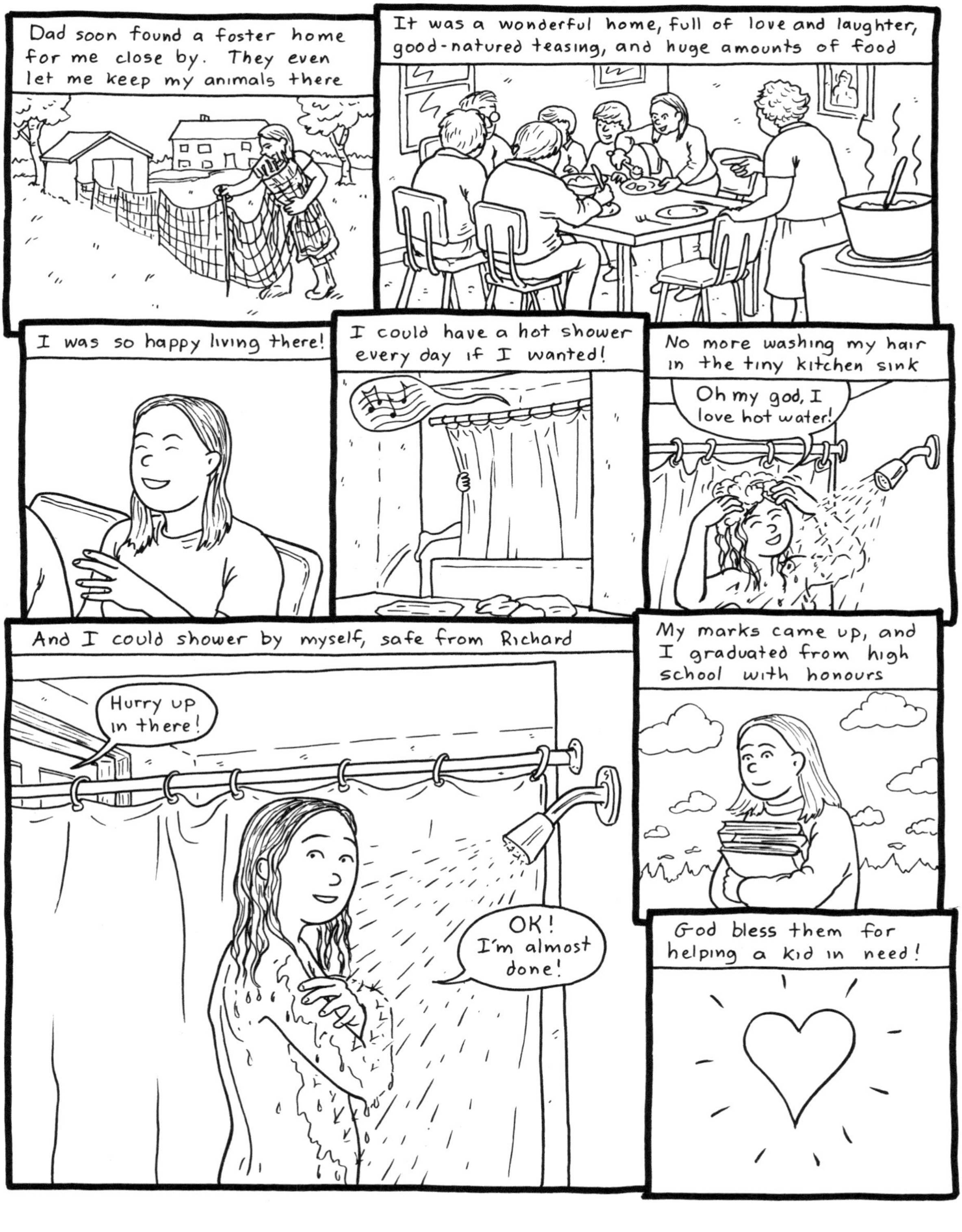
Dad soon found a foster home for me close by. They even let me keep my animals there
It was a wonderful home, full of love and laughter, good-natured teasing, and huge amounts of food
I was so happy living there!
I could have a hot shower every day if I wanted!
No more washing my hair in the tiny kitchen sink
Oh my god, I love hot water!
And I could shower by myself, safe from Richard
Hurry up in there!
OK! I'm almost done!
My marks came up, and I graduated from high school with honours
God bless them for helping a kid in need!

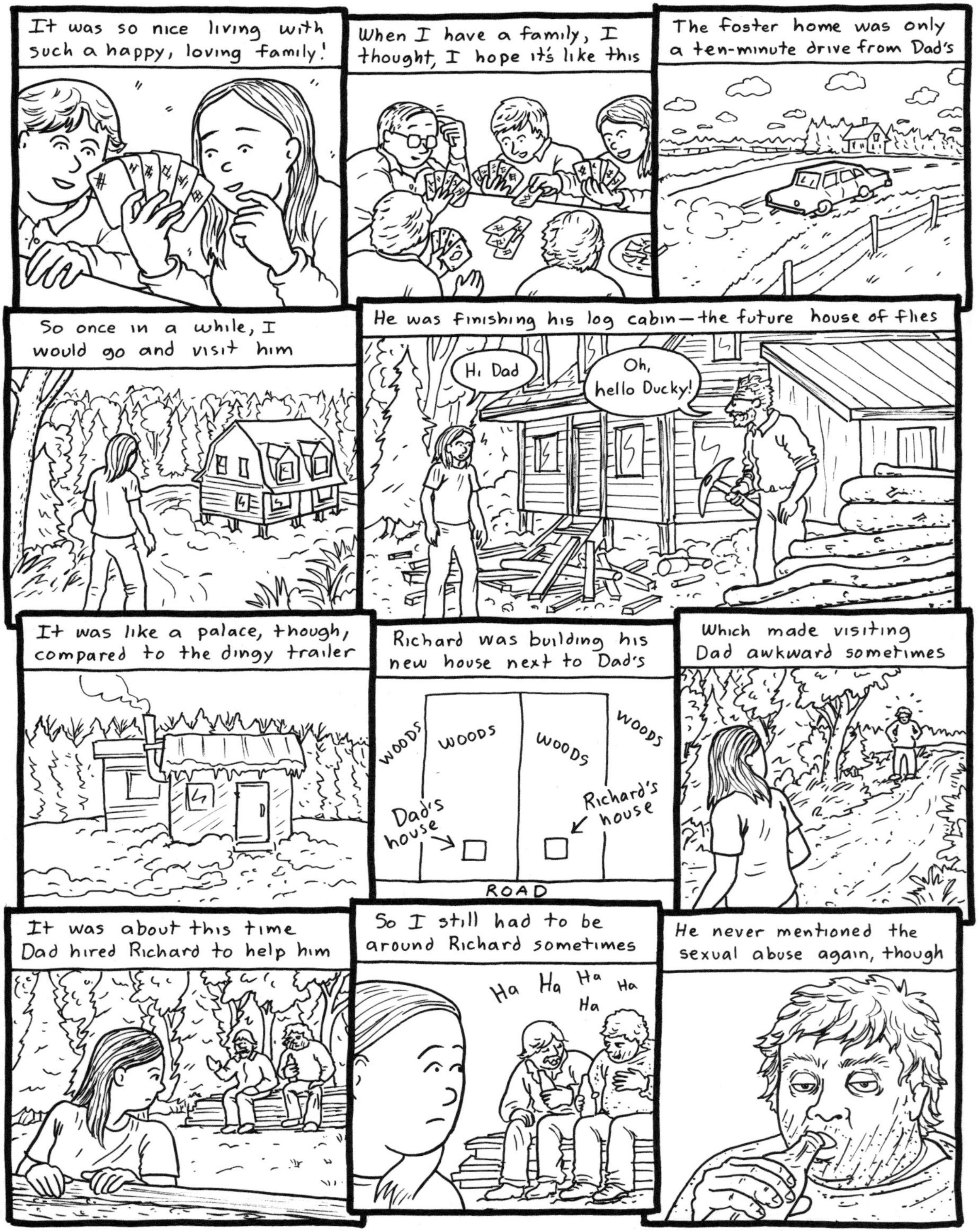
It was so nice living with such a happy, loving family!
When I have a family, I thought, I hope it's like this
The foster home was only a ten-minute drive from Dad's
So once in a while, I would go and visit him
He was finishing his log cabin—the future house of flies
Hi Dad
Oh, hello Ducky!
It was like a palace, though, compared to the dingy trailer
Richard was building his new house next to Dad's
WOODS
WOODS
WOODS
WOODS
Dad's house
Richard's house
ROAD
Which made visiting Dad awkward sometimes
It was about this time Dad hired Richard to help him
So I still had to be around Richard sometimes
Ha Ha Ha Ha Ha
He never mentioned the sexual abuse again, though

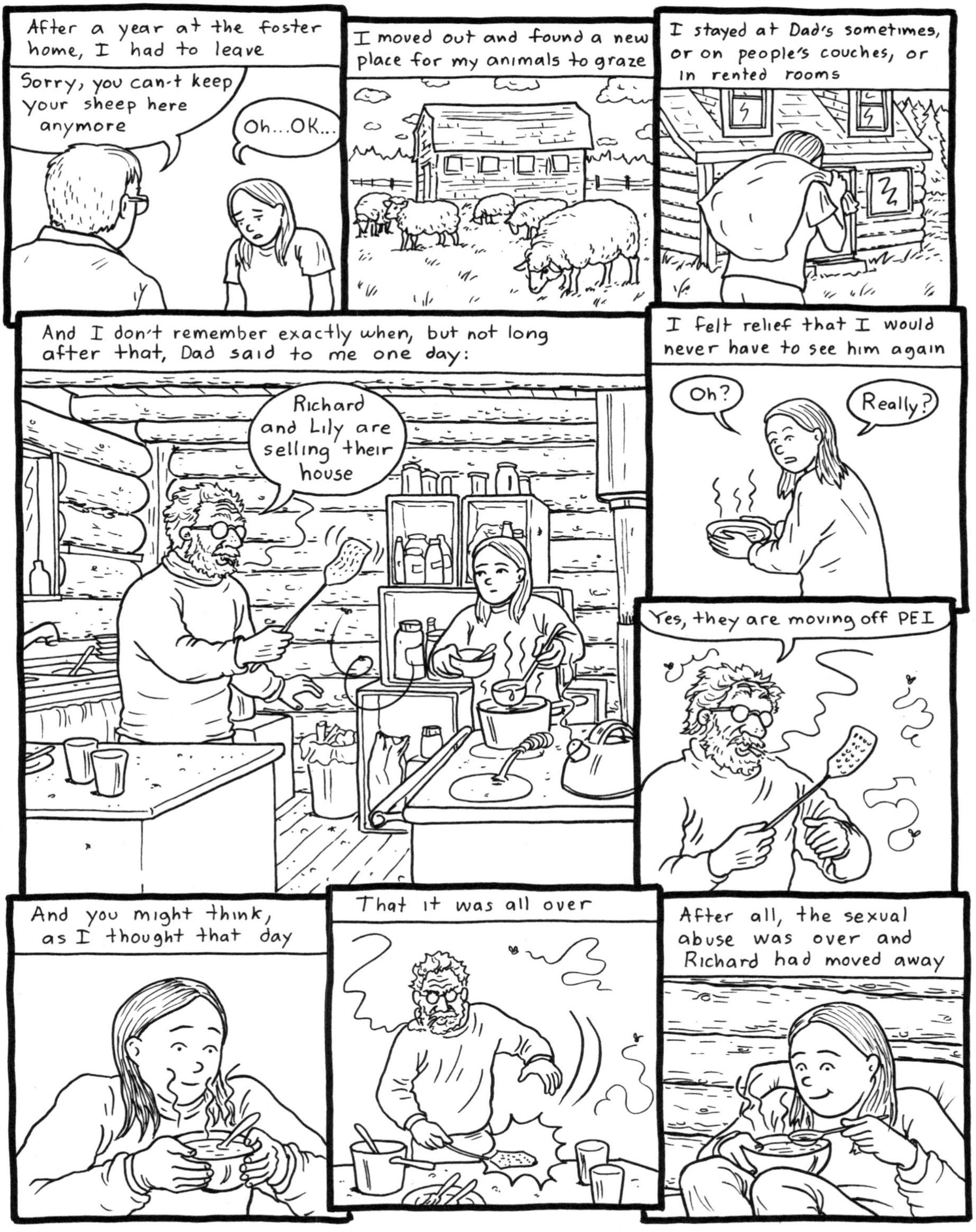
After a year at the foster home, I had to leave
Sorry, you can't keep your sheep here anymore
Oh...OK...
I moved out and found a new place for my animals to graze
I stayed at Dad's sometimes, or on people's couches, or in rented rooms
And I don't remember exactly when, but not long after that, Dad said to me one day:
Richard and Lily are selling their house
I felt relief that I would never have to see him again
Oh?
Really?
Yes, they are moving off PEI
And you might think, as I thought that day
That it was all over
After all, the sexual abuse was over and Richard had moved away

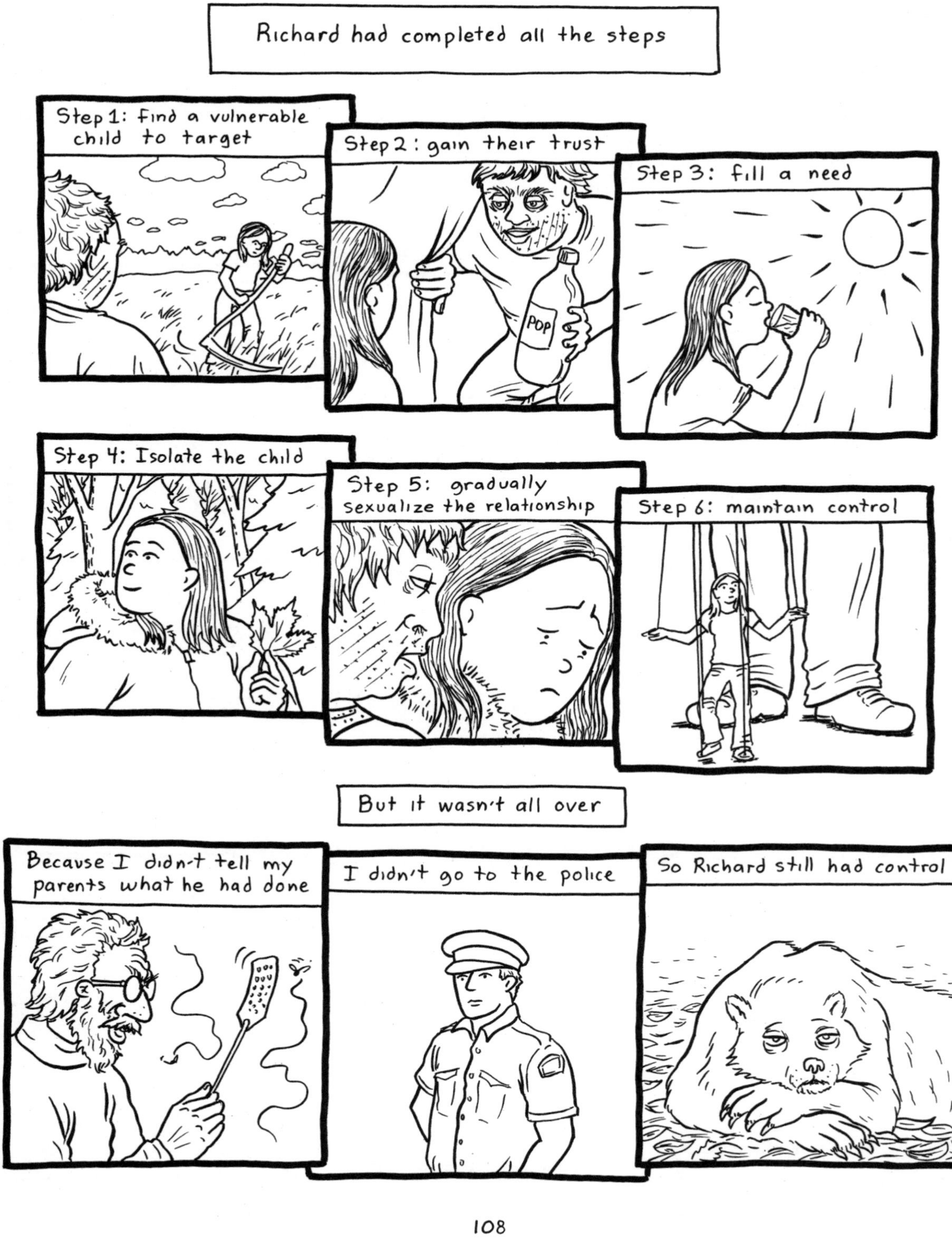
Richard had completed all the steps
Step 1: Find a vulnerable child to target
Step 2: gain their trust
POP
Step 3: fill a need
Step 4: Isolate the child
Step 5: gradually sexualize the relationship
Step 6: maintain control
But it wasn't all over
Because I didn't tell my parents what he had done
I didn't go to the police
So Richard still had control

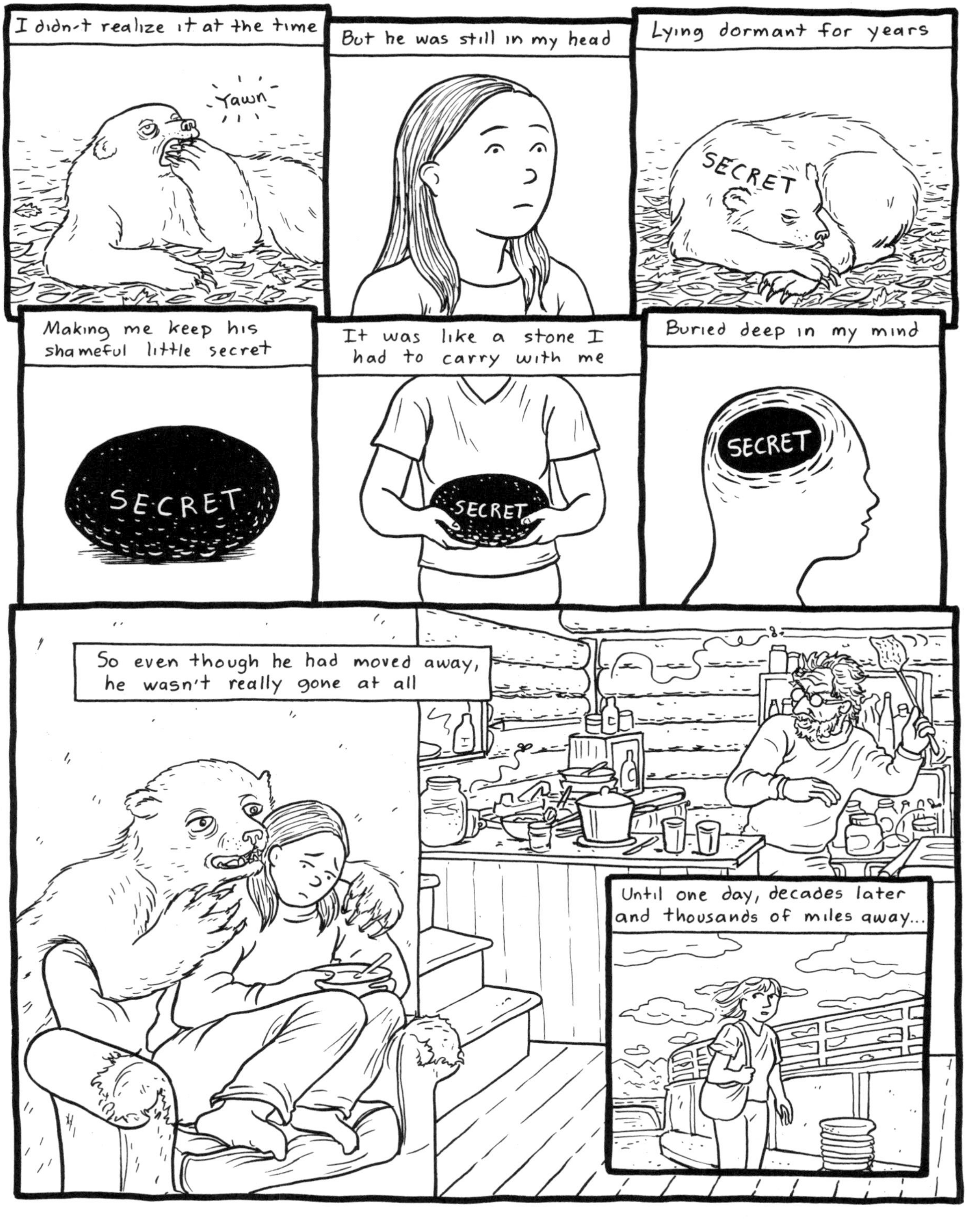

I didn't realize it at the time
Yawn
But he was still in my head
Lying dormant for years
SECRET
Making me keep his shameful little secret
SECRET
It was like a stone I had to carry with me
SECRET
Buried deep in my mind
SECRET
So even though he had moved away, he wasn't really gone at all
Until one day, decades later and thousands of miles away...

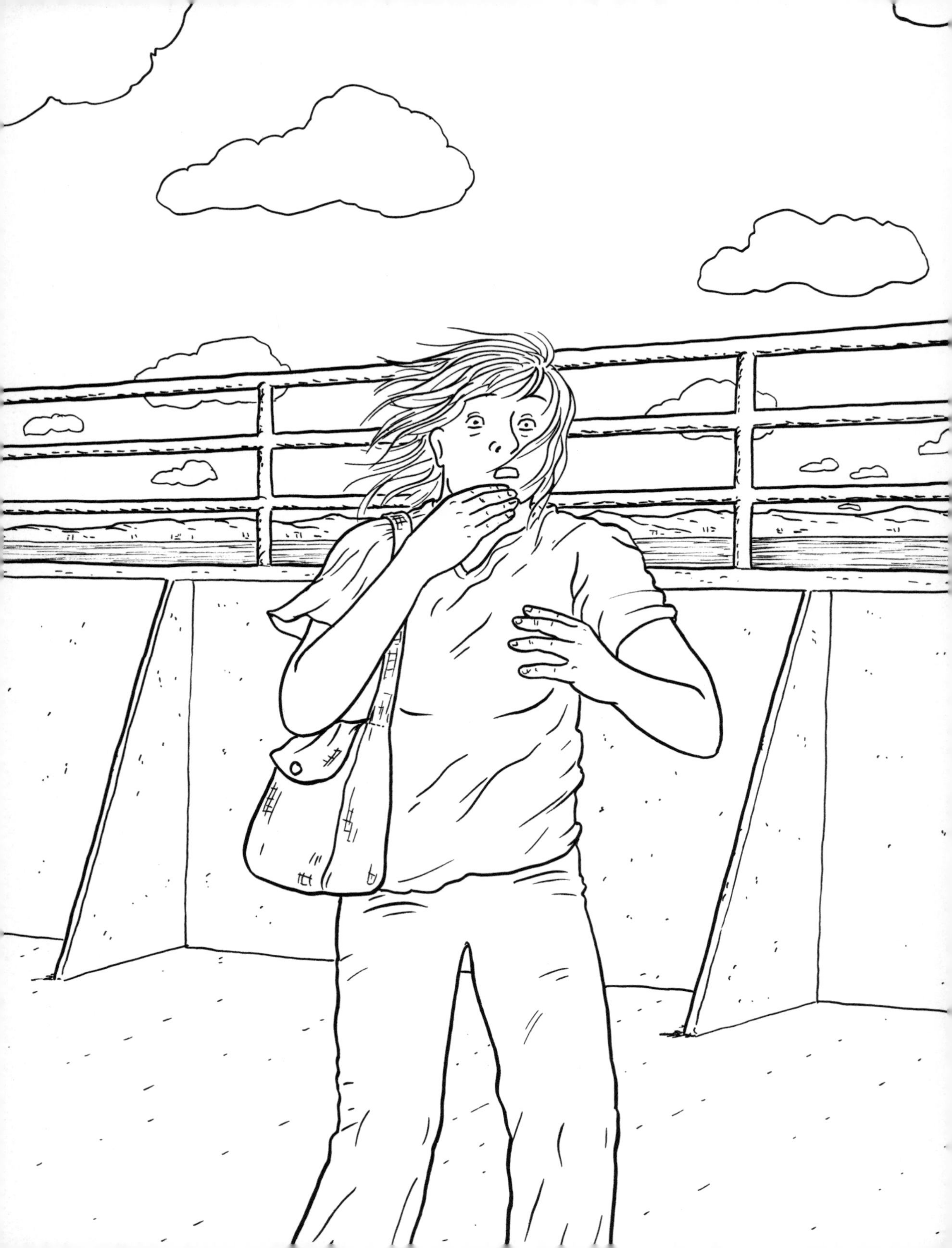

**July 15
2010**

27 years, 7 months, and 5 days
after Richard first raped me

I saw him
again

While on board
a ferry

For a moment, I was in shock

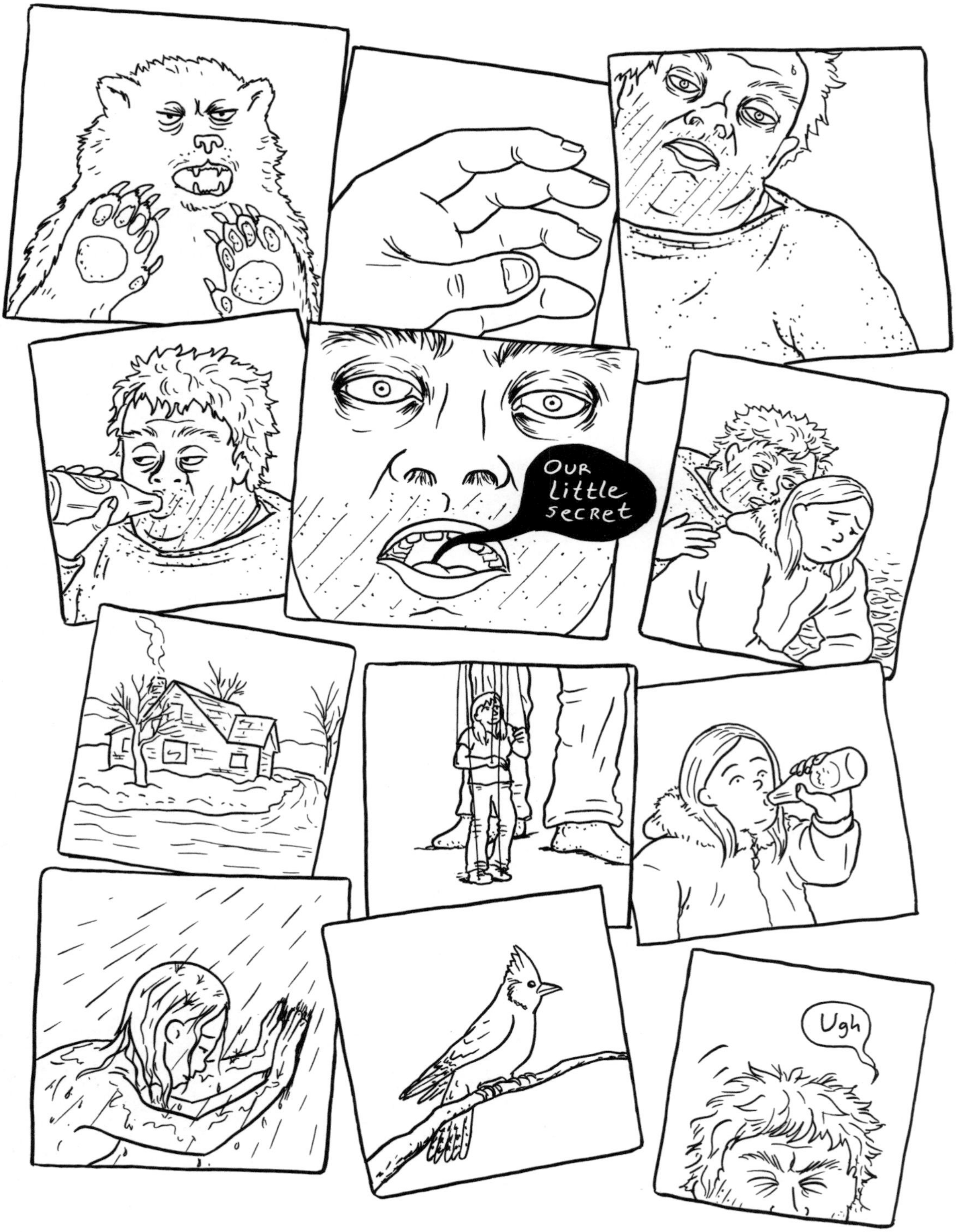
Our little secret
Ugh

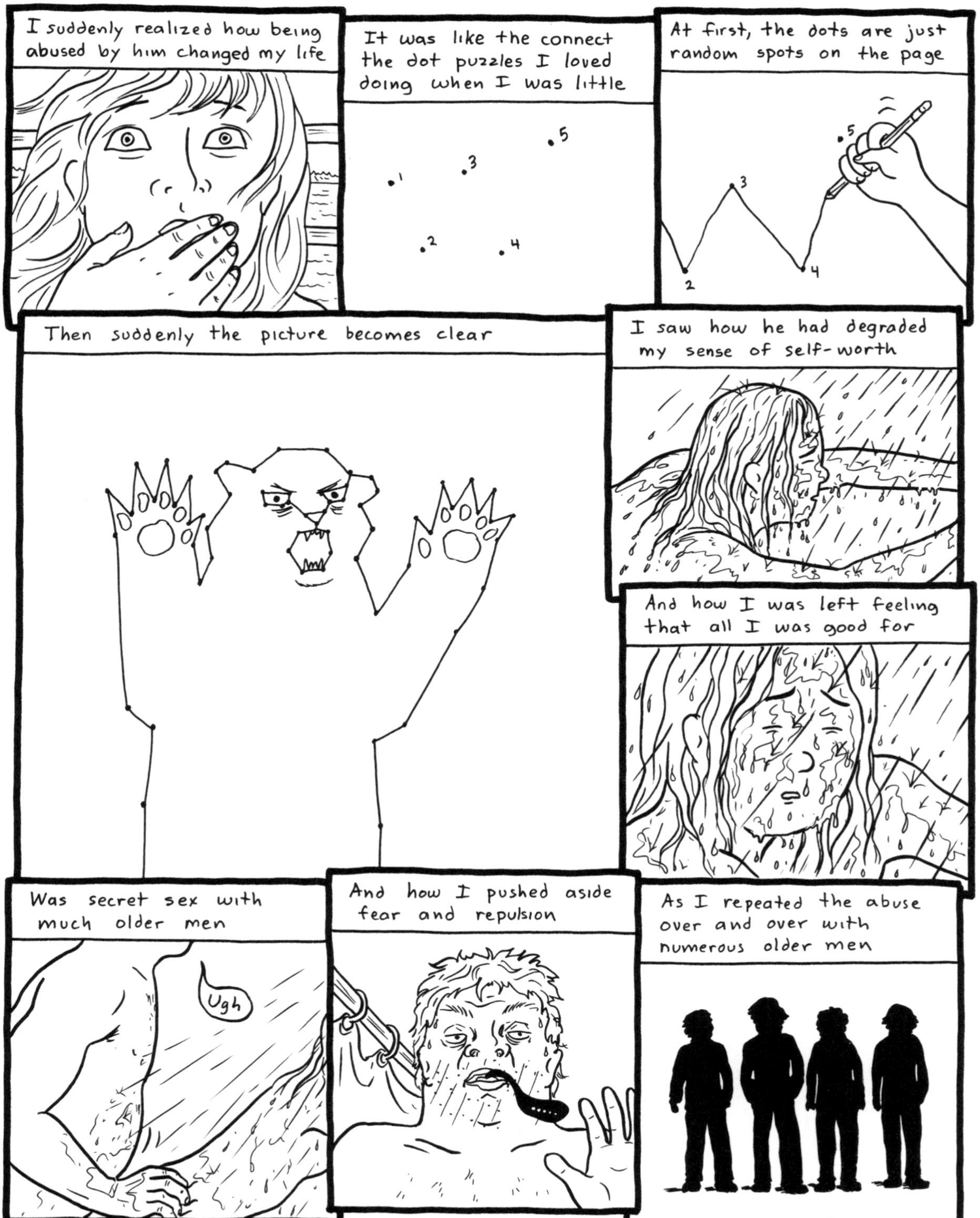
I suddenly realized how being abused by him changed my life
It was like the connect the dot puzzles I loved doing when I was little
1
2
3
4
5
At first, the dots are just random spots on the page
2
3
4
5
Then suddenly the picture becomes clear
I saw how he had degraded my sense of self-worth
And how I was left feeling that all I was good for
Was secret sex with much older men
Ugh
And how I pushed aside fear and repulsion
As I repeated the abuse over and over with numerous older men

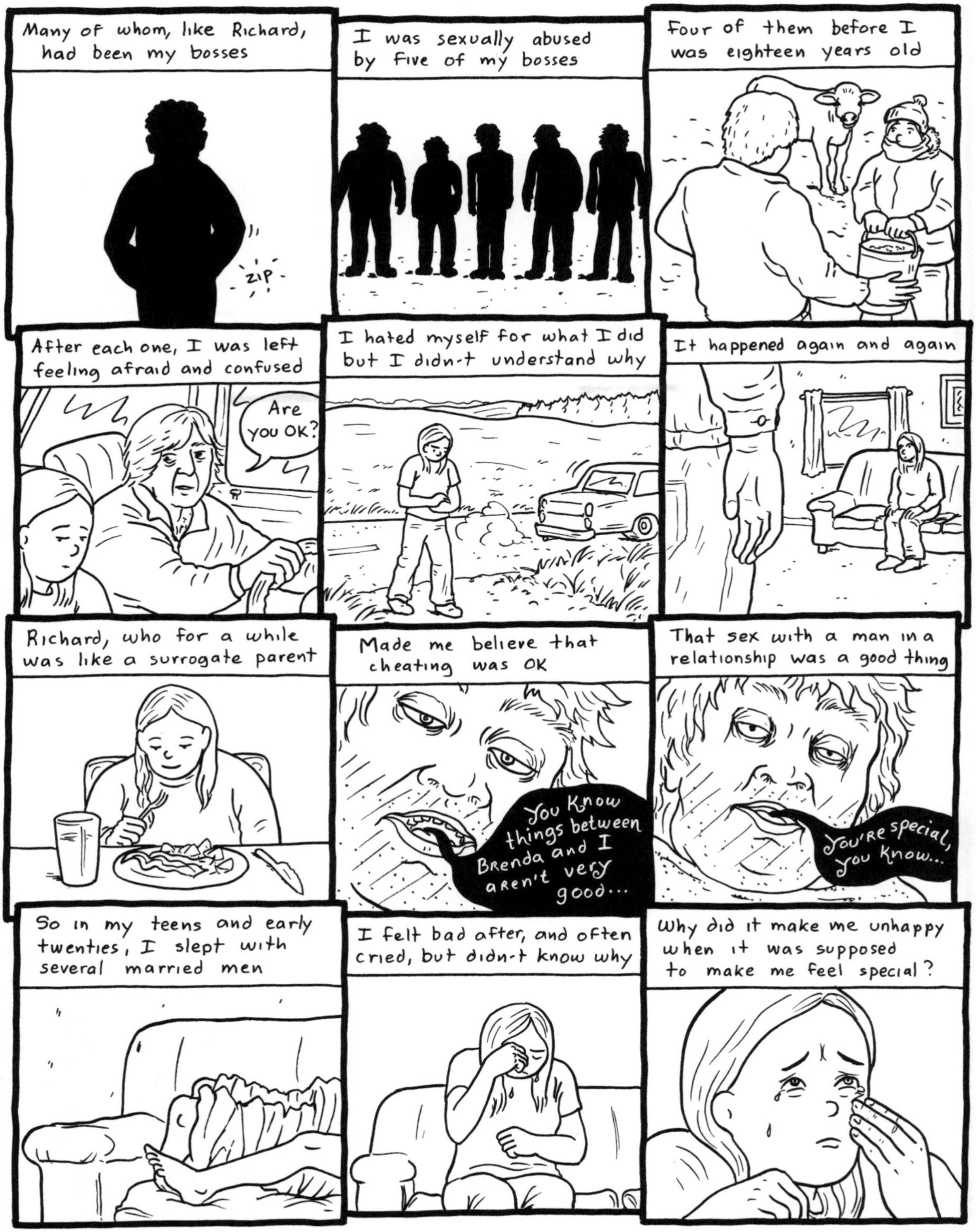
Many of whom, like Richard, had been my bosses
ZIP
I was sexually abused by five of my bosses
Four of them before I was eighteen years old
After each one, I was left feeling afraid and confused
Are you OK?
I hated myself for what I did but I didn't understand why
It happened again and again
Richard, who for a while was like a surrogate parent
Made me believe that cheating was OK
You know things between Brenda and I aren't very good...
That sex with a man in a relationship was a good thing
You're special, you know...
So in my teens and early twenties, I slept with several married men
I felt bad after, and often cried, but didn't know why
Why did it make me unhappy when it was supposed to make me feel special?

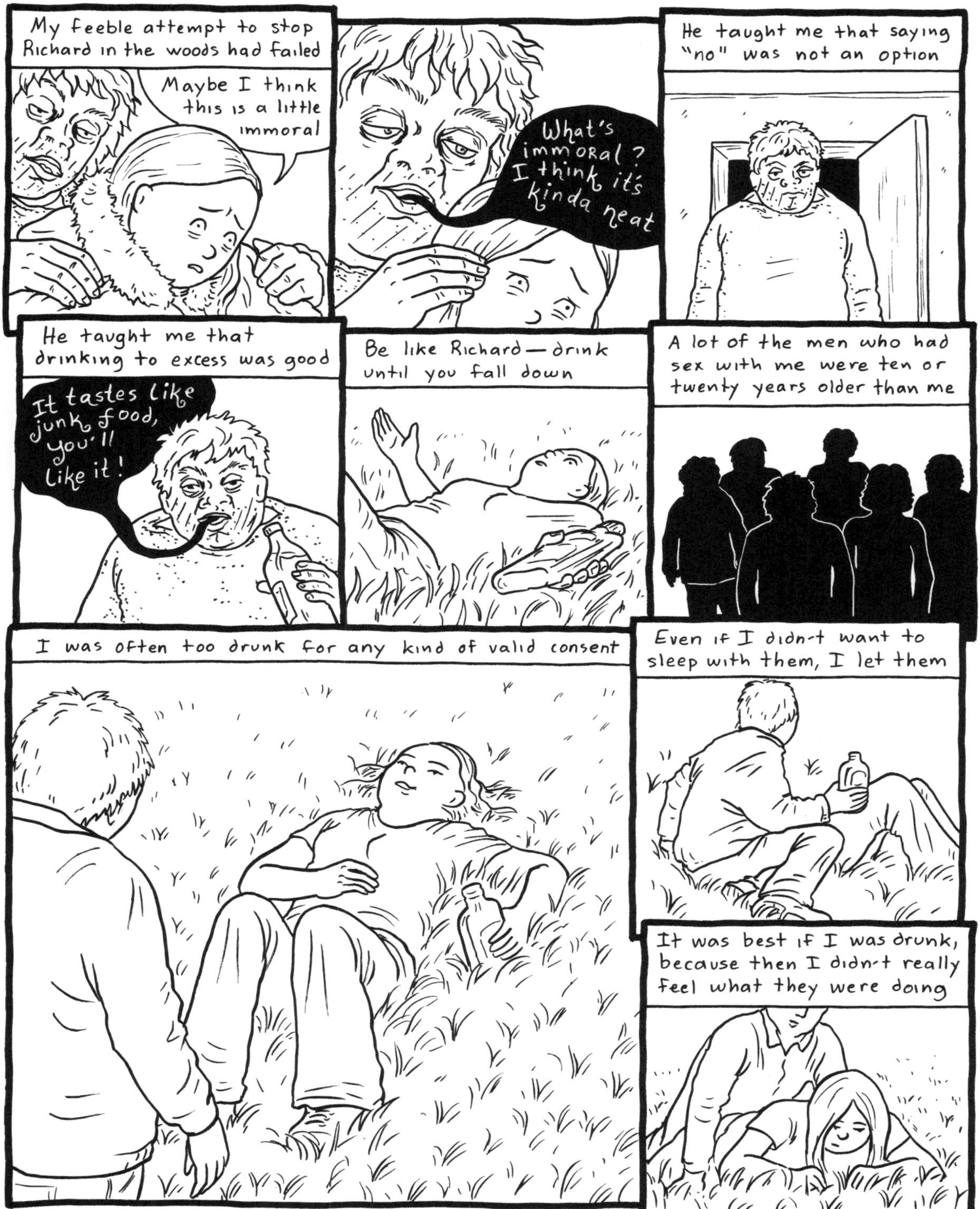
My feeble attempt to stop Richard in the woods had failed
Maybe I think this is a little immoral
What's immoral? I think it's kinda neat
He taught me that saying "no" was not an option
He taught me that drinking to excess was good
It tastes like junk food, you'll like it!
Be like Richard—drink until you fall down
A lot of the men who had sex with me were ten or twenty years older than me
I was often too drunk for any kind of valid consent
Even if I didn't want to sleep with them, I let them
It was best if I was drunk, because then I didn't really feel what they were doing

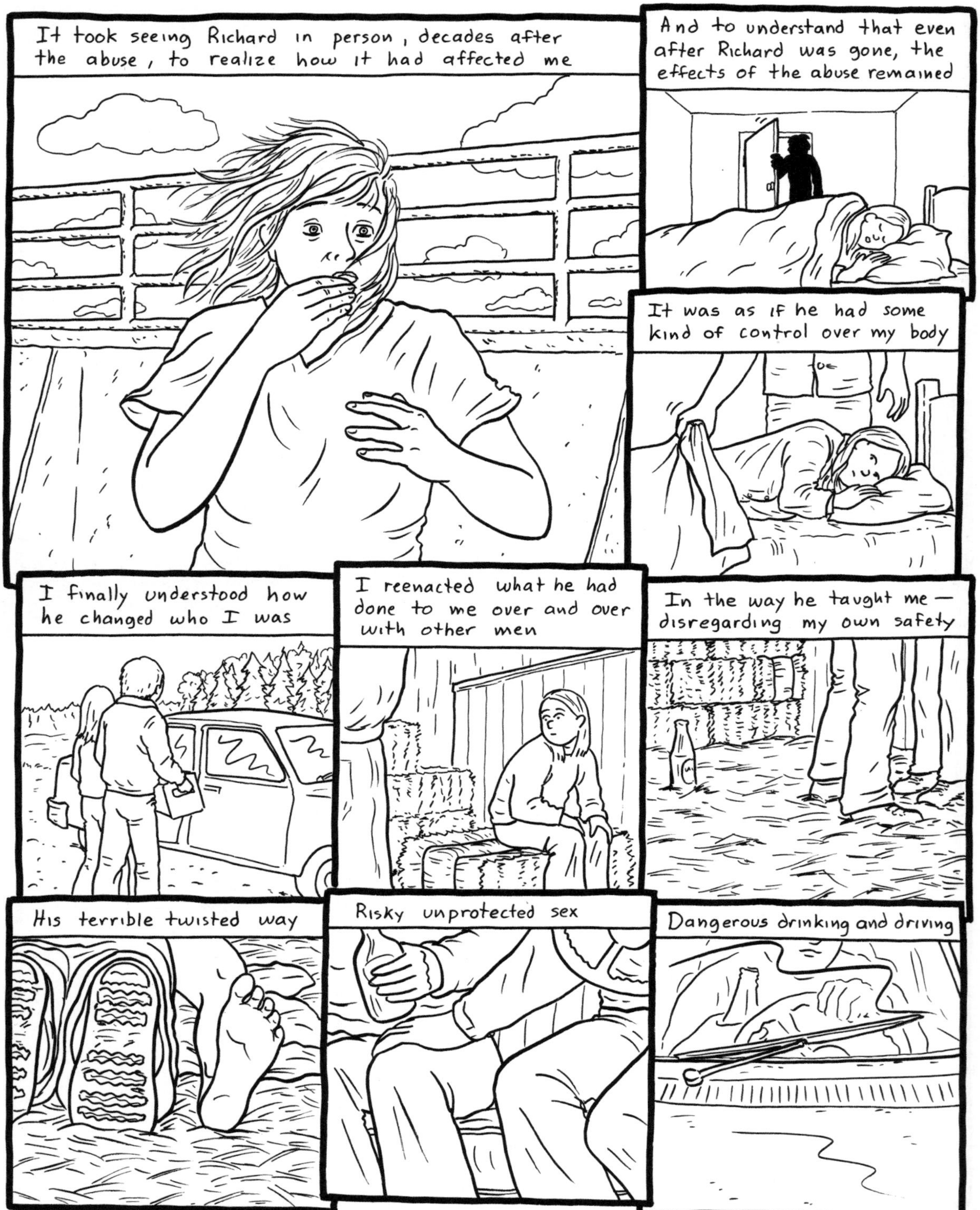
It took seeing Richard in person, decades after the abuse, to realize how it had affected me
And to understand that even after Richard was gone, the effects of the abuse remained
It was as if he had some kind of control over my body
I finally understood how he changed who I was
I reenacted what he had done to me over and over with other men
In the way he taught me — disregarding my own safety
His terrible twisted way
Risky unprotected sex
Dangerous drinking and driving

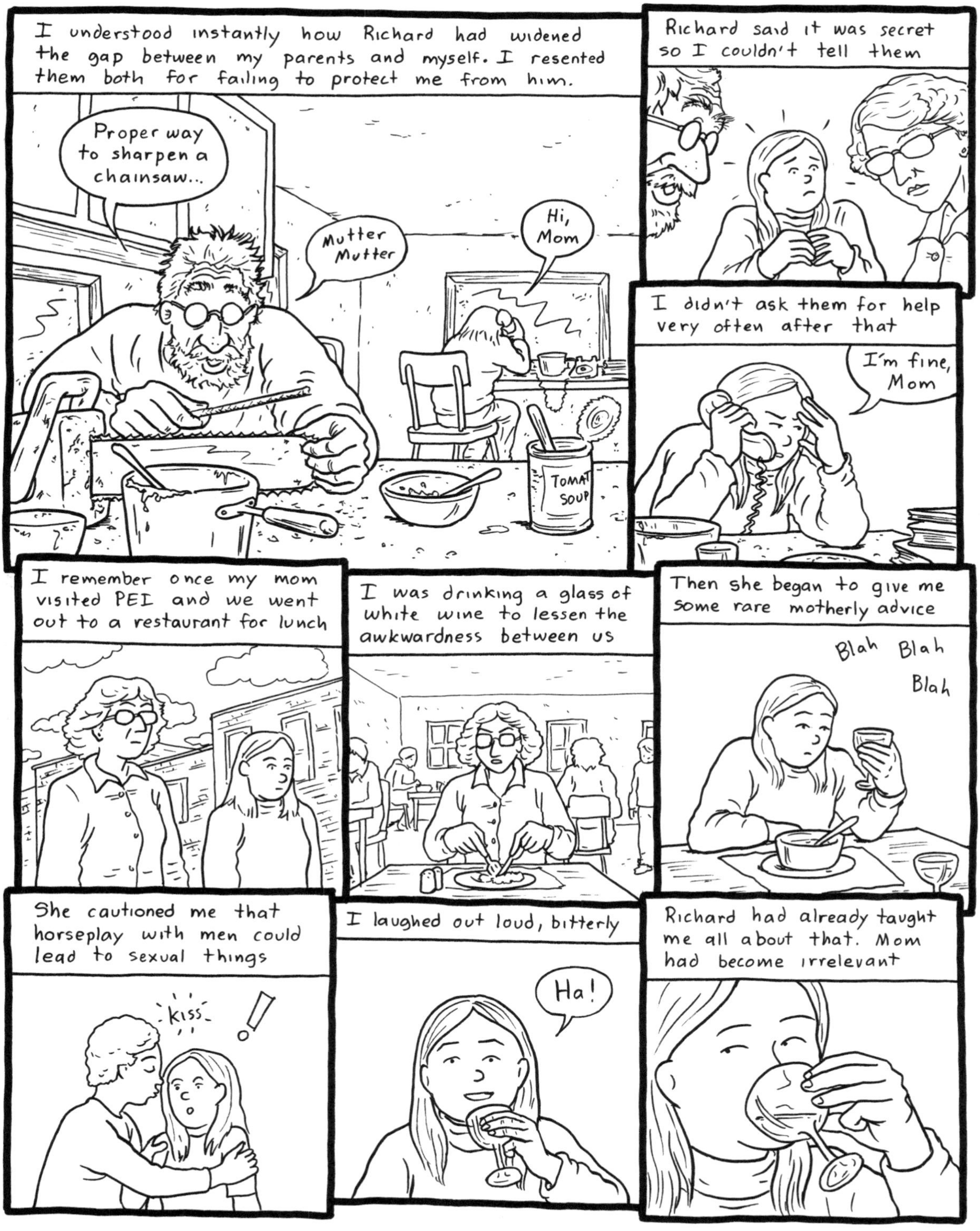

I understood instantly how Richard had widened the gap between my parents and myself. I resented them both for failing to protect me from him.
Proper way to sharpen a chainsaw...
Mutter Mutter
Hi, Mom
TOMAT SOUP
Richard said it was secret so I couldn't tell them
I didn't ask them for help very often after that
I'm fine, Mom
I remember once my mom visited PEI and we went out to a restaurant for lunch
I was drinking a glass of white wine to lessen the awkwardness between us
Then she began to give me some rare motherly advice
Blah Blah Blah
She cautioned me that horseplay with men could lead to sexual things
kiss
!
I laughed out loud, bitterly
Ha!
Richard had already taught me all about that. Mom had become irrelevant

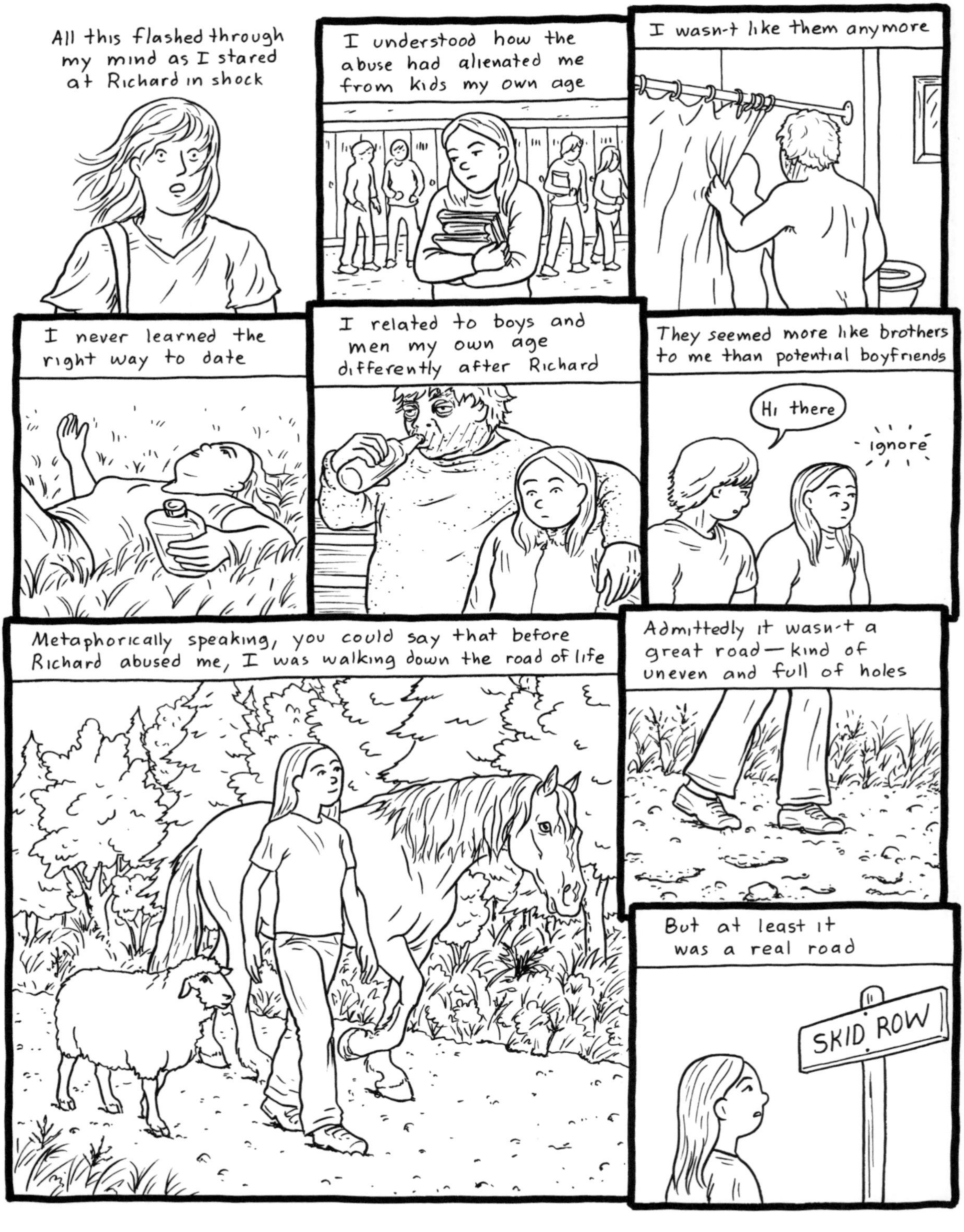
All this flashed through my mind as I stared at Richard in shock
I understood how the abuse had alienated me from kids my own age
I wasn-t like them anymore
I never learned the right way to date
I related to boys and men my own age differently after Richard
They seemed more like brothers to me than potential boyfriends
Hi there
ignore
Metaphorically speaking, you could say that before Richard abused me, I was walking down the road of life
Admittedly it wasn-t a great road—kind of uneven and full of holes
But at least it was a real road
SKID ROW

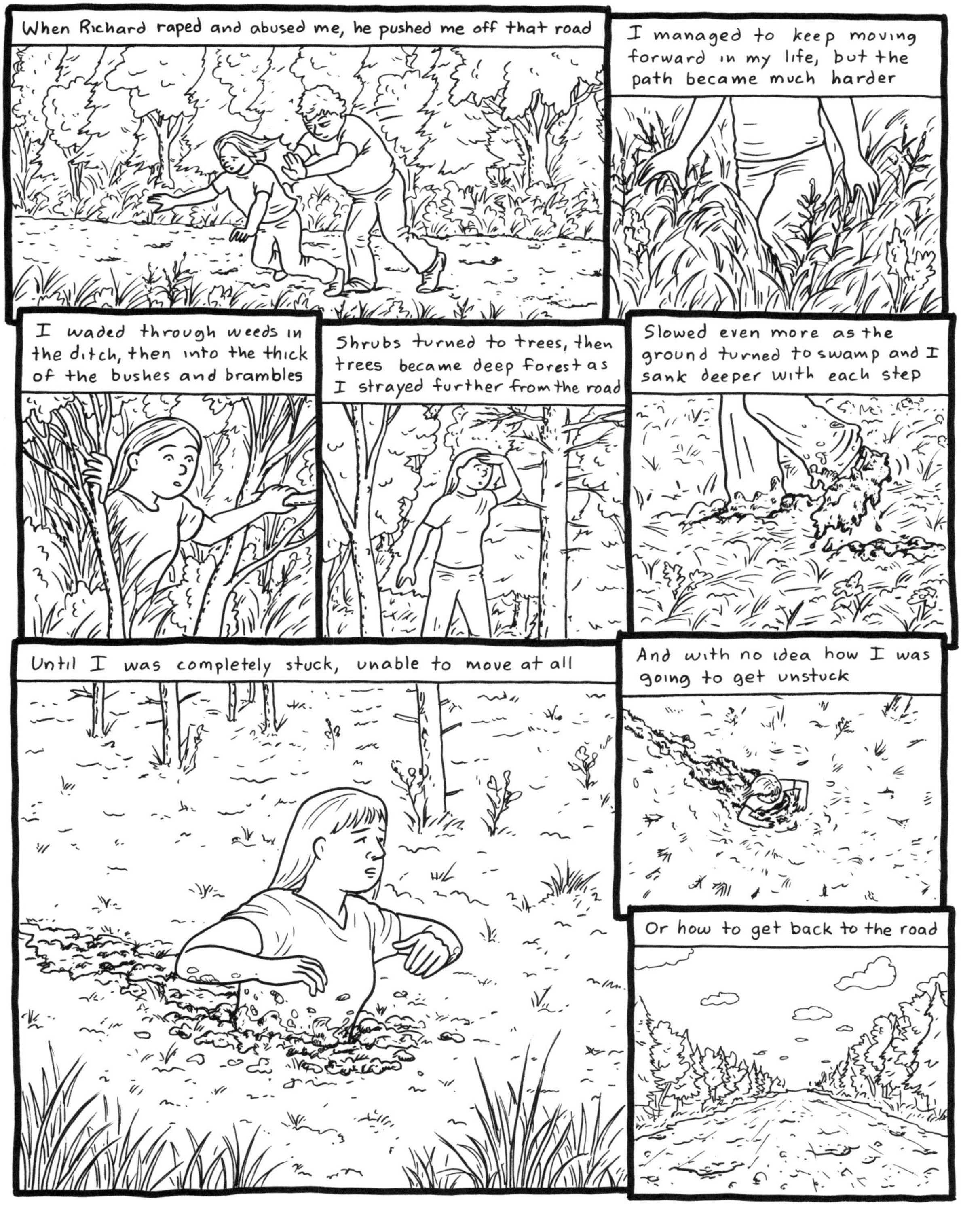
When Richard raped and abused me, he pushed me off that road
I managed to keep moving forward in my life, but the path became much harder
I waded through weeds in the ditch, then into the thick of the bushes and brambles
Shrubs turned to trees, then trees became deep forest as I strayed further from the road
Slowed even more as the ground turned to swamp and I sank deeper with each step
Until I was completely stuck, unable to move at all
And with no idea how I was going to get unstuck
Or how to get back to the road

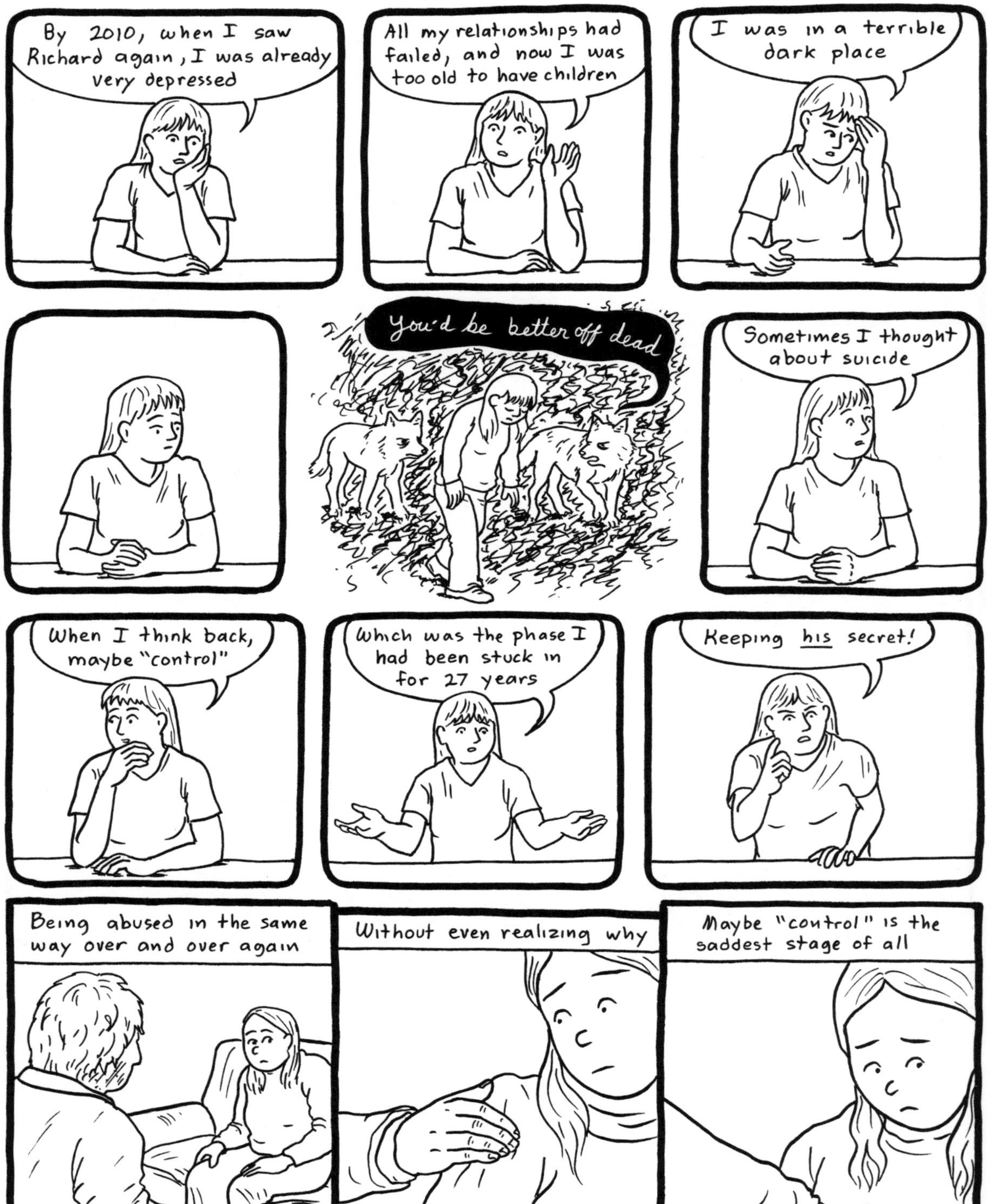

By 2010, when I saw Richard again, I was already very depressed
All my relationships had failed, and now I was too old to have children
I was in a terrible dark place
You'd be better off dead
Sometimes I thought about suicide
When I think back, maybe "control"
Which was the phase I had been stuck in for 27 years
Keeping his secret!
Being abused in the same way over and over again
Without even realizing why
Maybe "control" is the saddest stage of all

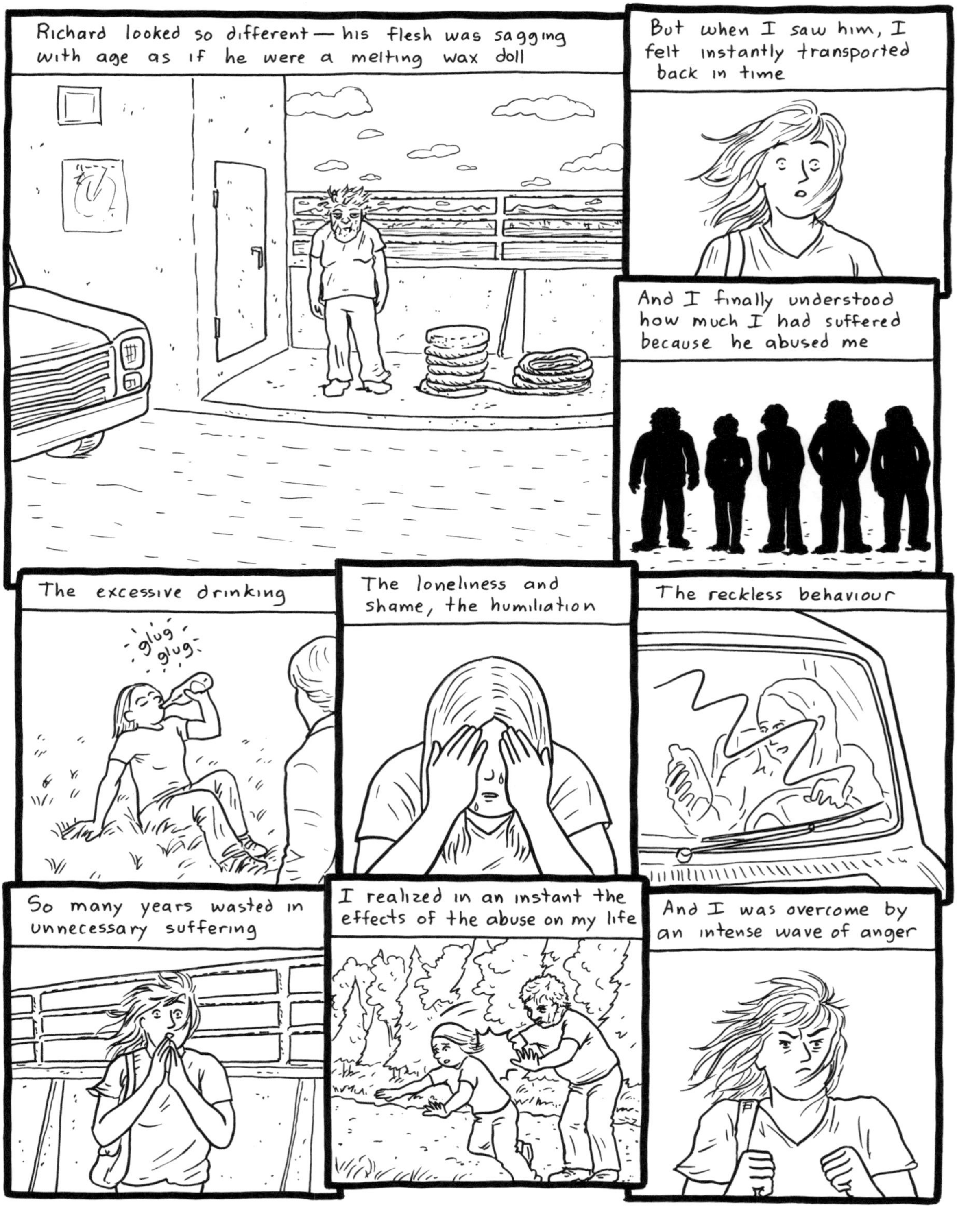
Richard looked so different — his flesh was sagging with age as if he were a melting wax doll
But when I saw him, I felt instantly transported back in time
And I finally understood how much I had suffered because he abused me
The excessive drinking
glug glug
The loneliness and shame, the humiliation
The reckless behaviour
So many years wasted in unnecessary suffering
I realized in an instant the effects of the abuse on my life
And I was overcome by an intense wave of anger

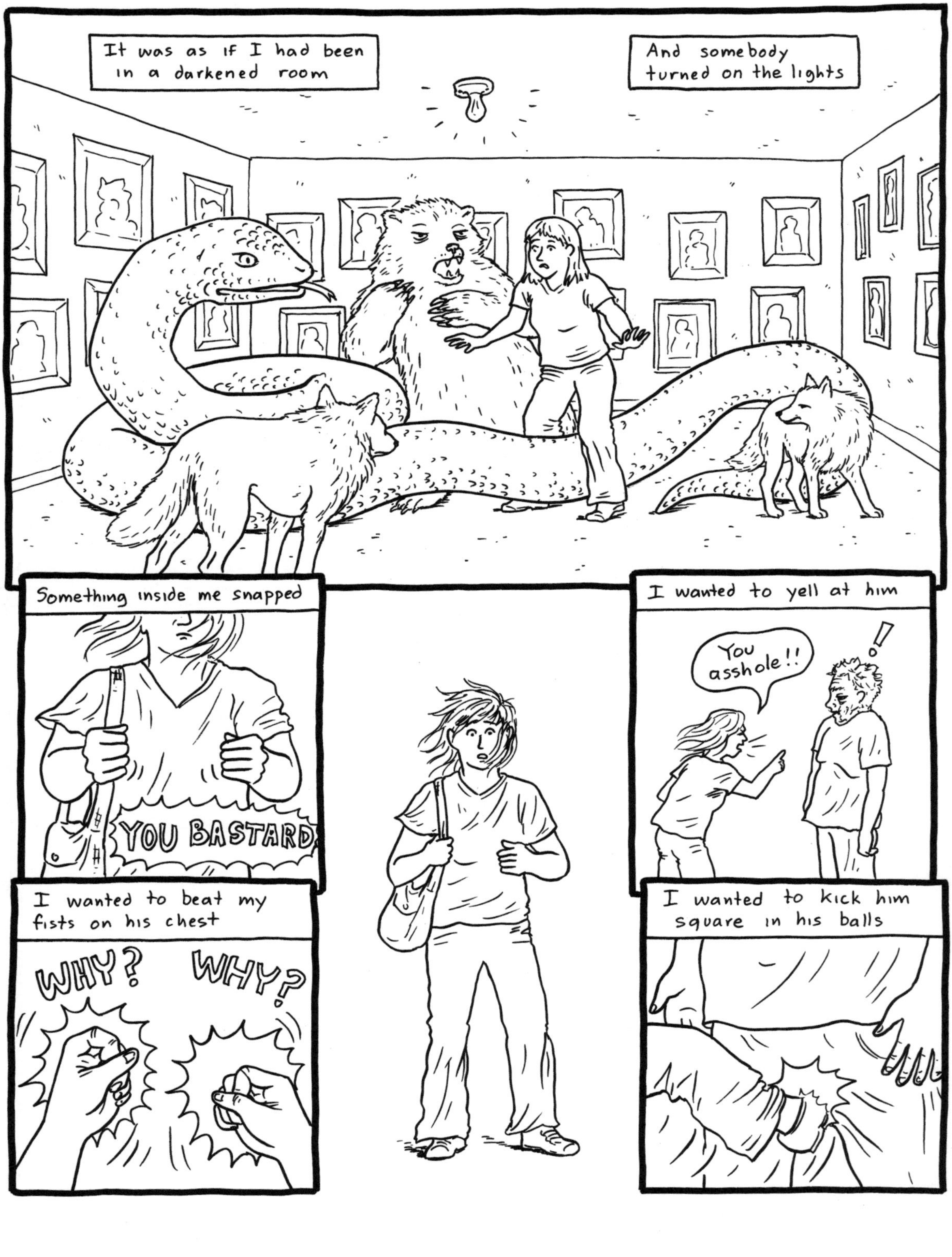
It was as if I had been in a darkened room
And somebody turned on the lights
Something inside me snapped
YOU BASTARD
I wanted to yell at him
You asshole!!
!
I wanted to beat my fists on his chest
WHY?
WHY?
I wanted to kick him square in his balls

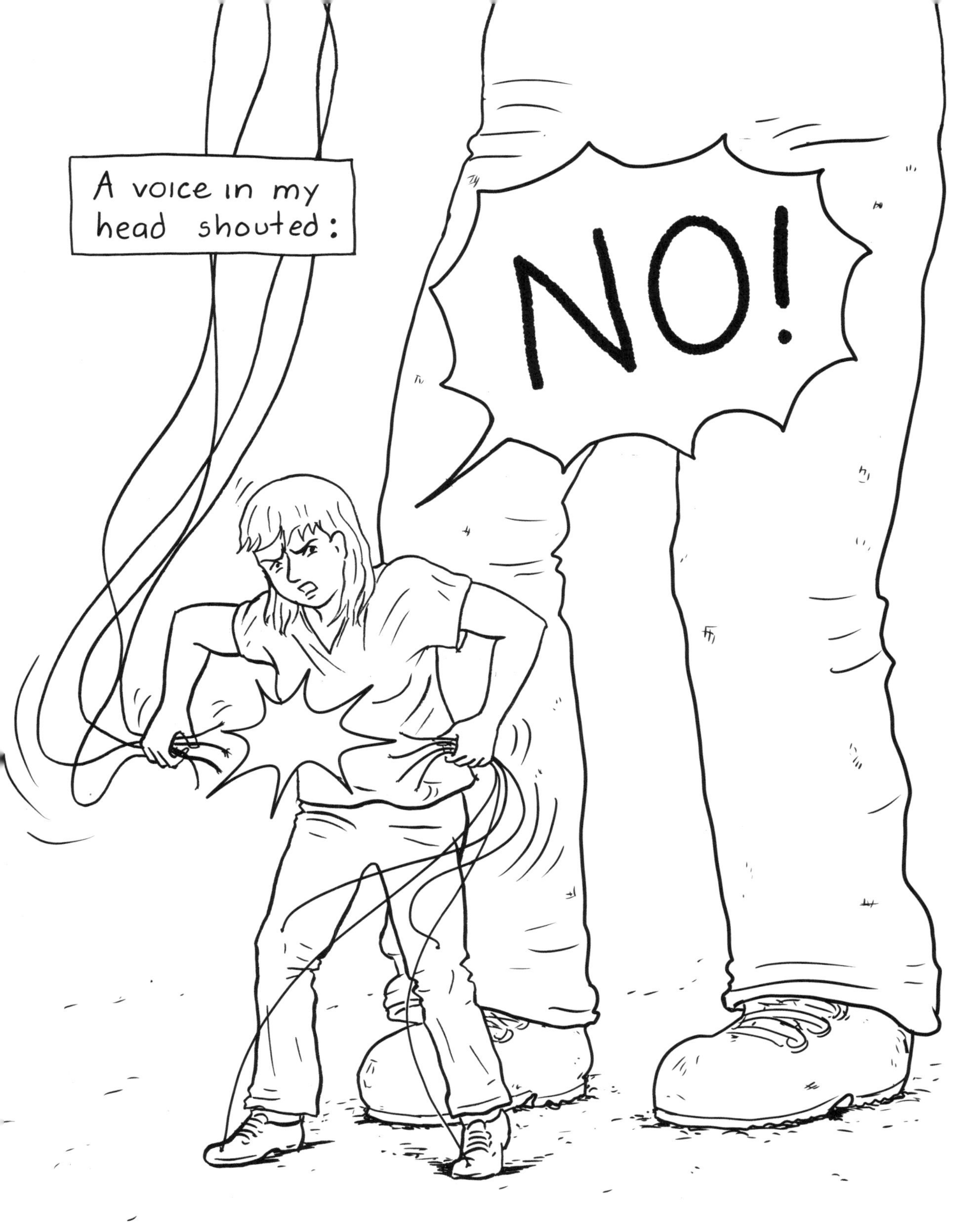
A voice in my head shouted:
NO!

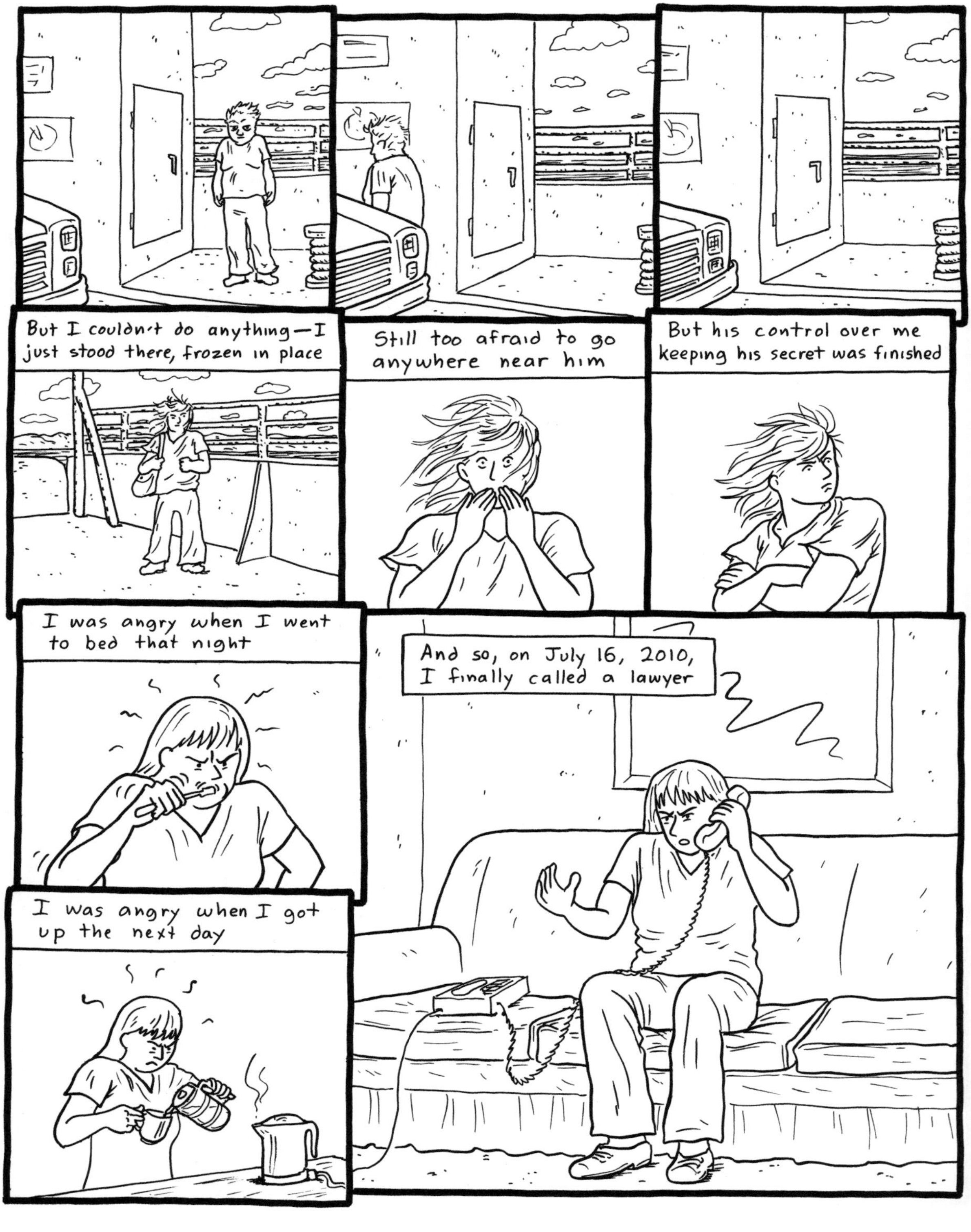
But I couldn't do anything—I just stood there, frozen in place
Still too afraid to go anywhere near him
But his control over me keeping his secret was finished
I was angry when I went to bed that night
And so, on July 16, 2010, I finally called a lawyer
I was angry when I got up the next day

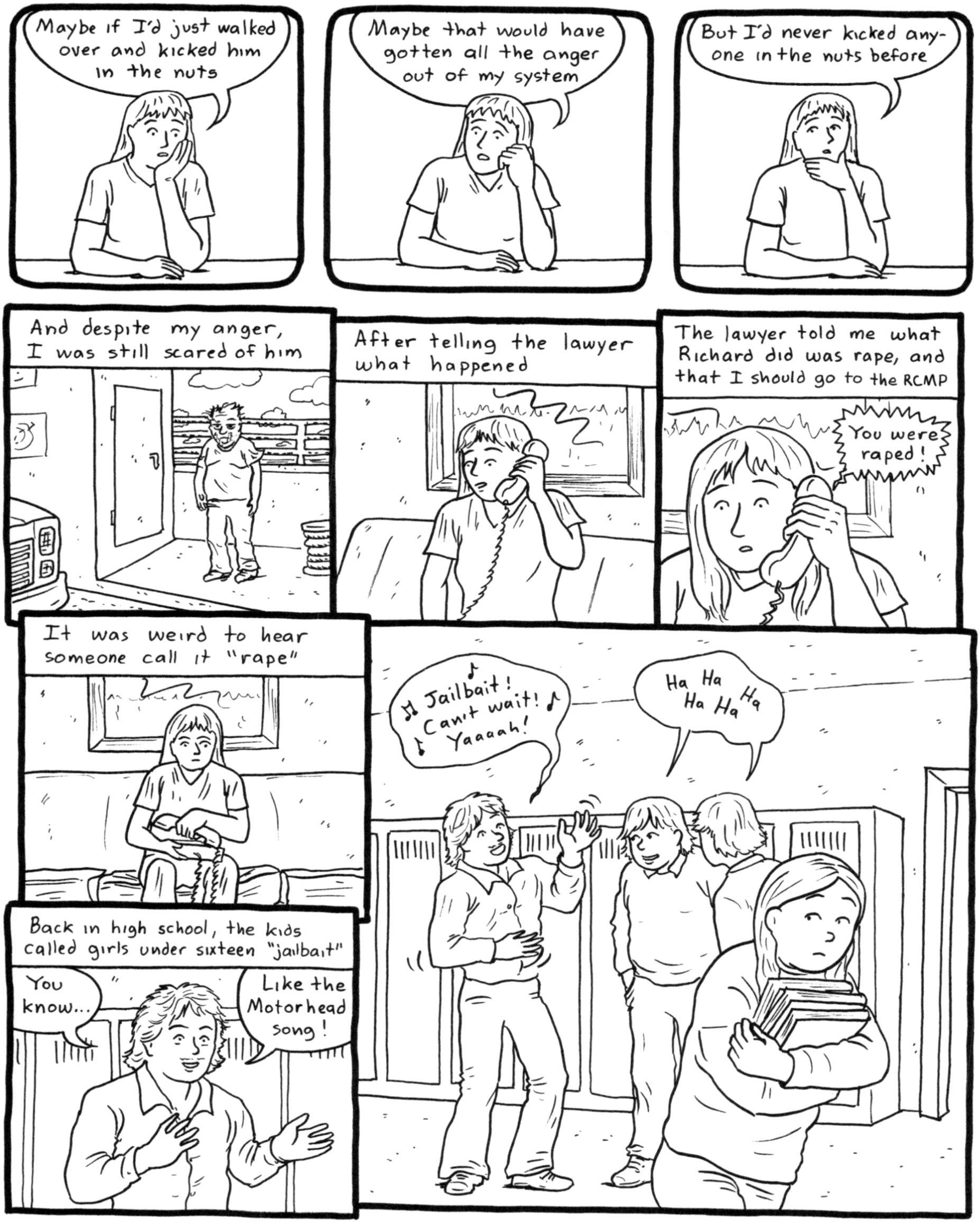
Maybe if I'd just walked over and kicked him in the nuts
Maybe that would have gotten all the anger out of my system
But I'd never kicked anyone in the nuts before
And despite my anger, I was still scared of him
After telling the lawyer what happened
The lawyer told me what Richard did was rape, and that I should go to the RCMP
You were raped!
It was weird to hear someone call it "rape"
Back in high school, the kids called girls under sixteen "jailbait"
You know...
Like the Motorhead song!
Jailbait! Can't wait! Yaaaah!
Ha Ha Ha Ha Ha

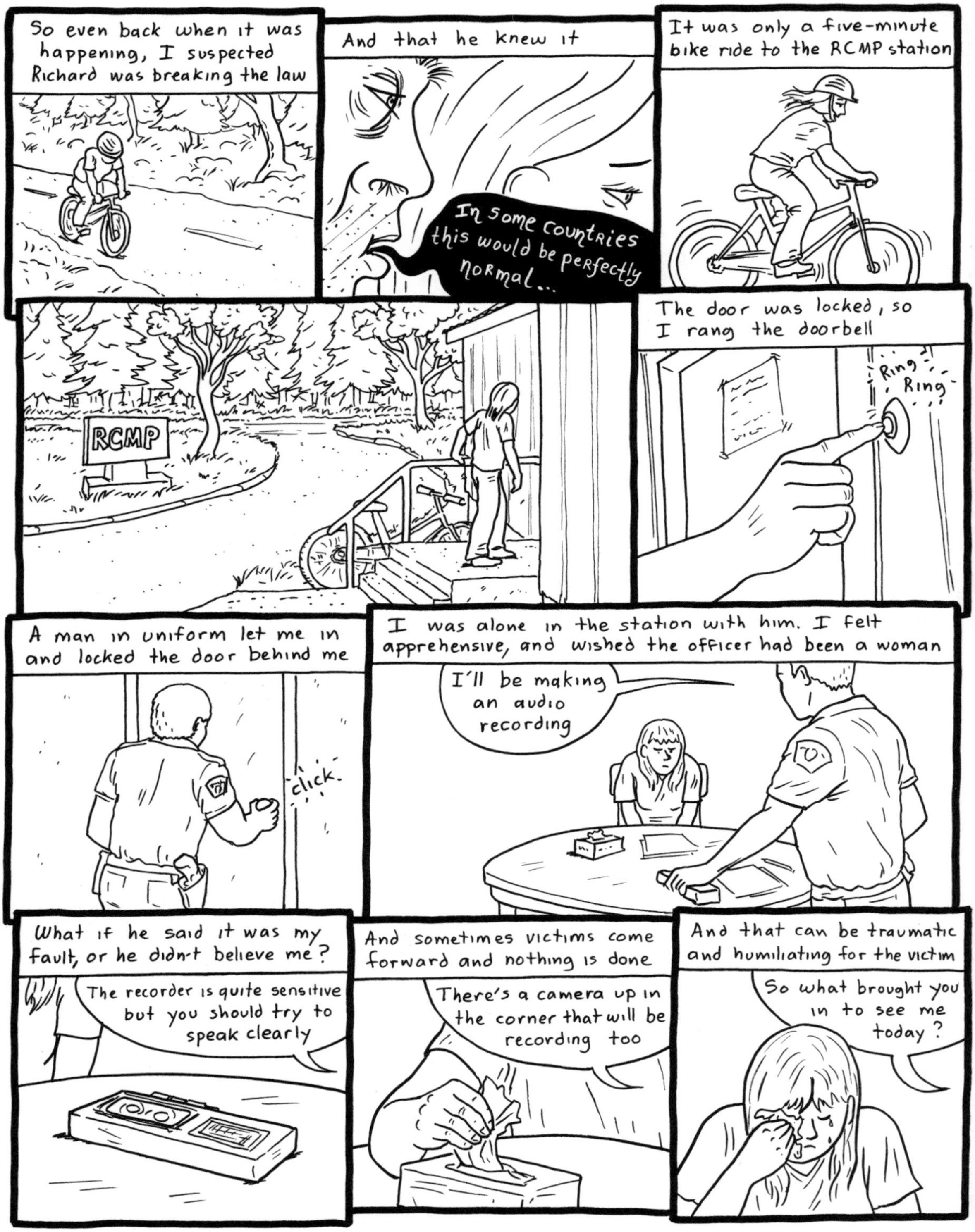
So even back when it was happening, I suspected Richard was breaking the law
And that he knew it
In some countries this would be perfectly normal...
It was only a five-minute bike ride to the RCMP station
RCMP
The door was locked, so I rang the doorbell
Ring Ring
A man in uniform let me in and locked the door behind me
click
I was alone in the station with him. I felt apprehensive, and wished the officer had been a woman
I'll be making an audio recording
What if he said it was my fault, or he didn't believe me?
The recorder is quite sensitive but you should try to speak clearly
And sometimes victims come forward and nothing is done
There's a camera up in the corner that will be recording too
And that can be traumatic and humiliating for the victim
So what brought you in to see me today?

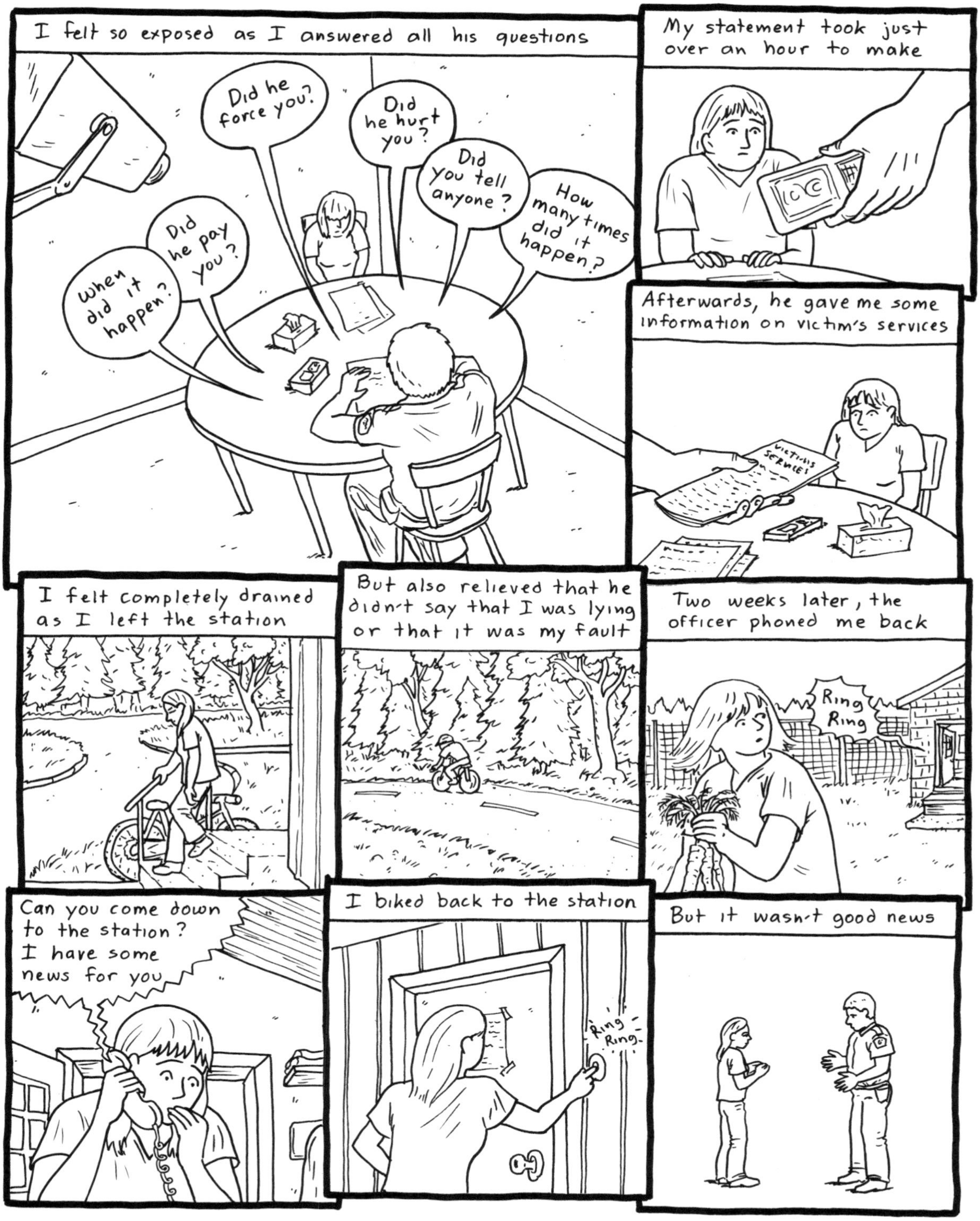
I felt so exposed as I answered all his questions
Did he force you?
Did he hurt you?
Did you tell anyone?
How many times did it happen?
Did he pay you?
When did it happen?
My statement took just over an hour to make
Afterwards, he gave me some information on victim's services
VICTIMS SERVICES
I felt completely drained as I left the station
But also relieved that he didn't say that I was lying or that it was my fault
Two weeks later, the officer phoned me back
Ring Ring
Can you come down to the station? I have some news for you
I biked back to the station
Ring Ring
But it wasn't good news

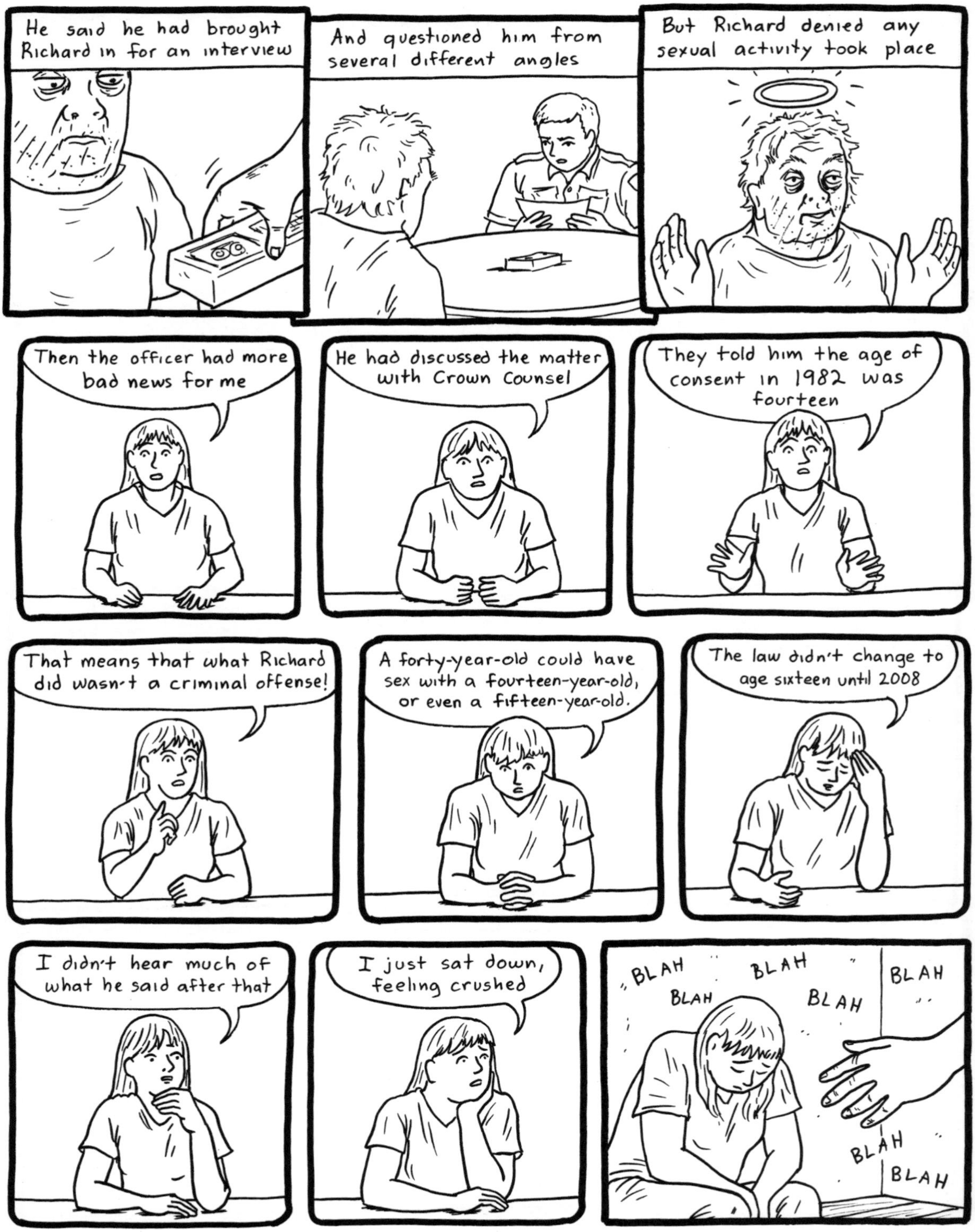
He said he had brought Richard in for an interview
And questioned him from several different angles
But Richard denied any sexual activity took place
Then the officer had more bad news for me
He had discussed the matter with Crown Counsel
They told him the age of consent in 1982 was fourteen
That means that what Richard did wasn't a criminal offense!
A forty-year-old could have sex with a fourteen-year-old, or even a fifteen-year-old.
The law didn't change to age sixteen until 2008
I didn't hear much of what he said after that
I just sat down, feeling crushed
BLAH BLAH BLAH BLAH BLAH BLAH BLAH

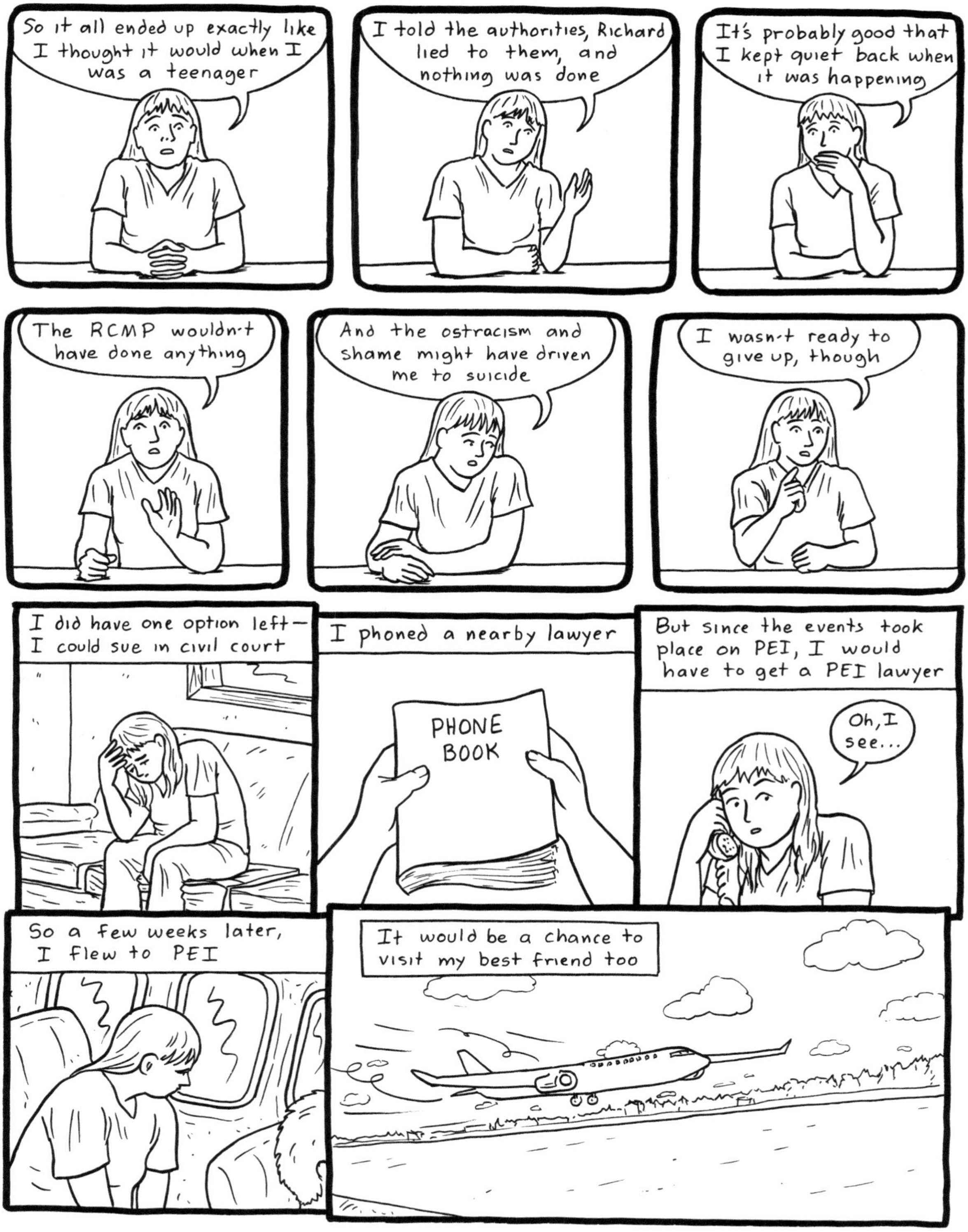
So it all ended up exactly like I thought it would when I was a teenager
I told the authorities, Richard lied to them, and nothing was done
It's probably good that I kept quiet back when it was happening
The RCMP wouldn't have done anything
And the ostracism and shame might have driven me to suicide
I wasn't ready to give up, though
I did have one option left— I could sue in civil court
I phoned a nearby lawyer
PHONE BOOK
But since the events took place on PEI, I would have to get a PEI lawyer
Oh, I see...
So a few weeks later, I flew to PEI
It would be a chance to visit my best friend too

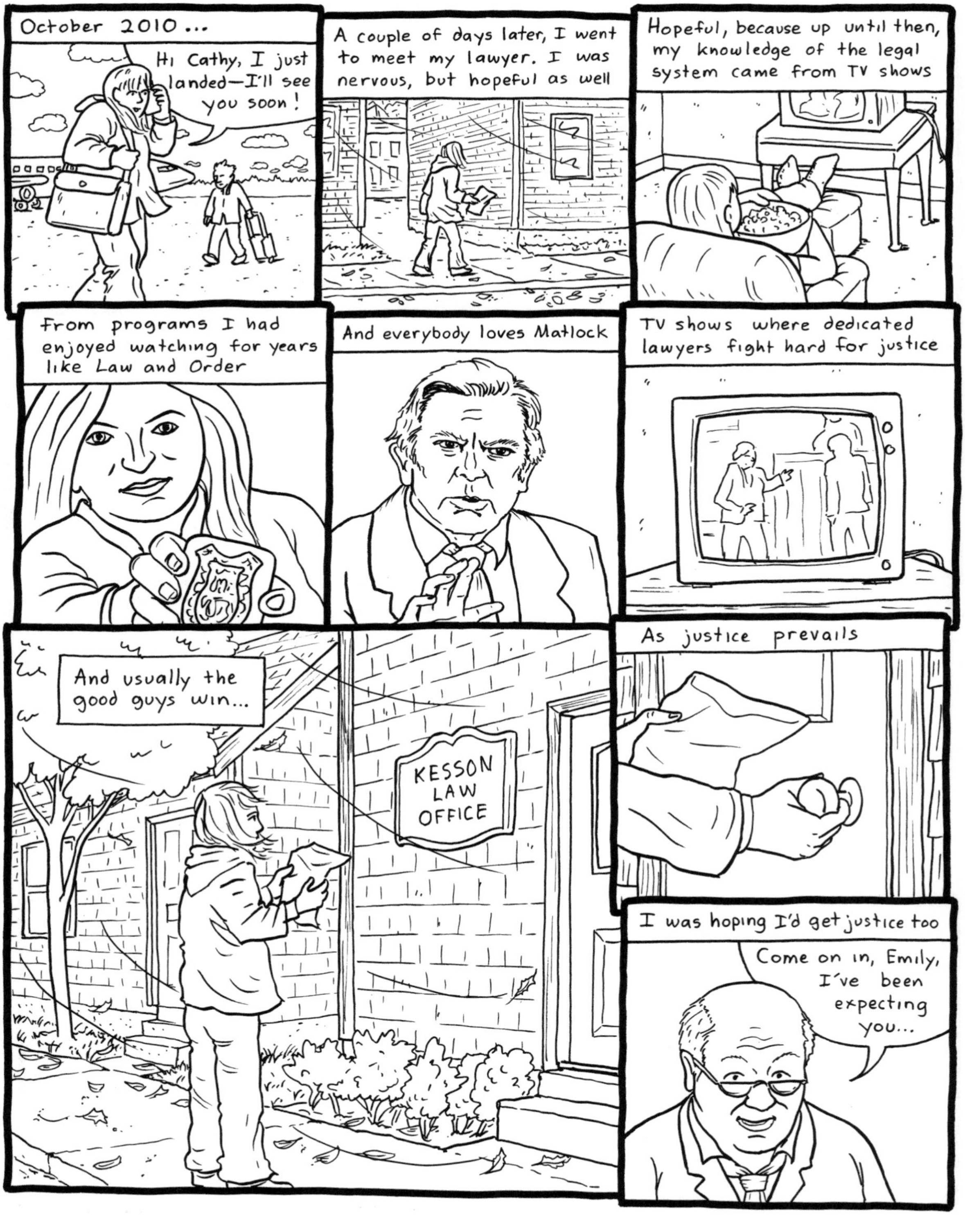
October 2010...
Hi Cathy, I just landed—I'll see you soon!
A couple of days later, I went to meet my lawyer. I was nervous, but hopeful as well
Hopeful, because up until then, my knowledge of the legal system came from TV shows
From programs I had enjoyed watching for years like Law and Order
And everybody loves Matlock
TV shows where dedicated lawyers fight hard for justice
And usually the good guys win...
KESSON LAW OFFICE
As justice prevails
I was hoping I'd get justice too
Come on in, Emily, I've been expecting you...

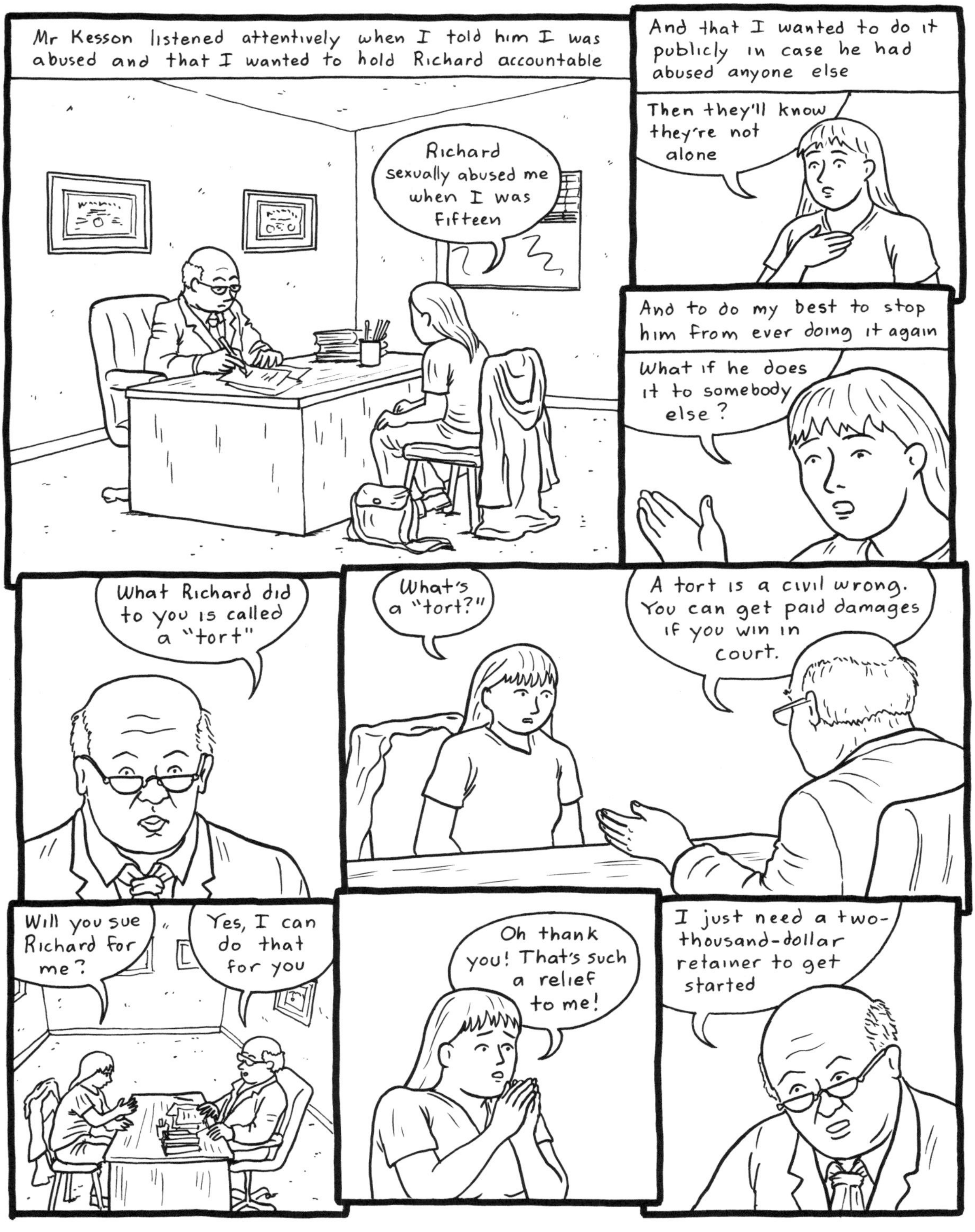
Mr Kesson listened attentively when I told him I was abused and that I wanted to hold Richard accountable
Richard sexually abused me when I was Fifteen
And that I wanted to do it publicly in case he had abused anyone else
Then they'll know they're not alone
And to do my best to stop him from ever doing it again
What if he does it to somebody else?
What Richard did to you is called a "tort"
What's a "tort?"
A tort is a civil wrong. You can get paid damages if you win in court.
Will you sue Richard for me?
Yes, I can do that for you
Oh thank you! That's such a relief to me!
I just need a two-thousand-dollar retainer to get started

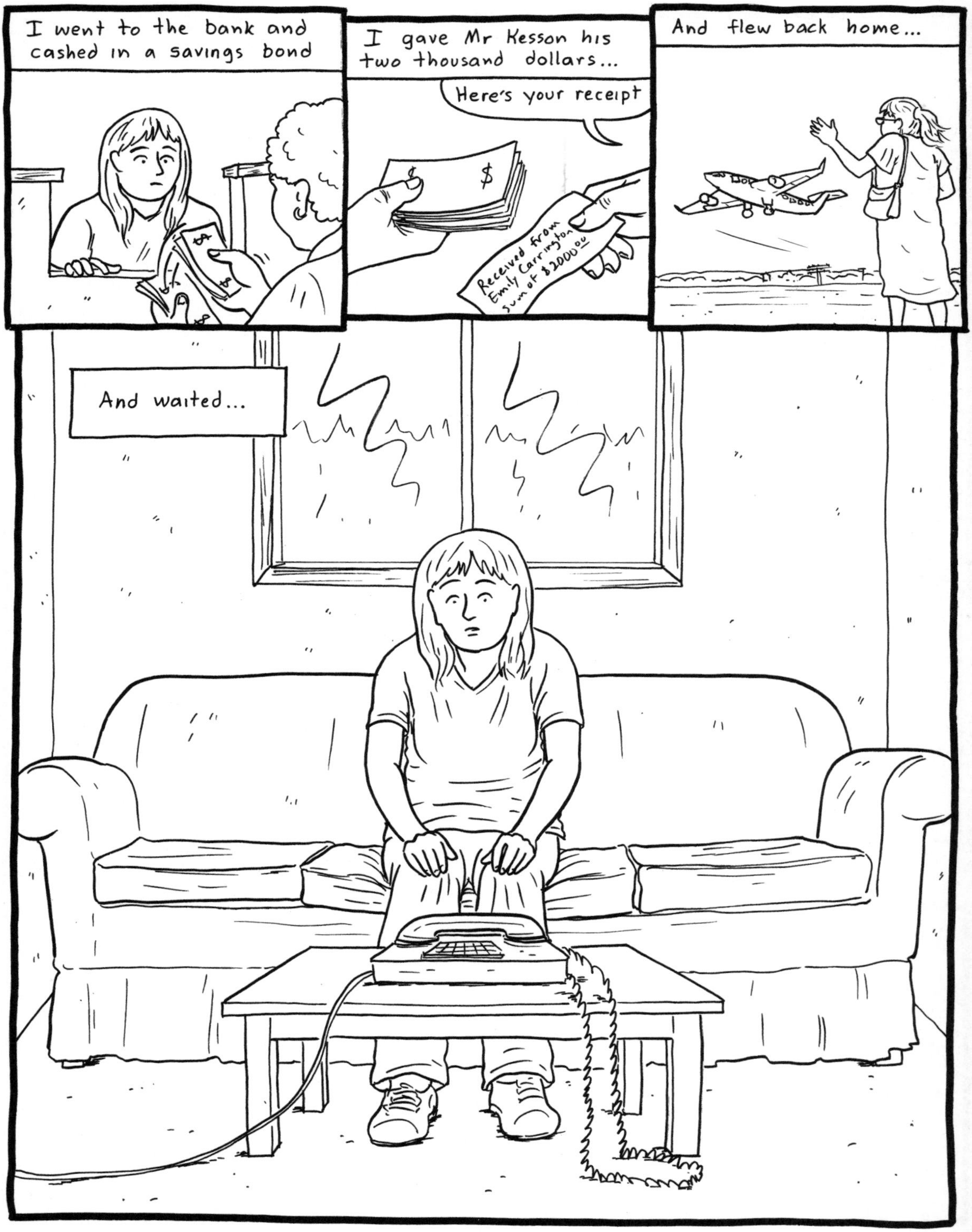
I went to the bank and cashed in a savings bond
I gave Mr Kesson his two thousand dollars...
Here's your receipt
Received from Emily Carrington sum of $2000.00
And flew back home...
And waited...

A couple of years ago when I first thought about drawing this book

I considered starting with an image of me in an airplane

Flying above the clouds

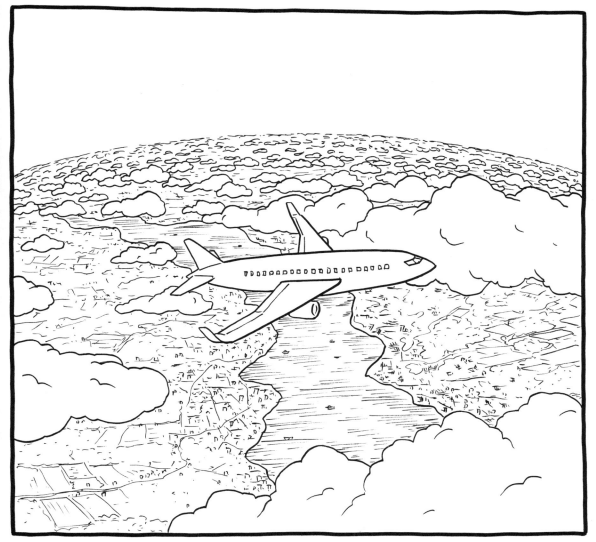

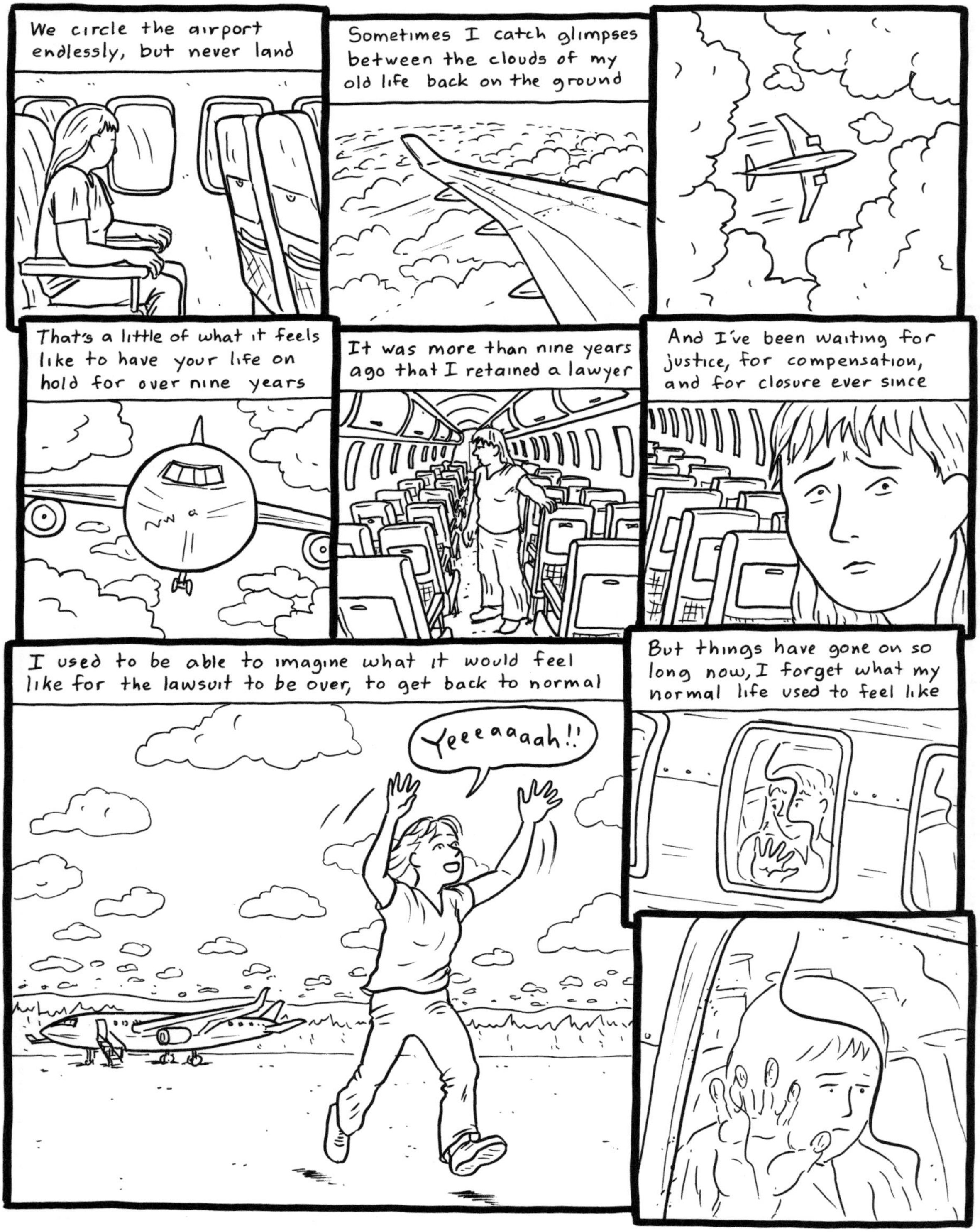

We circle the airport endlessly, but never land
Sometimes I catch glimpses between the clouds of my old life back on the ground
That's a little of what it feels like to have your life on hold for over nine years
It was more than nine years ago that I retained a lawyer
And I've been waiting for justice, for compensation, and for closure ever since
I used to be able to imagine what it would feel like for the lawsuit to be over, to get back to normal
Yeeeaaaaah!!
But things have gone on so long now, I forget what my normal life used to feel like

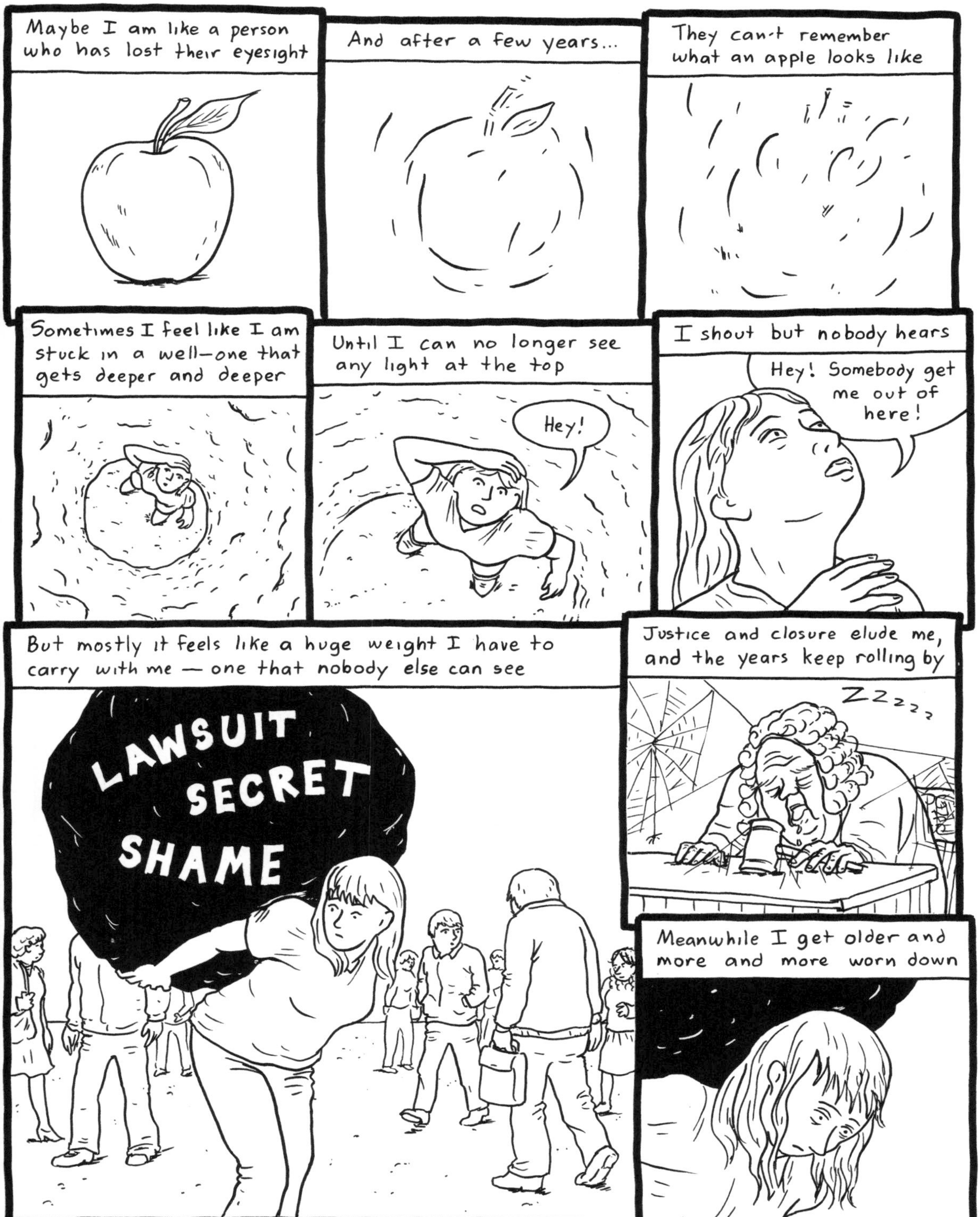
Maybe I am like a person who has lost their eyesight
And after a few years...
They can't remember what an apple looks like
Sometimes I feel like I am stuck in a well—one that gets deeper and deeper
Until I can no longer see any light at the top
Hey!
I shout but nobody hears
Hey! Somebody get me out of here!
But mostly it feels like a huge weight I have to carry with me — one that nobody else can see
LAWSUIT
SECRET
SHAME
Justice and closure elude me, and the years keep rolling by
ZZzzz
Meanwhile I get older and more and more worn down

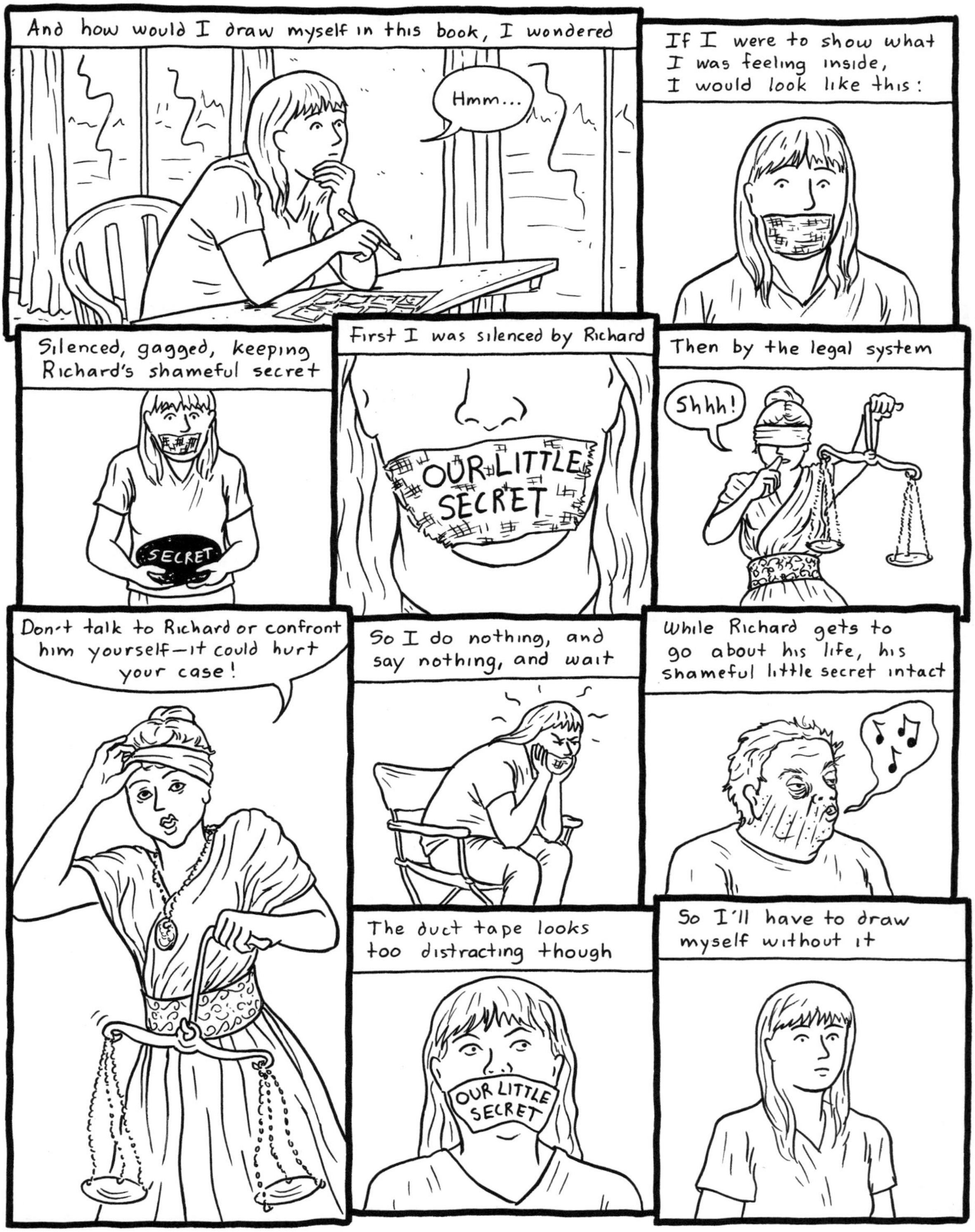

And how would I draw myself in this book, I wondered
Hmm...
If I were to show what I was feeling inside, I would look like this:
Silenced, gagged, keeping Richard's shameful secret
SECRET
First I was silenced by Richard
OUR LITTLE SECRET
Then by the legal system
Shhh!
Don't talk to Richard or confront him yourself—it could hurt your case!
So I do nothing, and say nothing, and wait
While Richard gets to go about his life, his shameful little secret intact
The duct tape looks too distracting though
OUR LITTLE SECRET
So I'll have to draw myself without it

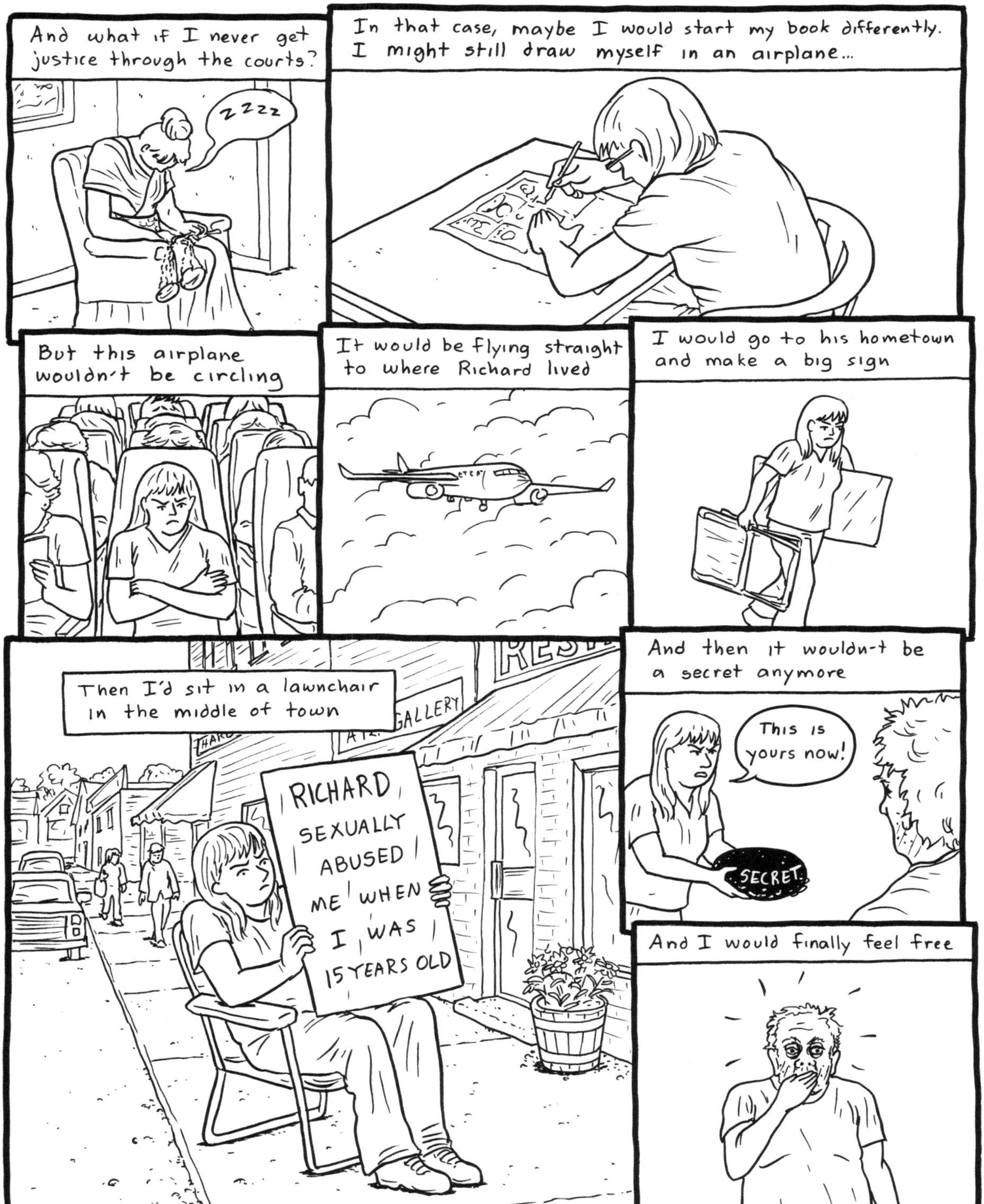
And what if I never get justice through the courts?
ZZZZ
In that case, maybe I would start my book differently. I might still draw myself in an airplane...
But this airplane wouldn't be circling
It would be flying straight to where Richard lived
I would go to his hometown and make a big sign
Then I'd sit in a lawnchair in the middle of town
GALLERY
RICHARD SEXUALLY ABUSED ME WHEN I WAS 15 YEARS OLD
And then it wouldn't be a secret anymore
This is yours now!
SECRET
And I would finally feel free

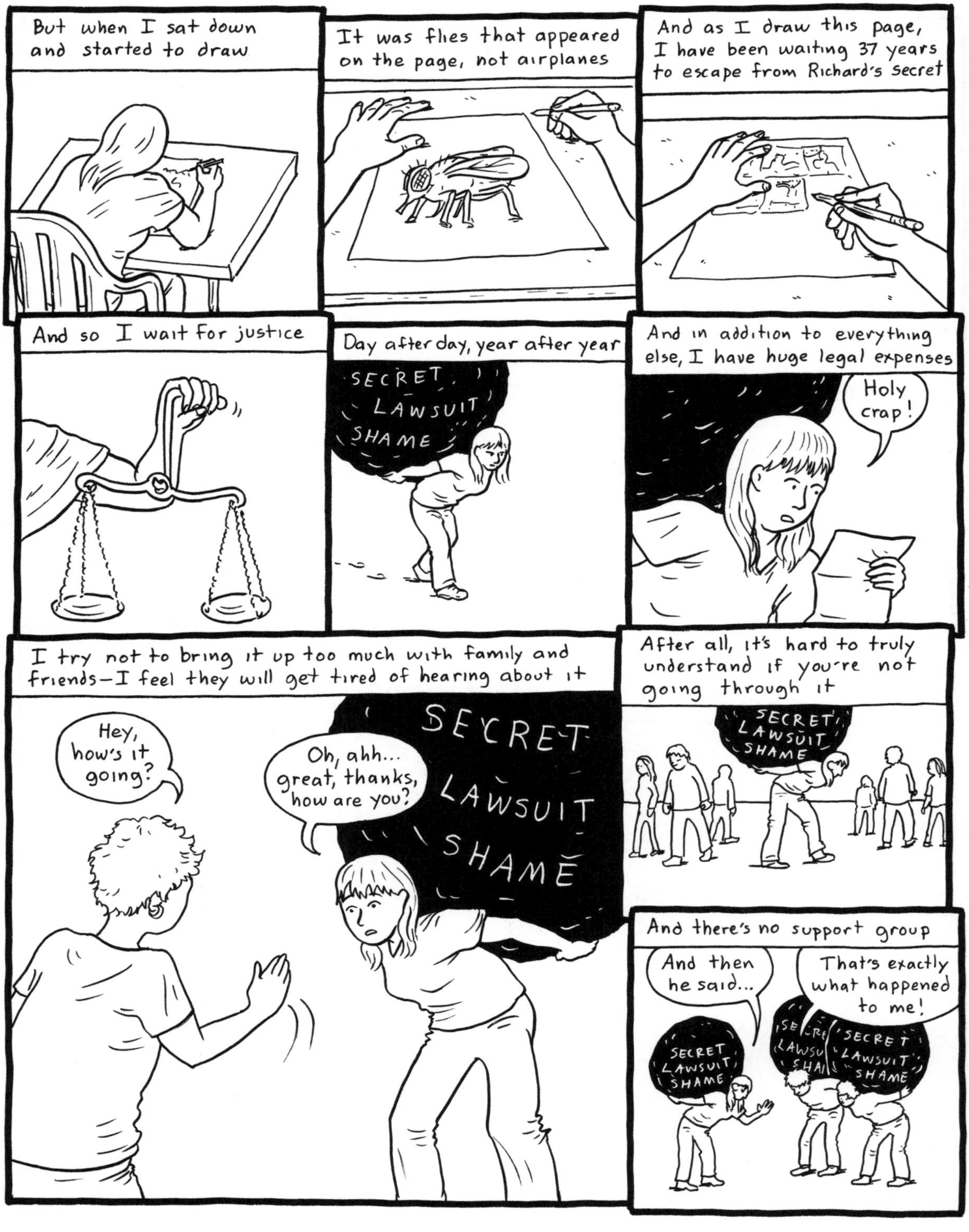
But when I sat down and started to draw
It was flies that appeared on the page, not airplanes
And as I draw this page, I have been waiting 37 years to escape from Richard's secret
And so I wait for justice
Day after day, year after year
SECRET
LAWSUIT
SHAME
And in addition to everything else, I have huge legal expenses
Holy crap!
I try not to bring it up too much with family and friends—I feel they will get tired of hearing about it
Hey, how's it going?
Oh, ahh... great, thanks, how are you?
SECRET
LAWSUIT
SHAME
After all, it's hard to truly understand if you're not going through it
SECRET
LAWSUIT
SHAME
And there's no support group
And then he said...
That's exactly what happened to me!
SECRET
LAWSUIT
SHAME
SECRET
LAWSUIT
SHAME

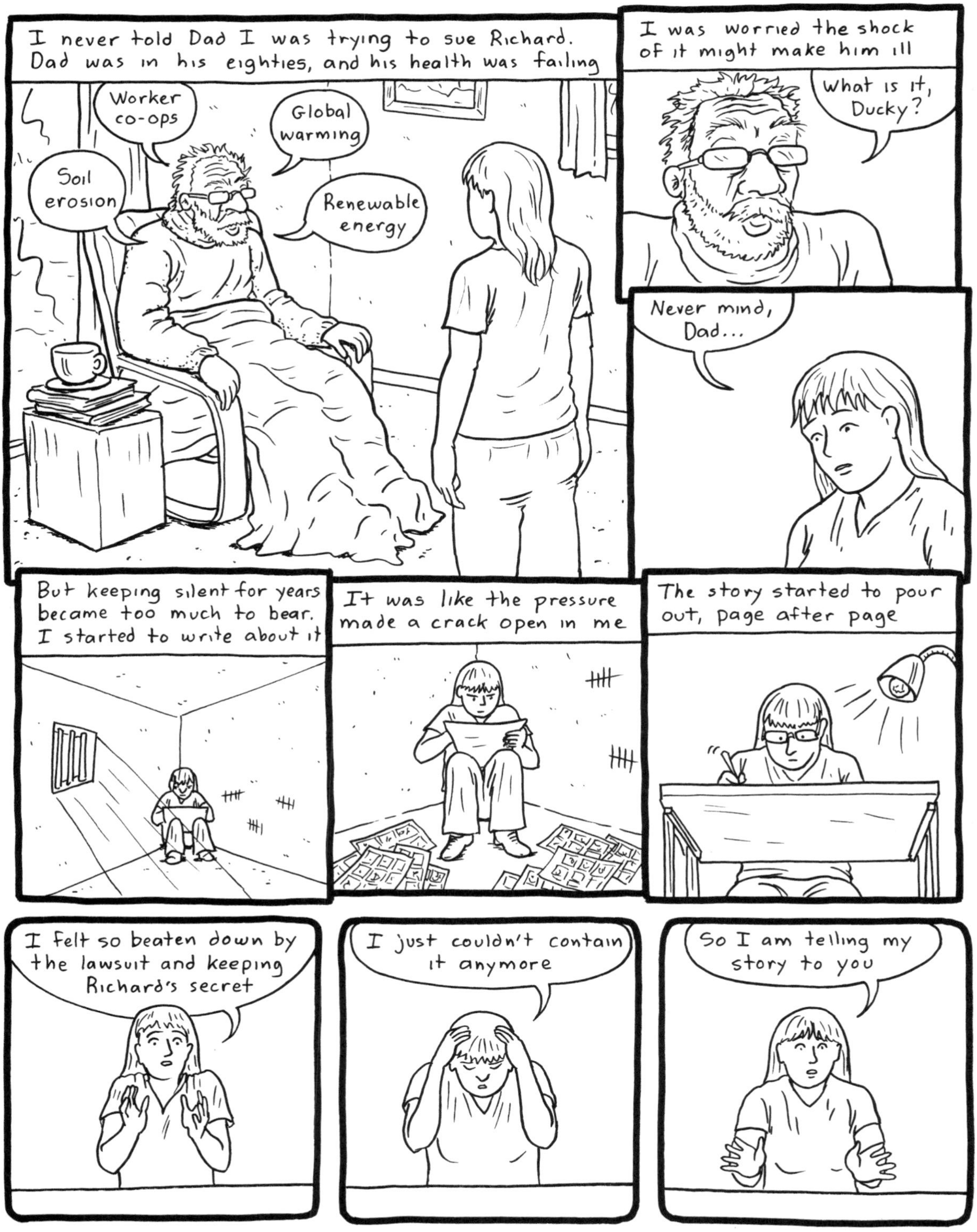
I never told Dad I was trying to sue Richard. Dad was in his eighties, and his health was failing
Worker co-ops
Global warming
Soil erosion
Renewable energy
I was worried the shock of it might make him ill
What is it, Ducky?
Never mind, Dad...
But keeping silent for years became too much to bear. I started to write about it
It was like the pressure made a crack open in me
The story started to pour out, page after page
I felt so beaten down by the lawsuit and keeping Richard's secret
I just couldn't contain it anymore
So I am telling my story to you

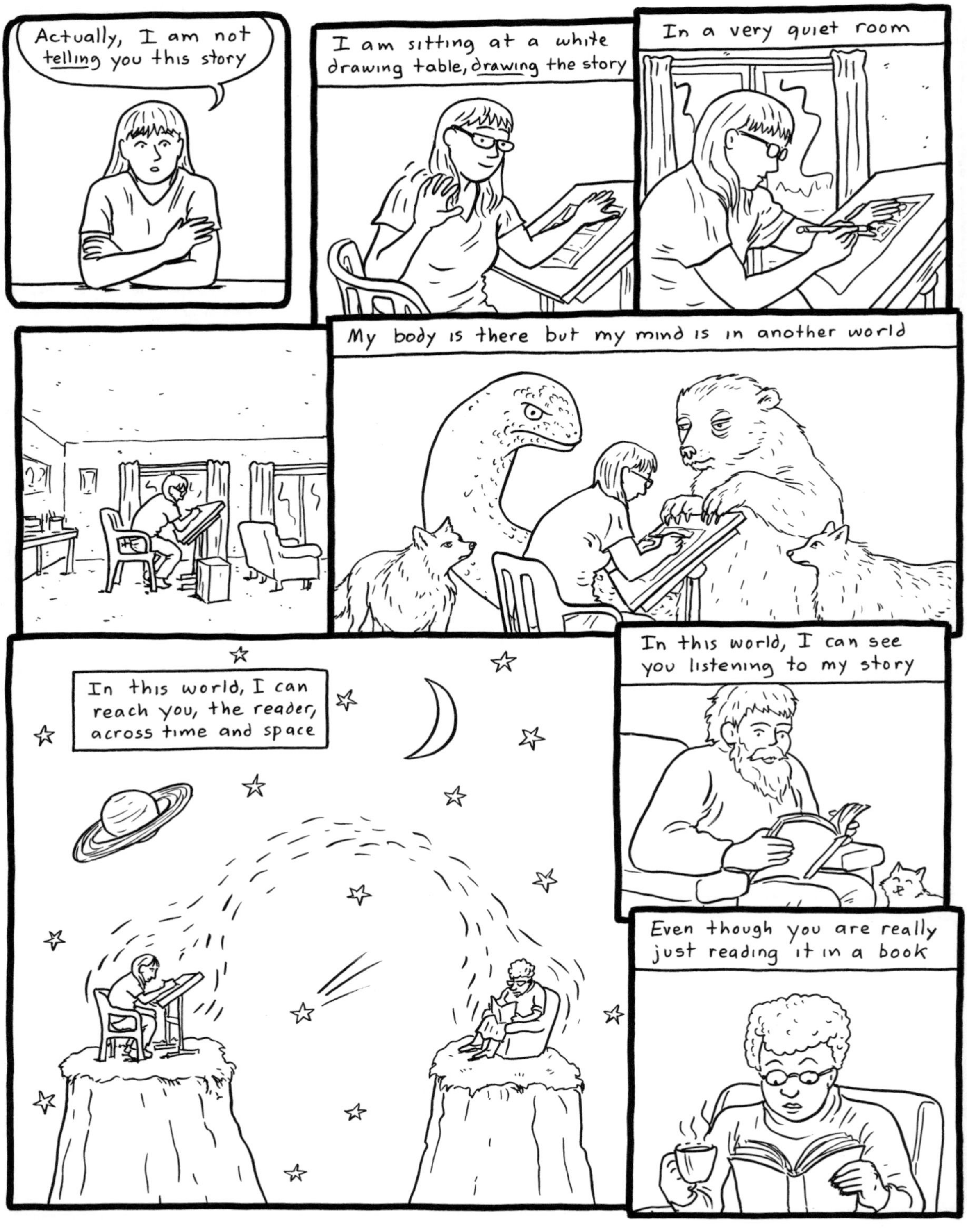
Actually, I am not telling you this story
I am sitting at a white drawing table, drawing the story
In a very quiet room
My body is there but my mind is in another world
In this world, I can reach you, the reader, across time and space
In this world, I can see you listening to my story
Even though you are really just reading it in a book

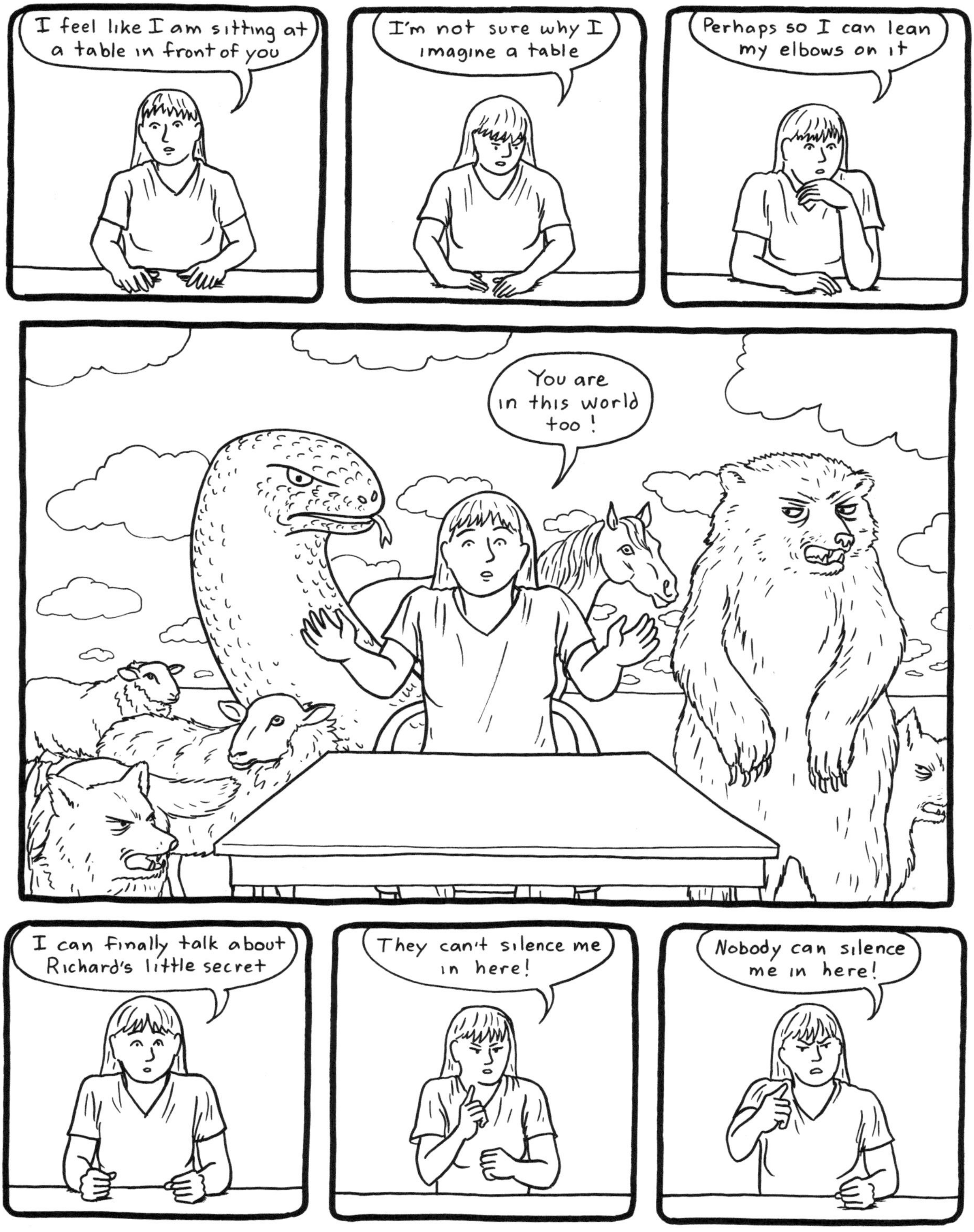
I feel like I am sitting at a table in front of you
I'm not sure why I imagine a table
Perhaps so I can lean my elbows on it
You are in this world too!
I can finally talk about Richard's little secret
They can't silence me in here!
Nobody can silence me in here!

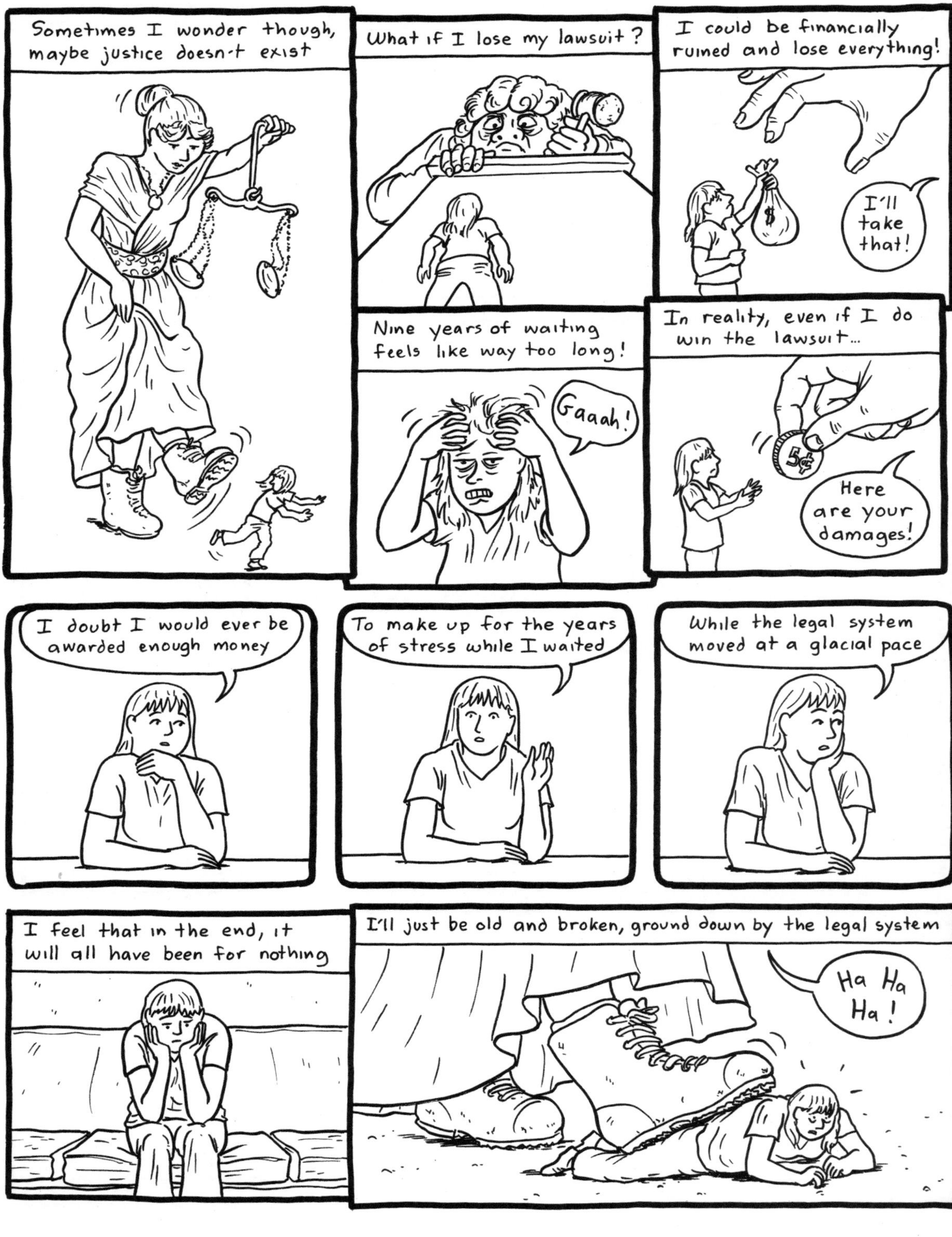

Sometimes I wonder though, maybe justice doesn't exist
What if I lose my lawsuit?
I could be financially ruined and lose everything!
I'll take that!
$
Nine years of waiting feels like way too long!
Gaaah!
In reality, even if I do win the lawsuit...
5¢
Here are your damages!
I doubt I would ever be awarded enough money
To make up for the years of stress while I waited
While the legal system moved at a glacial pace
I feel that in the end, it will all have been for nothing
I'll just be old and broken, ground down by the legal system
Ha Ha Ha!

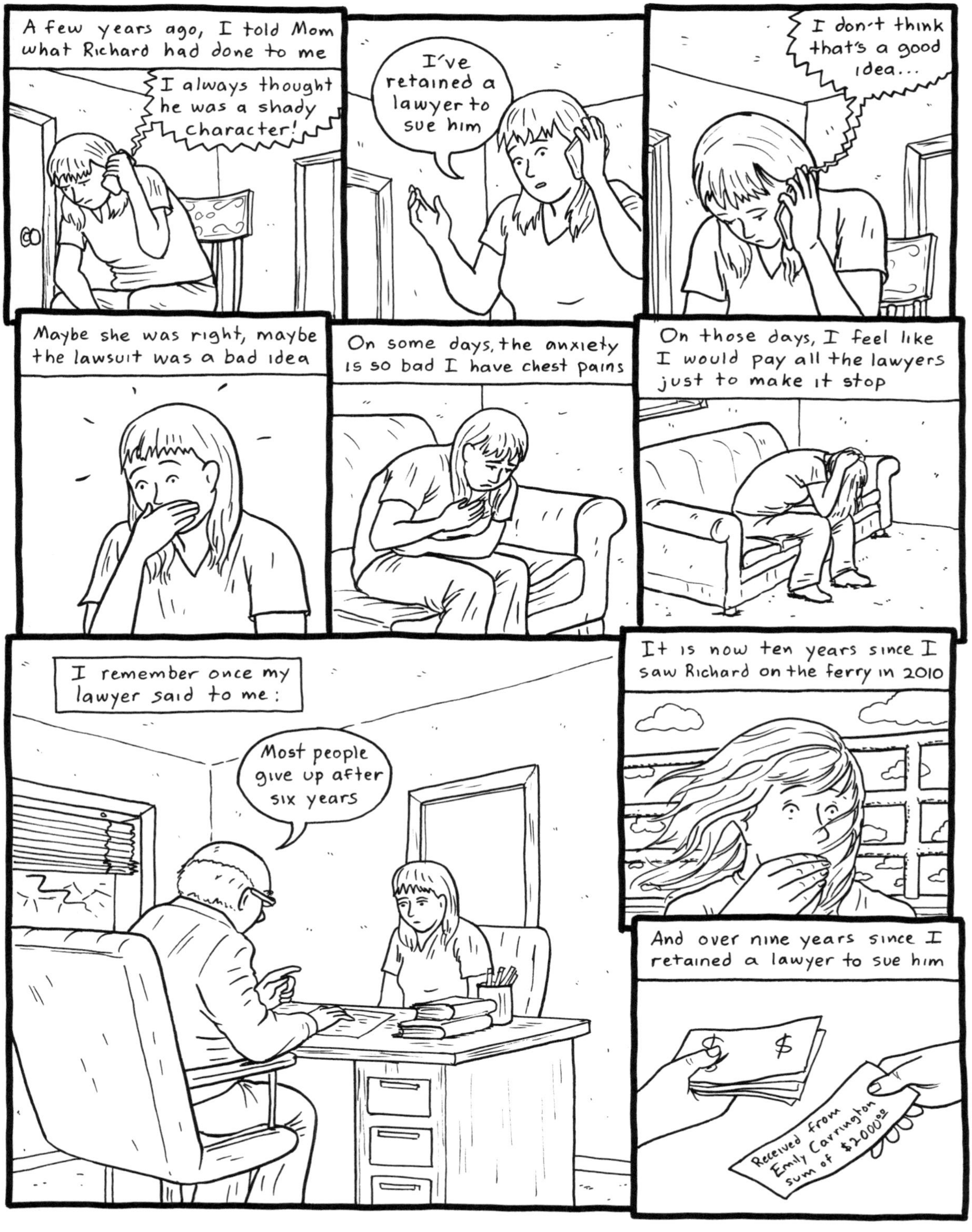
A few years ago, I told Mom what Richard had done to me
I always thought he was a shady character!
I've retained a lawyer to sue him
I don't think that's a good idea...
Maybe she was right, maybe the lawsuit was a bad idea
On some days, the anxiety is so bad I have chest pains
On those days, I feel like I would pay all the lawyers just to make it stop
I remember once my lawyer said to me:
Most people give up after six years
It is now ten years since I saw Richard on the ferry in 2010
And over nine years since I retained a lawyer to sue him
Received from Emily Carrington sum of $2000.00

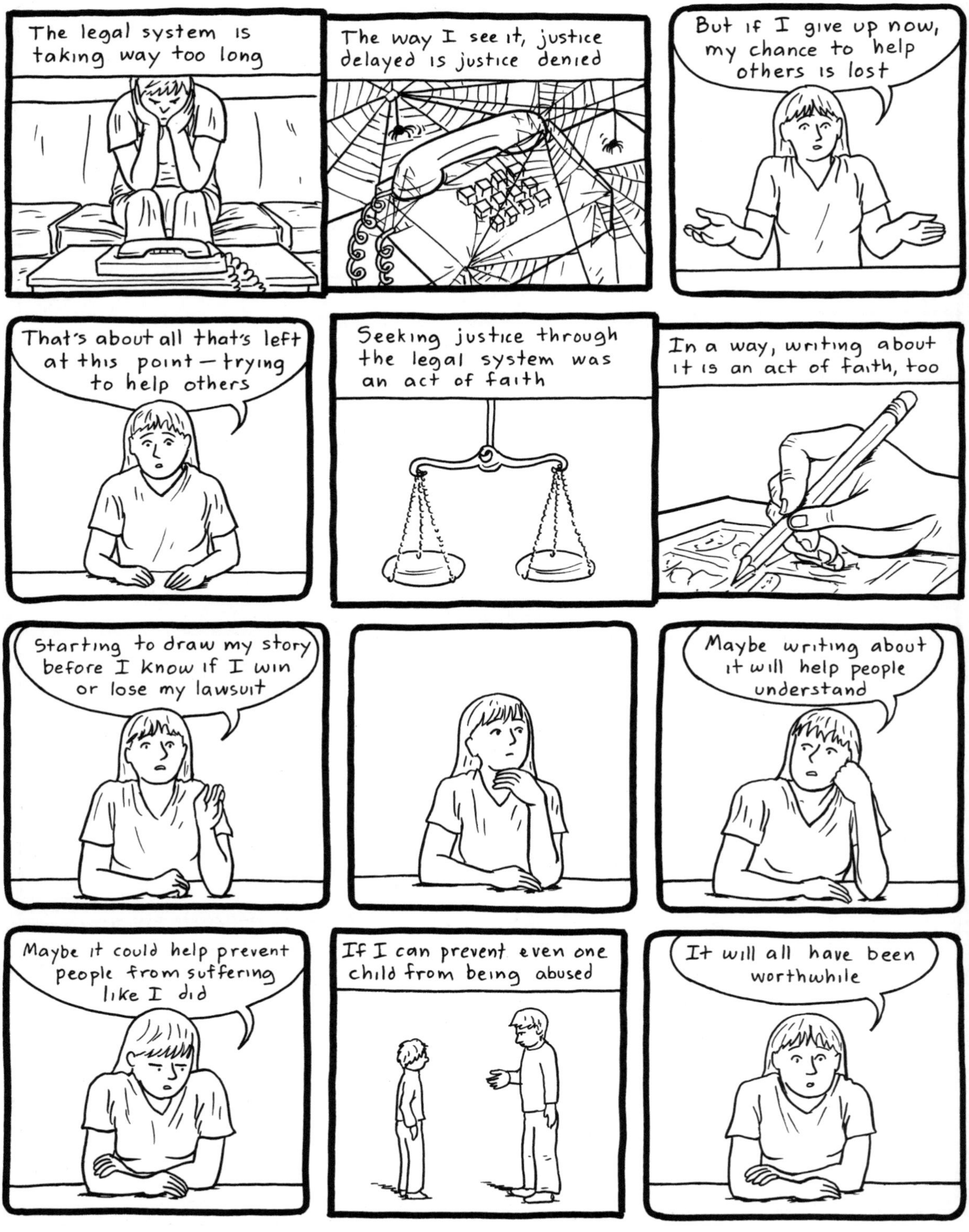
The legal system is taking way too long
The way I see it, justice delayed is justice denied
But if I give up now, my chance to help others is lost
That's about all that's left at this point — trying to help others
Seeking justice through the legal system was an act of faith
In a way, writing about it is an act of faith, too
Starting to draw my story before I know if I win or lose my lawsuit
Maybe writing about it will help people understand
Maybe it could help prevent people from suffering like I did
If I can prevent even one child from being abused
It will all have been worthwhile

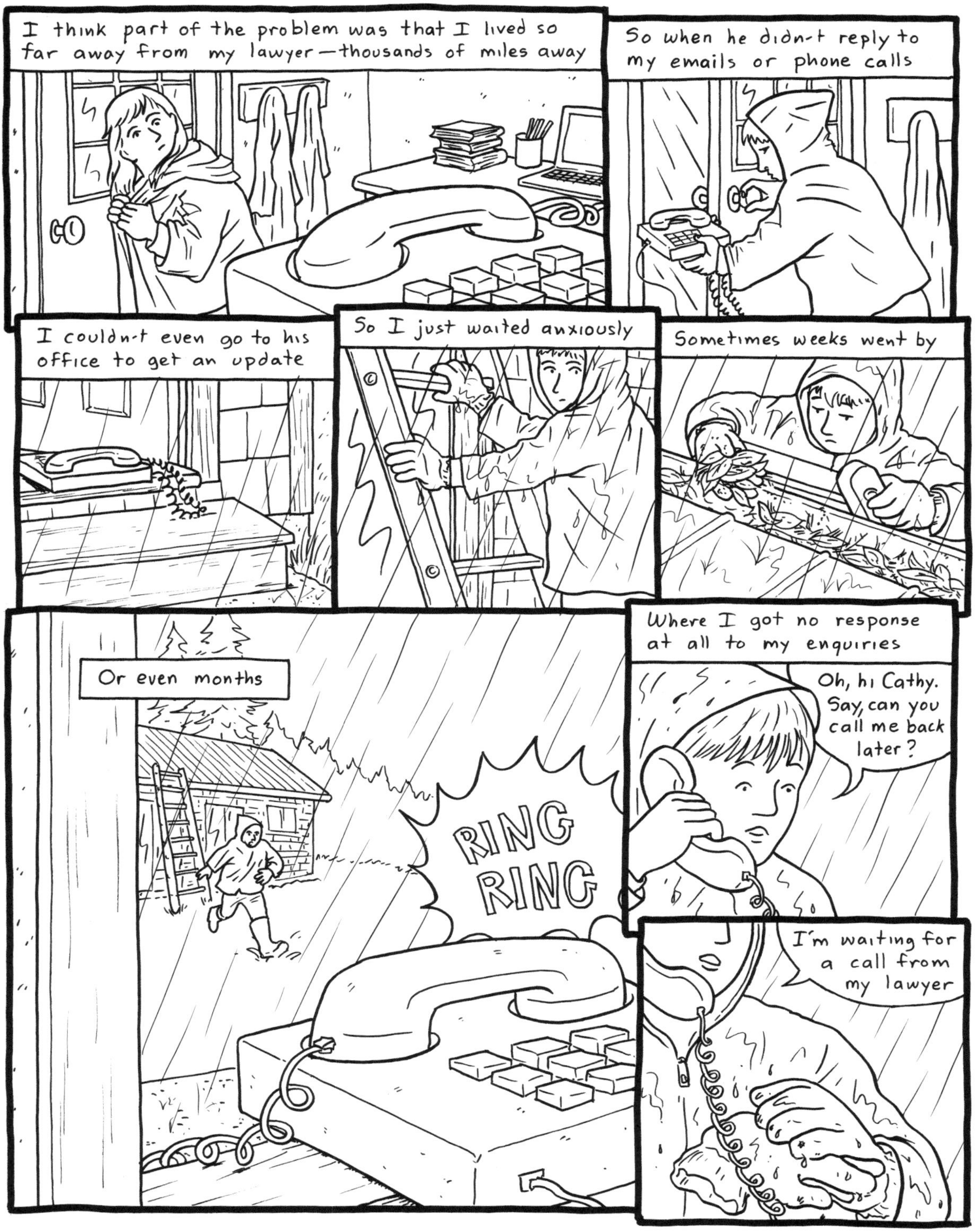
I think part of the problem was that I lived so far away from my lawyer—thousands of miles away
So when he didn't reply to my emails or phone calls
I couldn't even go to his office to get an update
So I just waited anxiously
Sometimes weeks went by
Or even months
RING RING
Where I got no response at all to my enquiries
Oh, hi Cathy. Say, can you call me back later?
I'm waiting for a call from my lawyer

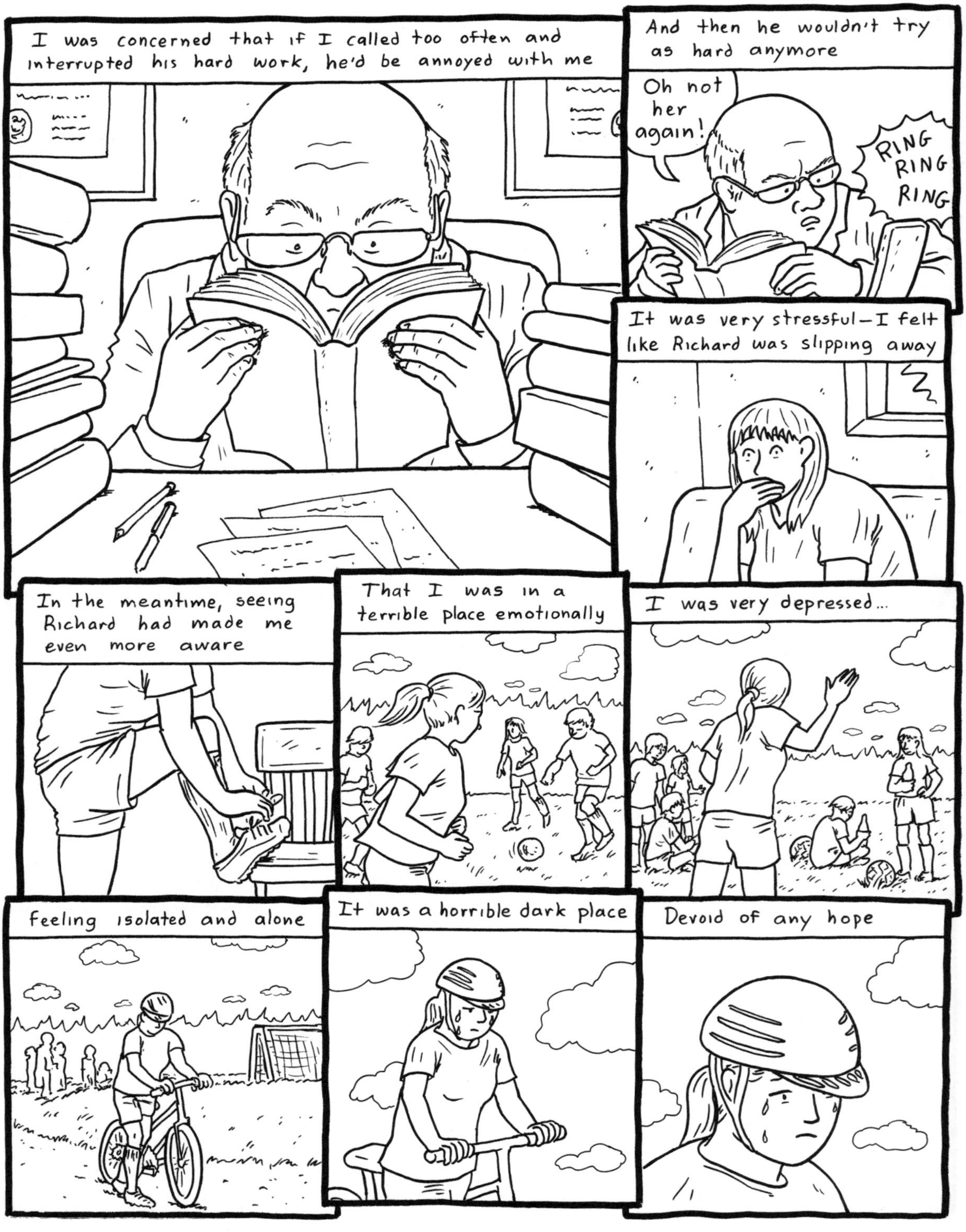
I was concerned that if I called too often and interrupted his hard work, he'd be annoyed with me
And then he wouldn't try as hard anymore
Oh not her again!
RING RING RING
It was very stressful—I felt like Richard was slipping away
In the meantime, seeing Richard had made me even more aware
That I was in a terrible place emotionally
I was very depressed...
Feeling isolated and alone
It was a horrible dark place
Devoid of any hope

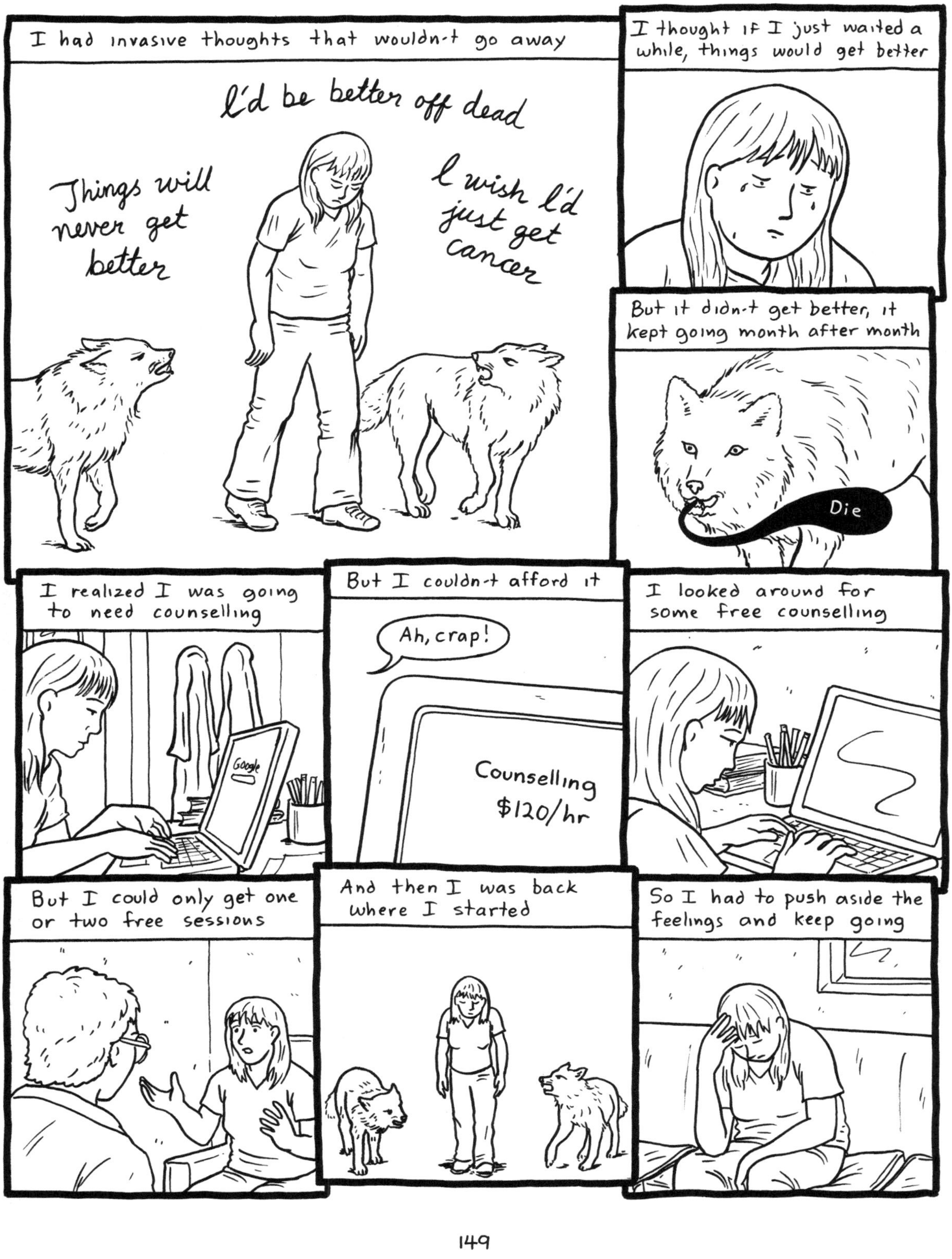
I had invasive thoughts that wouldn-t go away
I'd be better off dead
Things will never get better
I wish I'd just get cancer
I thought if I just waited a while, things would get better
But it didn-t get better, it kept going month after month
Die
I realized I was going to need counselling
Google
But I couldn-t afford it
Ah, crap!
Counselling $120/hr
I looked around for some free counselling
But I could only get one or two free sessions
And then I was back where I started
So I had to push aside the feelings and keep going

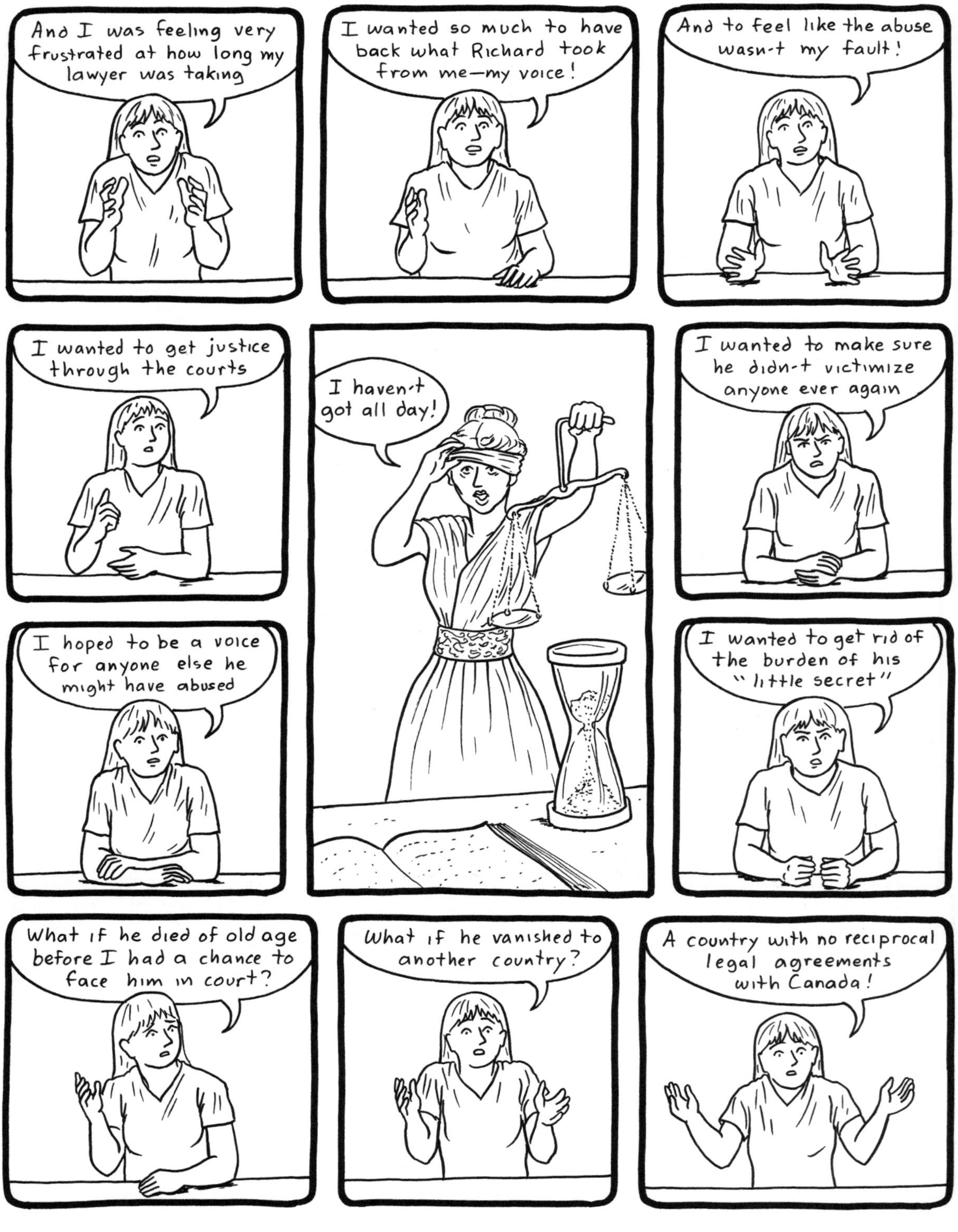
And I was feeling very frustrated at how long my lawyer was taking
I wanted so much to have back what Richard took from me—my voice!
And to feel like the abuse wasn't my fault!
I wanted to get justice through the courts
I haven't got all day!
I wanted to make sure he didn't victimize anyone ever again
I hoped to be a voice for anyone else he might have abused
I wanted to get rid of the burden of his "little secret"
What if he died of old age before I had a chance to face him in court?
What if he vanished to another country?
A country with no reciprocal legal agreements with Canada!

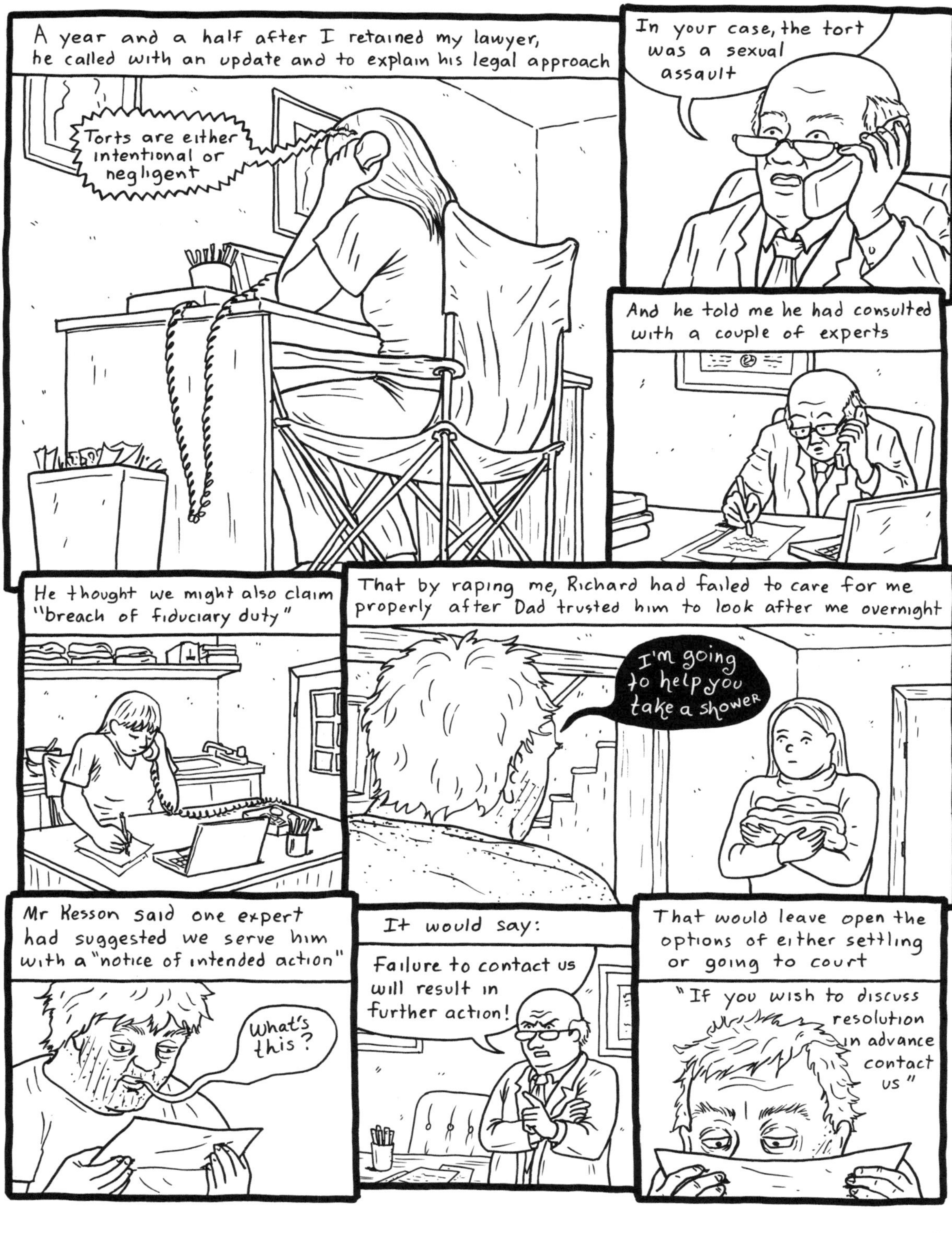

A year and a half after I retained my lawyer, he called with an update and to explain his legal approach
Torts are either intentional or negligent
In your case, the tort was a sexual assault
And he told me he had consulted with a couple of experts
He thought we might also claim "breach of fiduciary duty"
That by raping me, Richard had failed to care for me properly after Dad trusted him to look after me overnight
I'm going to help you take a shower
Mr Kesson said one expert had suggested we serve him with a "notice of intended action"
What's this?
It would say:
Failure to contact us will result in further action!
That would leave open the options of either settling or going to court
"If you wish to discuss resolution in advance contact us"

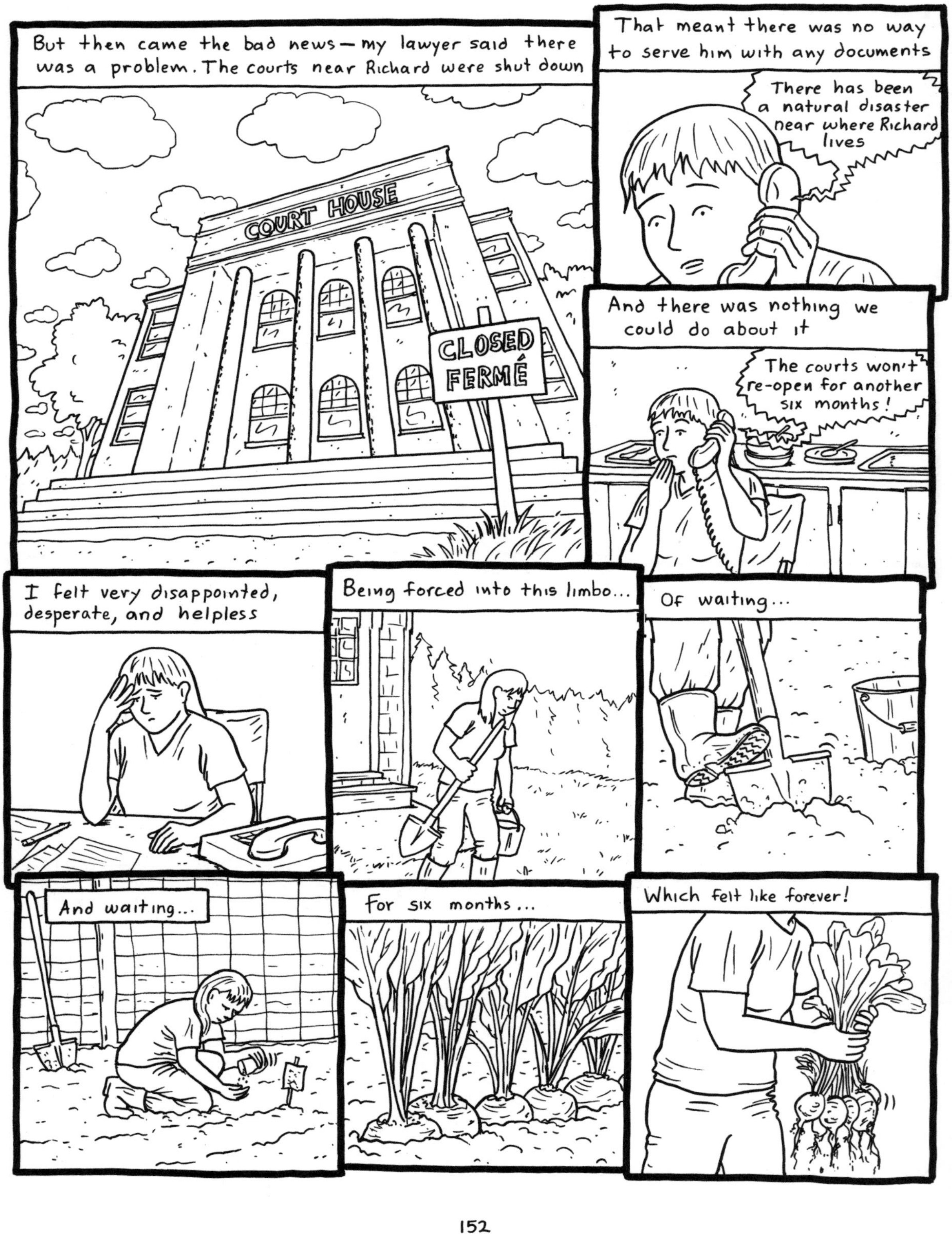
But then came the bad news—my lawyer said there was a problem. The courts near Richard were shut down
COURT HOUSE
CLOSED
FERMÉ
That meant there was no way to serve him with any documents
There has been a natural disaster near where Richard lives
And there was nothing we could do about it
The courts won't re-open for another six months!
I felt very disappointed, desperate, and helpless
Being forced into this limbo...
Of waiting...
And waiting...
For six months...
Which felt like forever!

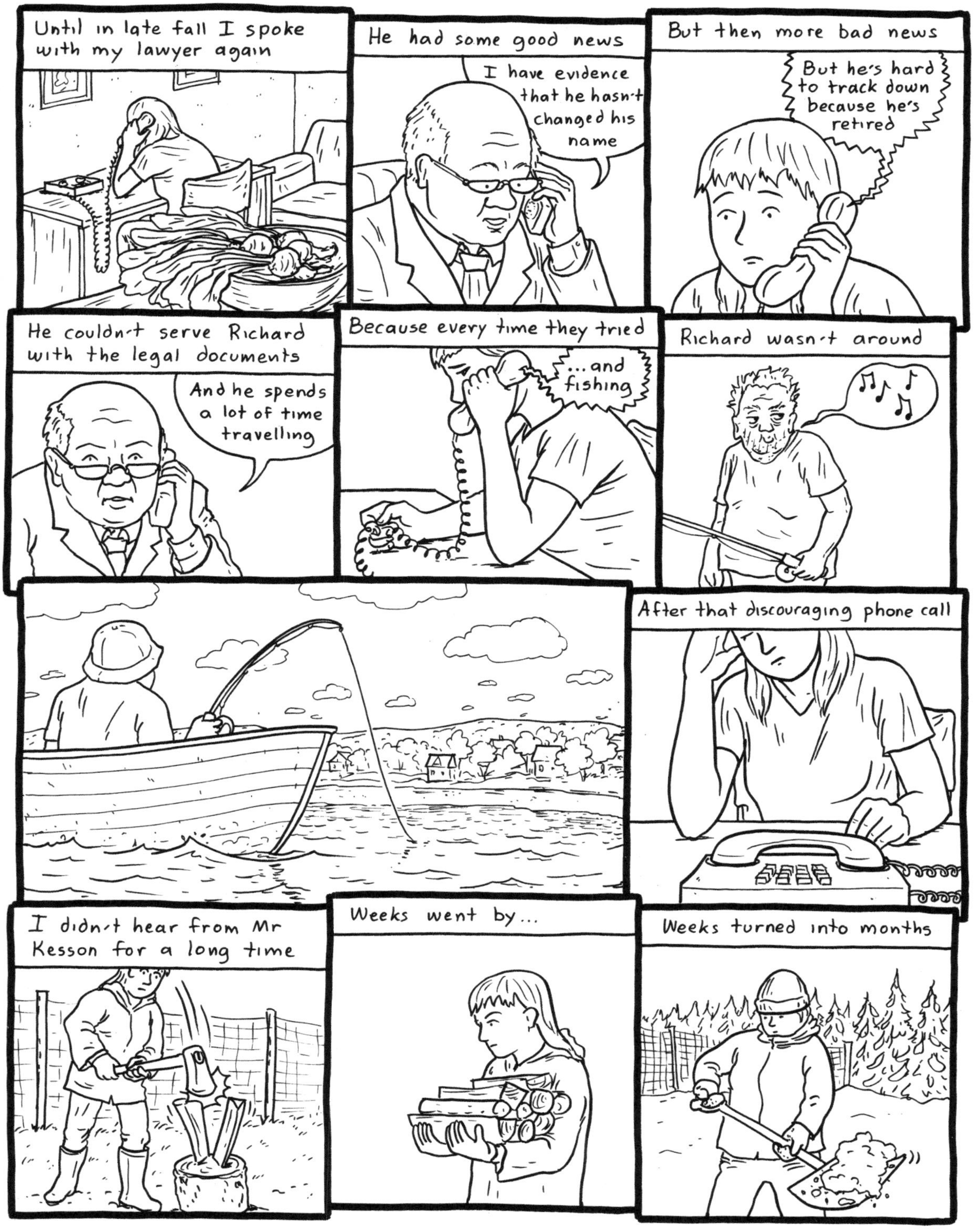
Until in late fall I spoke with my lawyer again
He had some good news
I have evidence that he hasn't changed his name
But then more bad news
But he's hard to track down because he's retired
He couldn't serve Richard with the legal documents
And he spends a lot of time travelling
Because every time they tried
...and fishing
Richard wasn't around
After that discouraging phone call
I didn't hear from Mr Kesson for a long time
Weeks went by...
Weeks turned into months

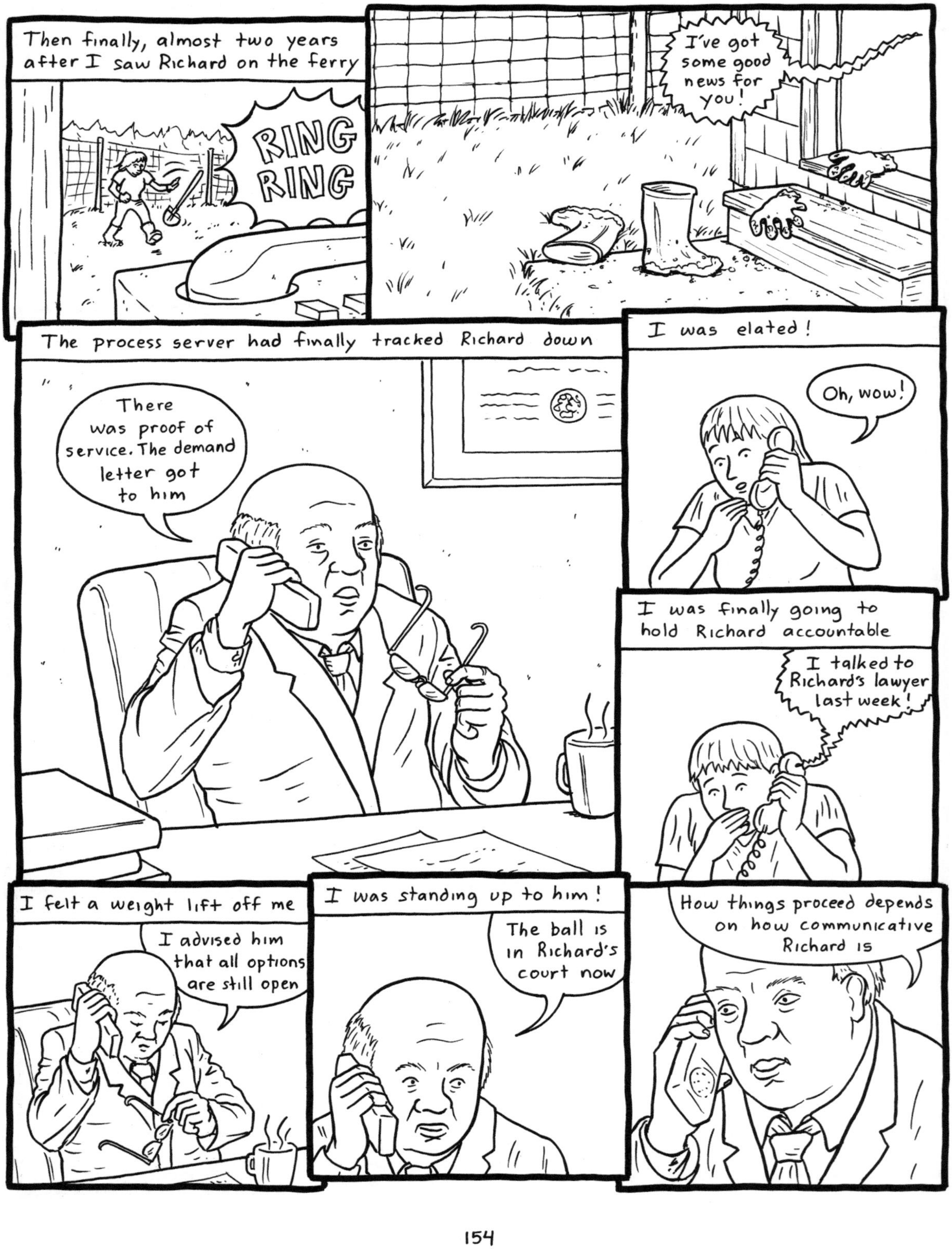
Then finally, almost two years after I saw Richard on the ferry
RING RING
I've got some good news for you!
The process server had finally tracked Richard down
There was proof of service. The demand letter got to him
I was elated!
Oh, wow!
I was finally going to hold Richard accountable
I talked to Richard's lawyer last week!
I felt a weight lift off me
I advised him that all options are still open
I was standing up to him!
The ball is in Richard's court now
How things proceed depends on how communicative Richard is

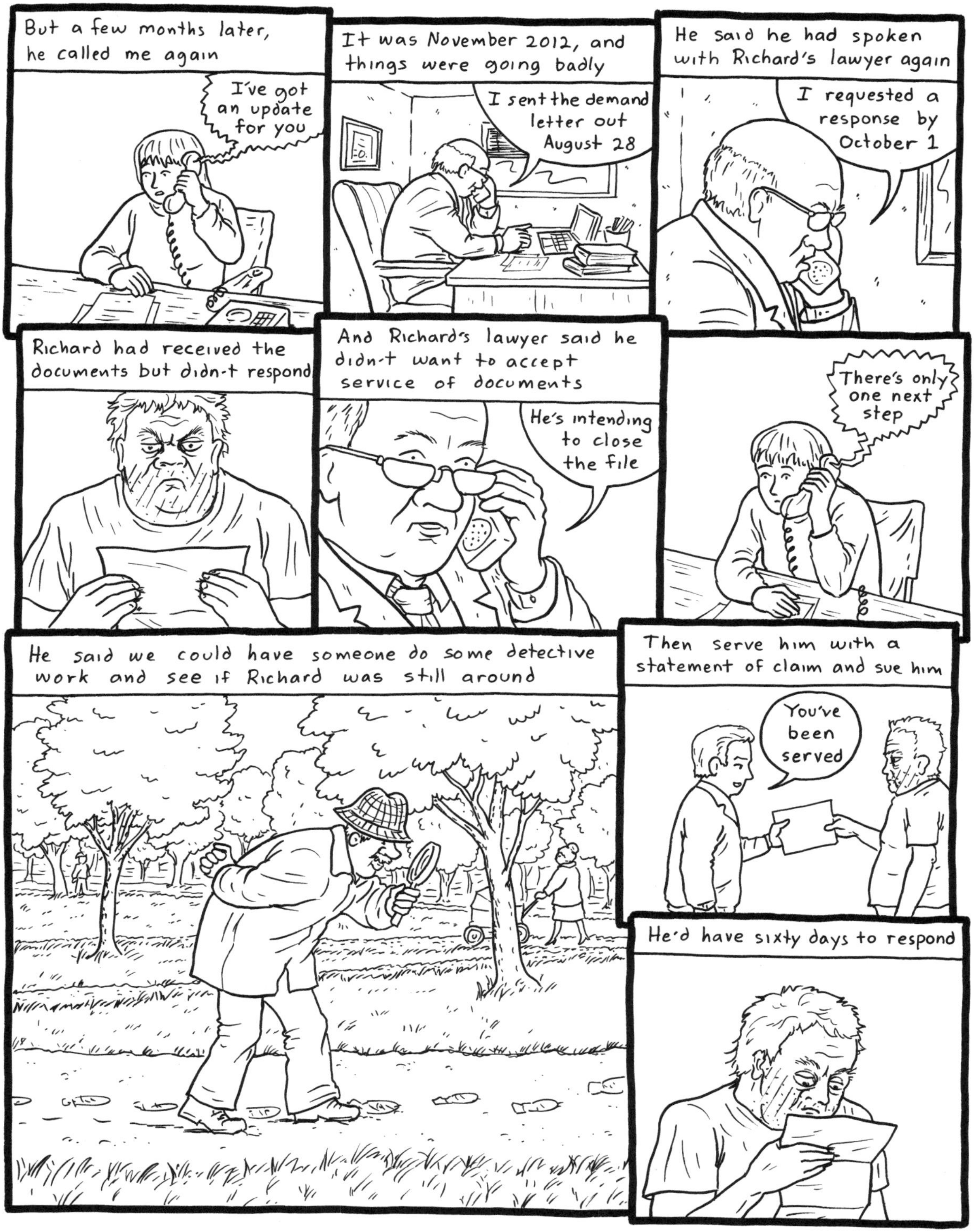
But a few months later, he called me again
I've got an update for you
It was November 2012, and things were going badly
I sent the demand letter out August 28
He said he had spoken with Richard's lawyer again
I requested a response by October 1
Richard had received the documents but didn't respond
And Richard's lawyer said he didn't want to accept service of documents
He's intending to close the file
There's only one next step
He said we could have someone do some detective work and see if Richard was still around
Then serve him with a statement of claim and sue him
You've been served
He'd have sixty days to respond

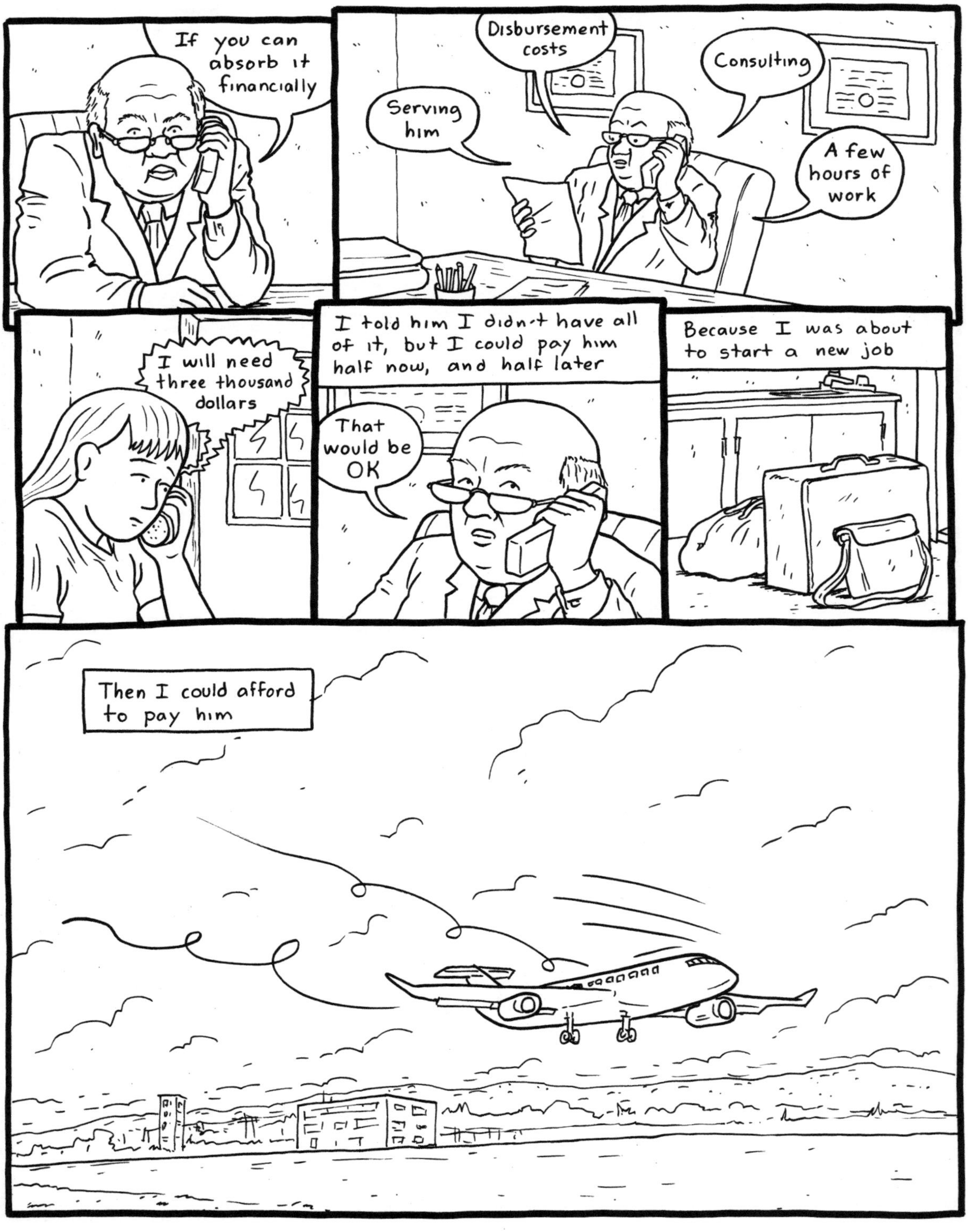
If you can absorb it financially
Disbursement costs
Consulting
Serving him
A few hours of work
I will need three thousand dollars
I told him I didn't have all of it, but I could pay him half now, and half later
That would be OK
Because I was about to start a new job
Then I could afford to pay him

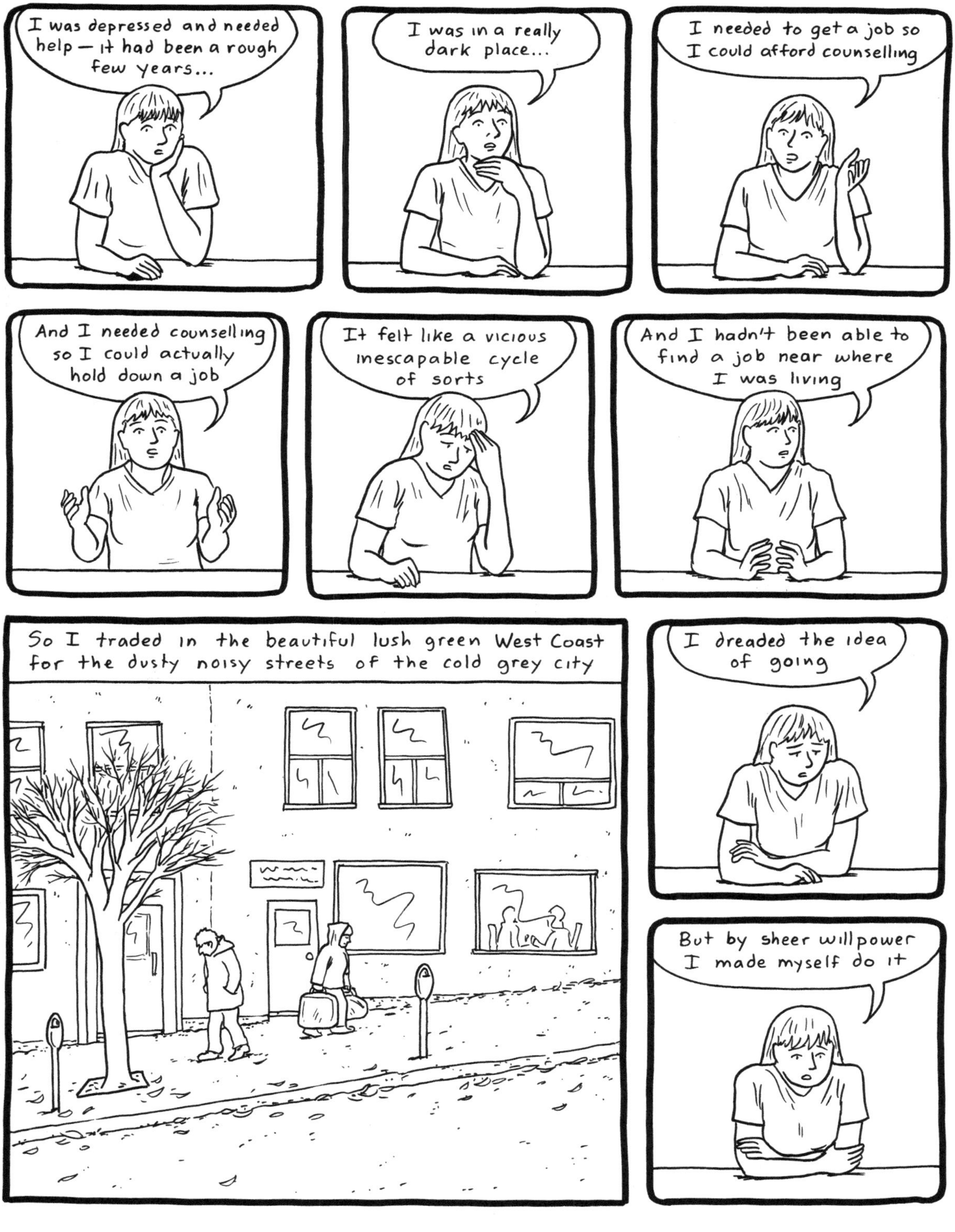
I was depressed and needed help — it had been a rough few years...
I was in a really dark place...
I needed to get a job so I could afford counselling
And I needed counselling so I could actually hold down a job
It felt like a vicious inescapable cycle of sorts
And I hadn't been able to find a job near where I was living
So I traded in the beautiful lush green West Coast for the dusty noisy streets of the cold grey city
I dreaded the idea of going
But by sheer willpower I made myself do it

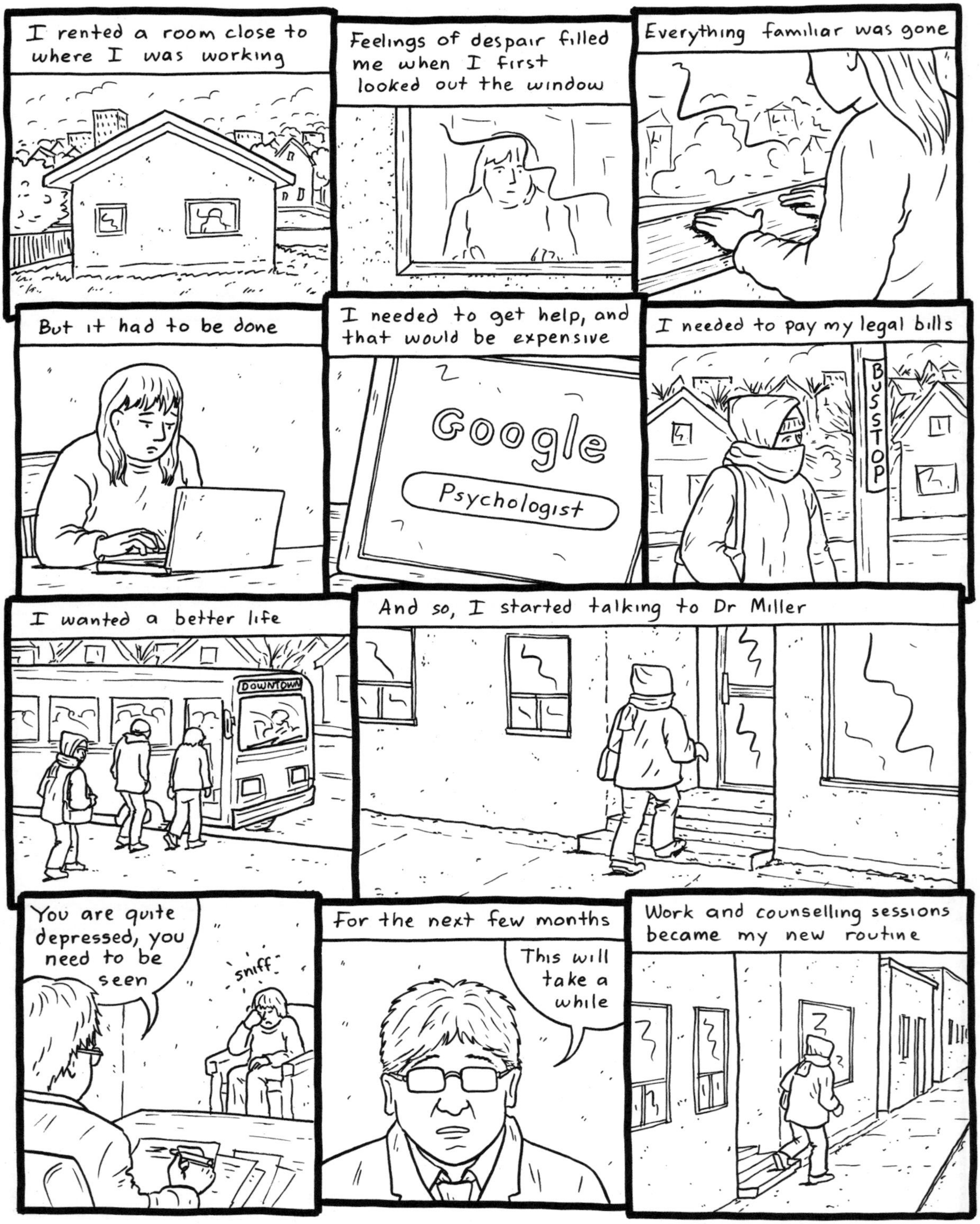
I rented a room close to where I was working
Feelings of despair filled me when I first looked out the window
Everything familiar was gone
But it had to be done
I needed to get help, and that would be expensive
Google
Psychologist
I needed to pay my legal bills
BUSSTOP
I wanted a better life
DOWNTOWN
And so, I started talking to Dr Miller
You are quite depressed, you need to be seen
sniff
For the next few months
This will take a while
Work and counselling sessions became my new routine

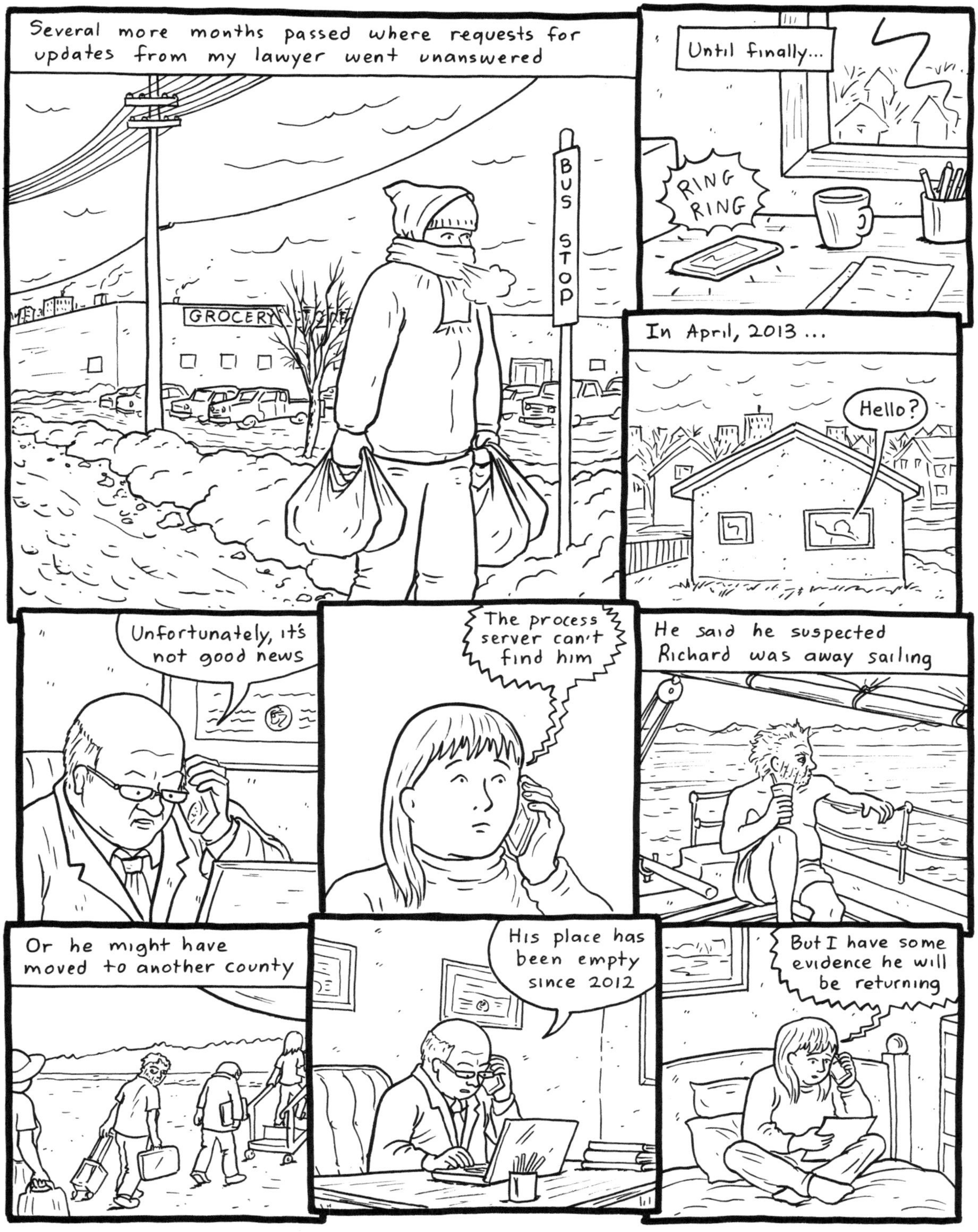
Several more months passed where requests for updates from my lawyer went unanswered
GROCERY
BUS STOP
Until finally...
RING RING
In April, 2013...
Hello?
Unfortunately, it's not good news
The process server can't find him
He said he suspected Richard was away sailing
Or he might have moved to another county
His place has been empty since 2012
But I have some evidence he will be returning

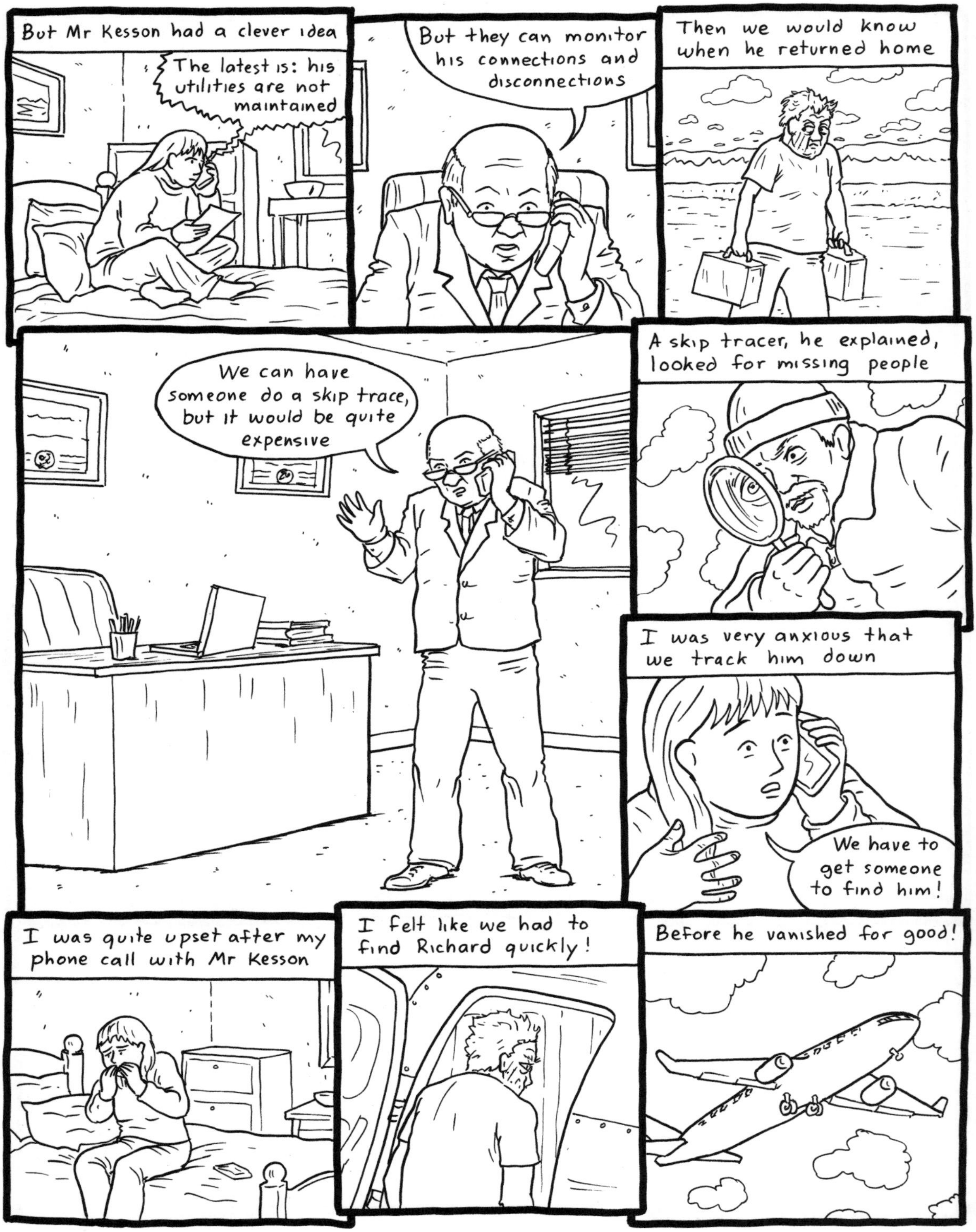
But Mr Kesson had a clever idea
The latest is: his utilities are not maintained
But they can monitor his connections and disconnections
Then we would know when he returned home
We can have someone do a skip trace, but it would be quite expensive
A skip tracer, he explained, looked for missing people
I was very anxious that we track him down
We have to get someone to find him!
I was quite upset after my phone call with Mr Kesson
I felt like we had to find Richard quickly!
Before he vanished for good!

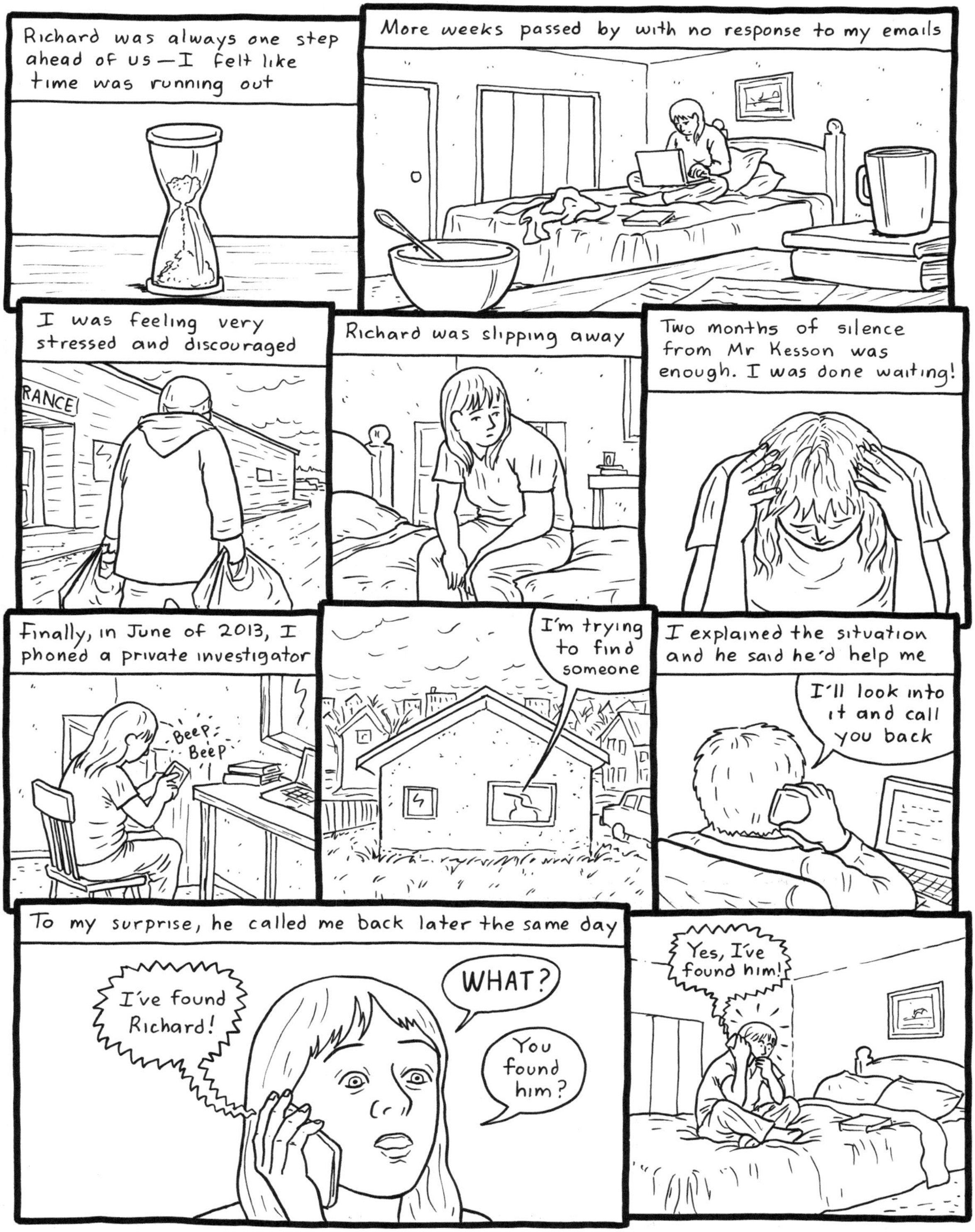
Richard was always one step ahead of us—I felt like time was running out
More weeks passed by with no response to my emails
I was feeling very stressed and discouraged
RANCE
Richard was slipping away
Two months of silence from Mr Kesson was enough. I was done waiting!
Finally, in June of 2013, I phoned a private investigator
Beep Beep
I'm trying to find someone
I explained the situation and he said he'd help me
I'll look into it and call you back
To my surprise, he called me back later the same day
I've found Richard!
WHAT?
You found him?
Yes, I've found him!

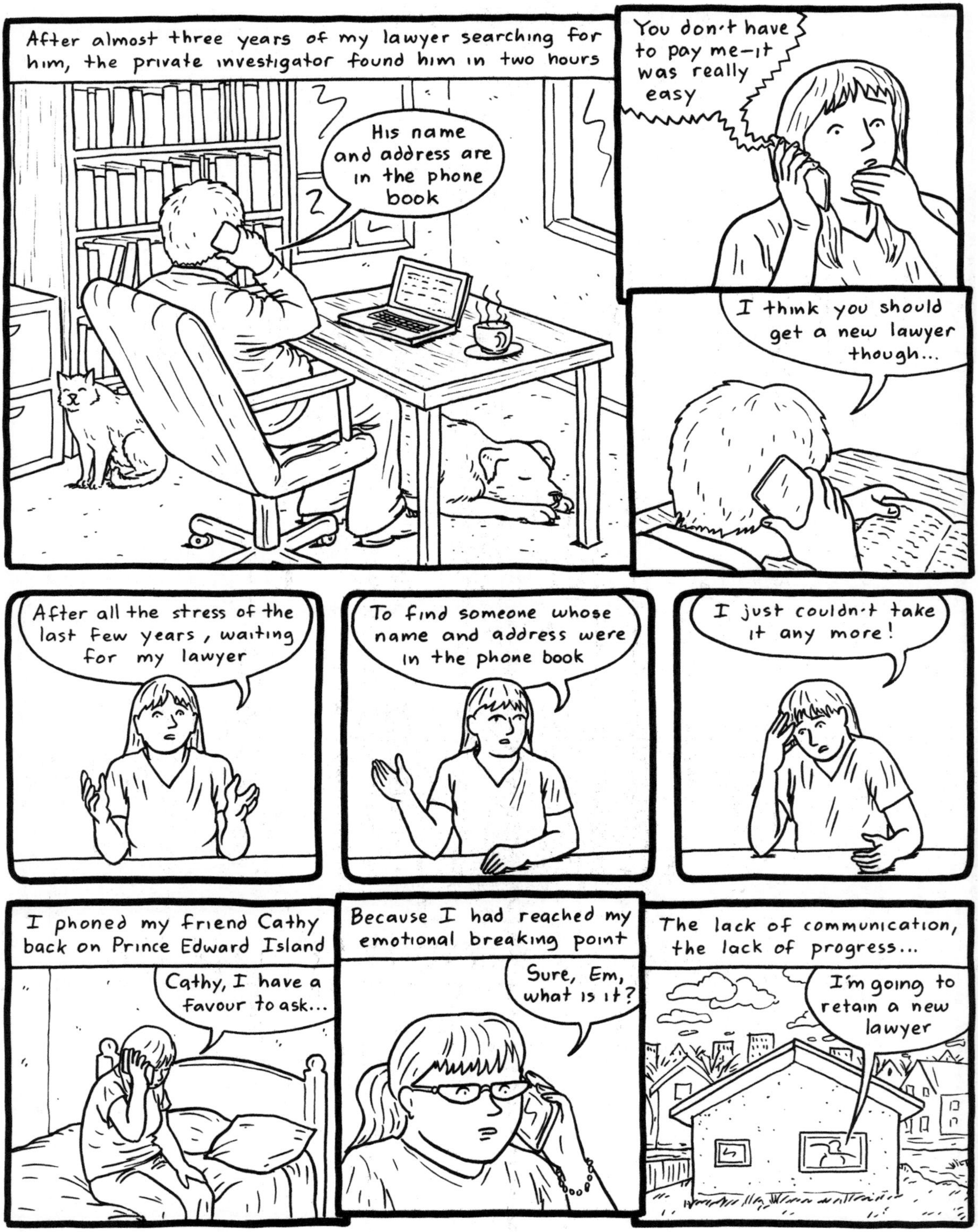
After almost three years of my lawyer searching for him, the private investigator found him in two hours
His name and address are in the phone book
You don't have to pay me—it was really easy
I think you should get a new lawyer though...
After all the stress of the last few years, waiting for my lawyer
To find someone whose name and address were in the phone book
I just couldn't take it any more!
I phoned my friend Cathy back on Prince Edward Island
Cathy, I have a favour to ask...
Because I had reached my emotional breaking point
Sure, Em, what is it?
The lack of communication, the lack of progress...
I'm going to retain a new lawyer

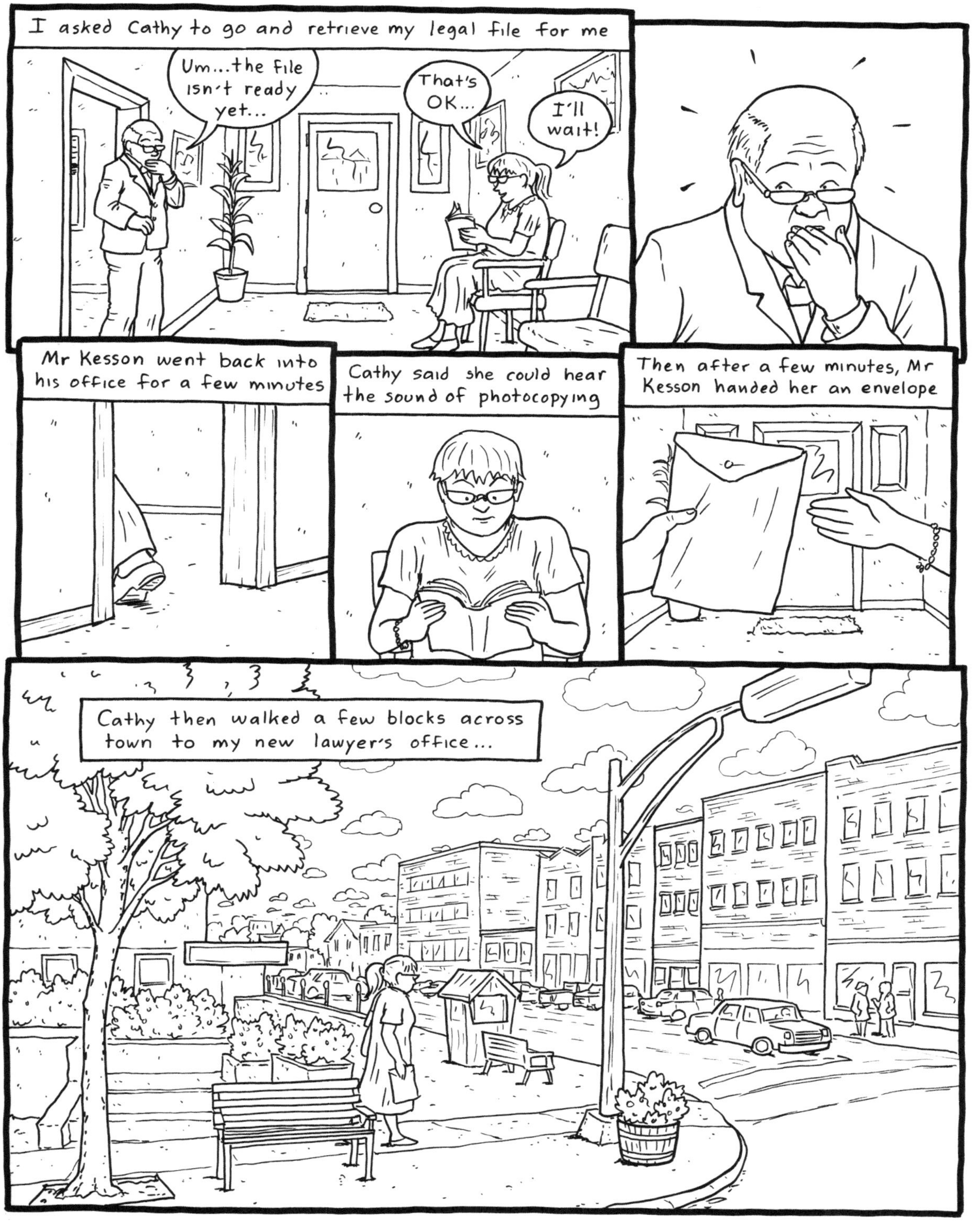
I asked Cathy to go and retrieve my legal file for me
Um...the file isn't ready yet...
That's OK...
I'll wait!
Mr Kesson went back into his office for a few minutes
Cathy said she could hear the sound of photocopying
Then after a few minutes, Mr Kesson handed her an envelope
Cathy then walked a few blocks across town to my new lawyer's office...

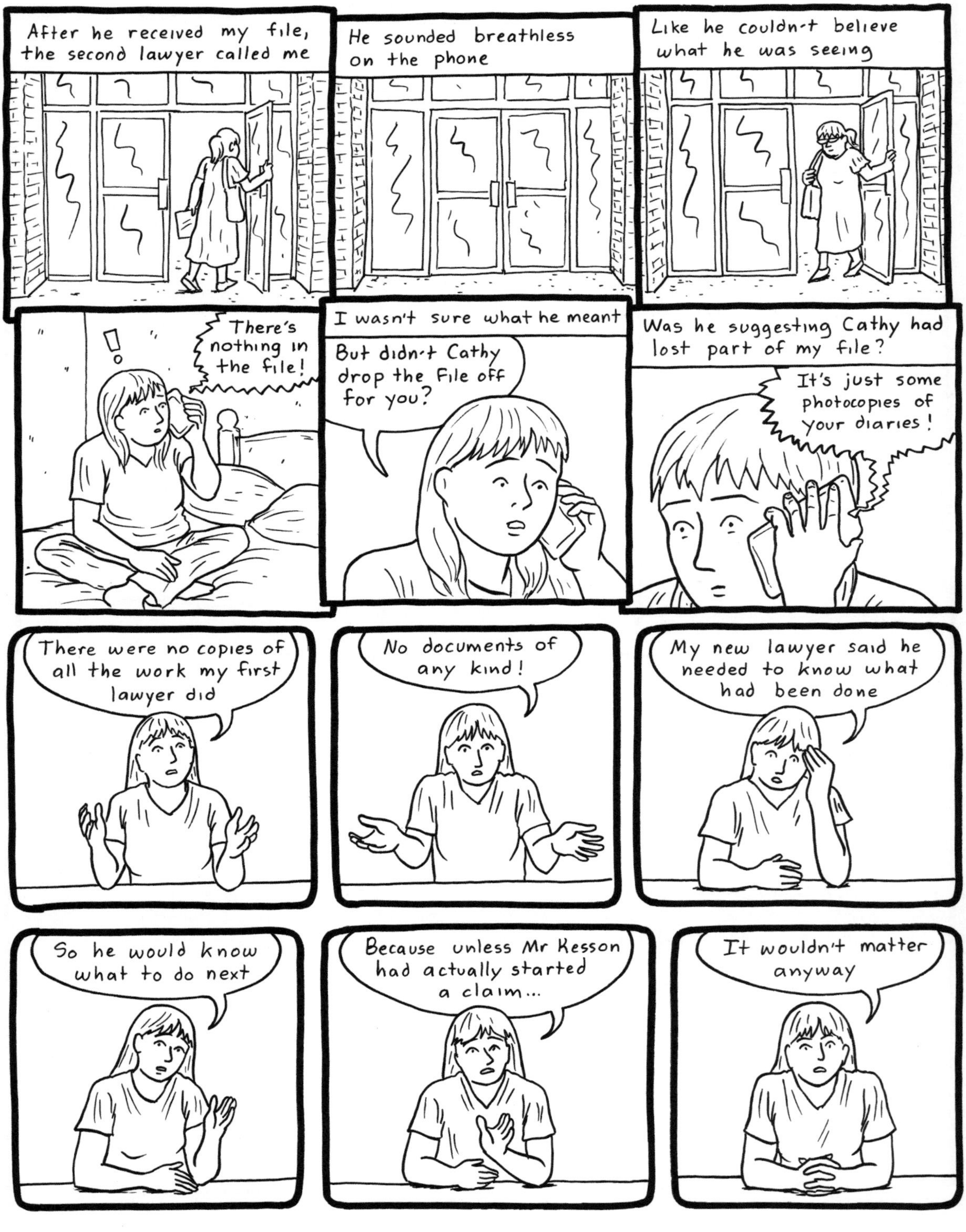
After he received my file, the second lawyer called me
He sounded breathless on the phone
Like he couldn't believe what he was seeing
There's nothing in the file!
I wasn't sure what he meant
But didn't Cathy drop the file off for you?
Was he suggesting Cathy had lost part of my file?
It's just some photocopies of your diaries!
There were no copies of all the work my first lawyer did
No documents of any kind!
My new lawyer said he needed to know what had been done
So he would know what to do next
Because unless Mr Kesson had actually started a claim...
It wouldn't matter anyway

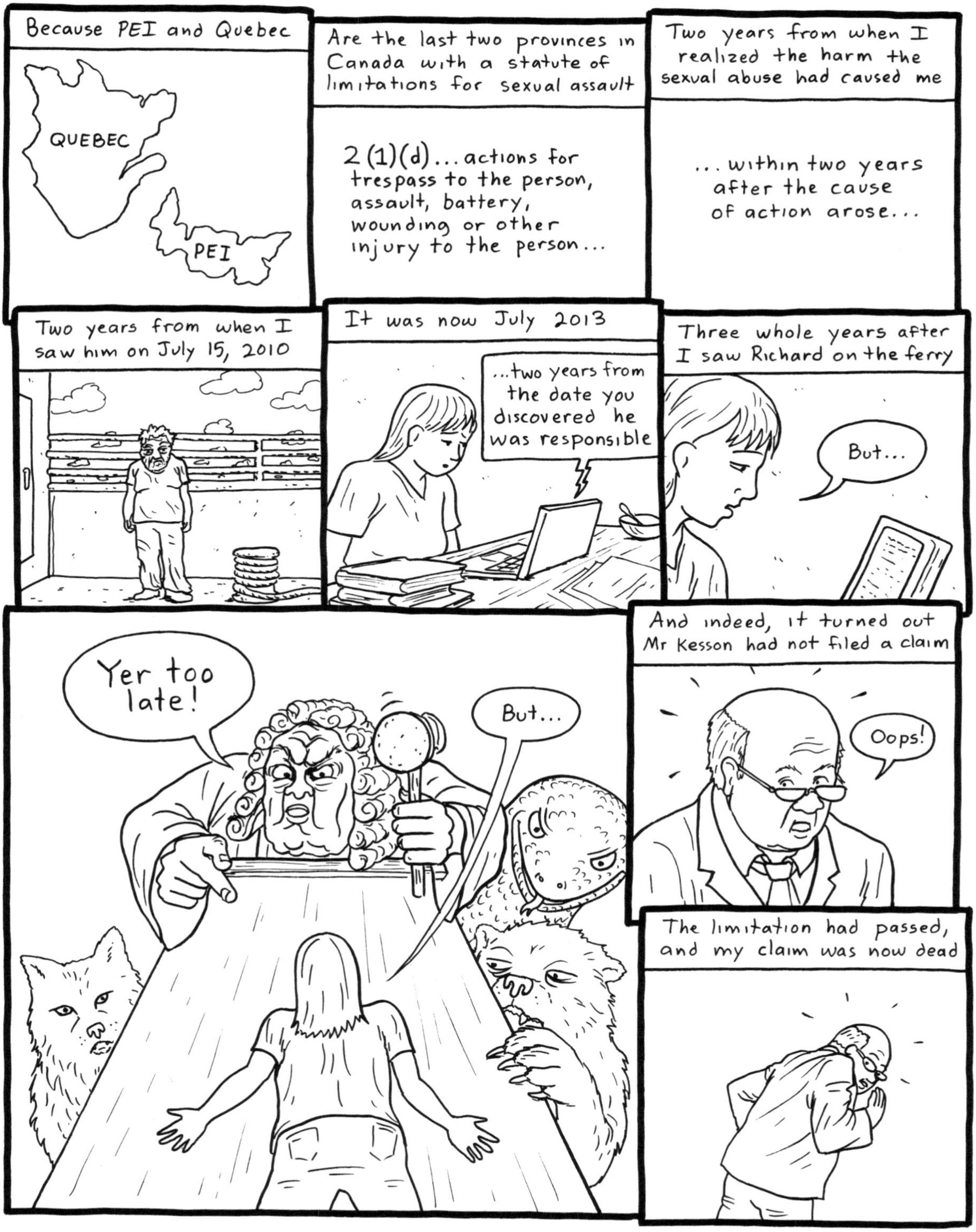

Because PEI and Quebec
QUEBEC
PEI
Are the last two provinces in Canada with a statute of limitations for sexual assault
2(1)(d)... actions for trespass to the person, assault, battery, wounding or other injury to the person...
Two years from when I realized the harm the sexual abuse had caused me
...within two years after the cause of action arose...
Two years from when I saw him on July 15, 2010
It was now July 2013
...two years from the date you discovered he was responsible
Three whole years after I saw Richard on the ferry
But...
Yer too late!
But...
And indeed, it turned out Mr Kesson had not filed a claim
Oops!
The limitation had passed, and my claim was now dead

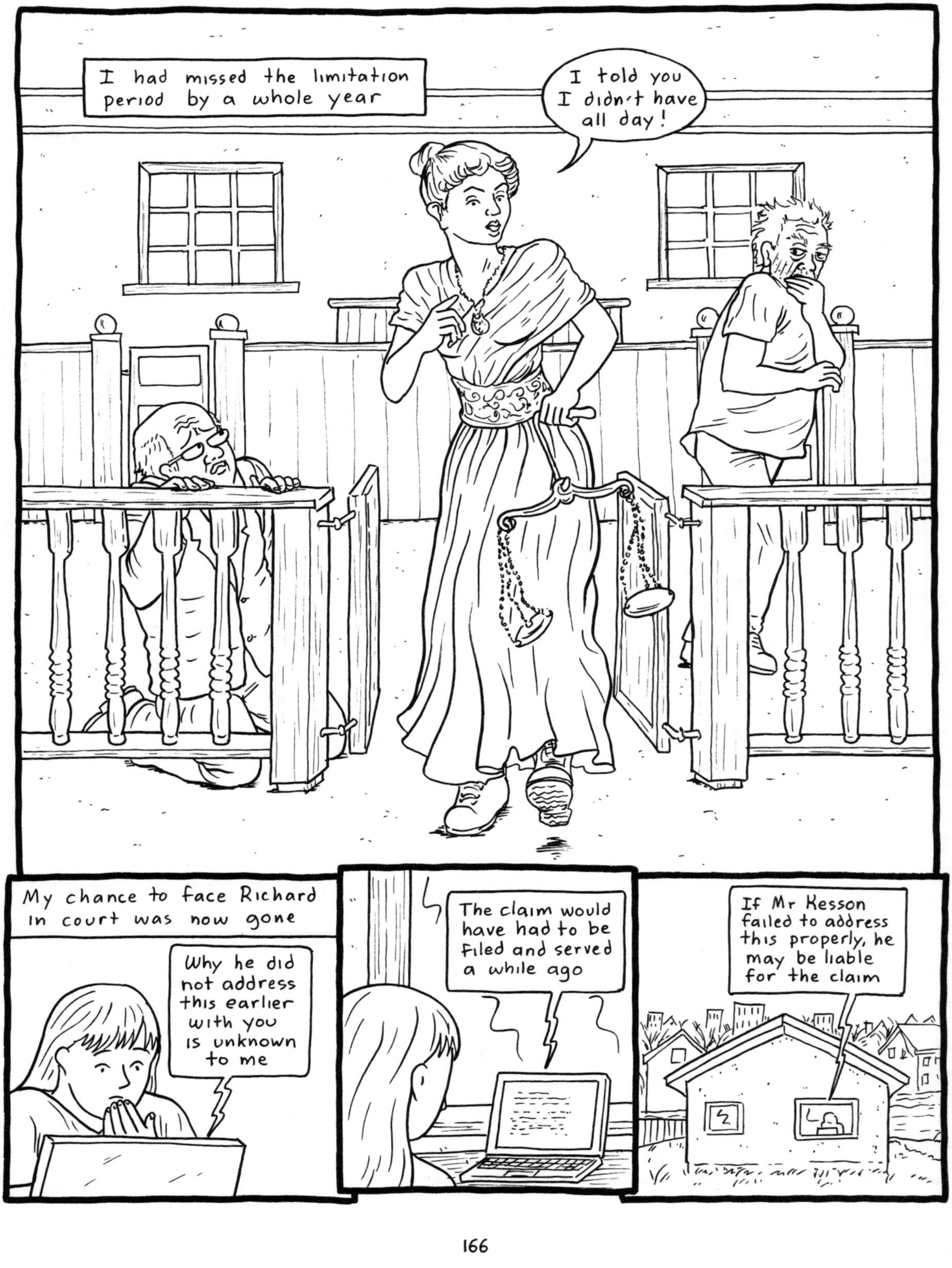

I had missed the limitation period by a whole year
I told you I didn't have all day!
My chance to face Richard in court was now gone
Why he did not address this earlier with you is unknown to me
The claim would have had to be filed and served a while ago
If Mr Kesson failed to address this properly, he may be liable for the claim

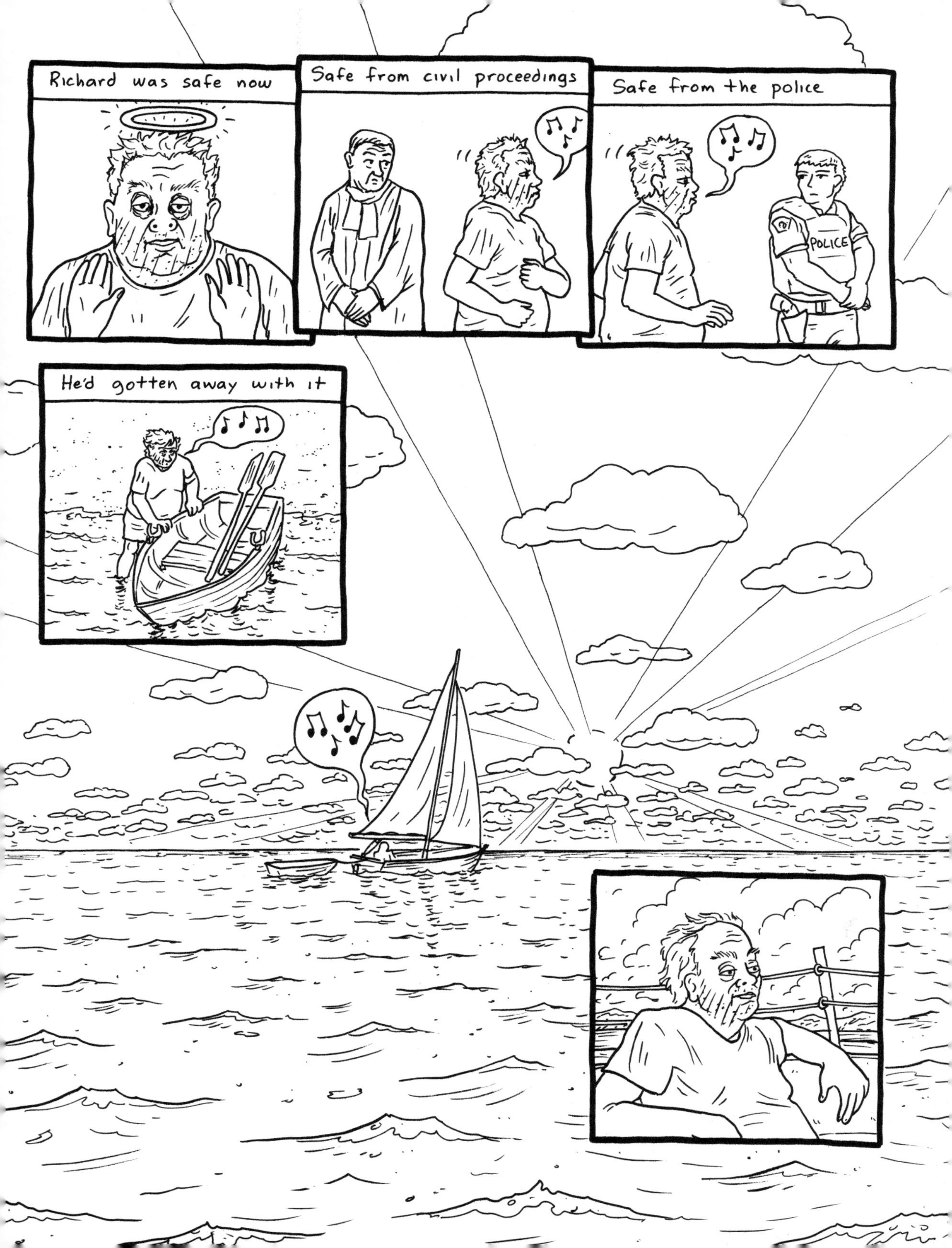
Richard was safe now
Safe from civil proceedings
Safe from the police
POLICE
He'd gotten away with it

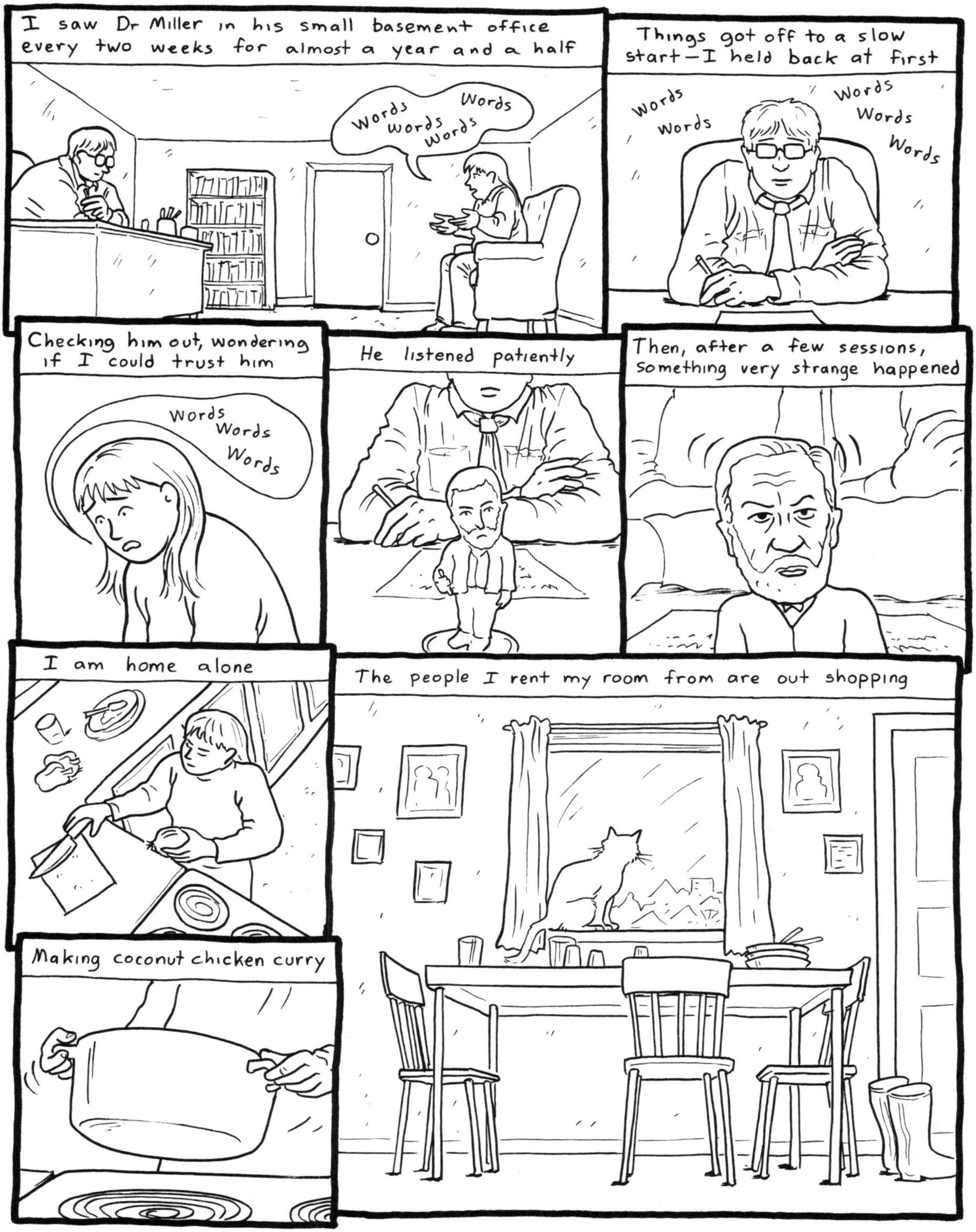
I saw Dr Miller in his small basement office every two weeks for almost a year and a half
Words Words Words Words
Things got off to a slow start—I held back at first
Words Words Words Words Words
Checking him out, wondering if I could trust him
Words Words Words
He listened patiently
Then, after a few sessions, something very strange happened
I am home alone
Making coconut chicken curry
The people I rent my room from are out shopping

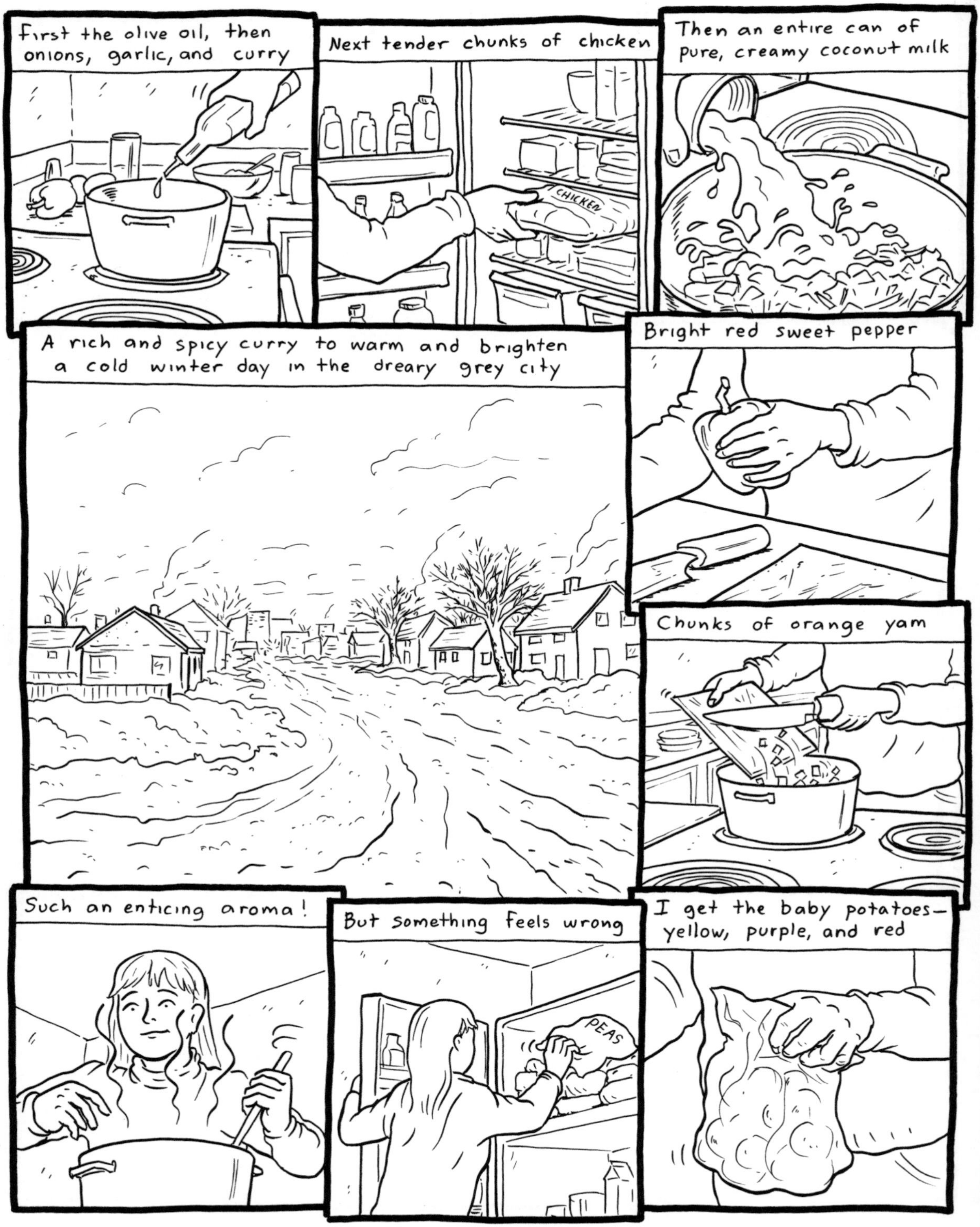
First the olive oil, then onions, garlic, and curry
Next tender chunks of chicken
CHICKEN
Then an entire can of pure, creamy coconut milk
A rich and spicy curry to warm and brighten a cold winter day in the dreary grey city
Bright red sweet pepper
Chunks of orange yam
Such an enticing aroma!
But something feels wrong
PEAS
I get the baby potatoes— yellow, purple, and red

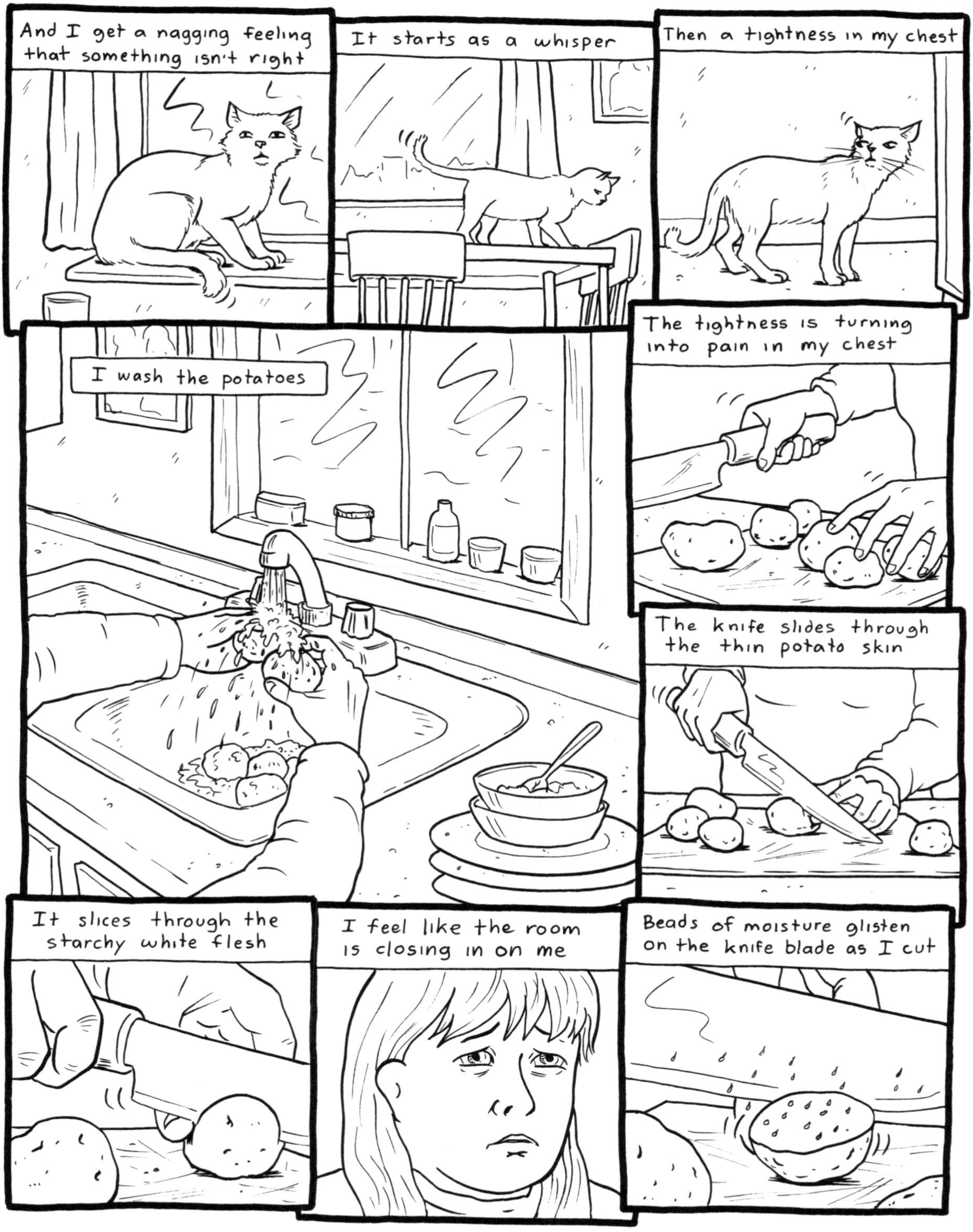
And I get a nagging feeling that something isn't right
It starts as a whisper
Then a tightness in my chest
I wash the potatoes
The tightness is turning into pain in my chest
The knife slides through the thin potato skin
It slices through the starchy white flesh
I feel like the room is closing in on me
Beads of moisture glisten on the knife blade as I cut

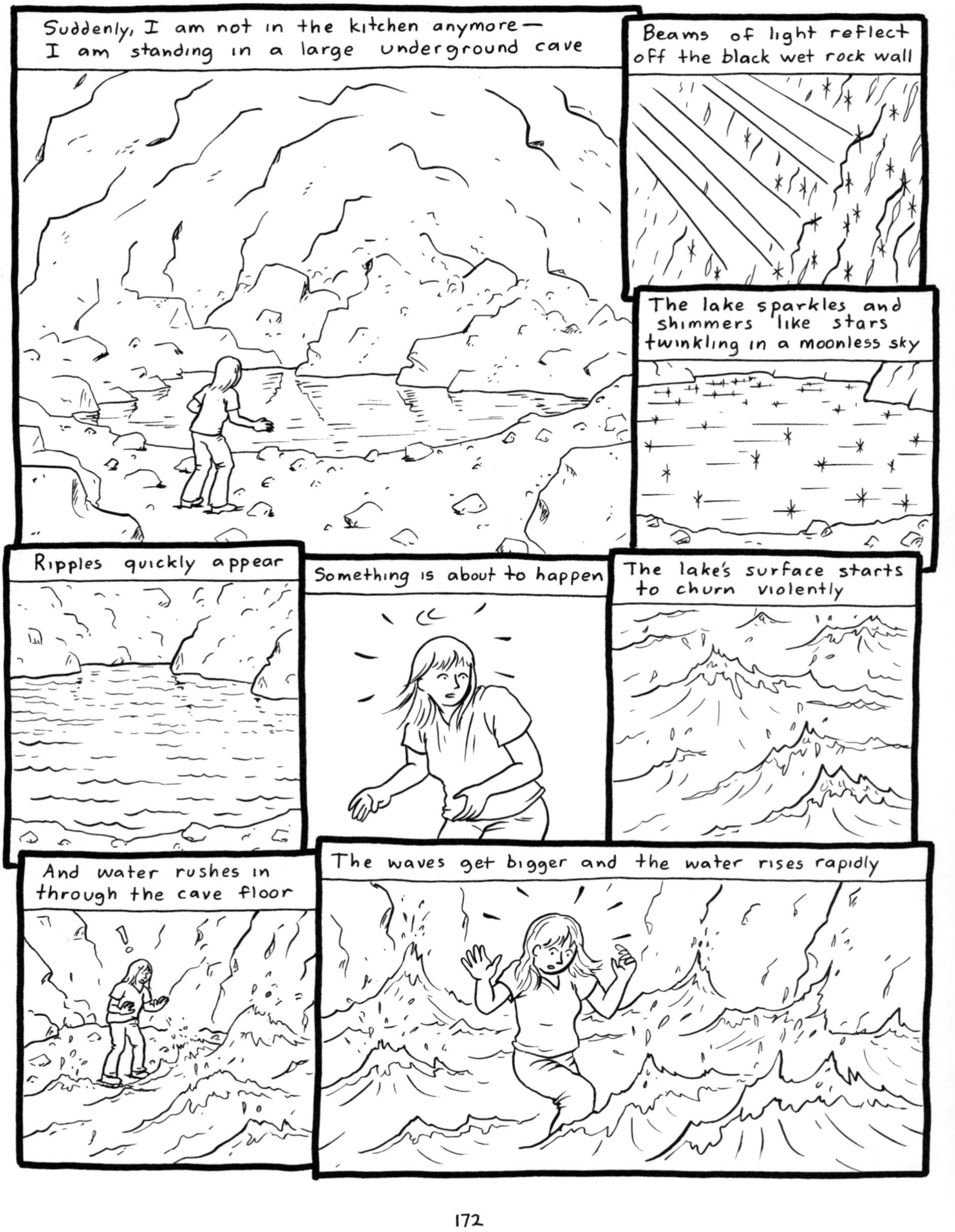
Suddenly, I am not in the kitchen anymore—
I am standing in a large underground cave
Beams of light reflect off the black wet rock wall
The lake sparkles and shimmers like stars twinkling in a moonless sky
Ripples quickly appear
Something is about to happen
The lake's surface starts to churn violently
And water rushes in through the cave floor
!
The waves get bigger and the water rises rapidly

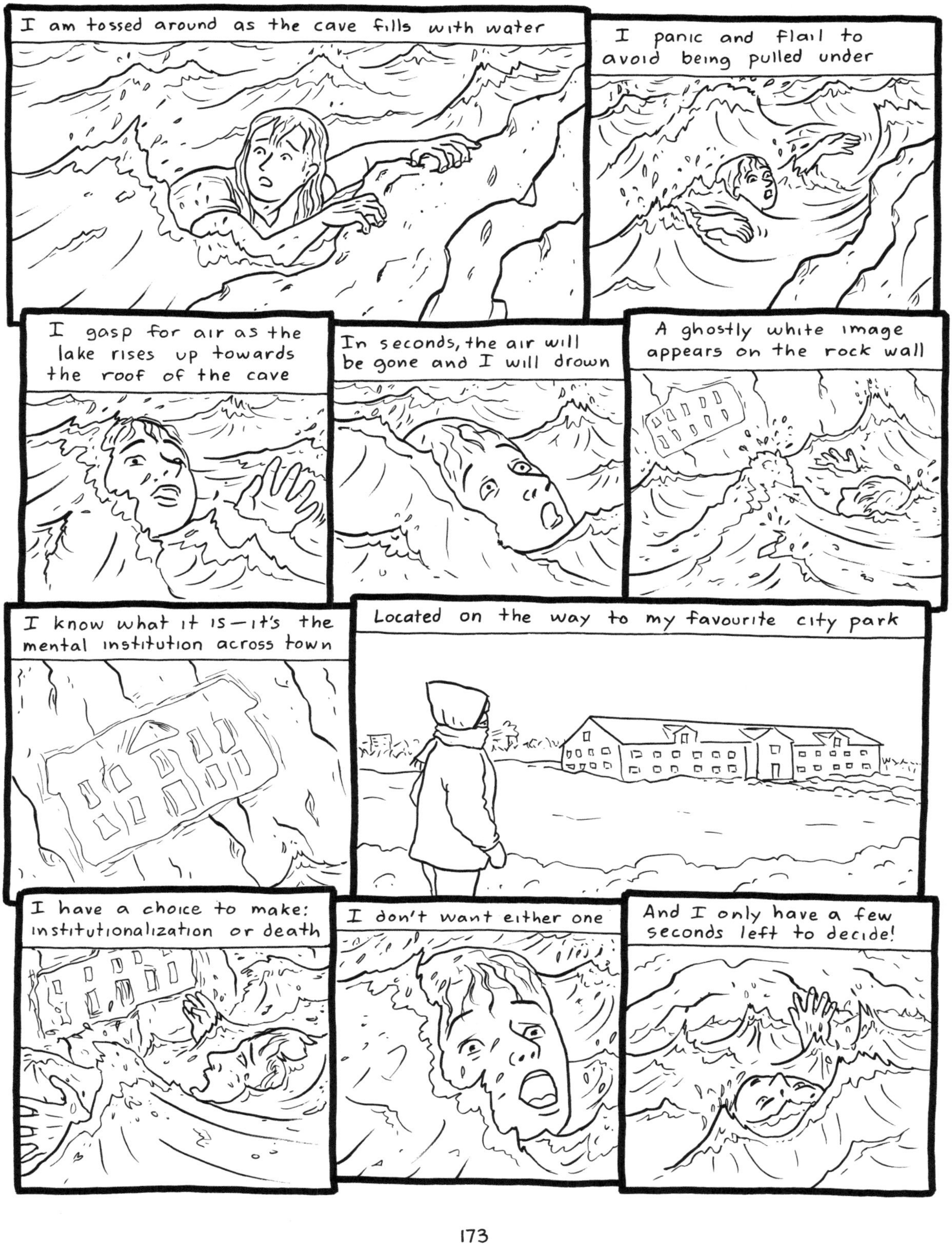
I am tossed around as the cave fills with water
I panic and flail to avoid being pulled under
I gasp for air as the lake rises up towards the roof of the cave
In seconds, the air will be gone and I will drown
A ghostly white image appears on the rock wall
I know what it is—it's the mental institution across town
Located on the way to my favourite city park
I have a choice to make: institutionalization or death
I don't want either one
And I only have a few seconds left to decide!

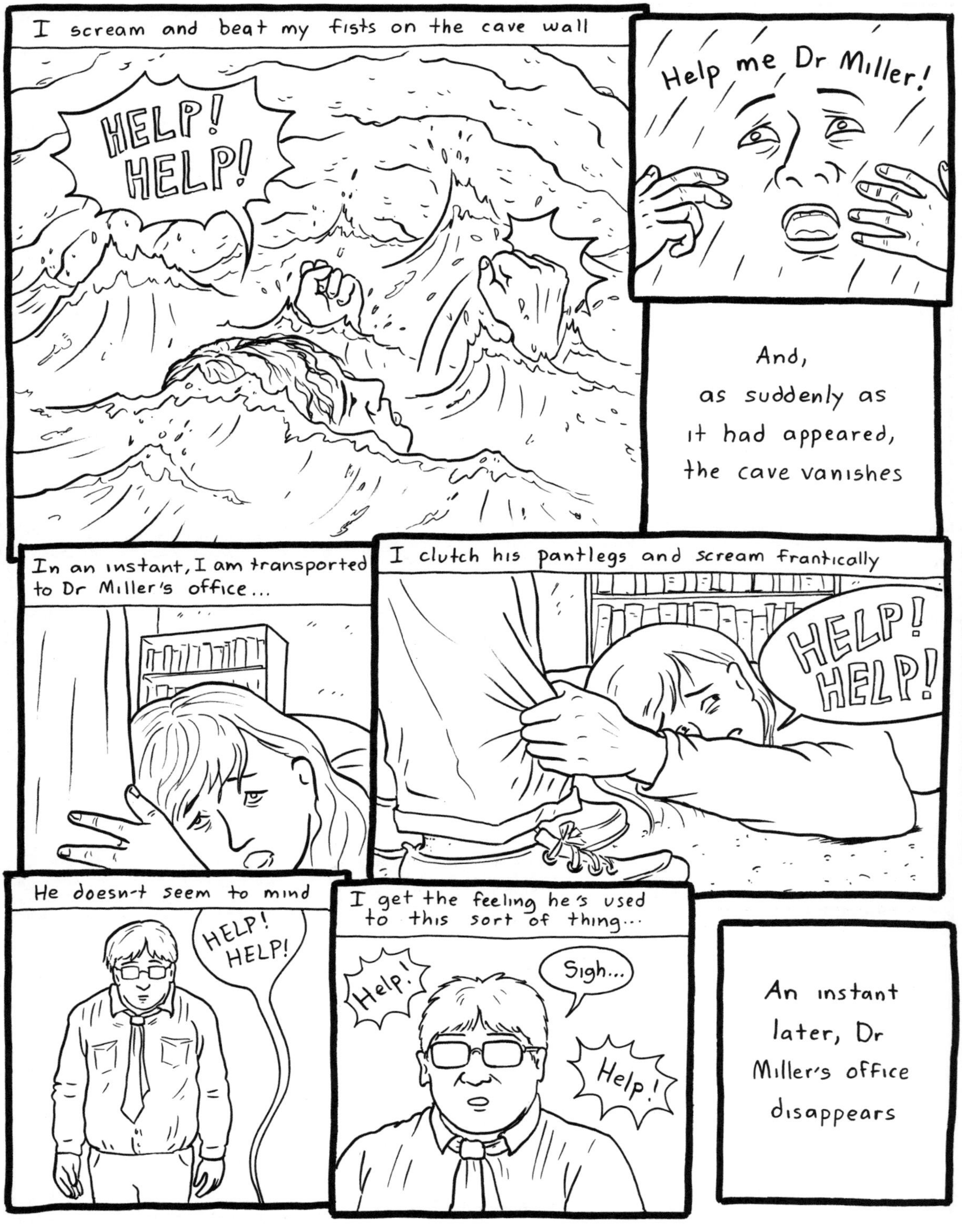
I scream and beat my fists on the cave wall
HELP! HELP!
Help me Dr Miller!
And, as suddenly as it had appeared, the cave vanishes
In an instant, I am transported to Dr Miller's office...
I clutch his pantlegs and scream frantically
HELP! HELP!
He doesn't seem to mind
HELP! HELP!
I get the feeling he's used to this sort of thing...
Help!
Sigh...
Help!
An instant later, Dr Miller's office disappears

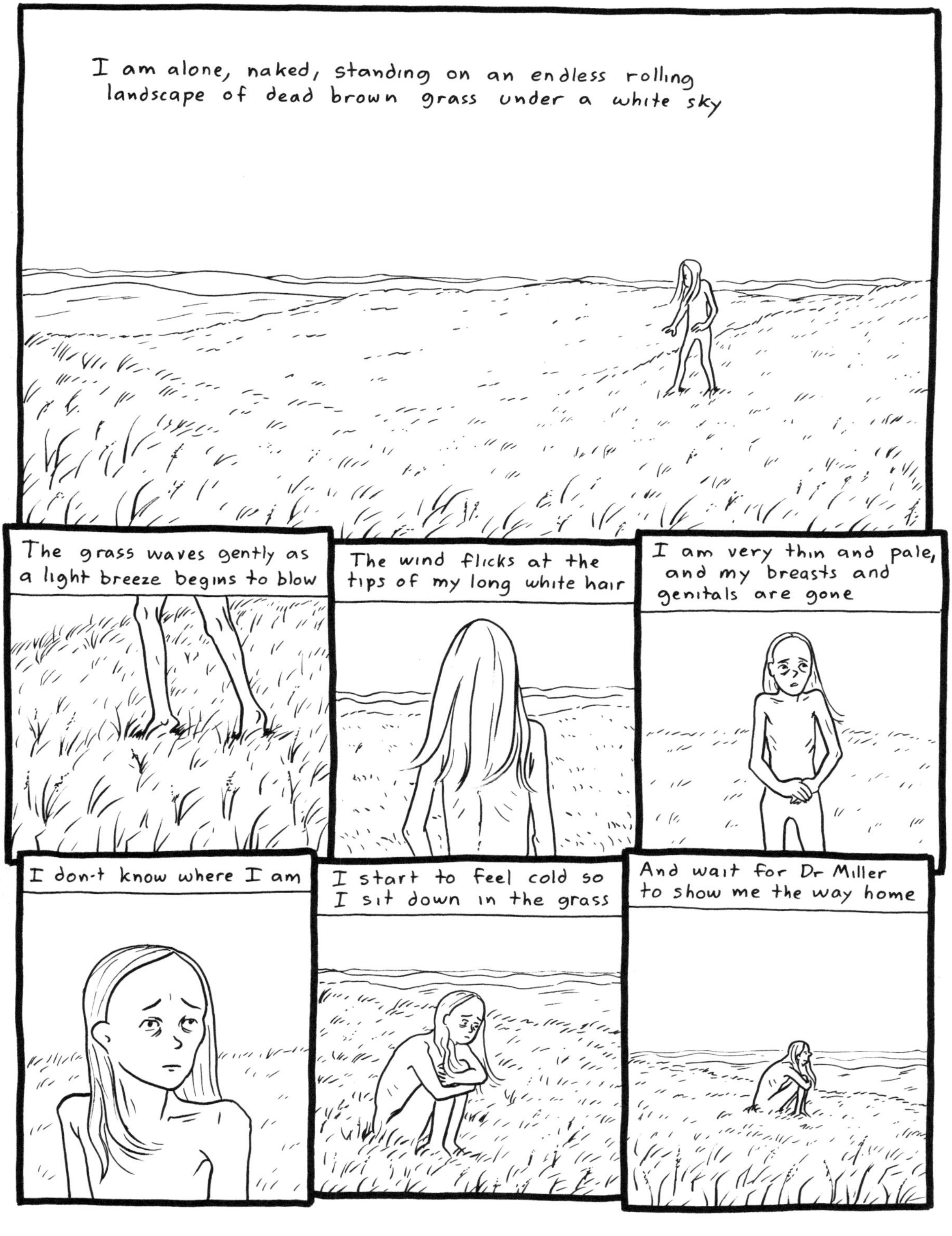
I am alone, naked, standing on an endless rolling landscape of dead brown grass under a white sky
The grass waves gently as a light breeze begins to blow
The wind flicks at the tips of my long white hair
I am very thin and pale, and my breasts and genitals are gone
I don't know where I am
I start to feel cold so I sit down in the grass
And wait for Dr Miller to show me the way home

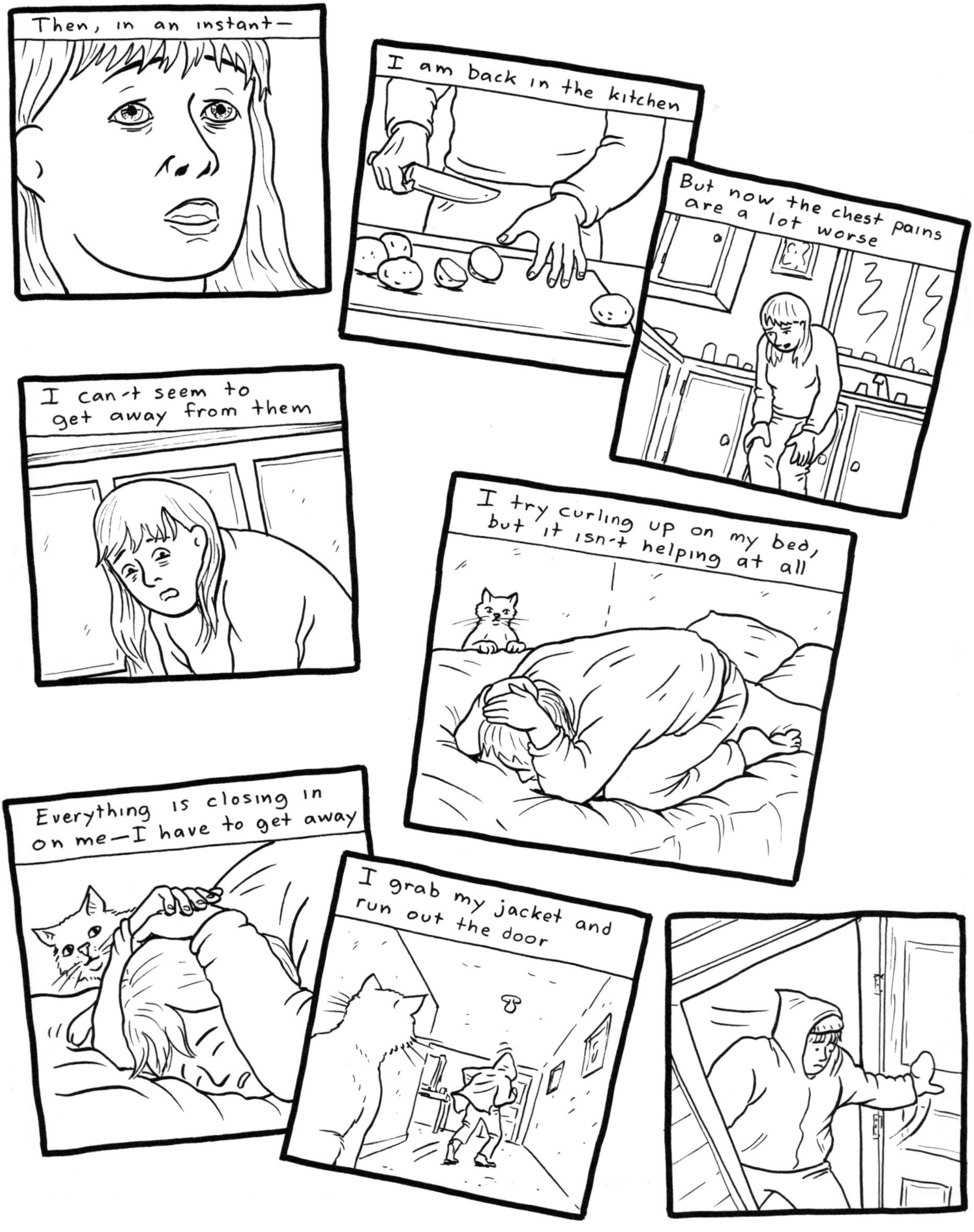

Then, in an instant—
I am back in the kitchen
But now the chest pains are a lot worse
I can't seem to get away from them
I try curling up on my bed, but it isn't helping at all
Everything is closing in on me—I have to get away
I grab my jacket and run out the door

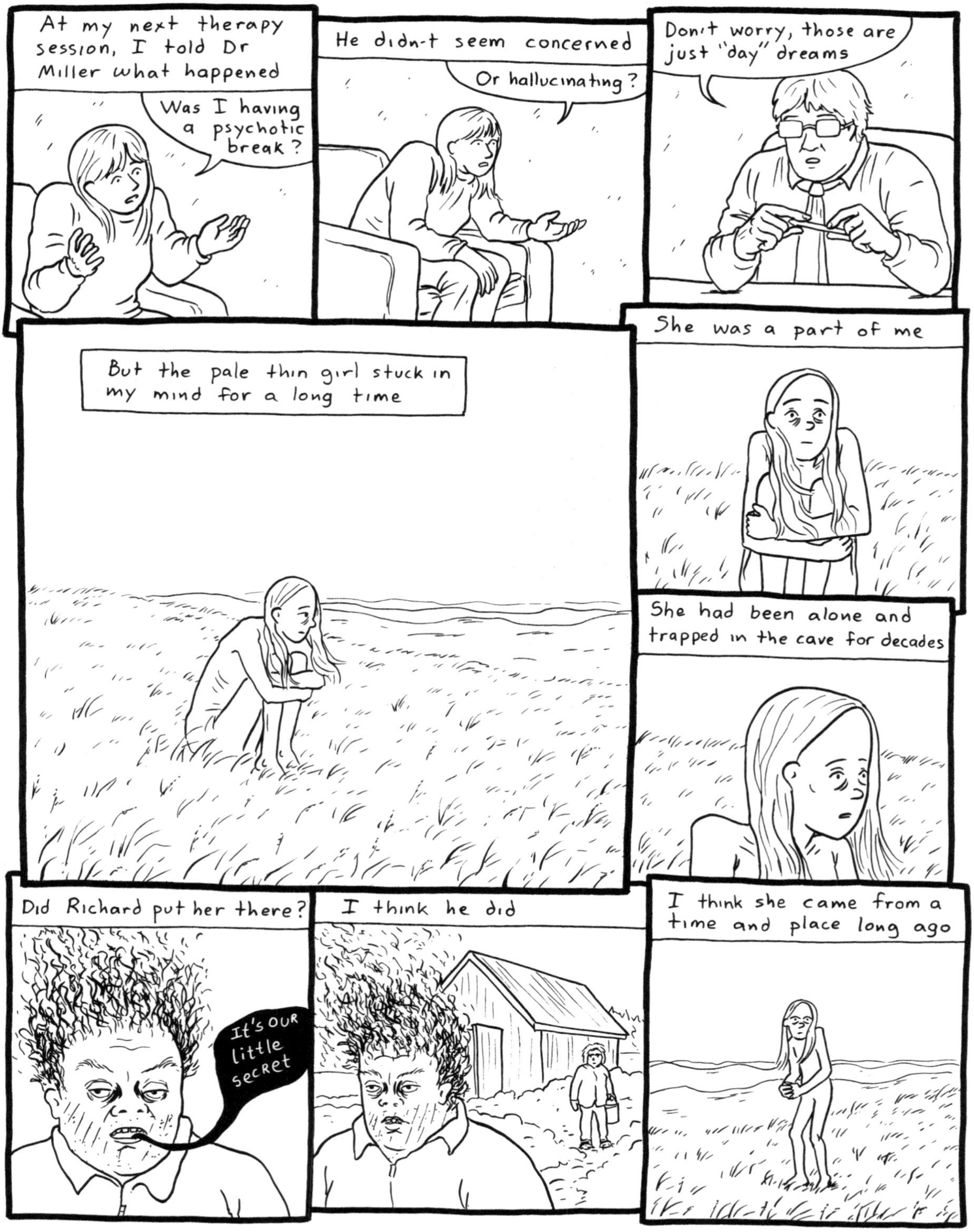
At my next therapy session, I told Dr Miller what happened
Was I having a psychotic break?
He didn't seem concerned
Or hallucinating?
Don't worry, those are just "day" dreams
But the pale thin girl stuck in my mind for a long time
She was a part of me
She had been alone and trapped in the cave for decades
Did Richard put her there?
It's OUR little secret
I think he did
I think she came from a time and place long ago

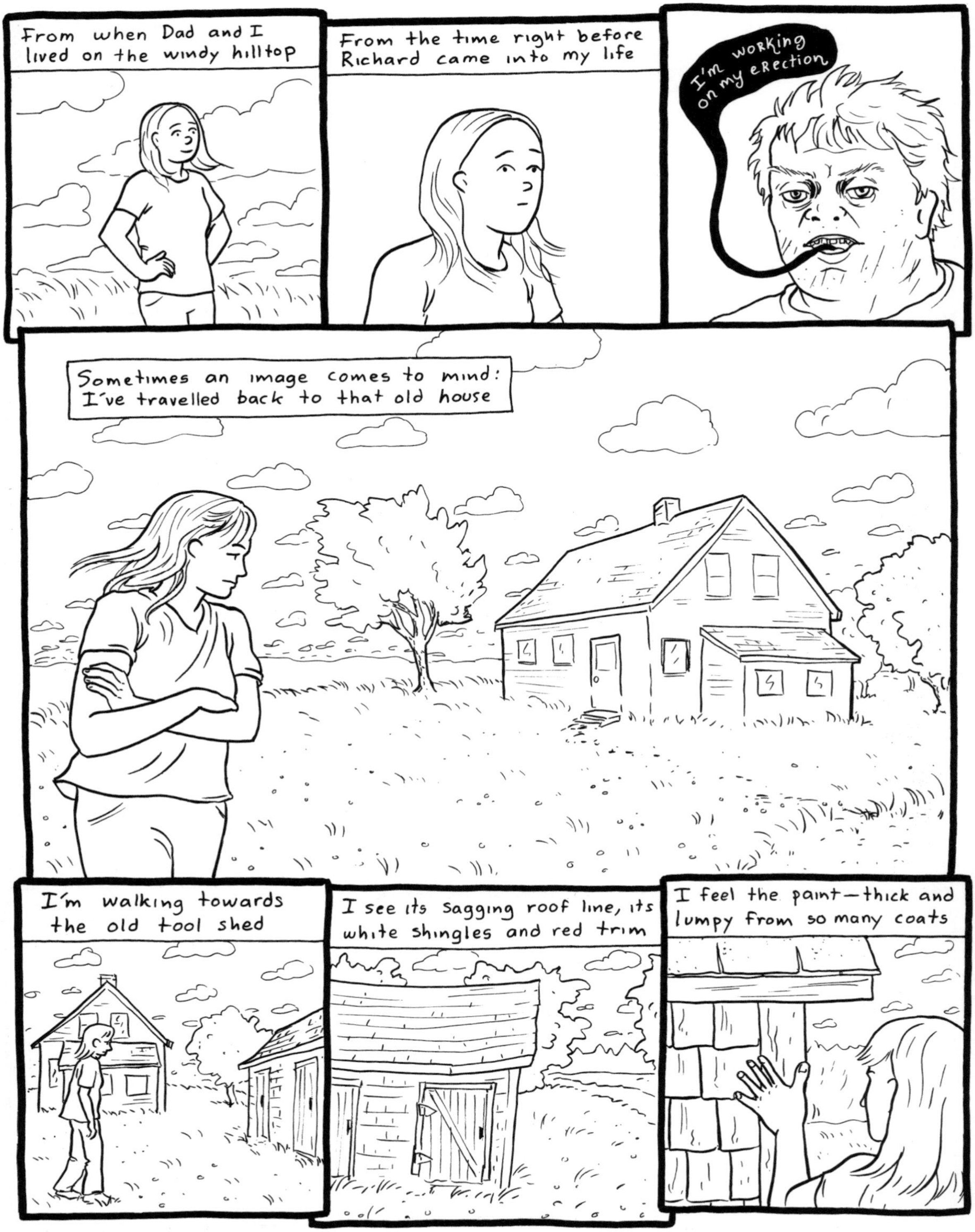
From when Dad and I lived on the windy hilltop
From the time right before Richard came into my life
I'm working on my erection
Sometimes an image comes to mind: I've travelled back to that old house
I'm walking towards the old tool shed
I see its sagging roof line, its white shingles and red trim
I feel the paint—thick and lumpy from so many coats

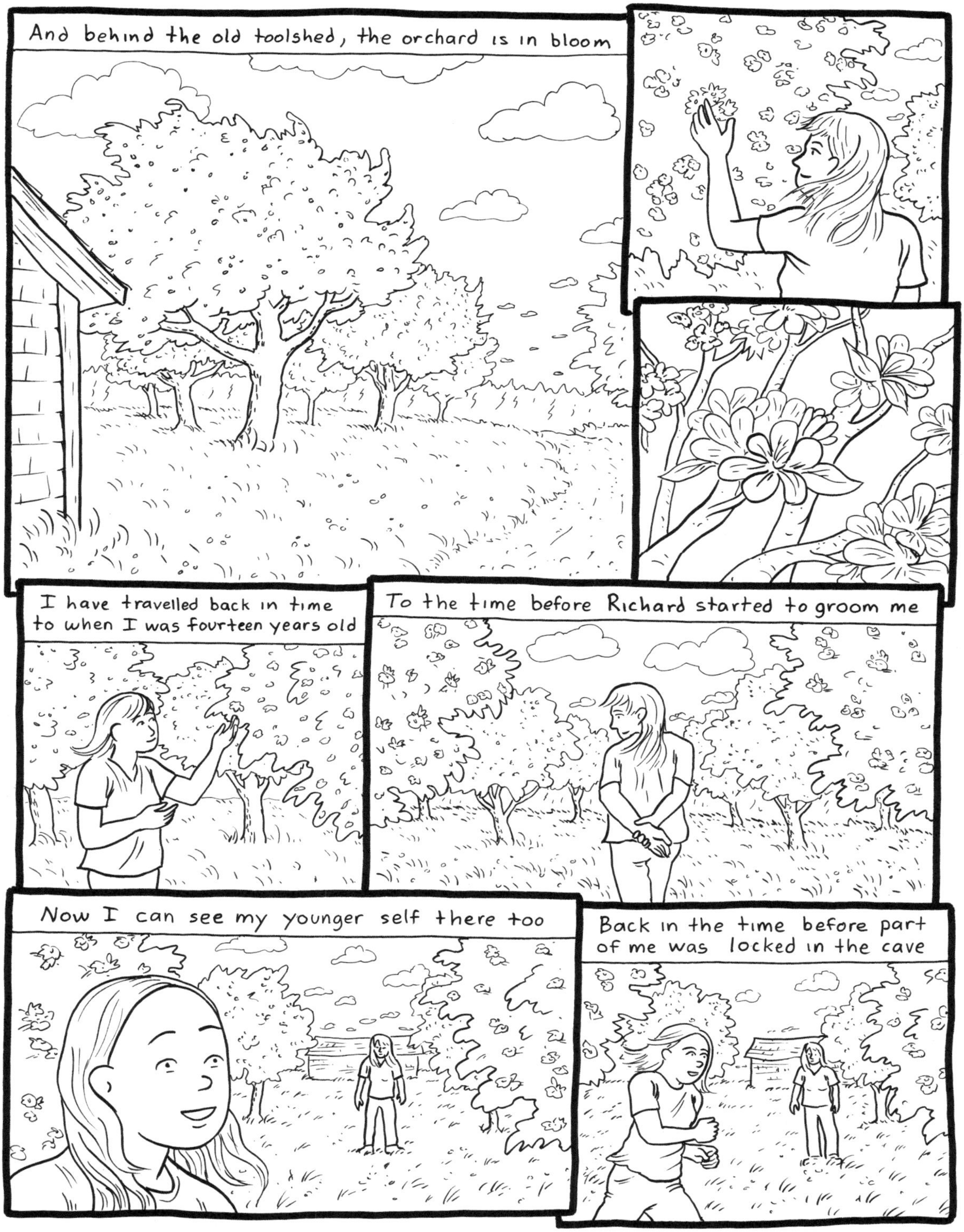

And behind the old toolshed, the orchard is in bloom
I have travelled back in time to when I was fourteen years old
To the time before Richard started to groom me
Now I can see my younger self there too
Back in the time before part of me was locked in the cave

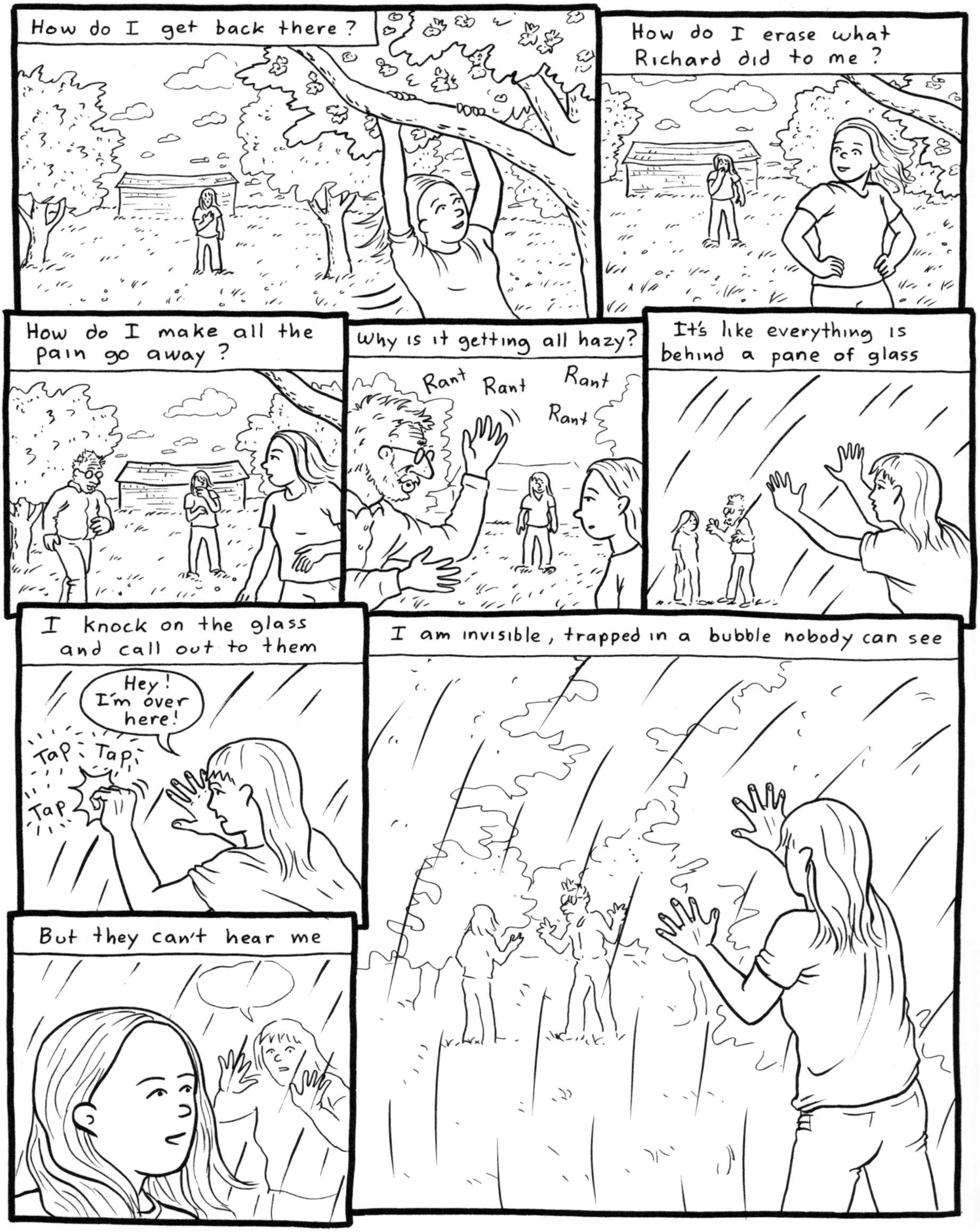
How do I get back there?
How do I erase what Richard did to me?
How do I make all the pain go away?
Why is it getting all hazy?
Rant Rant Rant Rant
It's like everything is behind a pane of glass
I knock on the glass and call out to them
Hey! I'm over here!
Tap Tap Tap
I am invisible, trapped in a bubble nobody can see
But they can't hear me

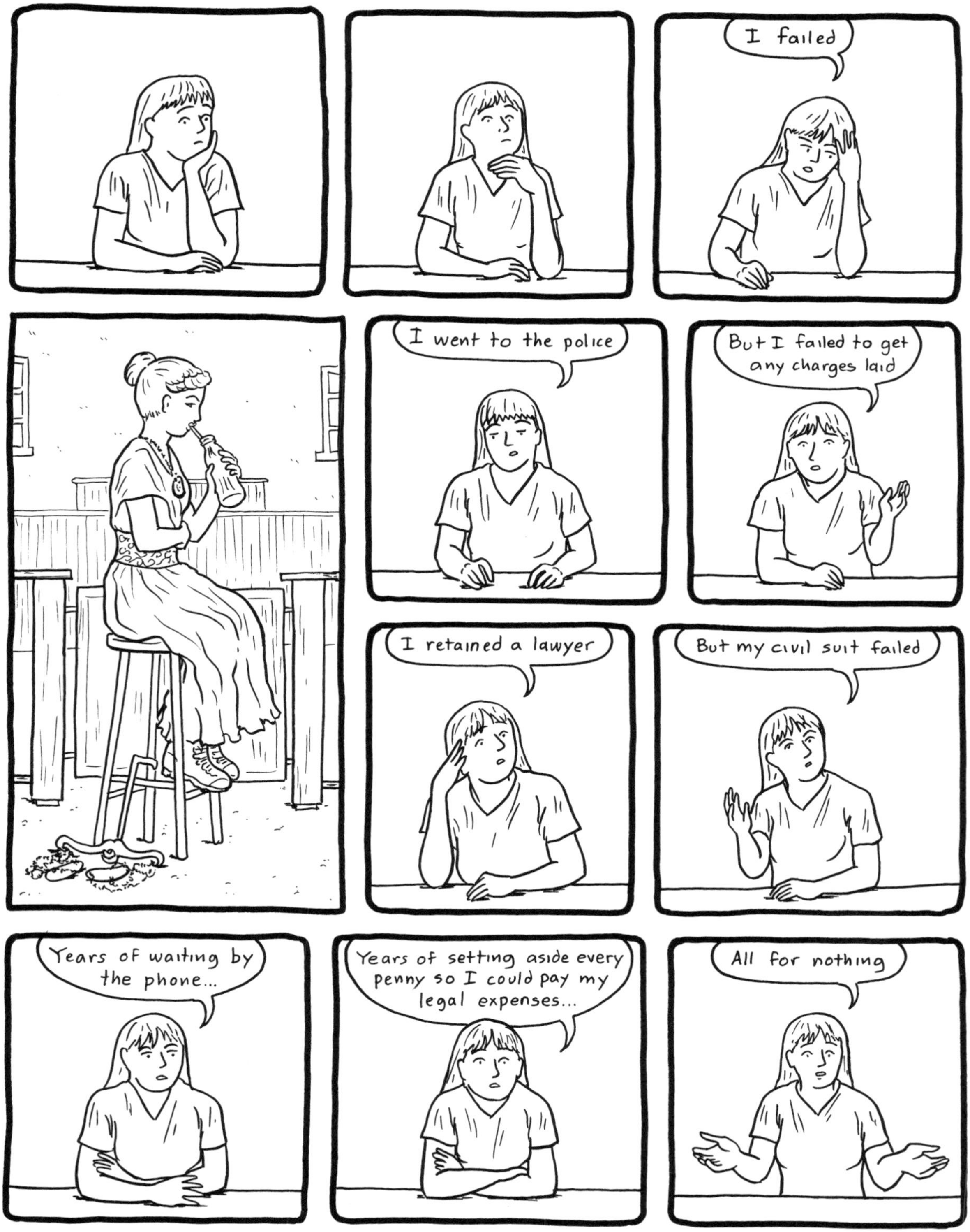
I failed
I went to the police
But I failed to get any charges laid
I retained a lawyer
But my civil suit failed
Years of waiting by the phone...
Years of setting aside every penny so I could pay my legal expenses...
All for nothing

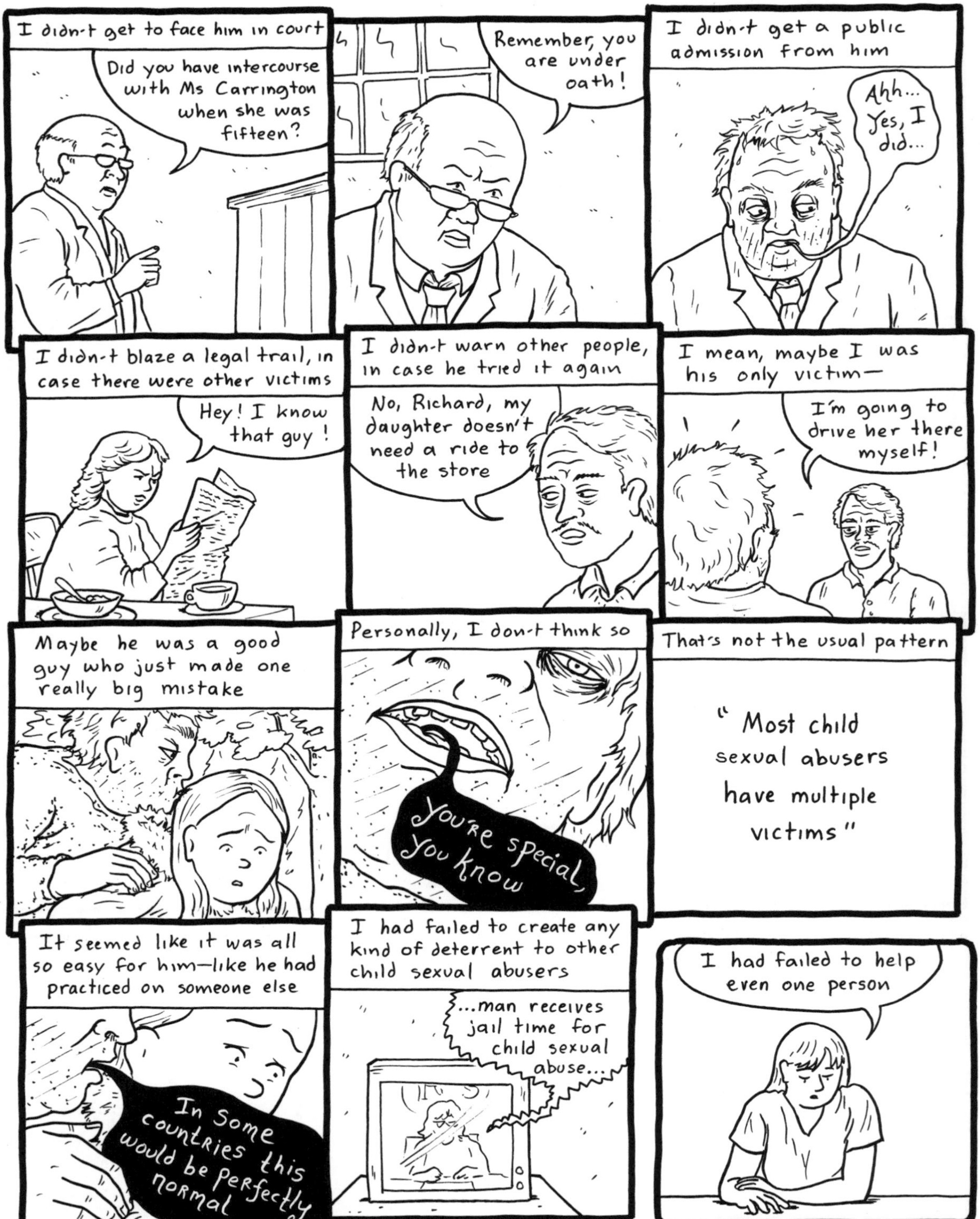

I didn't get to face him in court
Did you have intercourse with Ms Carrington when she was fifteen?
Remember, you are under oath!
I didn't get a public admission from him
Ahh... Yes, I did...
I didn't blaze a legal trail, in case there were other victims
Hey! I know that guy!
I didn't warn other people, in case he tried it again
No, Richard, my daughter doesn't need a ride to the store
I mean, maybe I was his only victim—
I'm going to drive her there myself!
Maybe he was a good guy who just made one really big mistake
Personally, I don't think so
You're special, you know
That's not the usual pattern
"Most child sexual abusers have multiple victims"
It seemed like it was all so easy for him—like he had practiced on someone else
In some countries this would be perfectly normal
I had failed to create any kind of deterrent to other child sexual abusers
...man receives jail time for child sexual abuse...
I had failed to help even one person

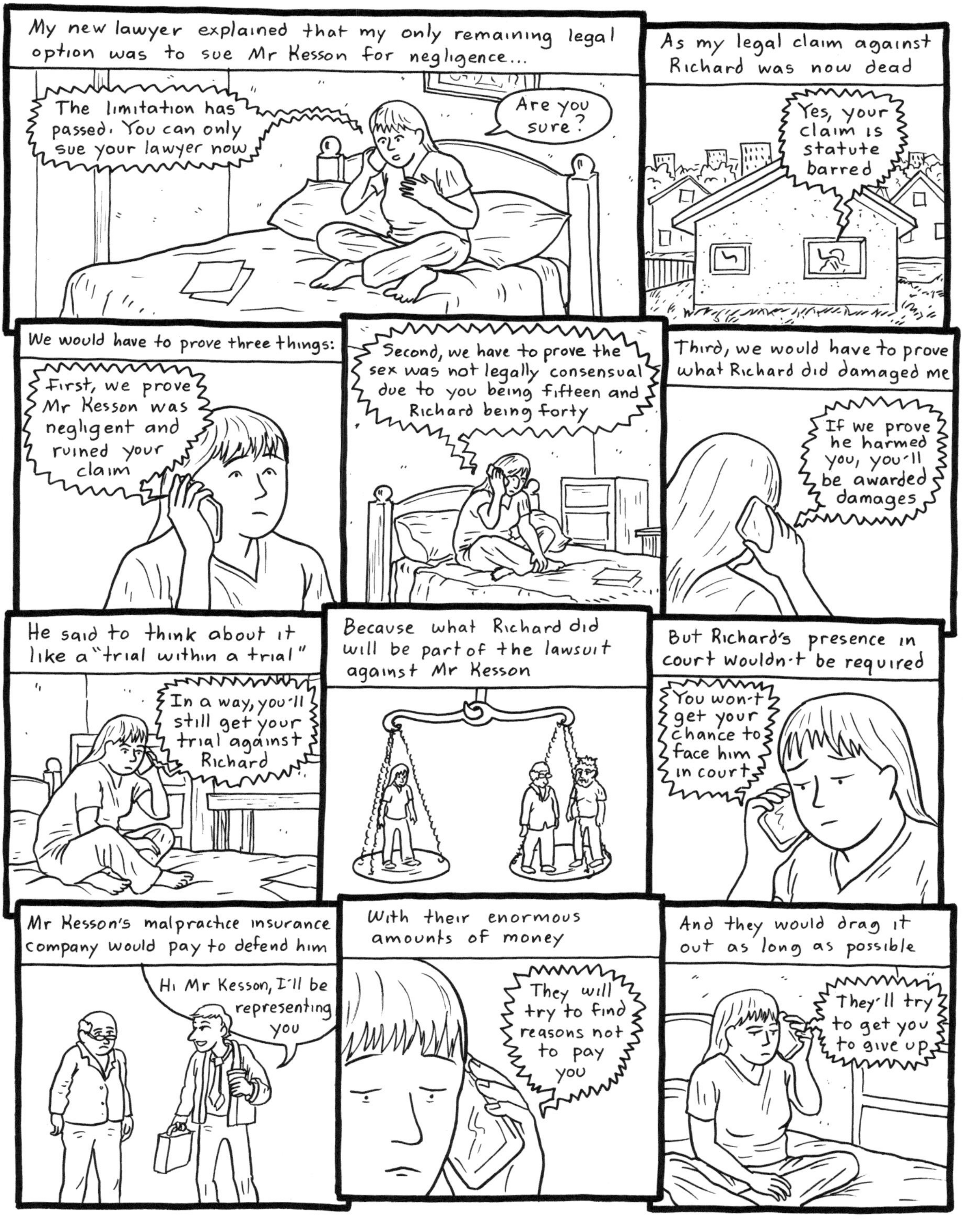
My new lawyer explained that my only remaining legal option was to sue Mr Kesson for negligence...
The limitation has passed. You can only sue your lawyer now
Are you sure?
As my legal claim against Richard was now dead
Yes, your claim is statute barred
We would have to prove three things:
First, we prove Mr Kesson was negligent and ruined your claim
Second, we have to prove the sex was not legally consensual due to you being fifteen and Richard being forty
Third, we would have to prove what Richard did damaged me
If we prove he harmed you, you'll be awarded damages
He said to think about it like a "trial within a trial"
In a way, you'll still get your trial against Richard
Because what Richard did will be part of the lawsuit against Mr Kesson
But Richard's presence in court wouldn't be required
You won't get your chance to face him in court
Mr Kesson's malpractice insurance company would pay to defend him
Hi Mr Kesson, I'll be representing you
With their enormous amounts of money
They will try to find reasons not to pay you
And they would drag it out as long as possible
They'll try to get you to give up

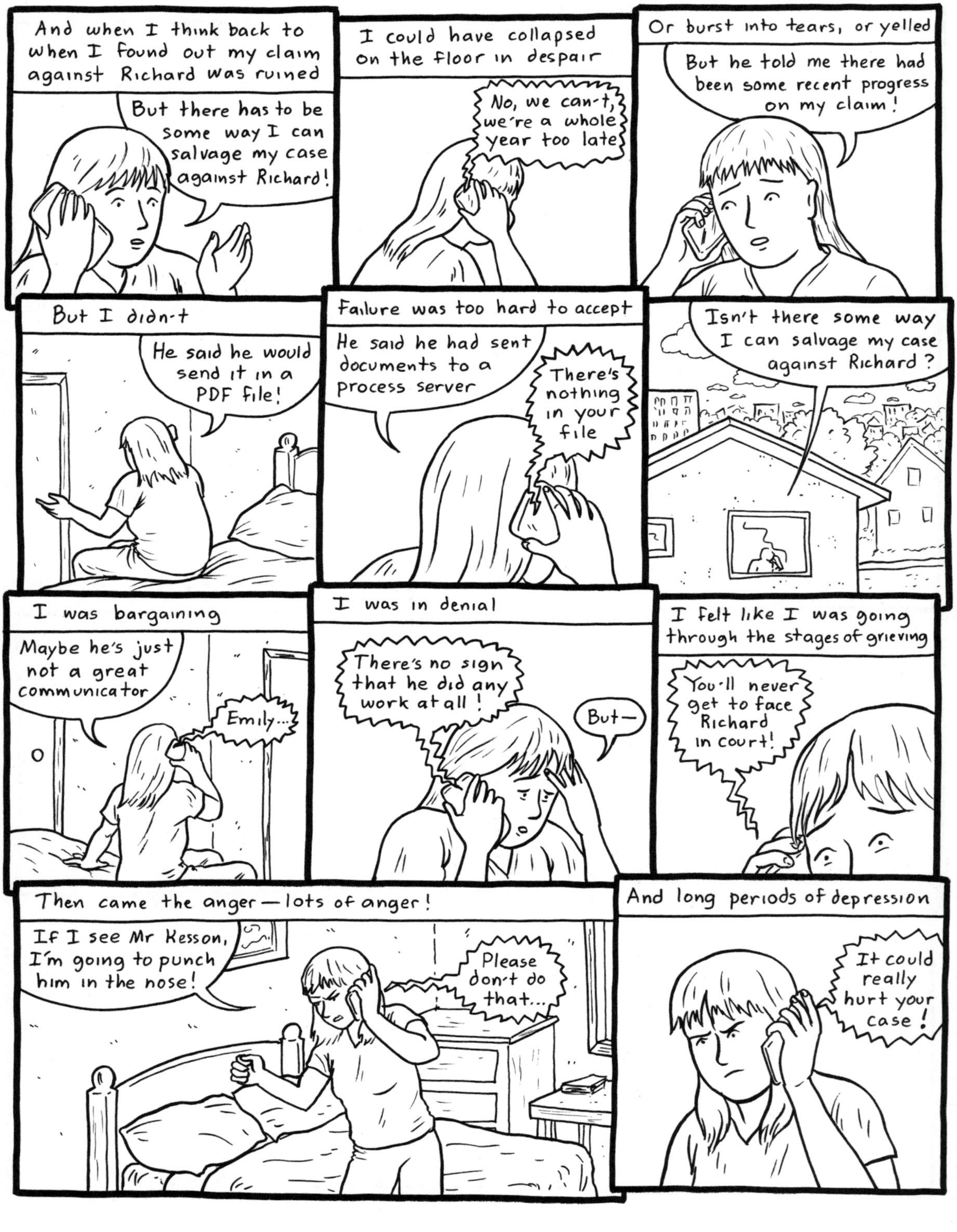
And when I think back to when I found out my claim against Richard was ruined
But there has to be some way I can salvage my case against Richard!
I could have collapsed on the floor in despair
No, we can't, we're a whole year too late
Or burst into tears, or yelled
But he told me there had been some recent progress on my claim!
But I didn't
He said he would send it in a PDF file!
Failure was too hard to accept
He said he had sent documents to a process server
There's nothing in your file
Isn't there some way I can salvage my case against Richard?
I was bargaining
Maybe he's just not a great communicator
Emily...
I was in denial
There's no sign that he did any work at all!
But—
I felt like I was going through the stages of grieving
You'll never get to face Richard in court!
Then came the anger—lots of anger!
If I see Mr Kesson, I'm going to punch him in the nose!
Please don't do that...
And long periods of depression
It could really hurt your case!

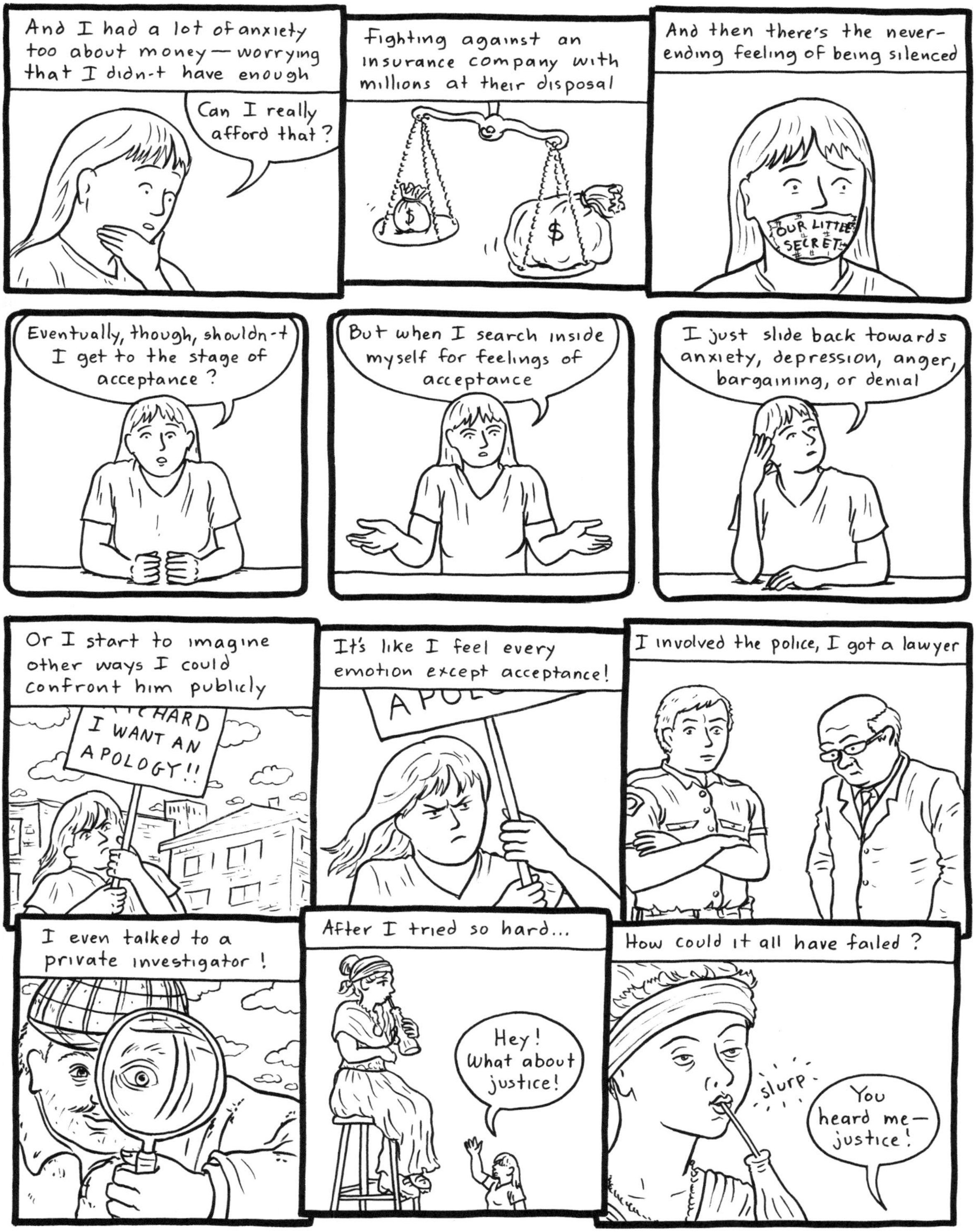
And I had a lot of anxiety too about money—worrying that I didn't have enough
Can I really afford that?
Fighting against an insurance company with millions at their disposal
$
$
And then there's the never-ending feeling of being silenced
OUR LITTLE SECRET
Eventually, though, shouldn't I get to the stage of acceptance?
But when I search inside myself for feelings of acceptance
I just slide back towards anxiety, depression, anger, bargaining, or denial
Or I start to imagine other ways I could confront him publicly
HARD I WANT AN APOLOGY!!
It's like I feel every emotion except acceptance!
I involved the police, I got a lawyer
I even talked to a private investigator!
After I tried so hard...
Hey! What about justice!
How could it all have failed?
slurp
You heard me—justice!

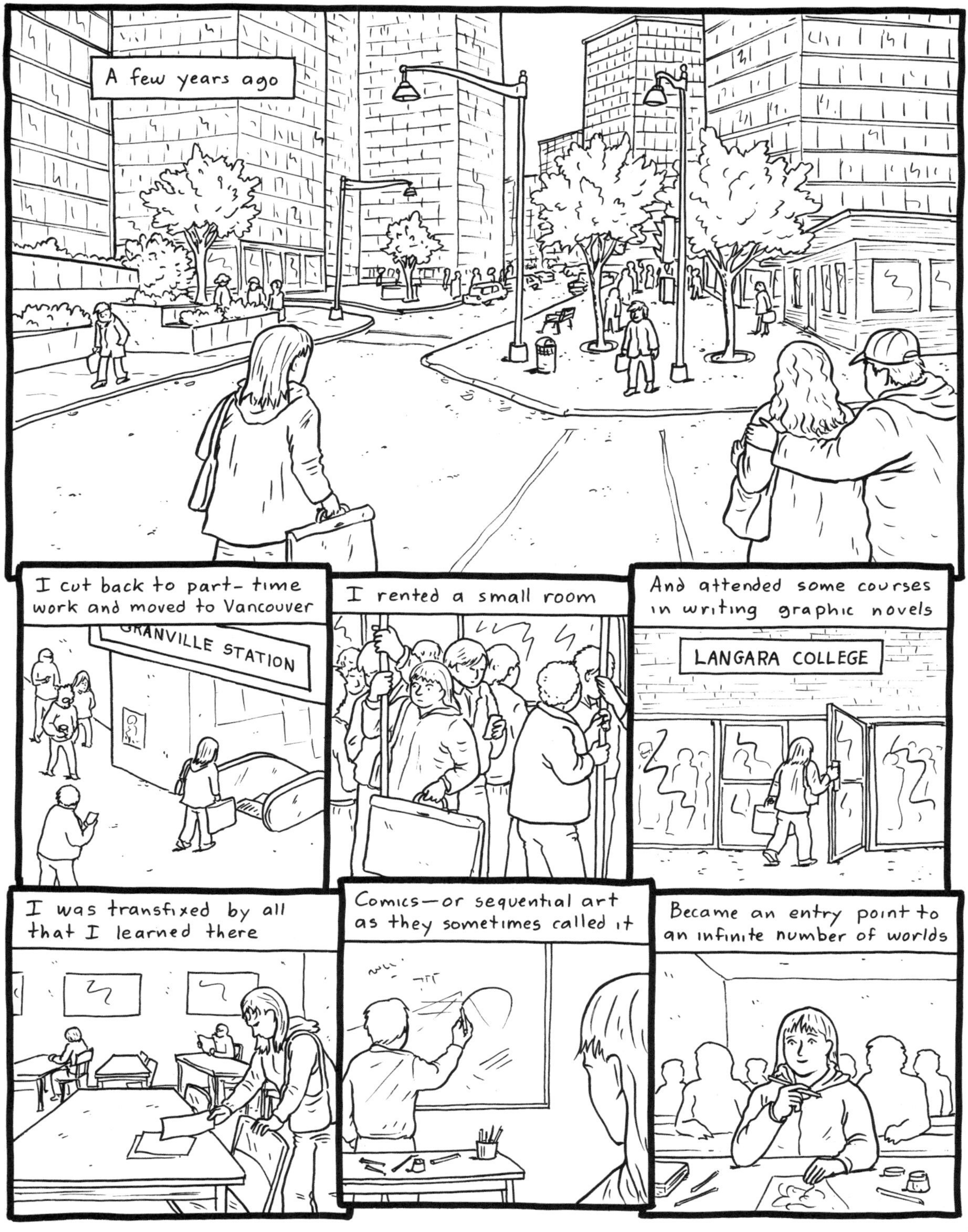
A few years ago
I cut back to part-time work and moved to Vancouver
GRANVILLE STATION
I rented a small room
And attended some courses in writing graphic novels
LANGARA COLLEGE
I was transfixed by all that I learned there
Comics—or sequential art as they sometimes called it
Became an entry point to an infinite number of worlds

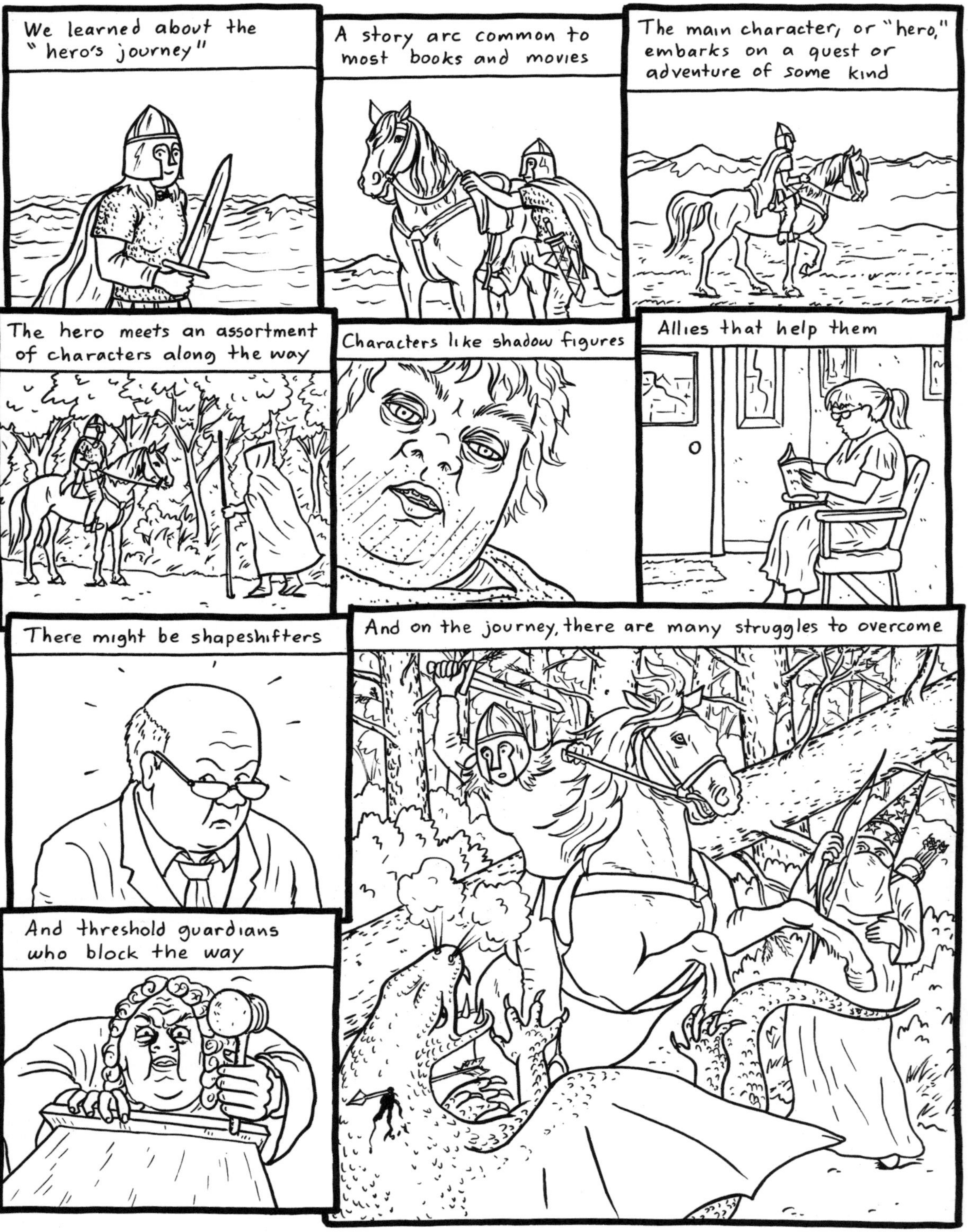

We learned about the "hero's journey"
A story arc common to most books and movies
The main character, or "hero," embarks on a quest or adventure of some kind
The hero meets an assortment of characters along the way
Characters like shadow figures
Allies that help them
There might be shapeshifters
And threshold guardians who block the way
And on the journey, there are many struggles to overcome

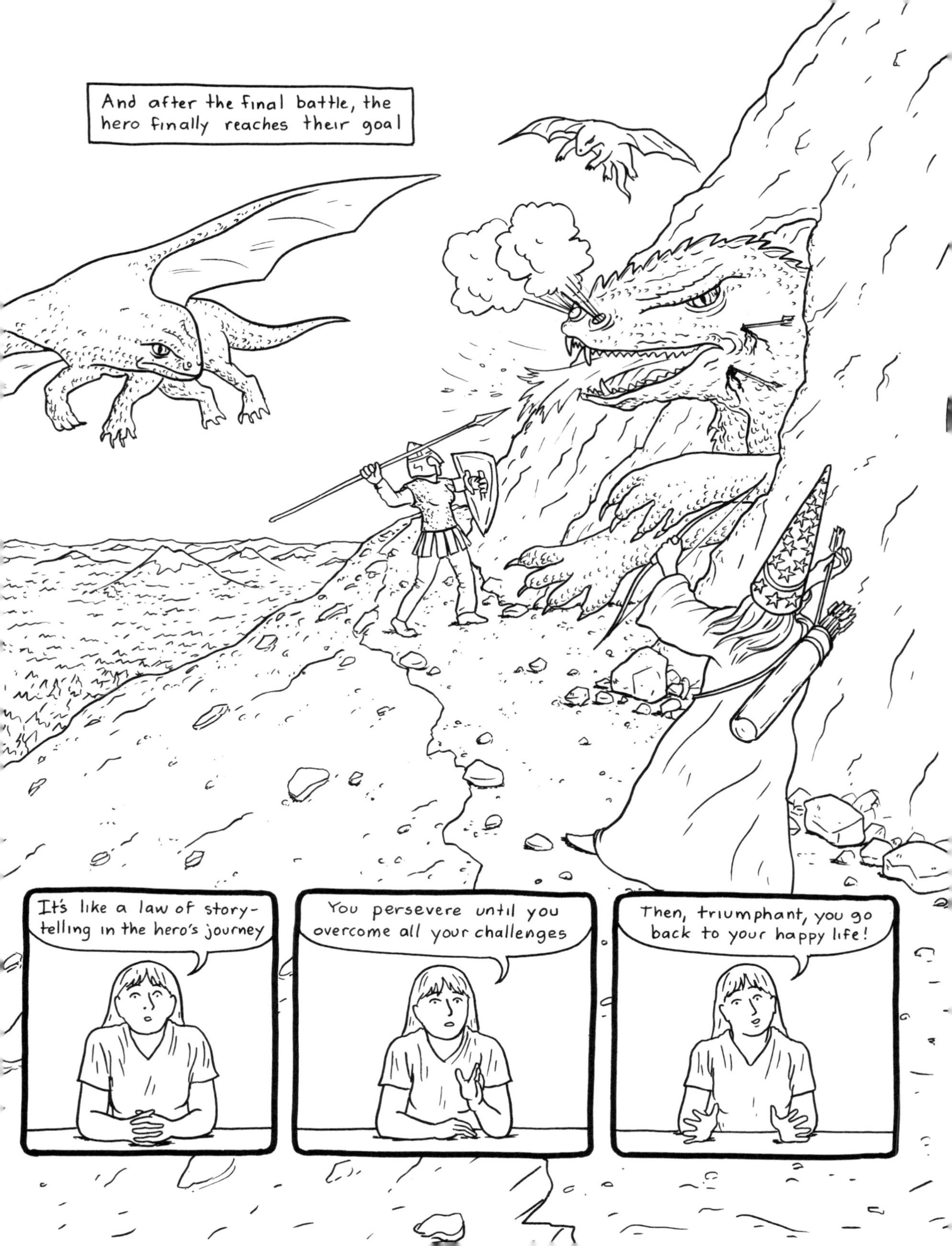

And after the final battle, the hero finally reaches their goal
It's like a law of story-telling in the hero's journey
You persevere until you overcome all your challenges
Then, triumphant, you go back to your happy life!

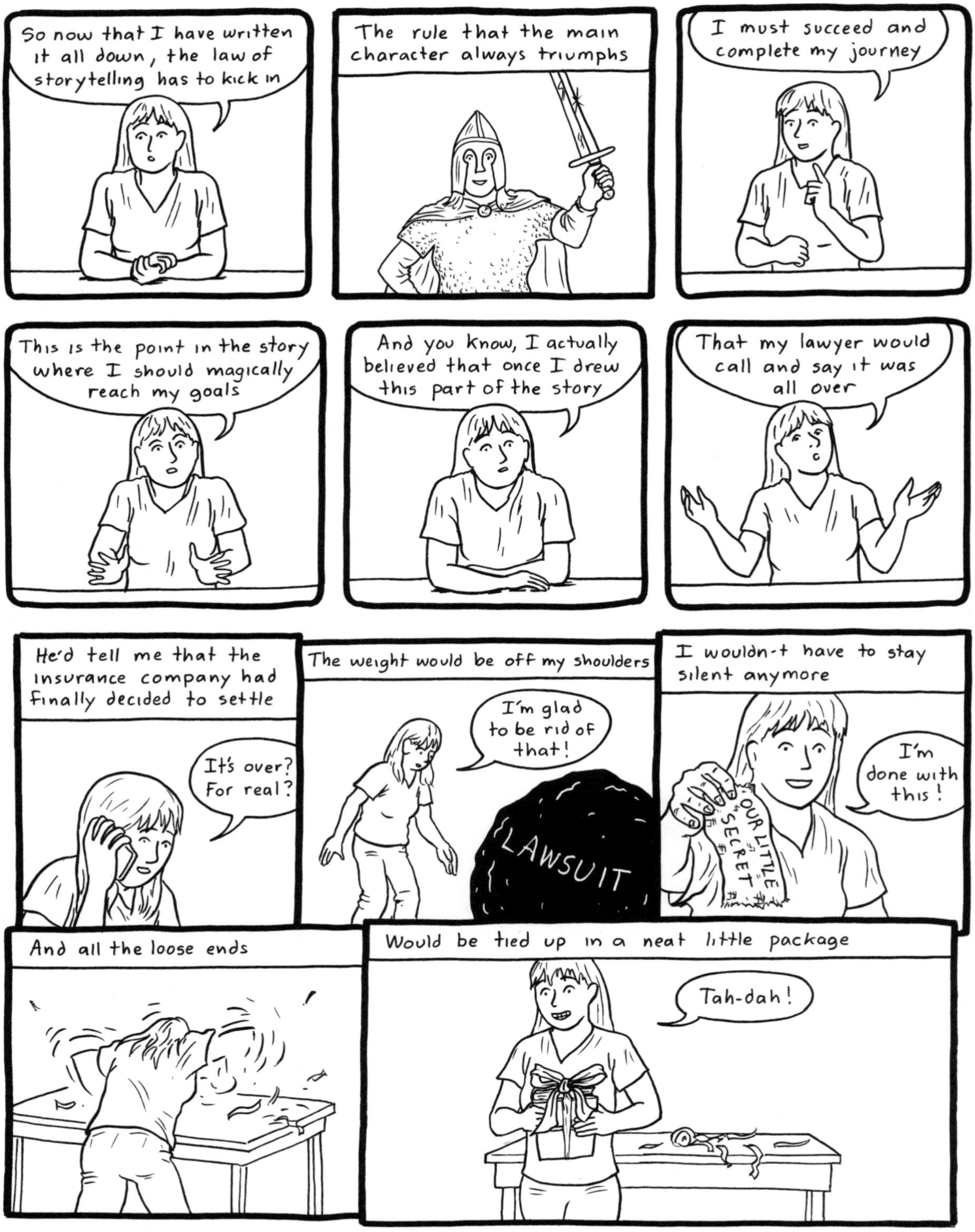
So now that I have written it all down, the law of storytelling has to kick in
The rule that the main character always triumphs
I must succeed and complete my journey
This is the point in the story where I should magically reach my goals
And you know, I actually believed that once I drew this part of the story
That my lawyer would call and say it was all over
He'd tell me that the insurance company had finally decided to settle
It's over? For real?
The weight would be off my shoulders
I'm glad to be rid of that!
LAWSUIT
I wouldn't have to stay silent anymore
I'm done with this!
OUR LITTLE SECRET
And all the loose ends
Would be tied up in a neat little package
Tah-dah!

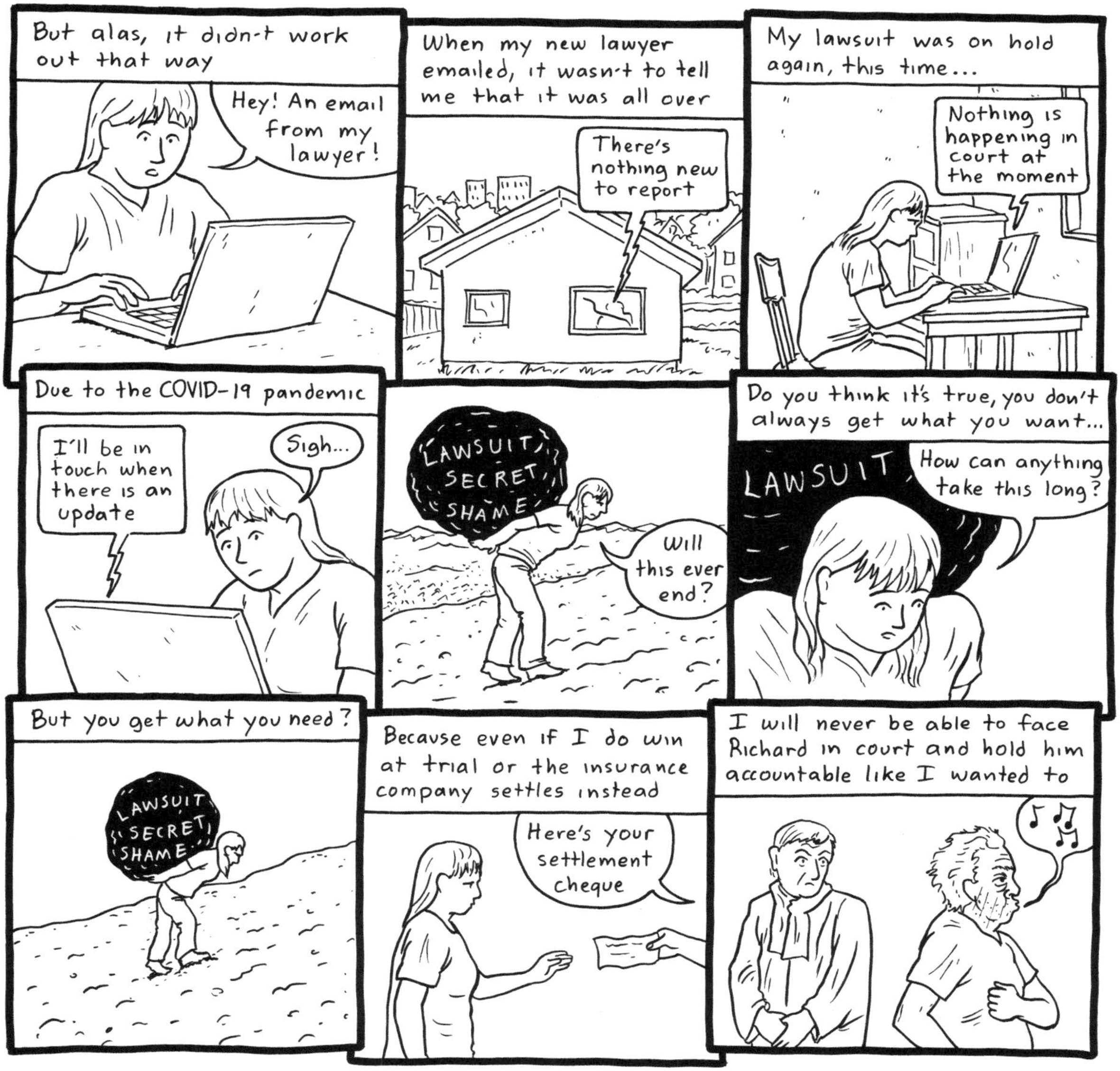
But alas, it didn't work out that way
Hey! An email from my lawyer!
When my new lawyer emailed, it wasn't to tell me that it was all over
There's nothing new to report
My lawsuit was on hold again, this time...
Nothing is happening in court at the moment
Due to the COVID-19 pandemic
I'll be in touch when there is an update
Sigh...
LAWSUIT SECRET SHAME
Will this ever end?
Do you think it's true, you don't always get what you want...
LAWSUIT
How can anything take this long?
But you get what you need?
LAWSUIT SECRET SHAME
Because even if I do win at trial or the insurance company settles instead
Here's your settlement cheque
I will never be able to face Richard in court and hold him accountable like I wanted to

In this story, the main character fails

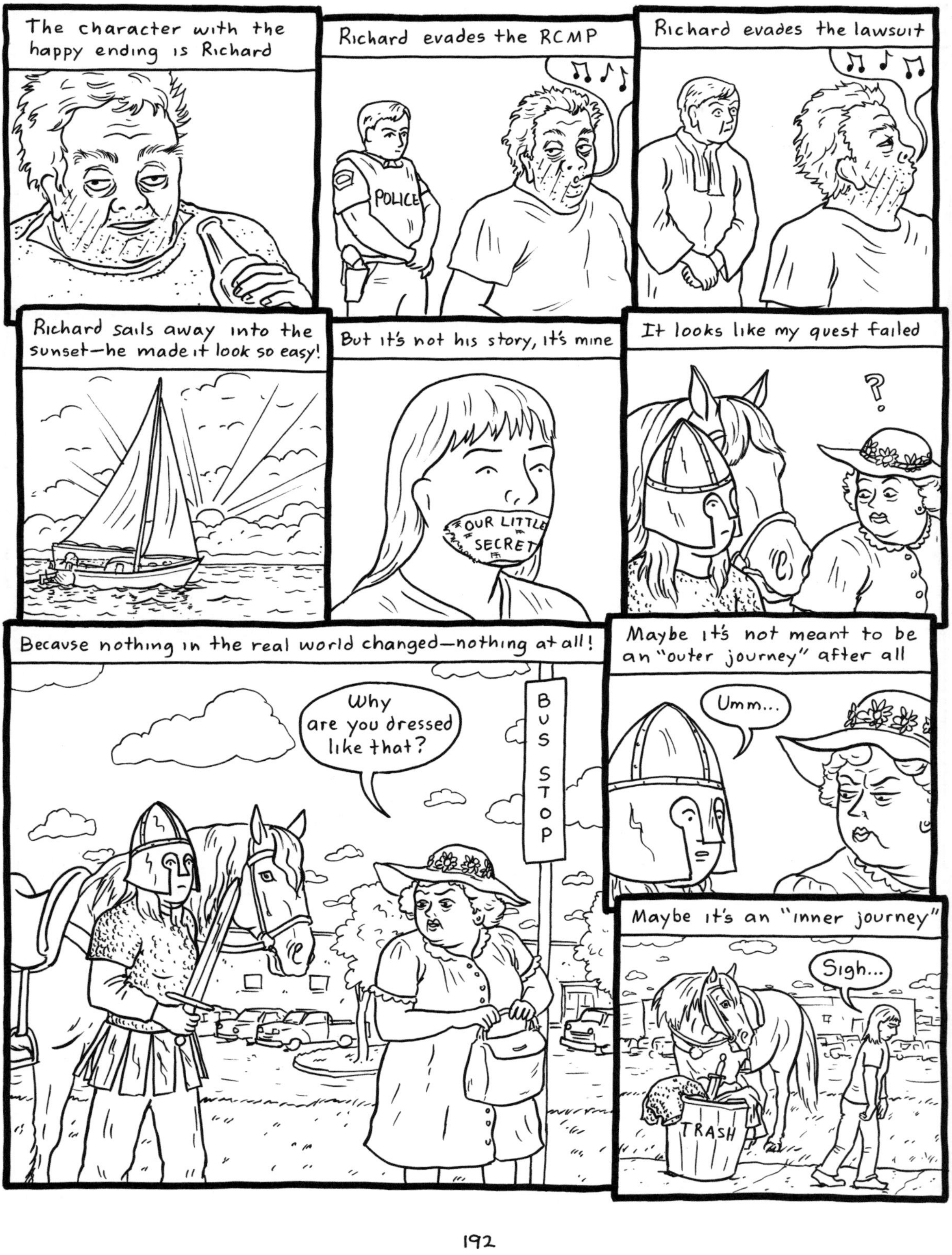
The character with the happy ending is Richard
Richard evades the RCMP
POLICE
Richard evades the lawsuit
Richard sails away into the sunset—he made it look so easy!
But it's not his story, it's mine
OUR LITTLE SECRET
It looks like my quest failed
?
Because nothing in the real world changed—nothing at all!
Why are you dressed like that?
BUS STOP
Maybe it's not meant to be an "outer journey" after all
Umm...
Maybe it's an "inner journey"
Sigh...
TRASH

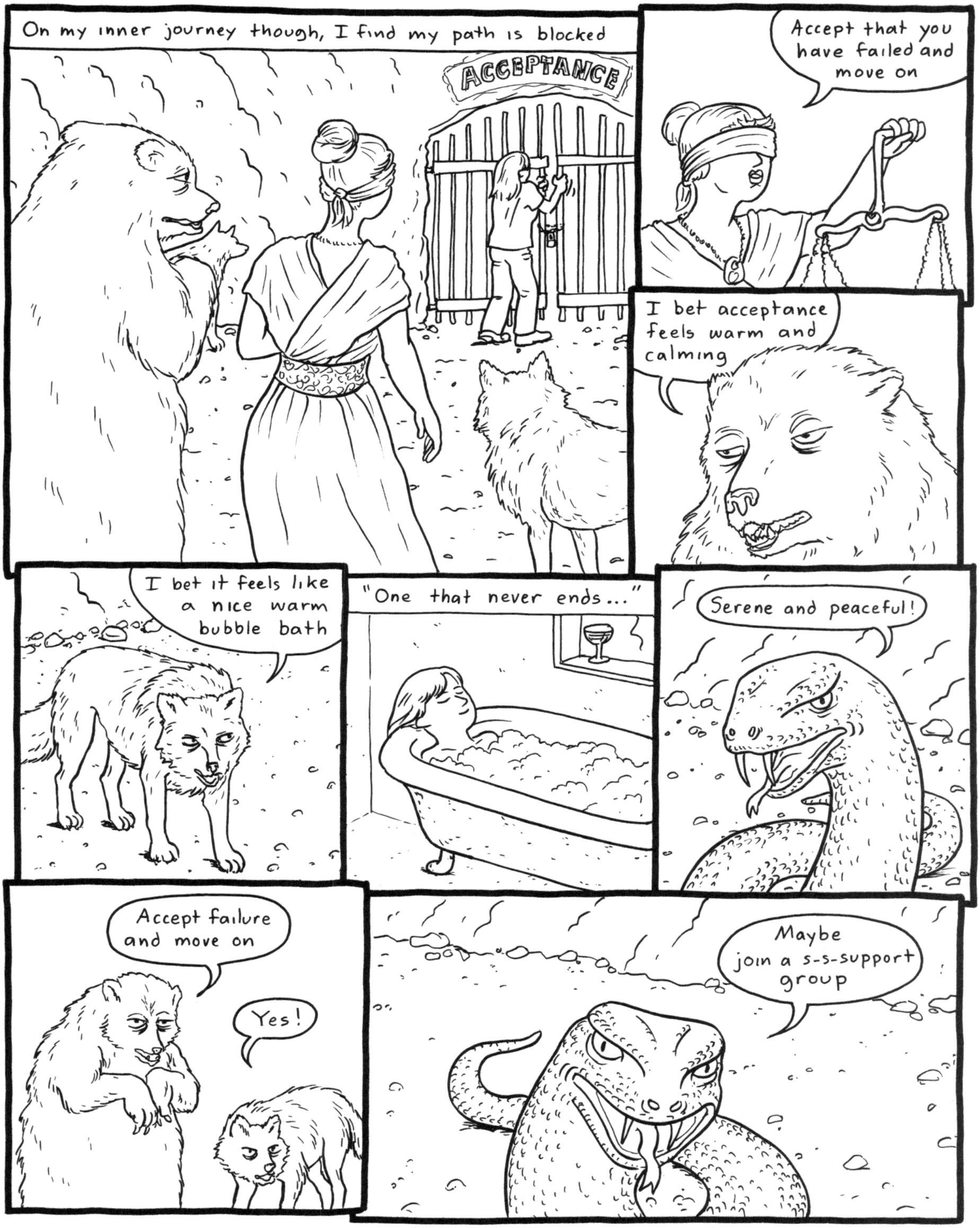
On my inner journey though, I find my path is blocked
ACCEPTANCE
Accept that you have failed and move on
I bet acceptance feels warm and calming
I bet it feels like a nice warm bubble bath
"One that never ends..."
Serene and peaceful!
Accept failure and move on
Yes!
Maybe join a s-s-support group

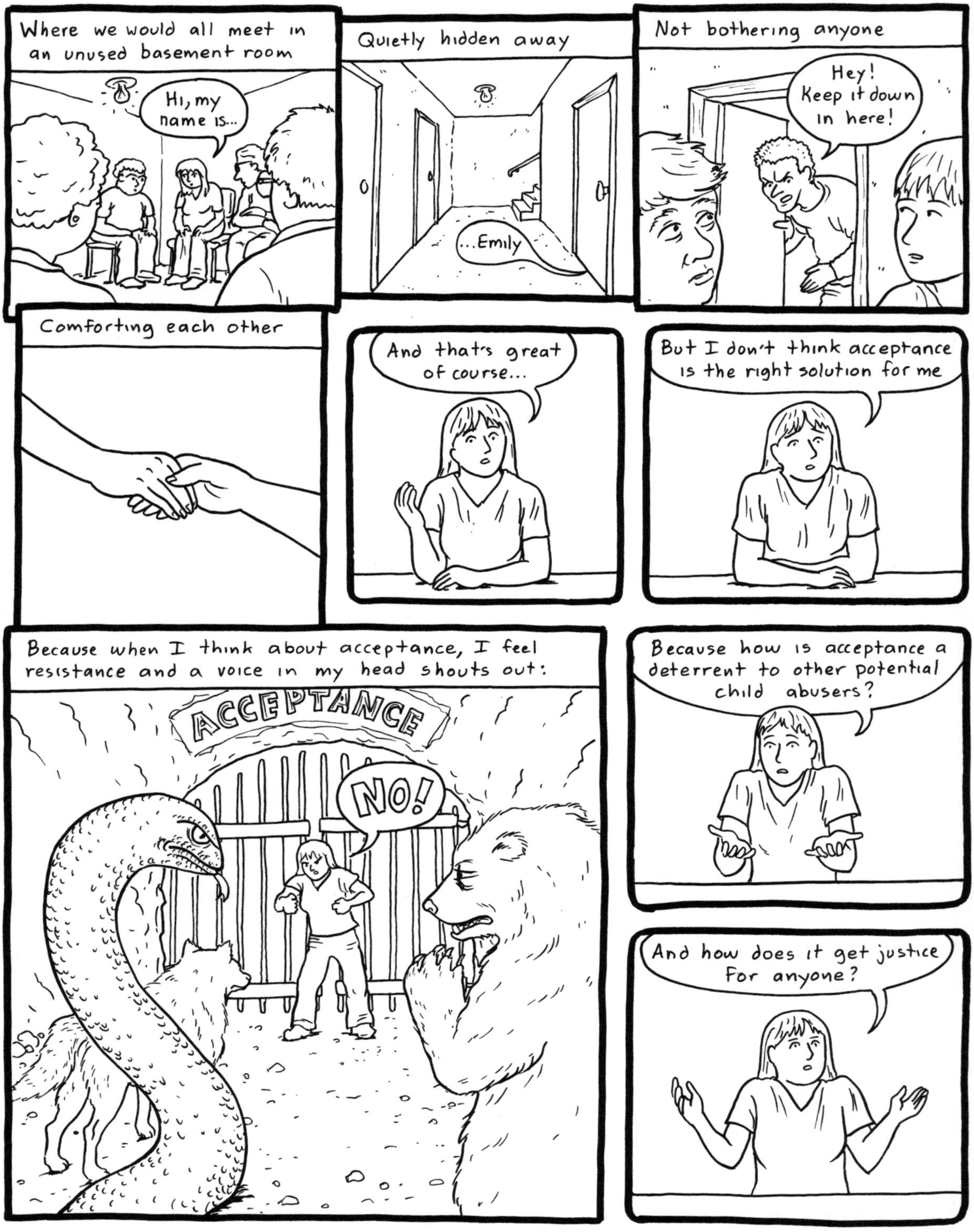
Where we would all meet in an unused basement room
Hi, my name is...
Quietly hidden away
...Emily
Not bothering anyone
Hey! Keep it down in here!
Comforting each other
And that's great of course...
But I don't think acceptance is the right solution for me
Because when I think about acceptance, I feel resistance and a voice in my head shouts out:
ACCEPTANCE
NO!
Because how is acceptance a deterrent to other potential child abusers?
And how does it get justice for anyone?

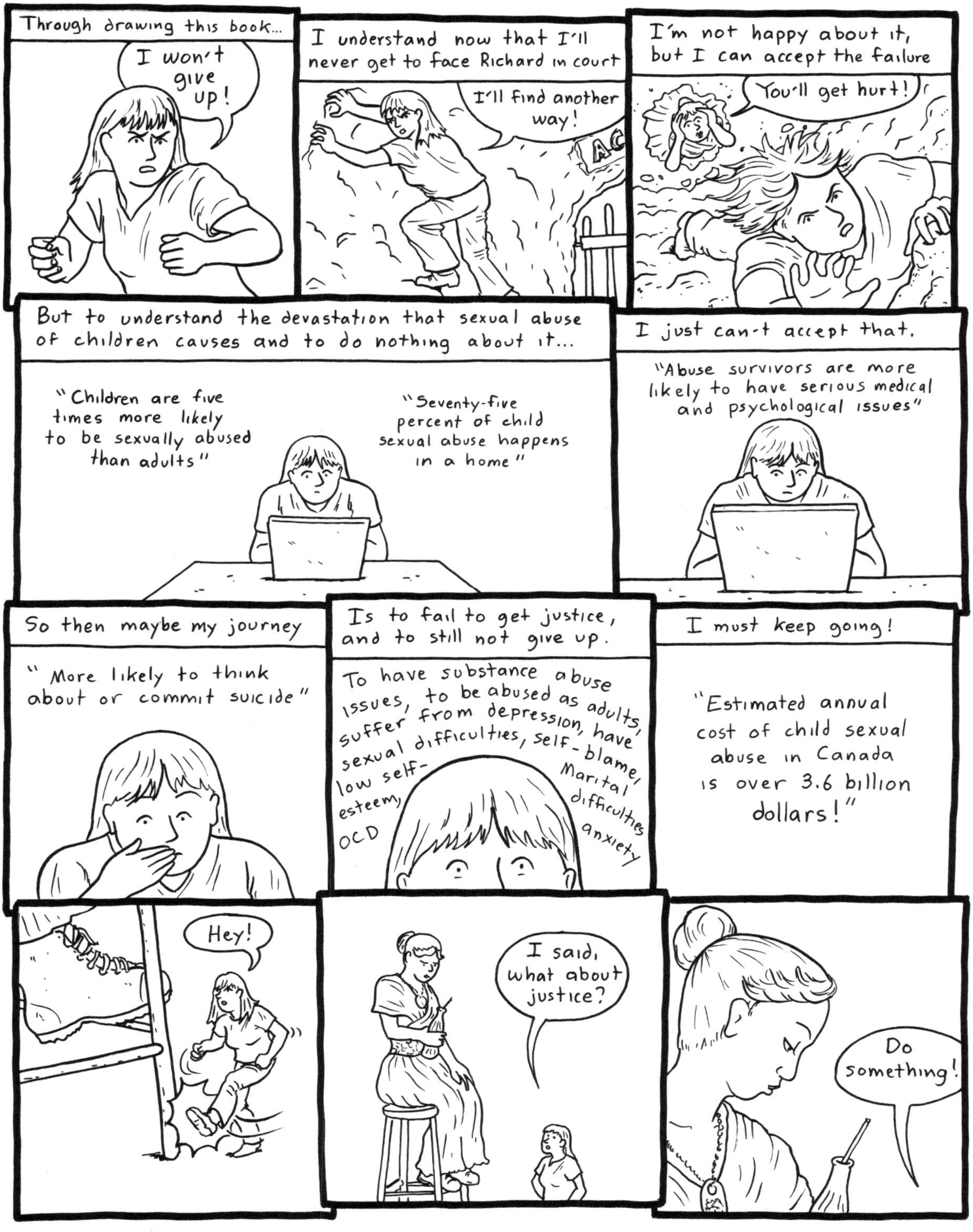

Through drawing this book...
I won't give up!
I understand now that I'll never get to face Richard in court
I'll find another way!
I'm not happy about it, but I can accept the failure
You'll get hurt!
But to understand the devastation that sexual abuse of children causes and to do nothing about it...
"Children are five times more likely to be sexually abused than adults"
"Seventy-five percent of child sexual abuse happens in a home"
I just can't accept that.
"Abuse survivors are more likely to have serious medical and psychological issues"
So then maybe my journey
"More likely to think about or commit suicide"
Is to fail to get justice, and to still not give up.
To have substance abuse issues, to be abused as adults, suffer from depression, have sexual difficulties, self-blame, low self-esteem,
Marital difficulties
anxiety
OCD
I must keep going!
"Estimated annual cost of child sexual abuse in Canada is over 3.6 billion dollars!"
Hey!
I said, what about justice?
Do something!

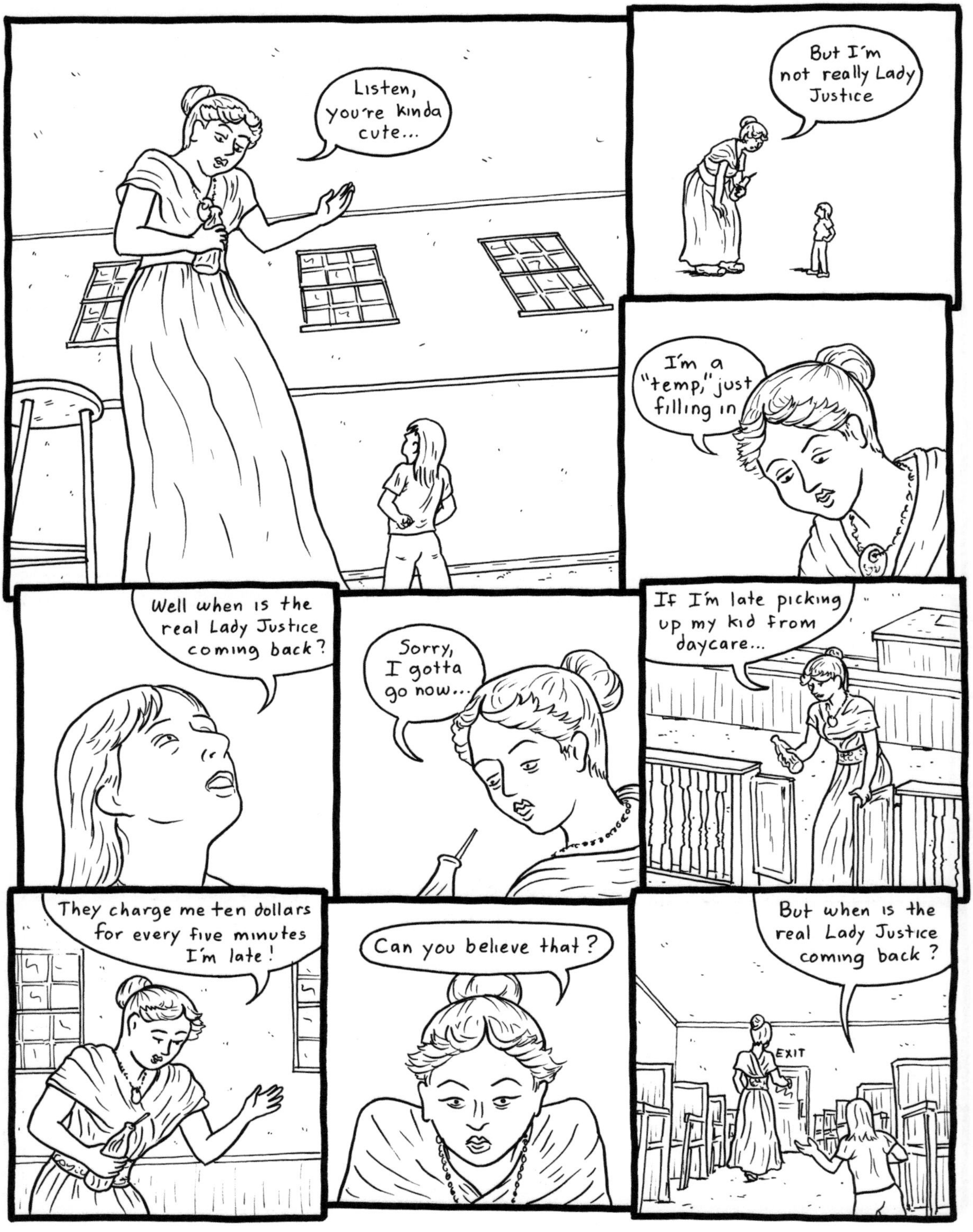
Listen, you're kinda cute...
But I'm not really Lady Justice
I'm a "temp," just filling in
Well when is the real Lady Justice coming back?
Sorry, I gotta go now...
If I'm late picking up my kid from daycare...
They charge me ten dollars for every five minutes I'm late!
Can you believe that?
But when is the real Lady Justice coming back?
EXIT

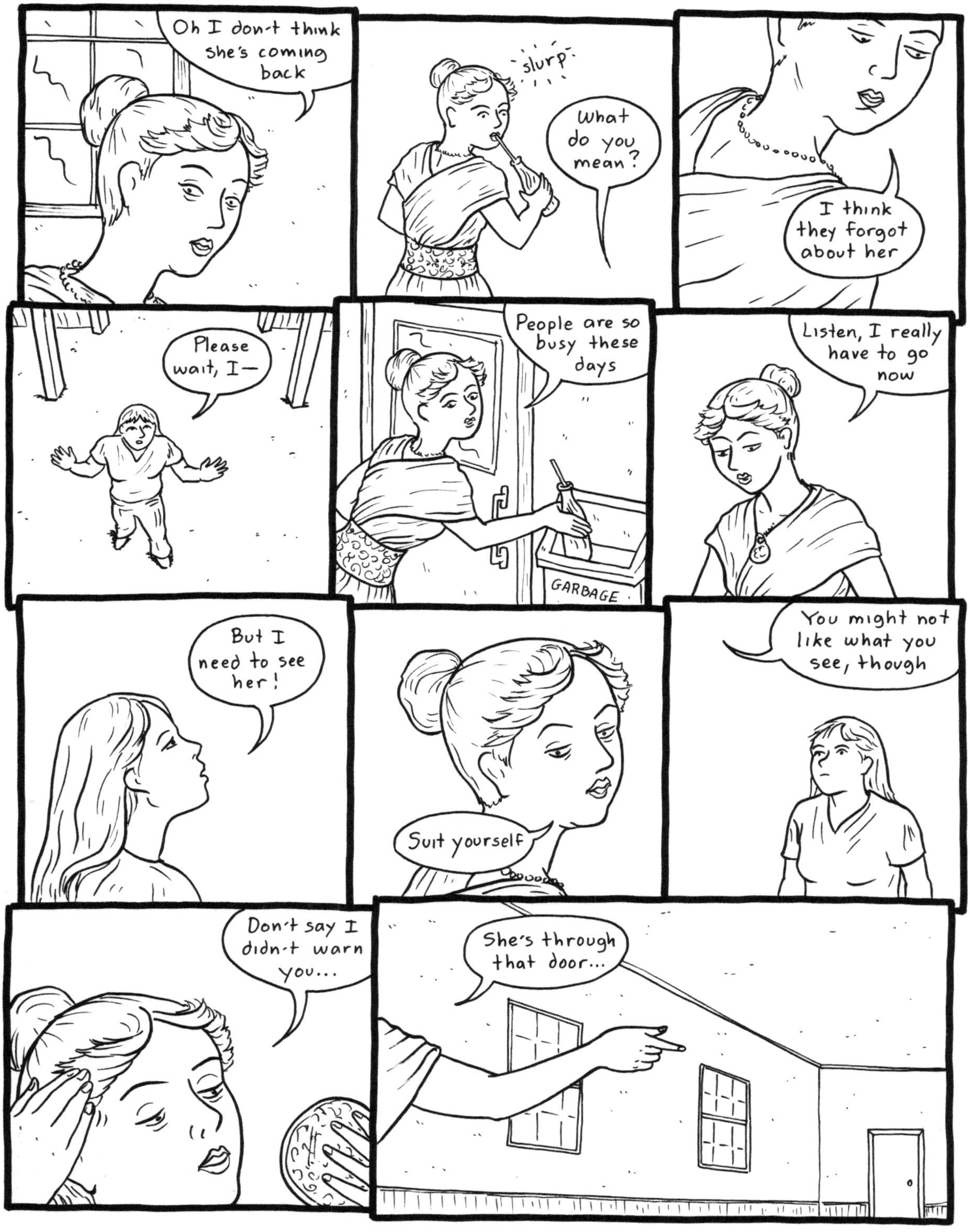

Oh I don't think she's coming back
slurp
What do you mean?
I think they forgot about her
Please wait, I—
People are so busy these days
GARBAGE
Listen, I really have to go now
But I need to see her!
Suit yourself
You might not like what you see, though
Don't say I didn't warn you...
She's through that door...

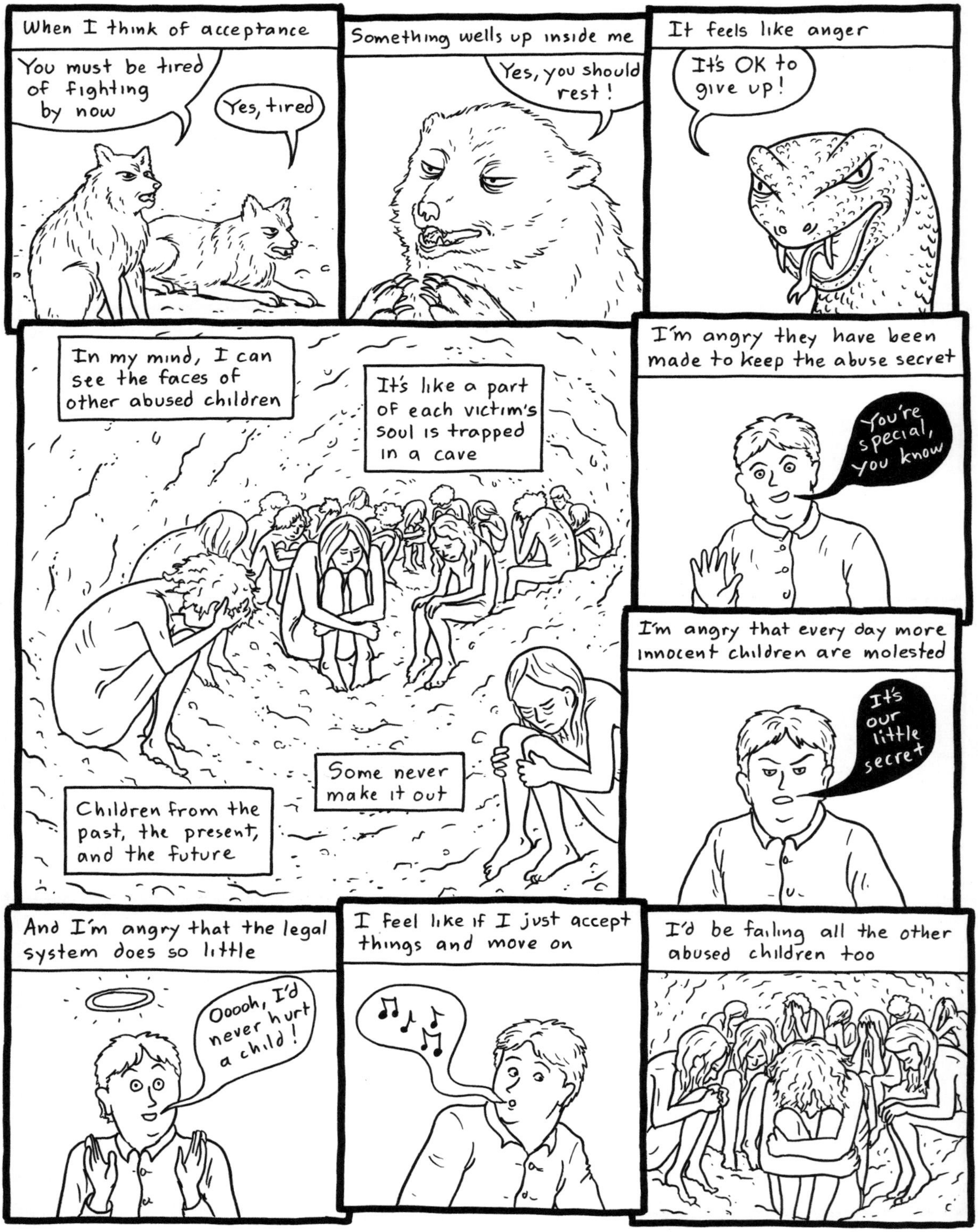
When I think of acceptance
You must be tired of fighting by now
Yes, tired
Something wells up inside me
Yes, you should rest!
It feels like anger
It's OK to give up!
In my mind, I can see the faces of other abused children
It's like a part of each victim's soul is trapped in a cave
Some never make it out
Children from the past, the present, and the future
I'm angry they have been made to keep the abuse secret
You're special, you know
I'm angry that every day more innocent children are molested
It's our little secret
And I'm angry that the legal system does so little
Ooooh, I'd never hurt a child!
I feel like if I just accept things and move on
I'd be failing all the other abused children too

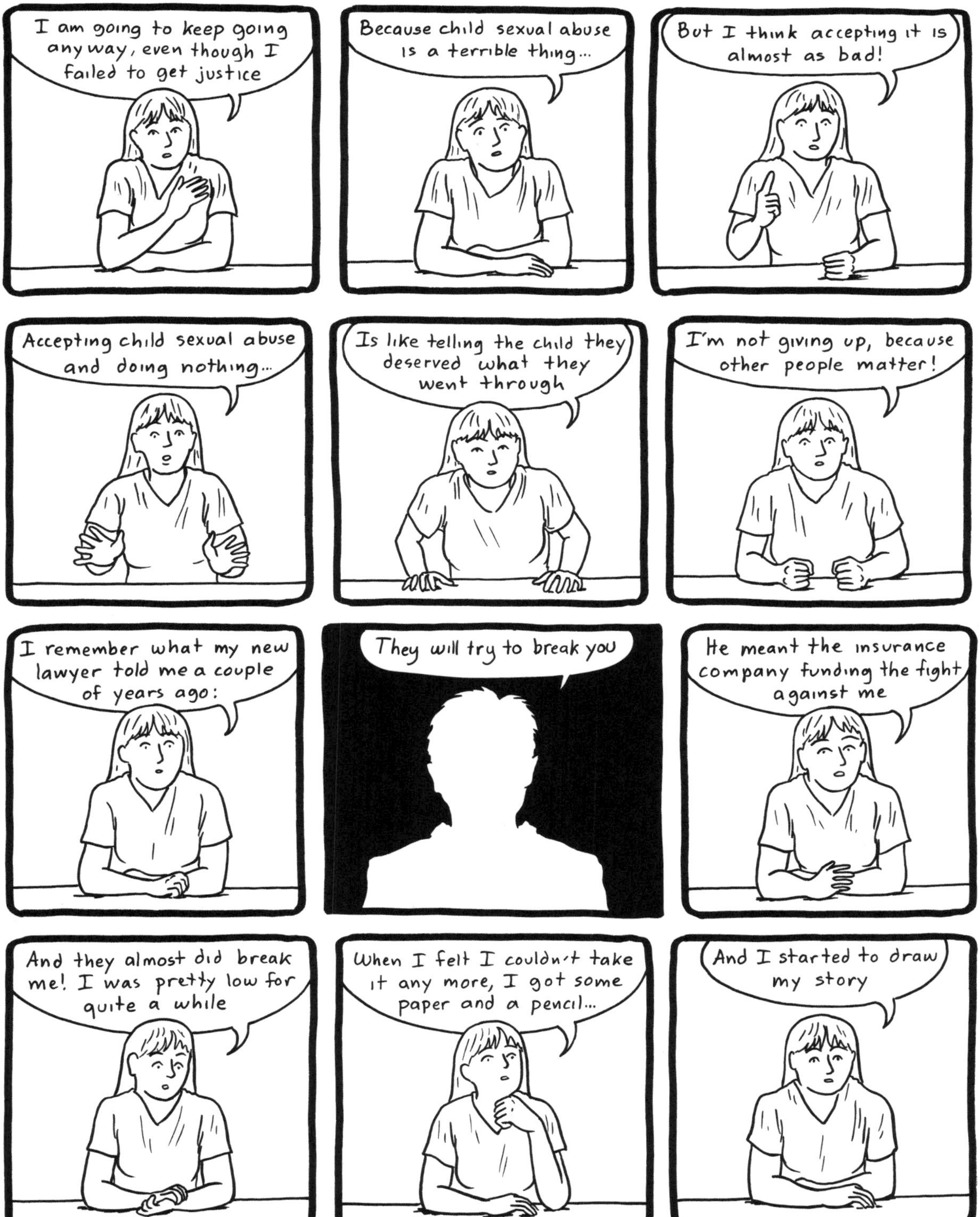
I am going to keep going anyway, even though I failed to get justice
Because child sexual abuse is a terrible thing...
But I think accepting it is almost as bad!
Accepting child sexual abuse and doing nothing...
Is like telling the child they deserved what they went through
I'm not giving up, because other people matter!
I remember what my new lawyer told me a couple of years ago:
They will try to break you
He meant the insurance company funding the fight against me
And they almost did break me! I was pretty low for quite a while
When I felt I couldn't take it any more, I got some paper and a pencil...
And I started to draw my story

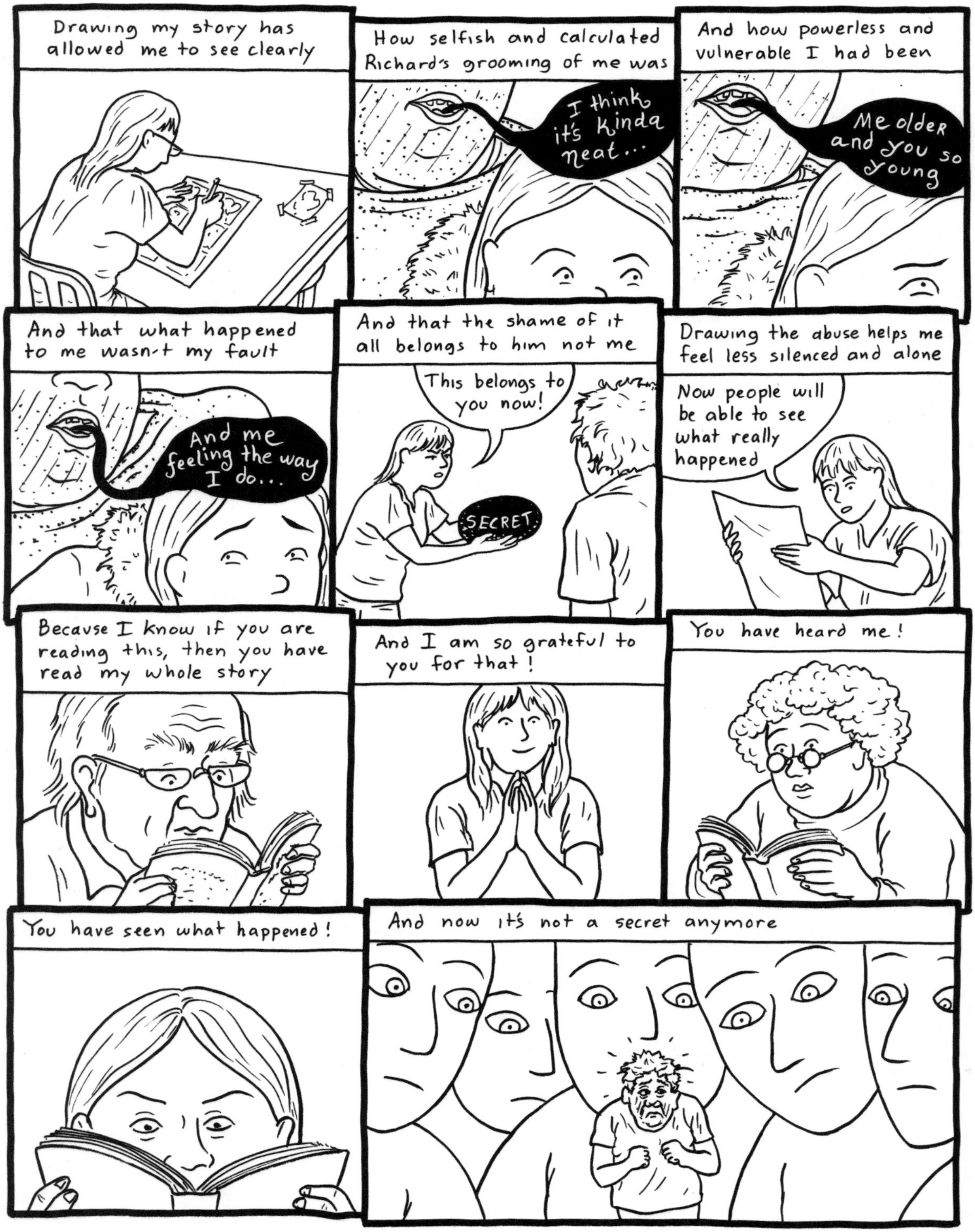

Drawing my story has allowed me to see clearly
How selfish and calculated Richard's grooming of me was
I think it's kinda neat...
And how powerless and vulnerable I had been
Me older and you so young
And that what happened to me wasn't my fault
And me feeling the way I do...
And that the shame of it all belongs to him not me
This belongs to you now!
SECRET
Drawing the abuse helps me feel less silenced and alone
Now people will be able to see what really happened
Because I know if you are reading this, then you have read my whole story
And I am so grateful to you for that!
You have heard me!
You have seen what happened!
And now it's not a secret anymore

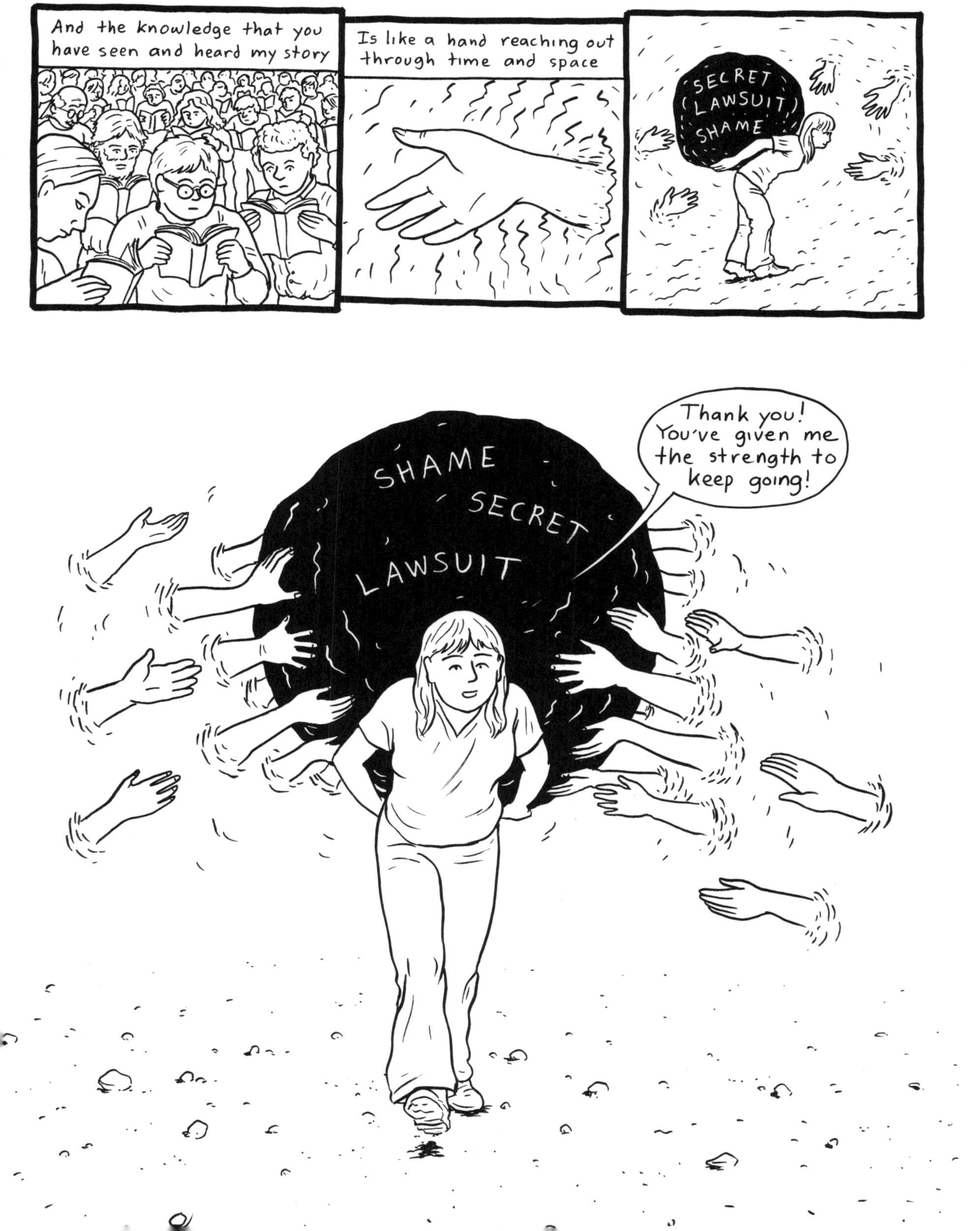

And the knowledge that you have seen and heard my story
Is like a hand reaching out through time and space
SECRET
LAWSUIT
SHAME
SHAME
SECRET
LAWSUIT
Thank you! You've given me the strength to keep going!

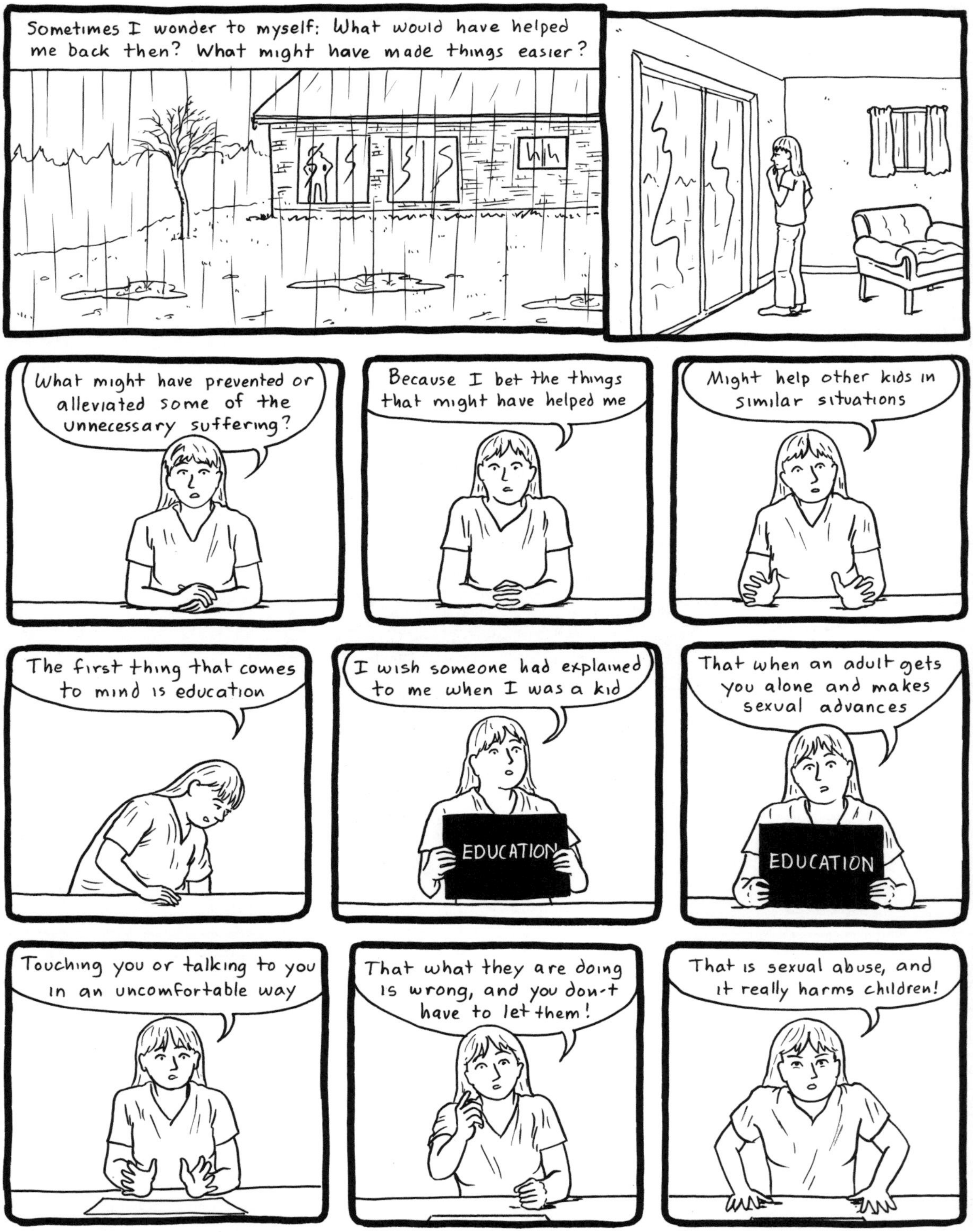
Sometimes I wonder to myself: What would have helped me back then? What might have made things easier?
What might have prevented or alleviated some of the unnecessary suffering?
Because I bet the things that might have helped me
Might help other kids in similar situations
The first thing that comes to mind is education
I wish someone had explained to me when I was a kid
EDUCATION
That when an adult gets you alone and makes sexual advances
EDUCATION
Touching you or talking to you in an uncomfortable way
That what they are doing is wrong, and you don-t have to let them!
That is sexual abuse, and it really harms children!

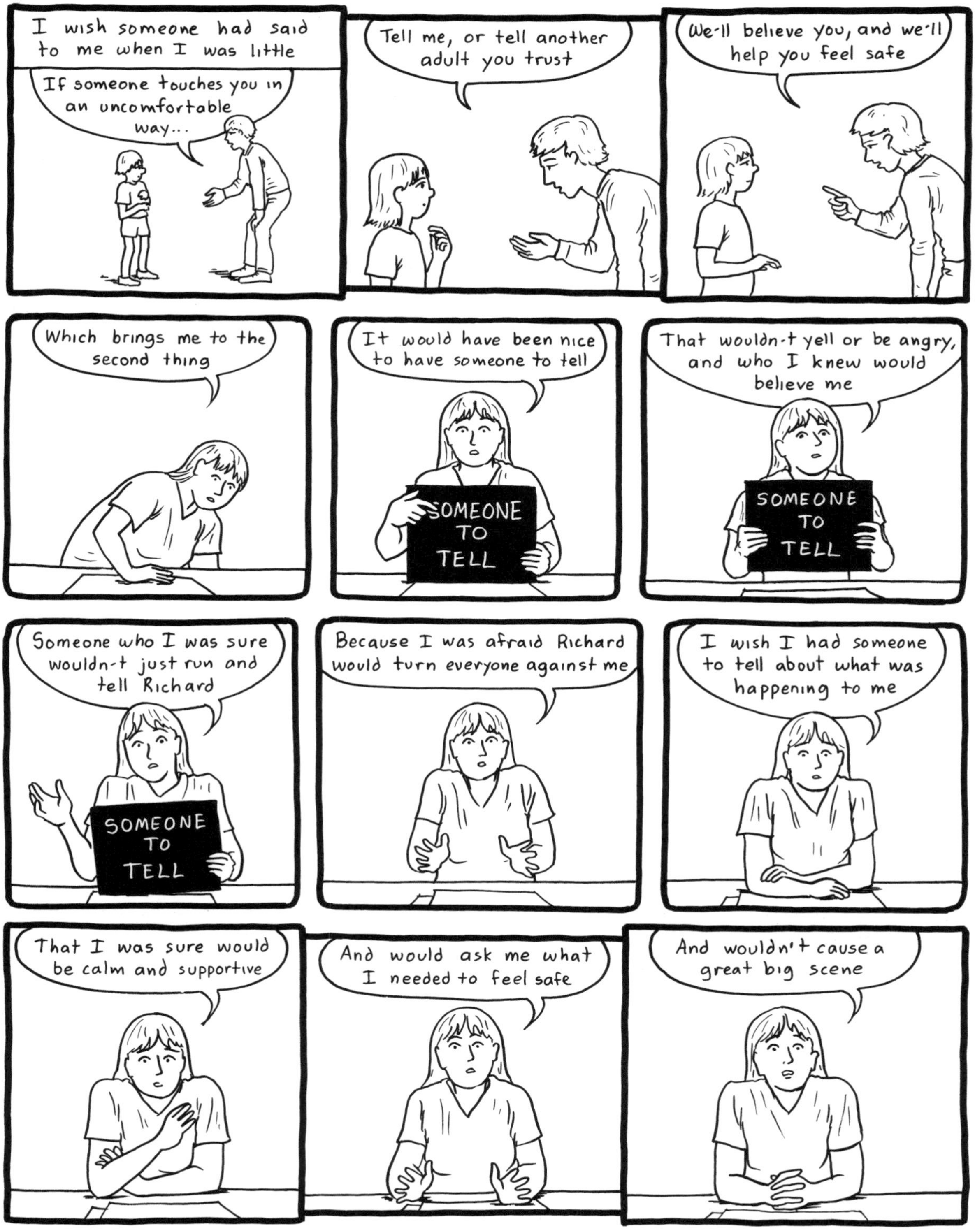
I wish someone had said to me when I was little
If someone touches you in an uncomfortable way...
Tell me, or tell another adult you trust
We'll believe you, and we'll help you feel safe
Which brings me to the second thing
It would have been nice to have someone to tell
SOMEONE TO TELL
That wouldn't yell or be angry, and who I knew would believe me
SOMEONE TO TELL
Someone who I was sure wouldn't just run and tell Richard
SOMEONE TO TELL
Because I was afraid Richard would turn everyone against me
I wish I had someone to tell about what was happening to me
That I was sure would be calm and supportive
And would ask me what I needed to feel safe
And wouldn't cause a great big scene

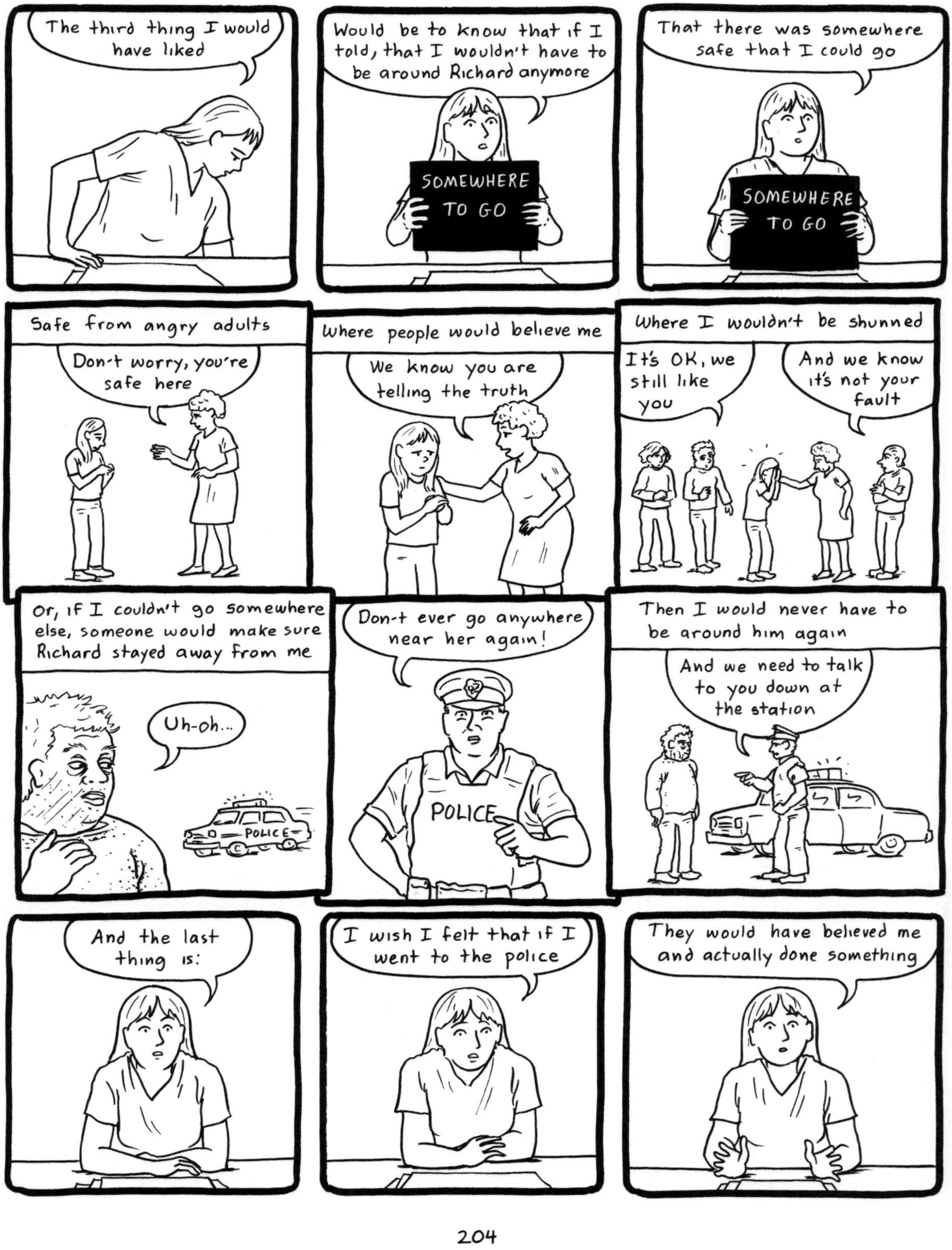

The third thing I would have liked
Would be to know that if I told, that I wouldn't have to be around Richard anymore
SOMEWHERE TO GO
That there was somewhere safe that I could go
SOMEWHERE TO GO
Safe from angry adults
Don't worry, you're safe here
Where people would believe me
We know you are telling the truth
Where I wouldn't be shunned
It's OK, we still like you
And we know it's not your fault
Or, if I couldn't go somewhere else, someone would make sure Richard stayed away from me
Uh-oh...
POLICE
Don't ever go anywhere near her again!
POLICE
Then I would never have to be around him again
And we need to talk to you down at the station
And the last thing is:
I wish I felt that if I went to the police
They would have believed me and actually done something

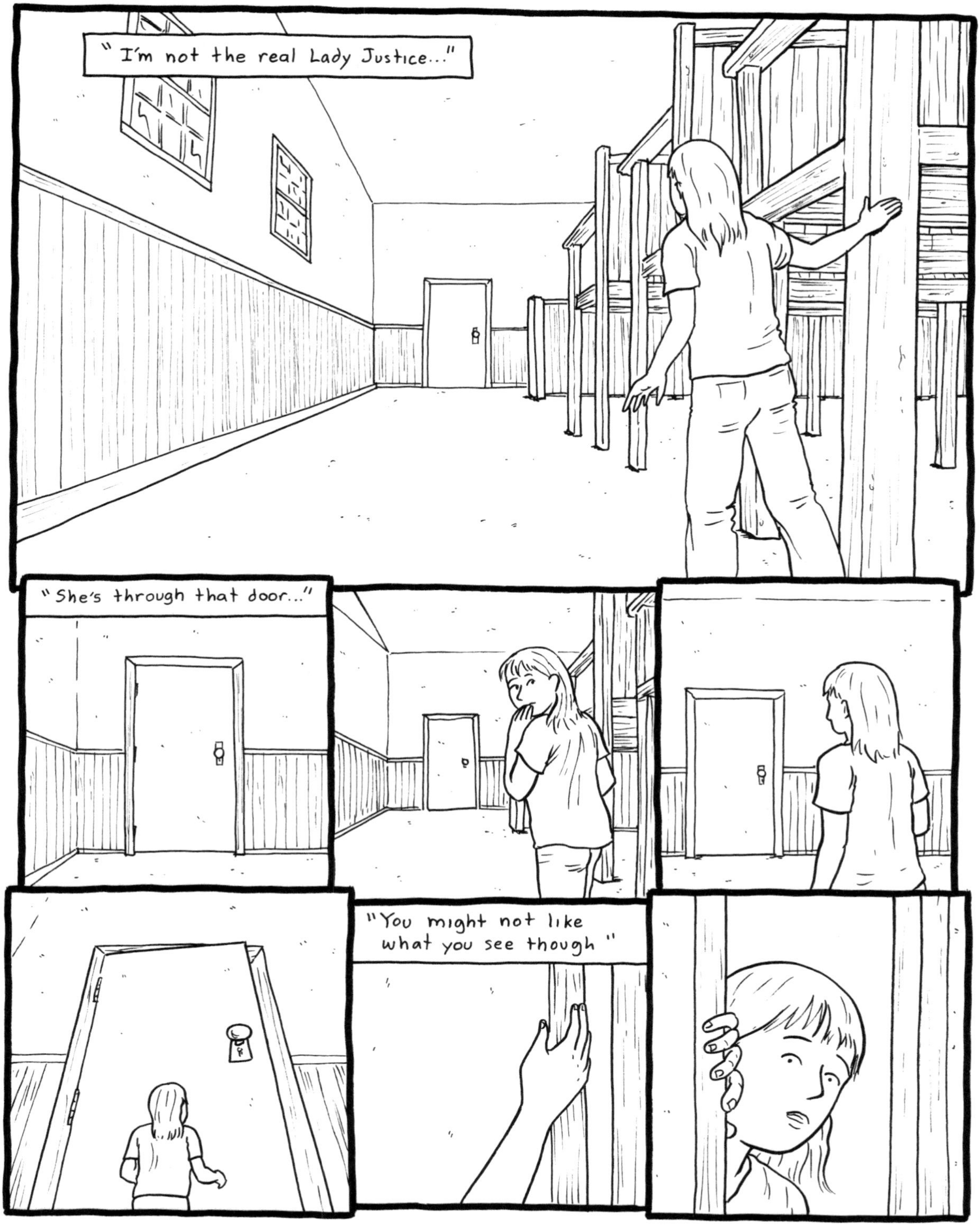
"I'm not the real Lady Justice..."
"She's through that door..."
"You might not like what you see though"

And so, the inner journey continues...

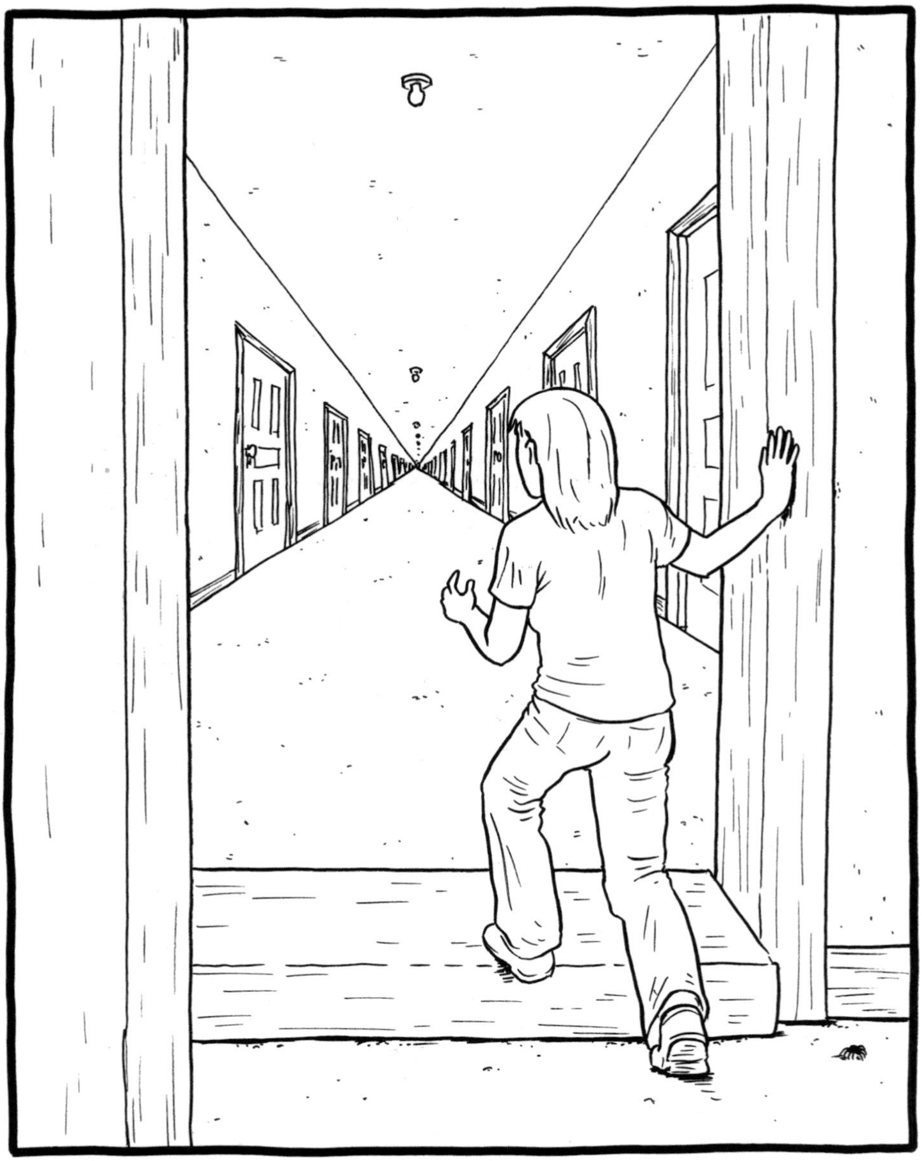

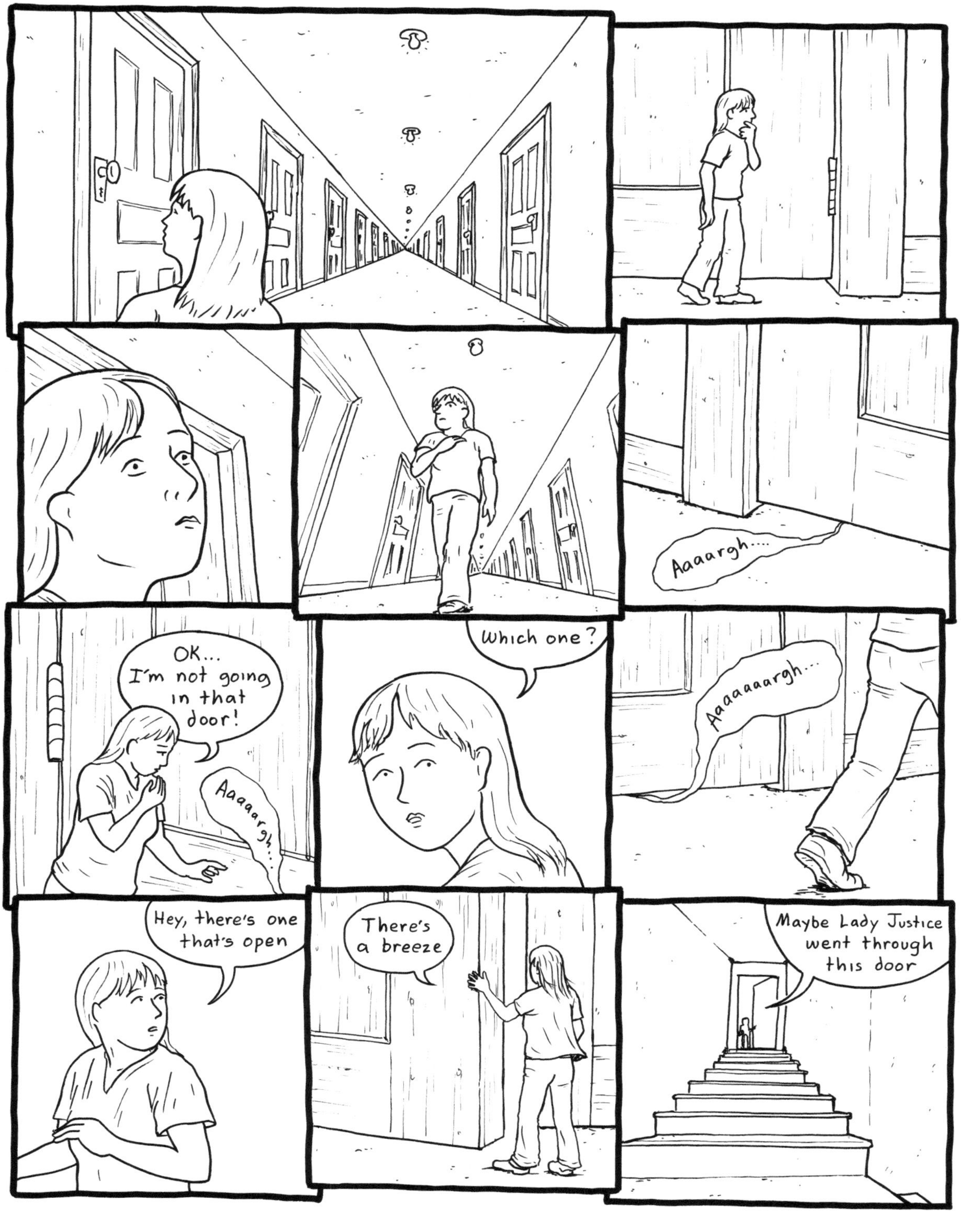
Aaaargh....
OK... I'm not going in that door!
Aaaaargh...
Which one?
Aaaaaaargh...
Hey, there's one that's open
There's a breeze
Maybe Lady Justice went through this door

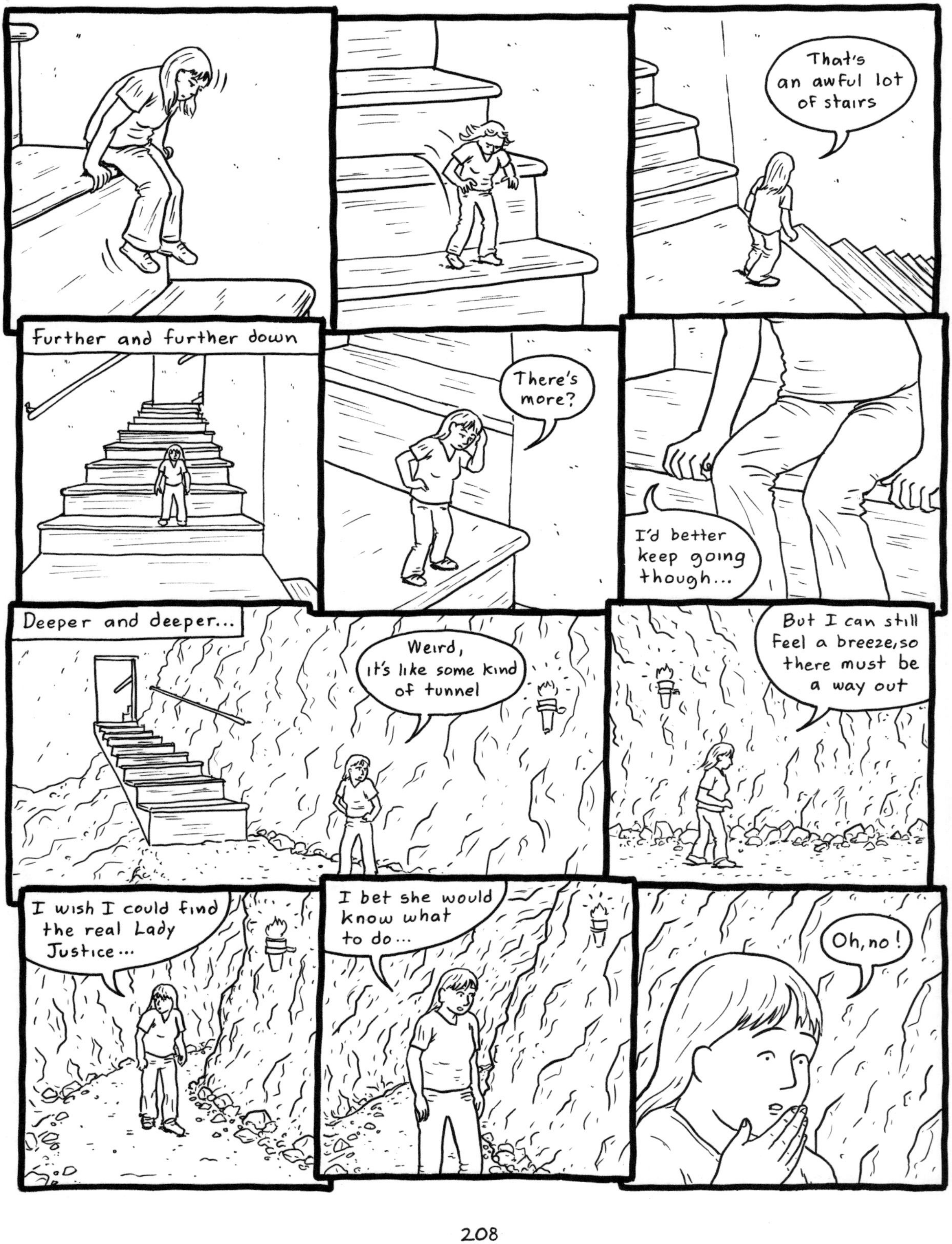

That's an awful lot of stairs
Further and further down
There's more?
I'd better keep going though...
Deeper and deeper...
Weird, it's like some kind of tunnel
But I can still feel a breeze, so there must be a way out
I wish I could find the real Lady Justice...
I bet she would know what to do...
Oh, no!

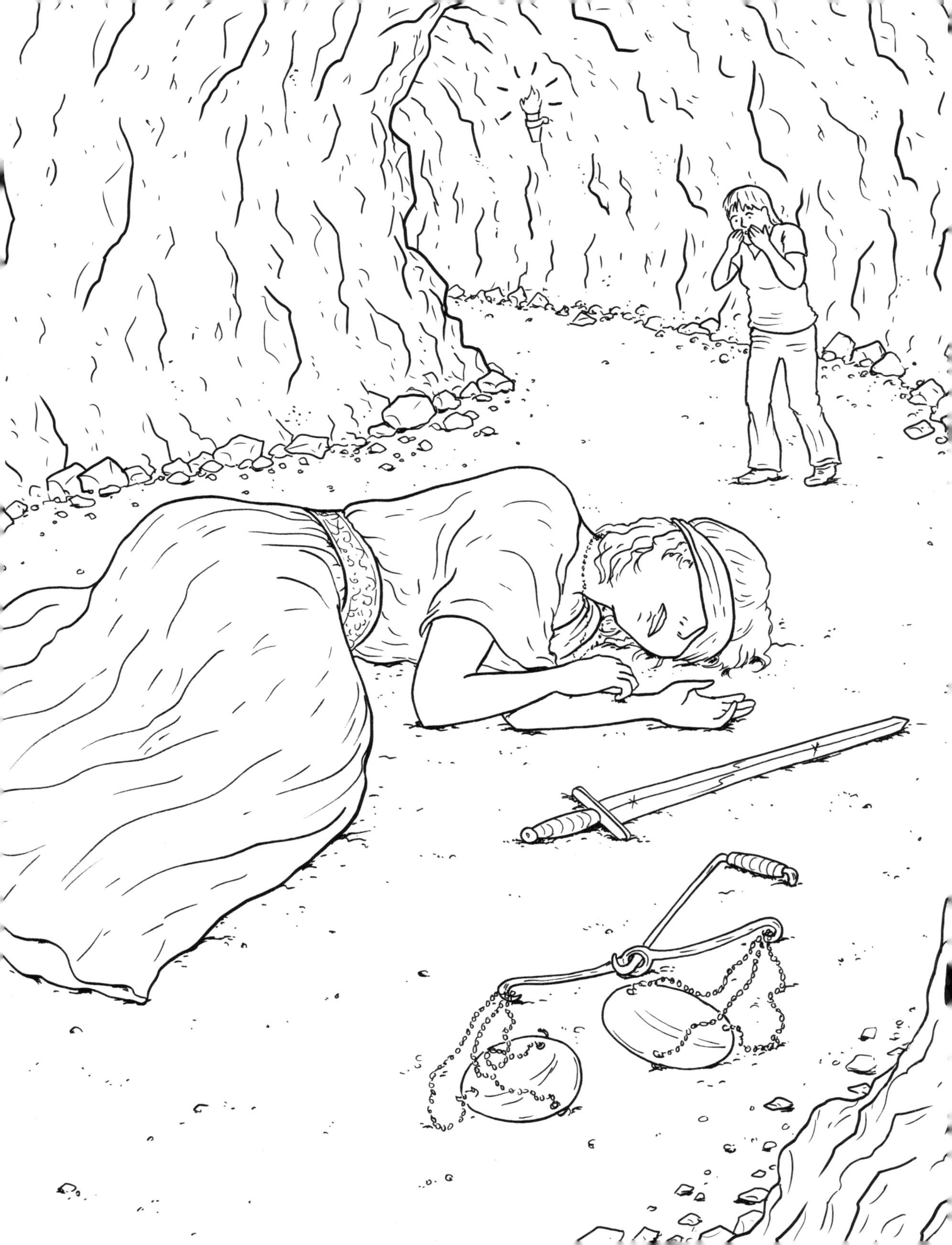

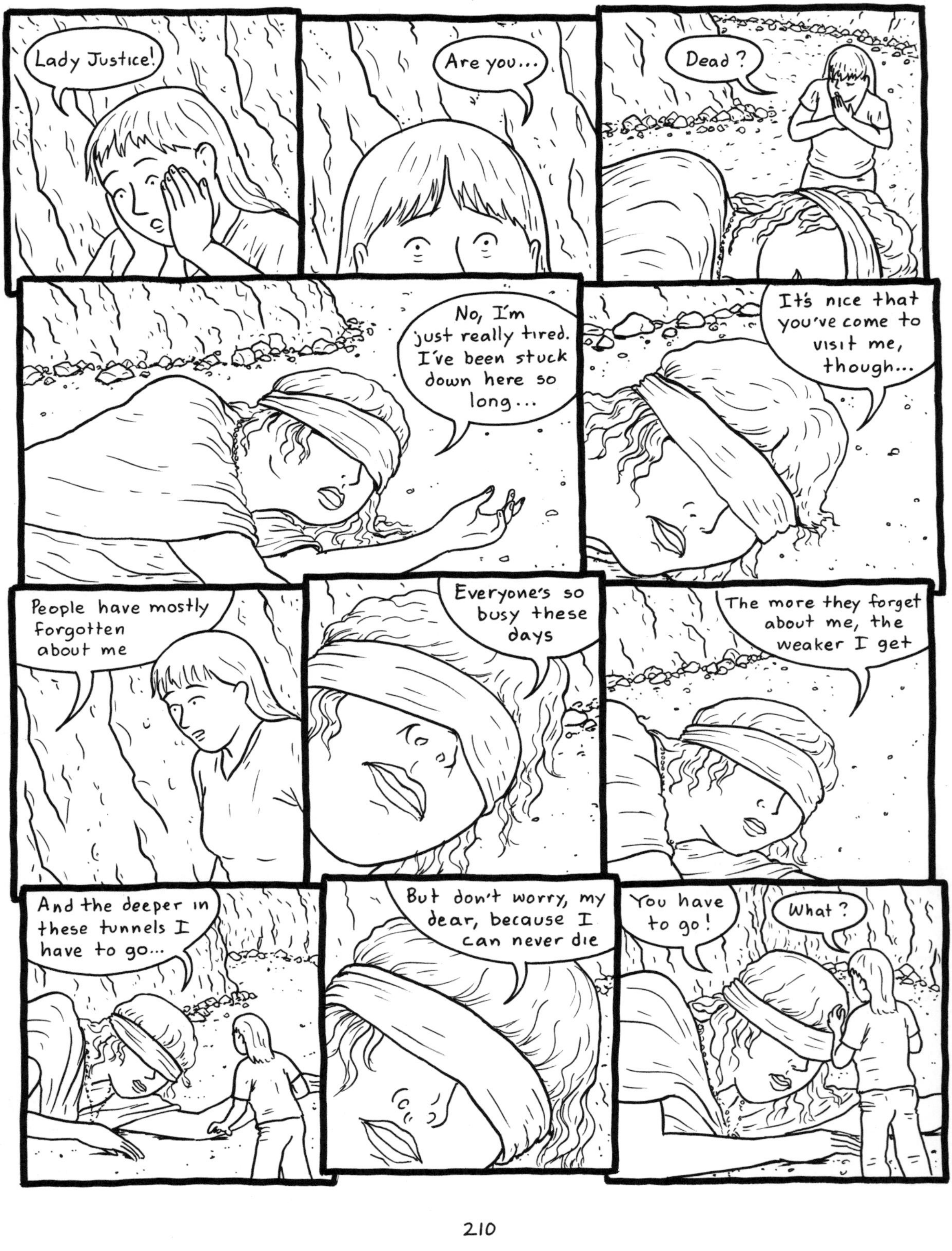
Lady Justice!
Are you...
Dead?
No, I'm just really tired. I've been stuck down here so long...
It's nice that you've come to visit me, though...
People have mostly forgotten about me
Everyone's so busy these days
The more they forget about me, the weaker I get
And the deeper in these tunnels I have to go...
But don't worry, my dear, because I can never die
You have to go!
What?

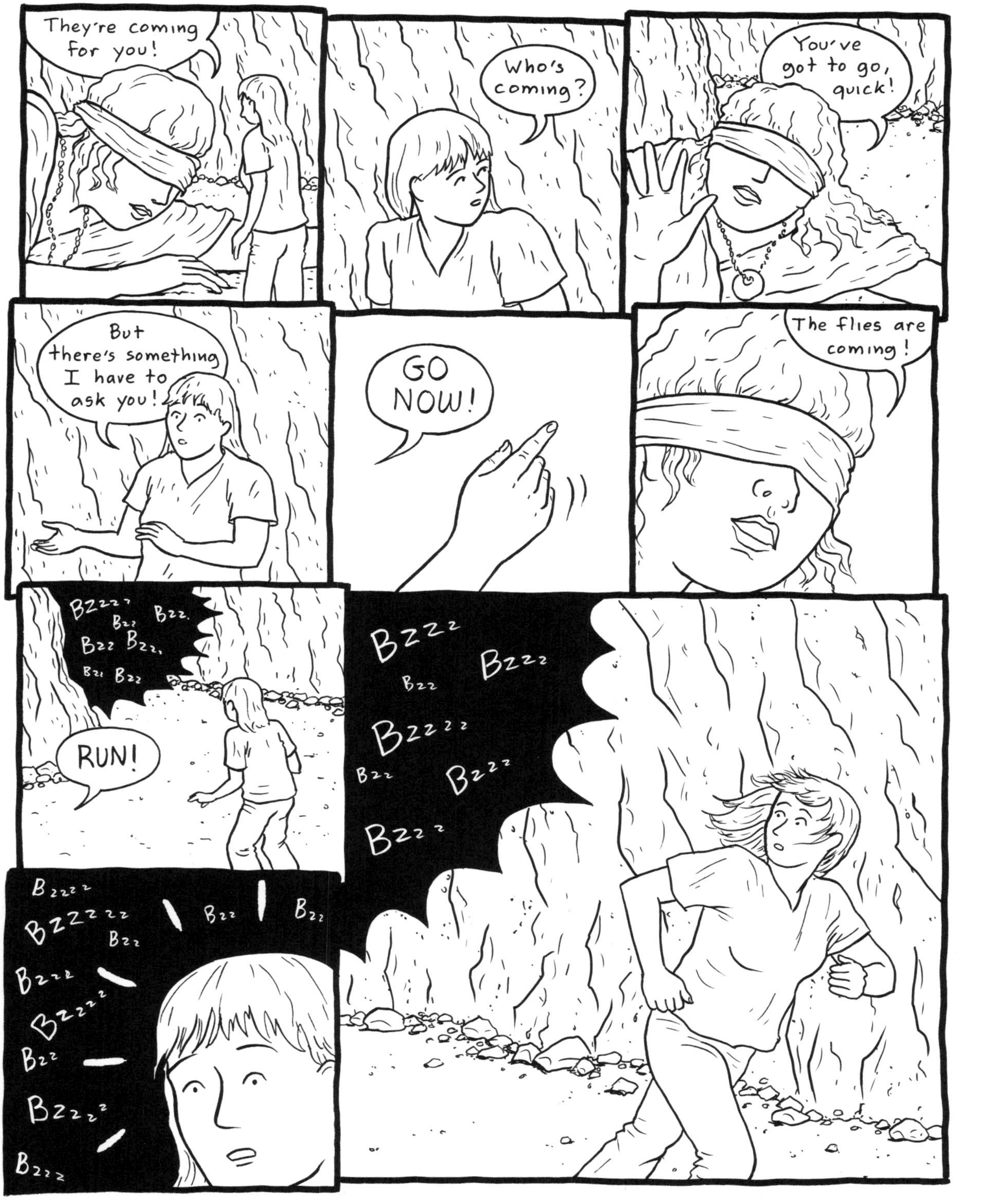
They're coming for you!
Who's coming?
You've got to go, quick!
But there's something I have to ask you!
GO NOW!
The flies are coming!
Bzzz Bzz Bzz. Bzz Bzz. Bzz Bzz
RUN!
Bzzz Bzzz Bzz Bzzzz Bzz Bzzz Bzzz
Bzzzz Bzzzzz Bzz Bzz Bzz Bzzz Bzzzz Bzz Bzzzz Bzzz

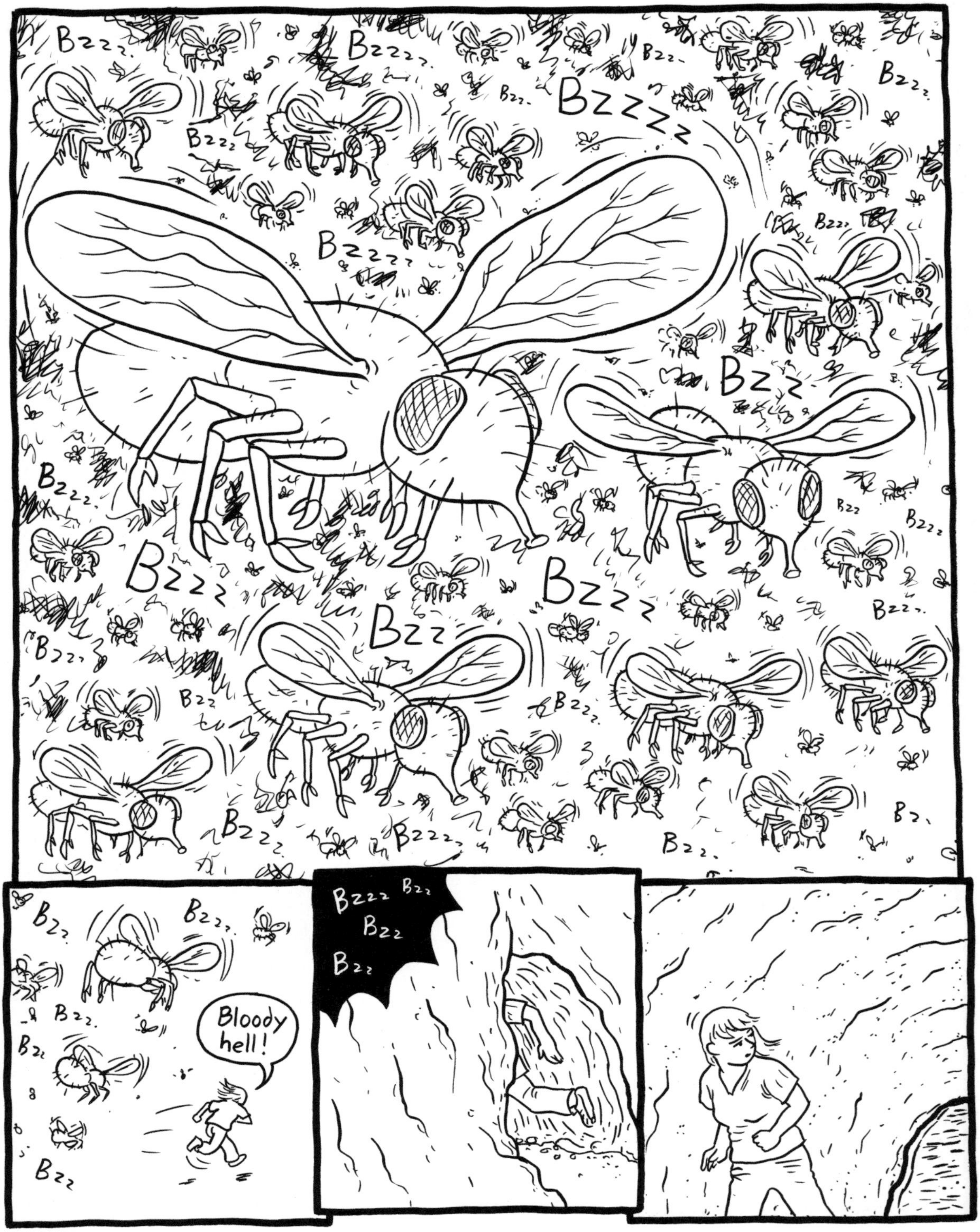
Bzzzz
Bzzzzzz
Bzzz
Bloody hell!
Bzzz Bzz
Bzz
Bzz

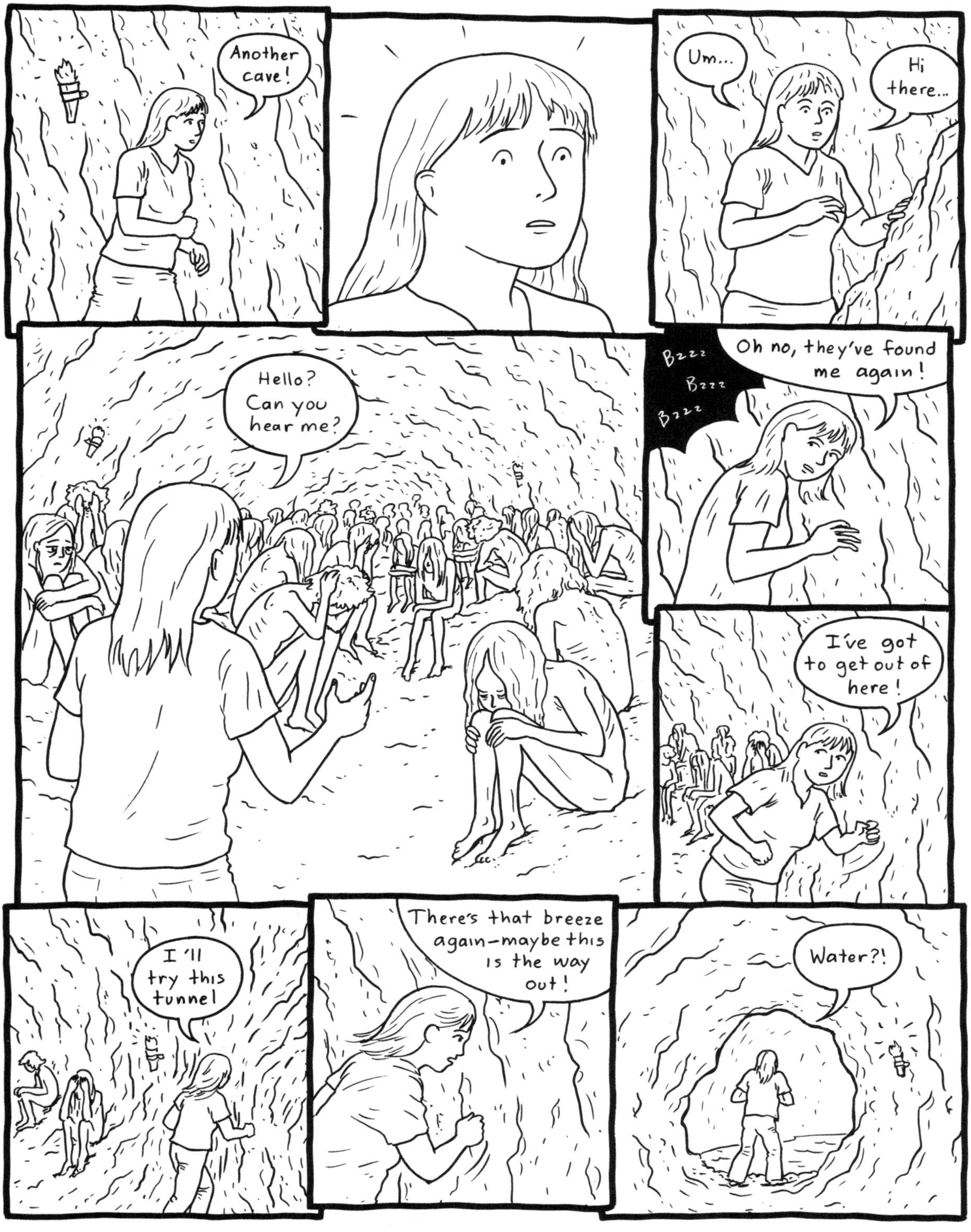
Another cave!
Um...
Hi there...
Hello? Can you hear me?
Bzzz Bzzz Bzzz
Oh no, they've found me again!
I've got to get out of here!
I'll try this tunnel
There's that breeze again—maybe this is the way out!
Water?!

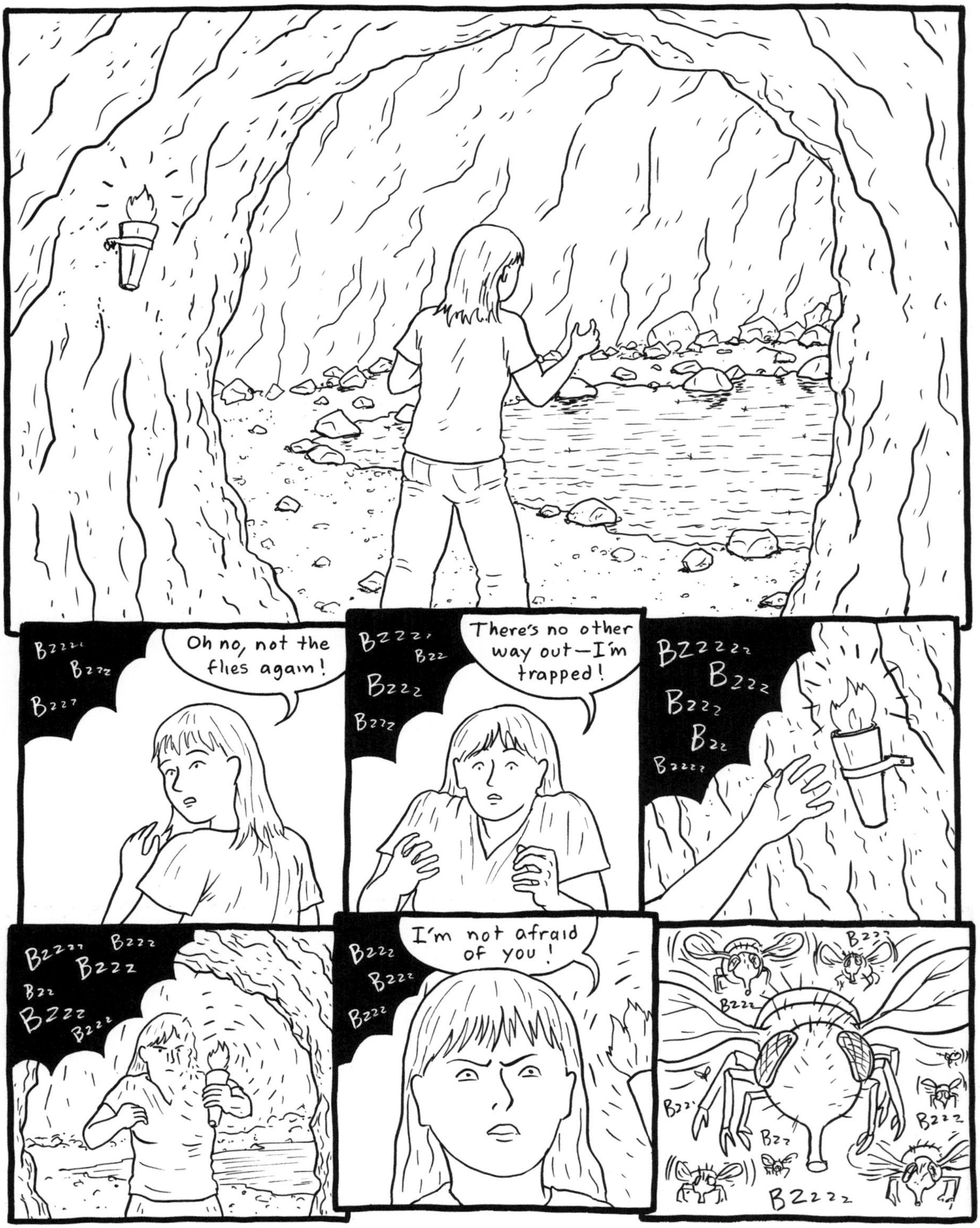
Bzzz
Bzzz
Bzzz
Oh no, not the flies again!
Bzzz
Bzz
Bzzz
Bzzz
There's no other way out—I'm trapped!
Bzzzzz
Bzzz
Bzzz
Bzz
Bzzzz
Bzzzz
Bzzz
Bzzz
Bzz
Bzzz
Bzzz
Bzzz
Bzzz
Bzzz
I'm not afraid of you!
Bzzz
Bzzz
Bzz
Bzzz
Bzz
Bzzzz

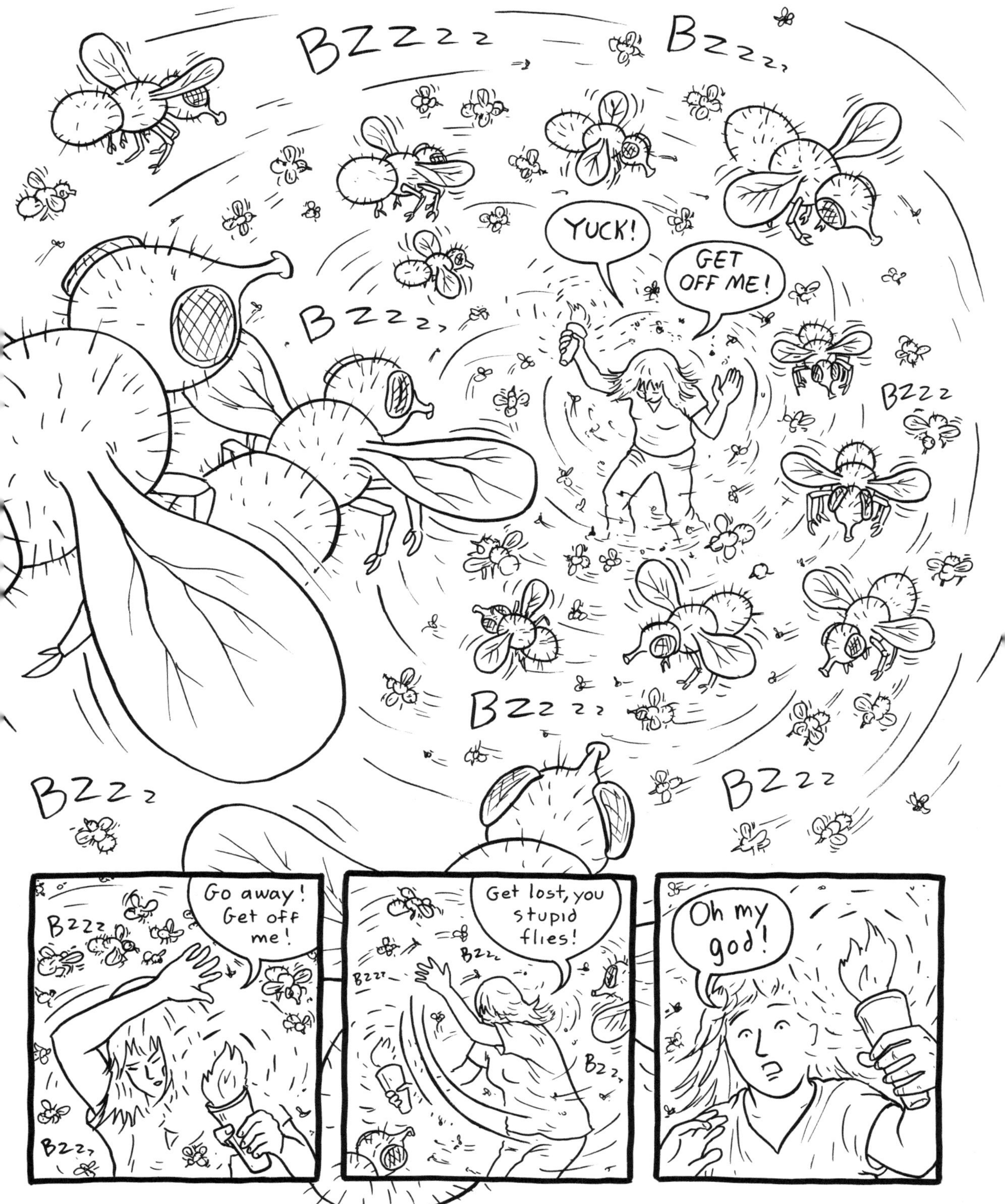
BZZzzz
Bzzzz
YUCK!
GET OFF ME!
Bzzzz
BZzz
BZzzzz
BZzz
BZzzz
Bzzz
Go away! Get off me!
Bzzz
Bzz
Get lost, you stupid flies!
Bzzz
Bzzz
Bzz
Oh my god!

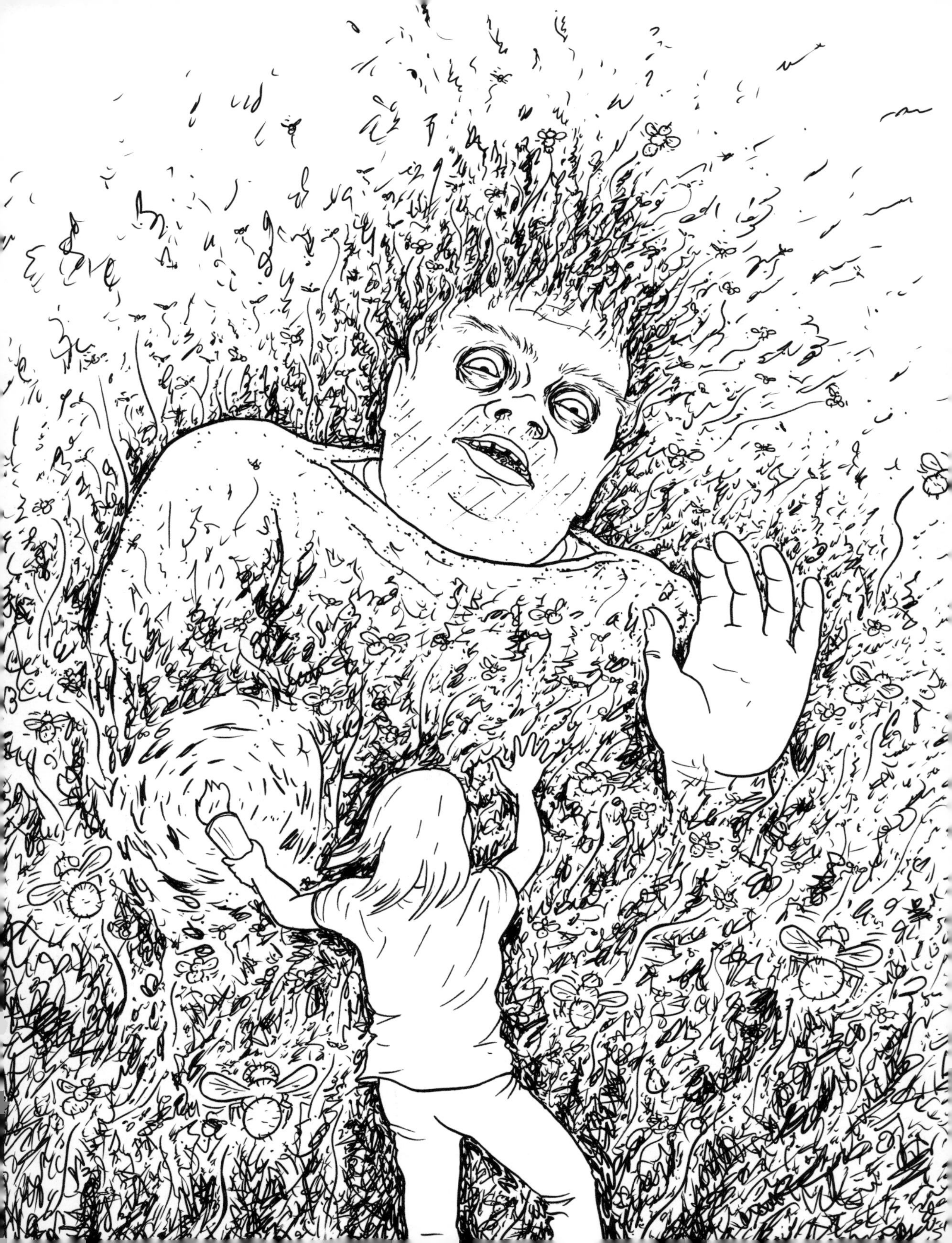

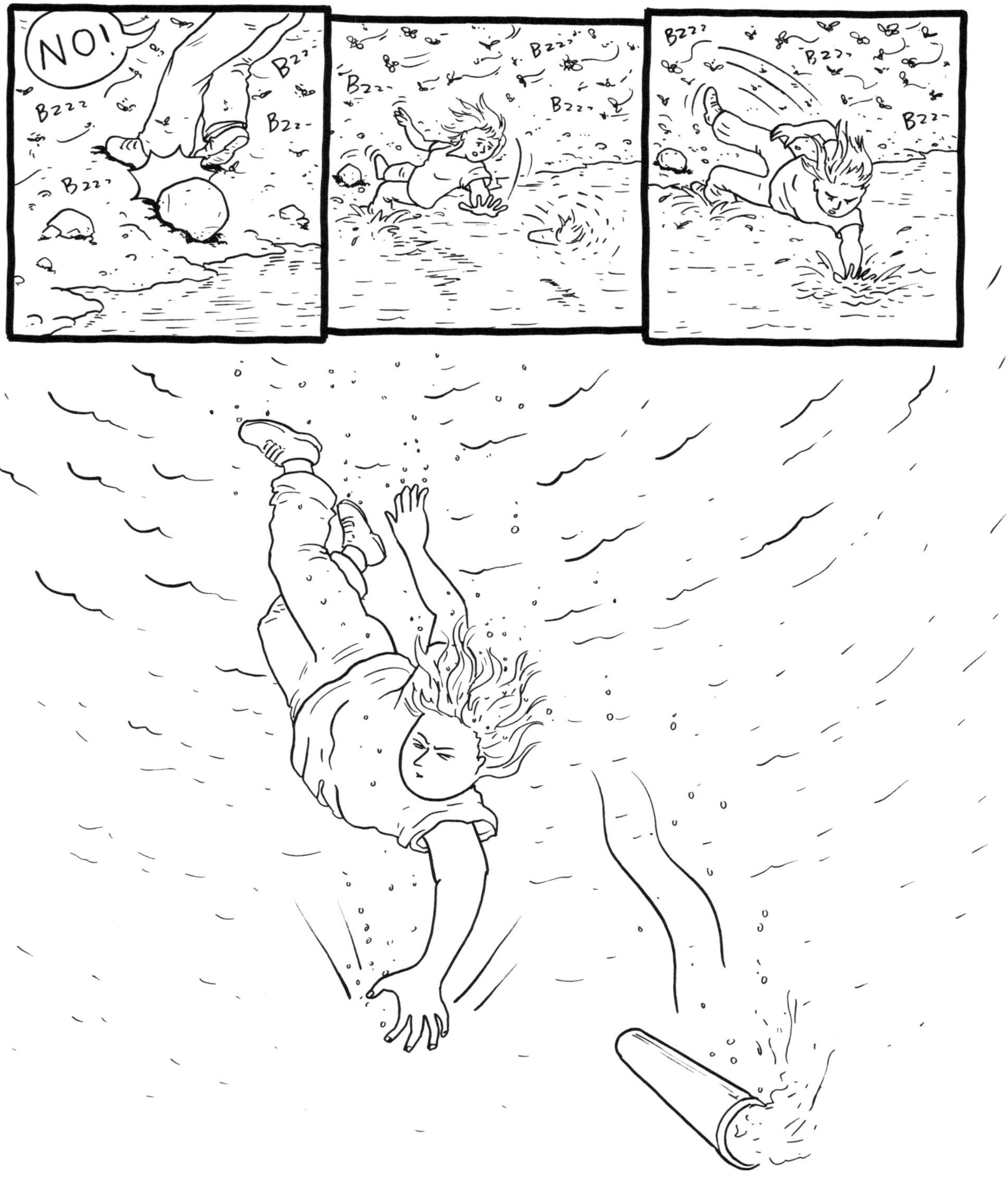
NO!
Bzzz
Bzz
Bzzz
Bzz
Bzzz
Bzz
Bzzz
Bzzz
Bzzz
Bzz

And then everything went white

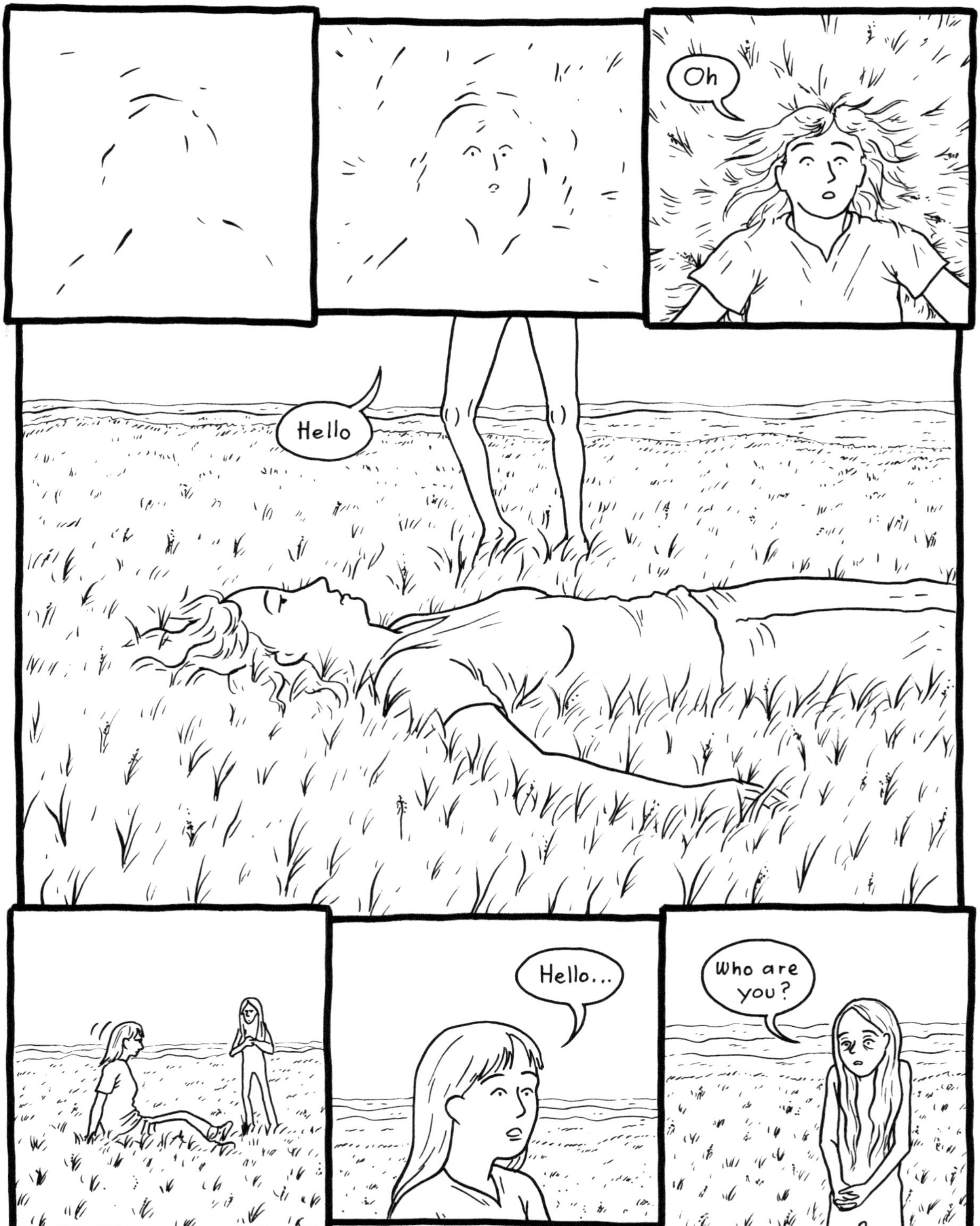
Oh
Hello
Hello...
Who are you?

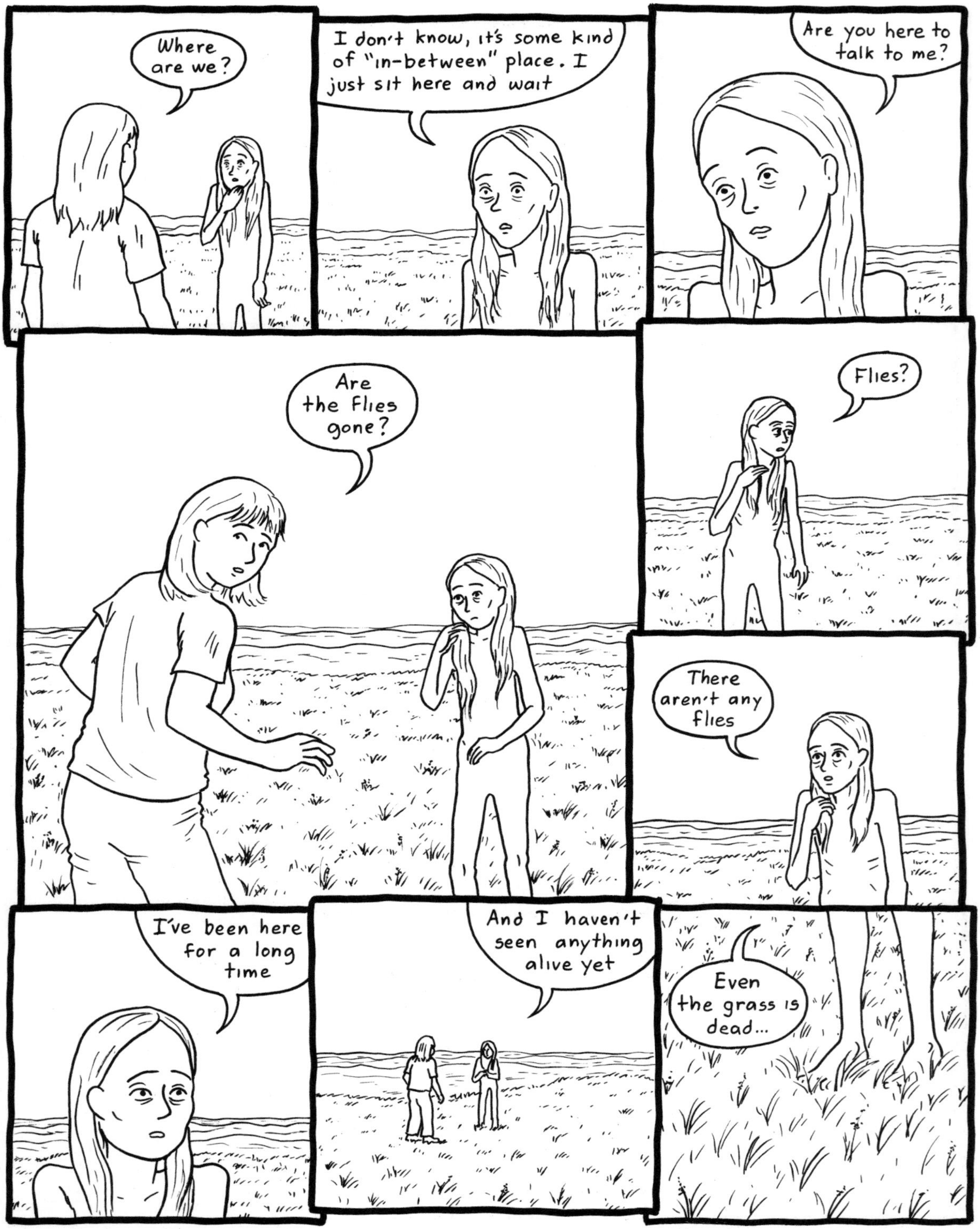
Where are we?
I don't know, it's some kind of "in-between" place. I just sit here and wait
Are you here to talk to me?
Are the flies gone?
Flies?
There aren't any flies
I've been here for a long time
And I haven't seen anything alive yet
Even the grass is dead...

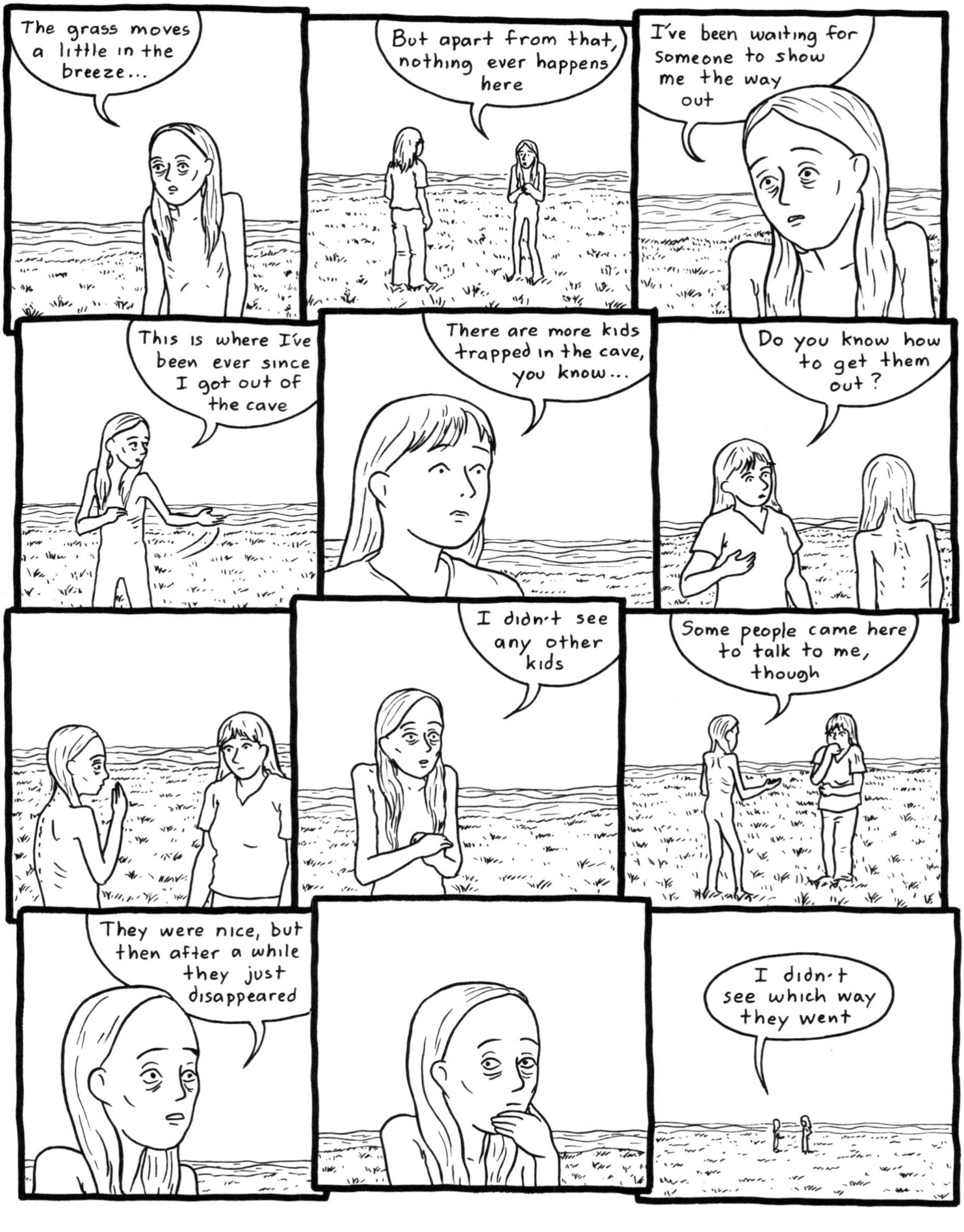
The grass moves a little in the breeze...
But apart from that, nothing ever happens here
I've been waiting for someone to show me the way out
This is where I've been ever since I got out of the cave
There are more kids trapped in the cave, you know...
Do you know how to get them out?
I didn't see any other kids
Some people came here to talk to me, though
They were nice, but then after a while they just disappeared
I didn't see which way they went

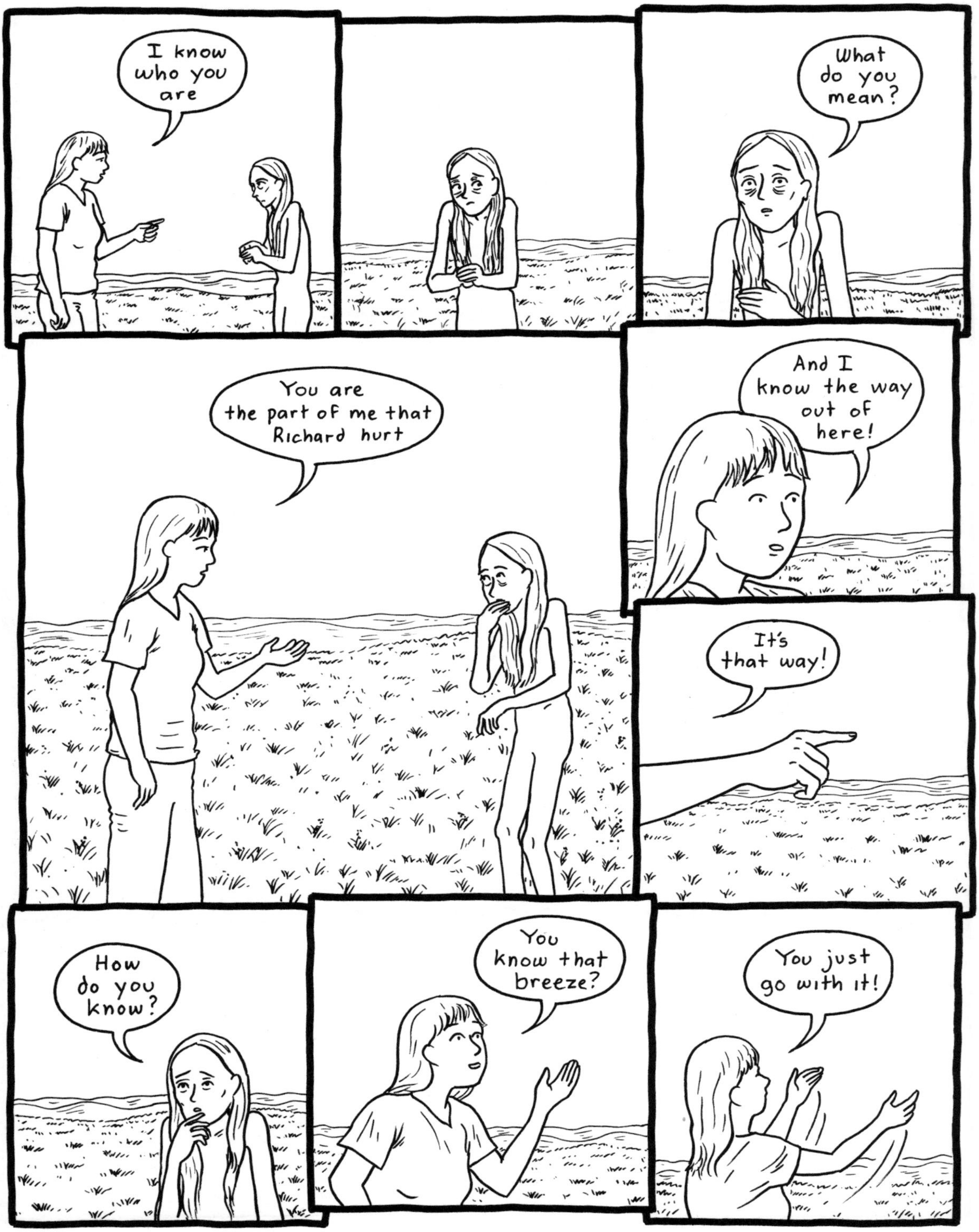
I know who you are
What do you mean?
You are the part of me that Richard hurt
And I know the way out of here!
It's that way!
How do you know?
You know that breeze?
You just go with it!

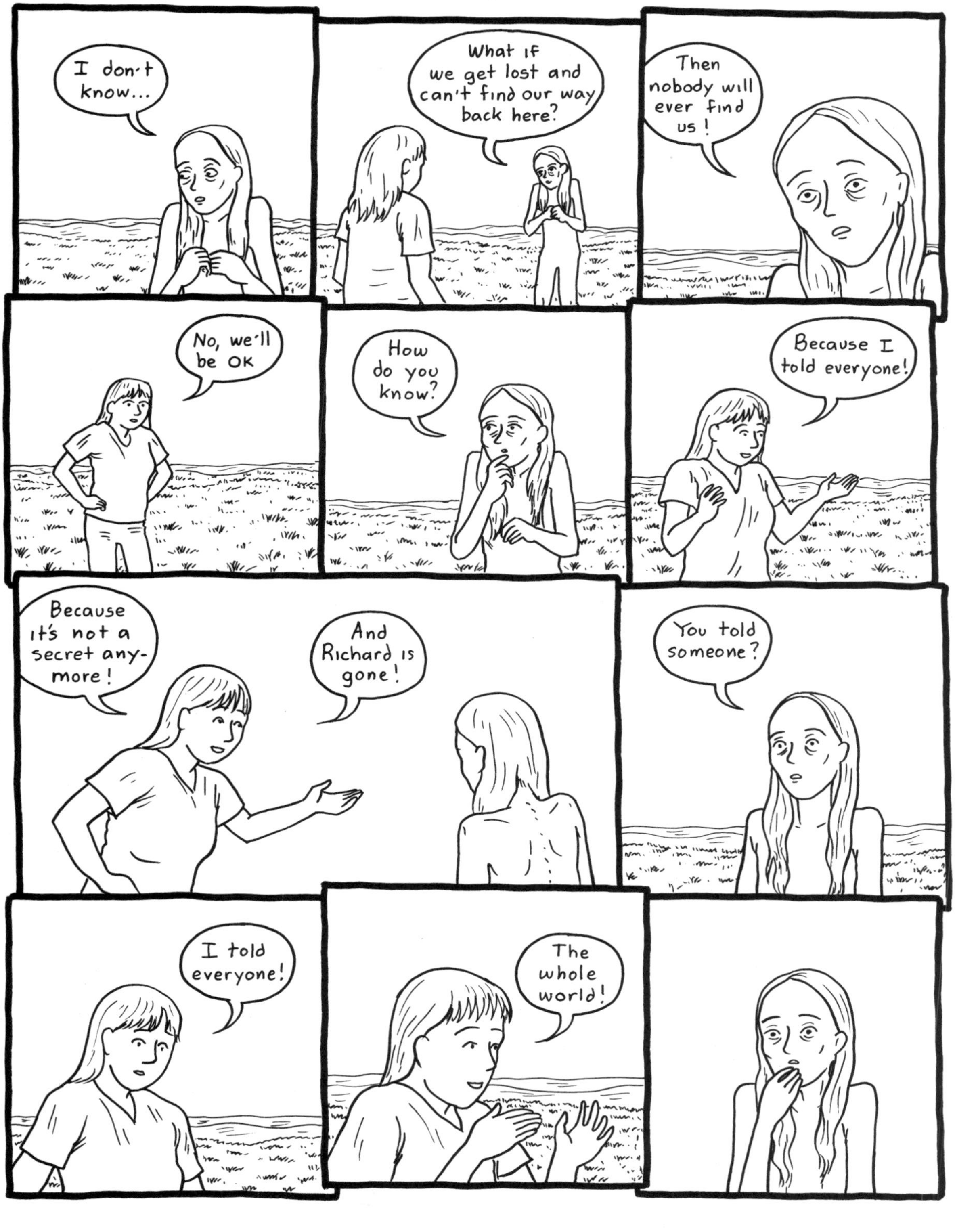
I don't know...
What if we get lost and can't find our way back here?
Then nobody will ever find us!
No, we'll be OK
How do you know?
Because I told everyone!
Because it's not a secret any-more!
And Richard is gone!
You told someone?
I told everyone!
The whole world!

When someone abuses or hurts you, it doesn't make you bad
It was never about you
It was always about him

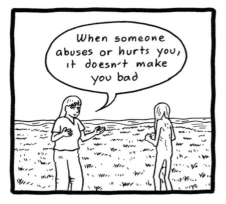

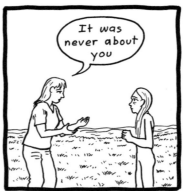

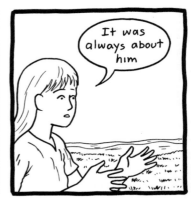

It's a sickness that lives inside them—a sickness of the soul

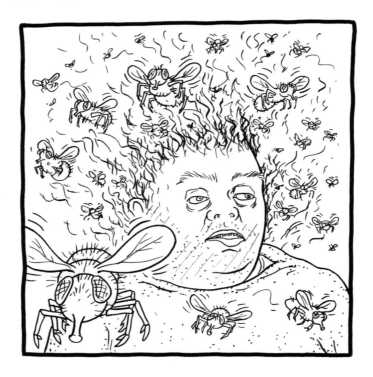

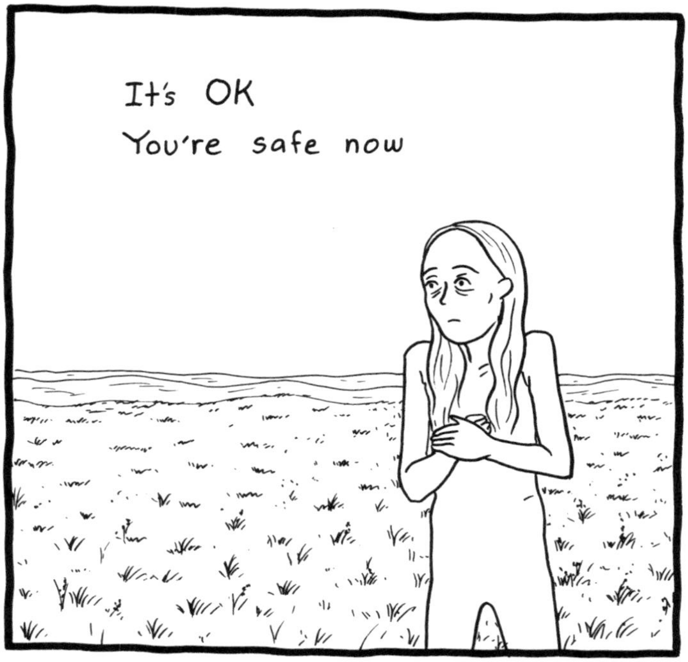
It's OK
You're safe now

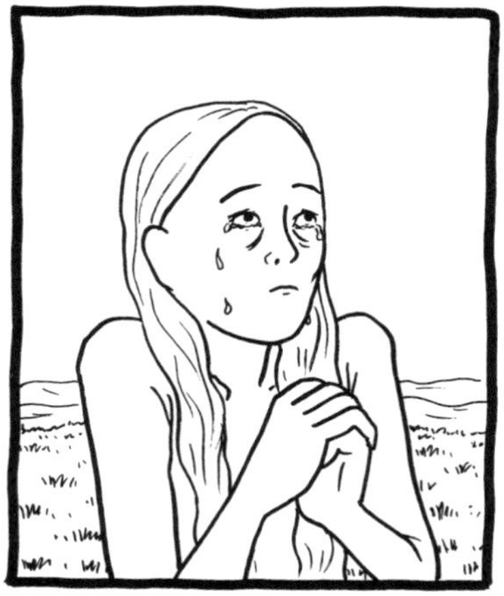

Come on, it's this way
Just a little bit further...

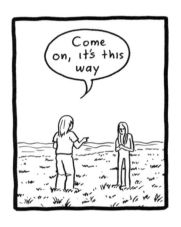

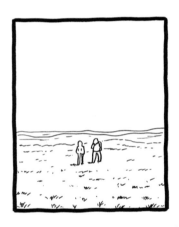

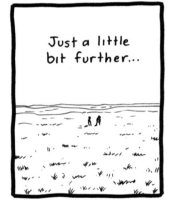

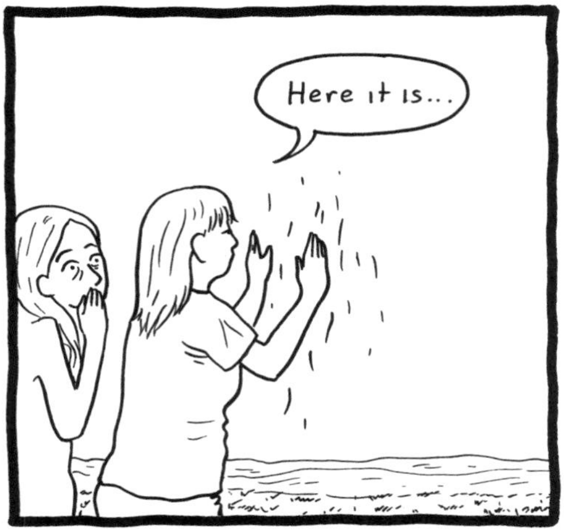
Here it is...

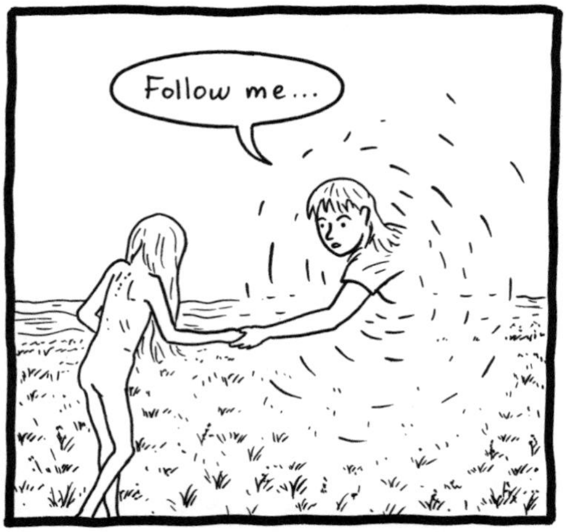
Follow me...

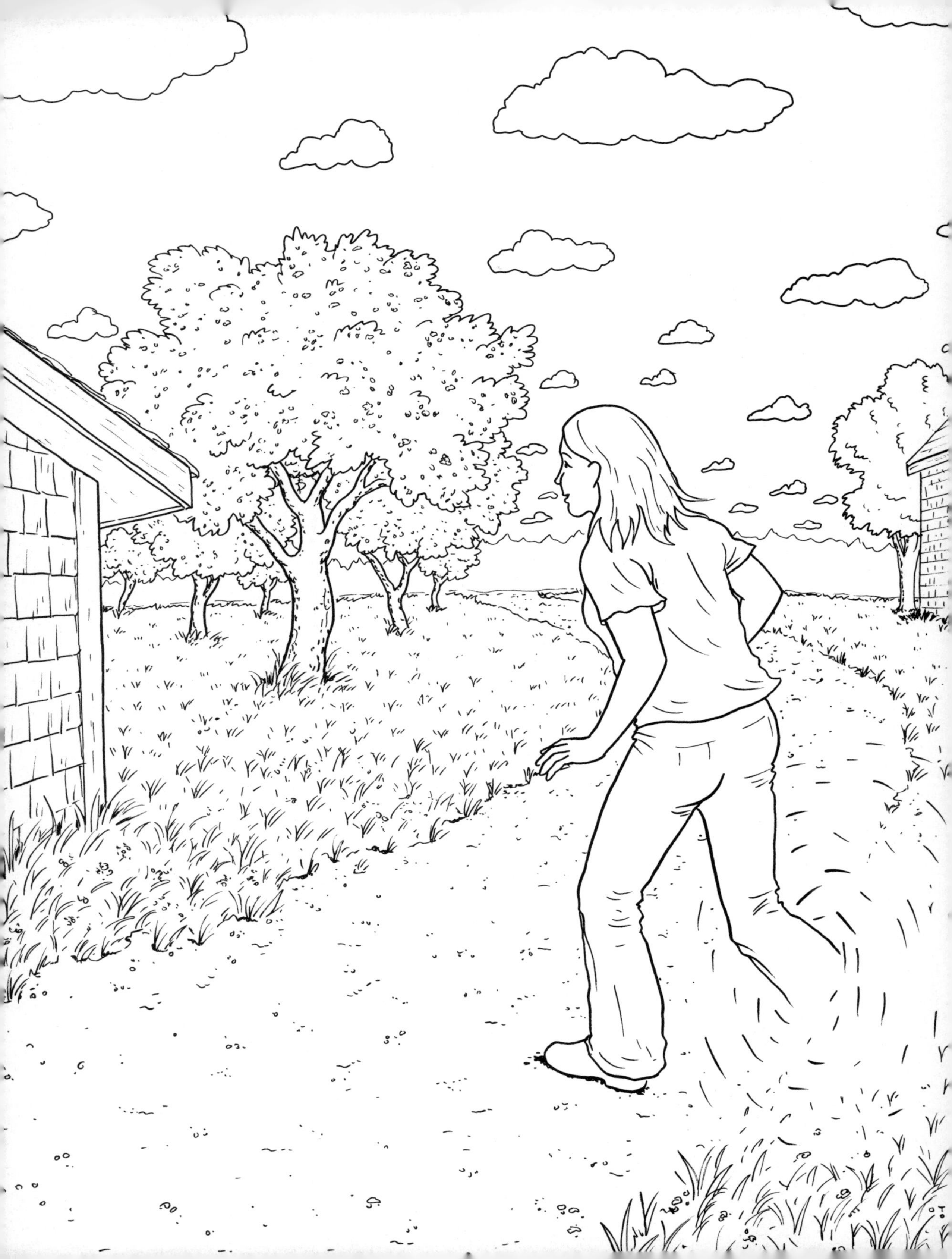

AFTERWORD

When I drew the initial pencil sketches for this book, I didn't follow an outline but rather allowed the story to unfold on its own, never knowing where it would take me next. But once I had put to paper the final image of me leaving the barren prairie and returning to the orchard in bloom, I knew my journey was complete, and I didn't need to draw anymore.

But there were still some loose ends that weren't tied up...

The reader might want to know that in the time between those first pencil sketches and the finished book, my new lawyer arranged a settlement hearing, and I decided to settle the lawsuit against my first lawyer rather than go to court. This freed up my energy to work on this book. The legal part, thankfully, is over.

My new lawyer pointed out that since I was a virgin (while this seems outdated in 2021, this hard-to-define word is used legally) when Richard first had intercourse with me, the age of consent in the criminal code at the time was actually 16 in my case, not 14. This means that what Richard did was a crime and the RCMP could have charged him. When I went to them for the third time asking for charges to be laid, they finally conceded that I was correct about the age of consent, and that their new reason for not laying charges was that "it wasn't in the public interest." After that, I abandoned any idea of getting the RCMP to lay charges as Richard is an old man now, and I am tired of dealing with the legal system.

Child abuse and child sexual abuse tear apart the lives of their victims. I'm still picking up the pieces even now, in my fifties. The legal system utterly failed to give me justice or closure over what Richard did to me. It also failed its citizens and even Richard himself by not holding him accountable. I am not alone in being failed by the legal system. Without the ability to effectively prosecute child sexual abuse, it is not a deterrent to abusers.

If you know of a child in your community that isn't doing well, maybe you could do something to help them. You never know what is going on behind the scenes in a vulnerable child's life. Even the smallest bit of help or kind gesture makes a difference to a child in need.

And if you are a victim, get all the help you can. Group support, therapists, friends and family— whatever it takes. Healing is possible.

SOURCES

PAGE 128, PANEL 9:
Bill C-22, *An Act to amend the Criminal Code (age of protection) and to make consequential amendments to the Criminal Records Act*, 1st sess., 39th Parliament, 2007, SC 2006. Accessed from Parliament of Canada website. (Although Bill C-22 was passed in 2006, the amendment was in effect only in 2008.)

PAGE 165, PANELS 2–3:
Statute of Limitations, Chapters S-7, Section 3: Part I – Limitation Periods; Section 2(1)(d). Accessed from the Prince of Edward Island's Legislative Counsel Office, p. 6.

PAGE 182, PANEL 9:
Child and Youth Mental Health Services, British Columbia Ministry of Health; Health and Welfare Canada: *Multiple Victim Child Sexual Abuse: The impact on Communities and Implications for the Intervention Planning*, Health Canada, Supply and Services Canada (1994), p. 6.

PAGE 195, PANEL 4:
Canadian Centre for Justice Statistics. Edited by Lucie Ogrodnik, *Family Violence in Canada: A Statistical Profile 2007* (2007), p. 20.

Statistics Canada, Rebecca Kong, Holly Johnson, Sara Beattie, and Andrew Cardillo, *Sexual Offences in Canada, Canadian Centre for Justice Statistics*, Vol. 23. no. 6. Released July 2003, p. 9.

PAGE 195, PANEL 5:
C. Cahill, S. P. Llewelyn, and C. Pearson. "Long-Term Effects of Sexual Abuse Which Occurred in Childhood: A Review." *British Journal of Clinical Psychology* 30, no. 2 (1991): pp. 117–130.

PAGE 195, PANEL 6:
Nancy Talbot, Paul Duberstein, Christopher Cox, Diane Denning, and Yeates Conwell. "Preliminary Report on Childhood Sexual Abuse, Suicidal Ideation, and Suicide Attempts among Middle-Aged and Older Depressed Women." *The American Journal of Geriatric Psychiatry* 12, no. 5 (2004): pp. 536–38

PAGE 195, PANEL 7:
Tracy Simpson, and William Miller. "Concomitance between Childhood Sexual and Physical Abuse and Substance Use Problems." *Clinical Psychology Review* 22, no. 1 (2002): pp. 27-77.

Benjamin Sadock, and Virginia Sadock. *Kaplan and Sadock's Synopsis of Psychiatry: Behavioral Sciences/Clinical Psychiatry*, 10th ed. (2007).

Kathryn Hill, and Sandra Butler. *Adult Survivors of Child Sexual Abuse, Information from The National Clearinghouse on Family Violence* (1993), pp. 3–4.

PAGE 195, PANEL 8:
Olena Hankivsky, and D. A. Draker. "The Economic Costs of Child Sexual Abuse in Canada." *Journal of Health & Social Policy* 17, no. 2 (2003): pp. 1–33.

AFTERWORD, PARAGRAPH 4:
Canada, and John C. Martin. *Martin's Annual Criminal Code Regular, 1982 edition*. "Sexual Intercourse with Female under Fourteen," Section 146(2). (1957): p. 136

AUTHOR'S NOTE

The following names are pseudonyms: Brenda, Peter, Steve, Lily, Mr. Kesson, Dr. Miller.

ACKNOWLEDGMENTS

Thank you to the instructors at Langara College's Graphic Novel & Comix Program, with special thanks to James Lloyd for his encouragement and feedback, and Bevan Thomas for his help with editing and page design.

Thank you to friends and family—Cathy, Beth, Cliff, Ian, Bonnie, to name a few—who supported and encouraged me during the difficult process of writing this book.

I appreciate the work everyone at Drawn & Quarterly does and am eternally grateful for the opportunity they have given me to finally, after all this time, be able to tell my story.